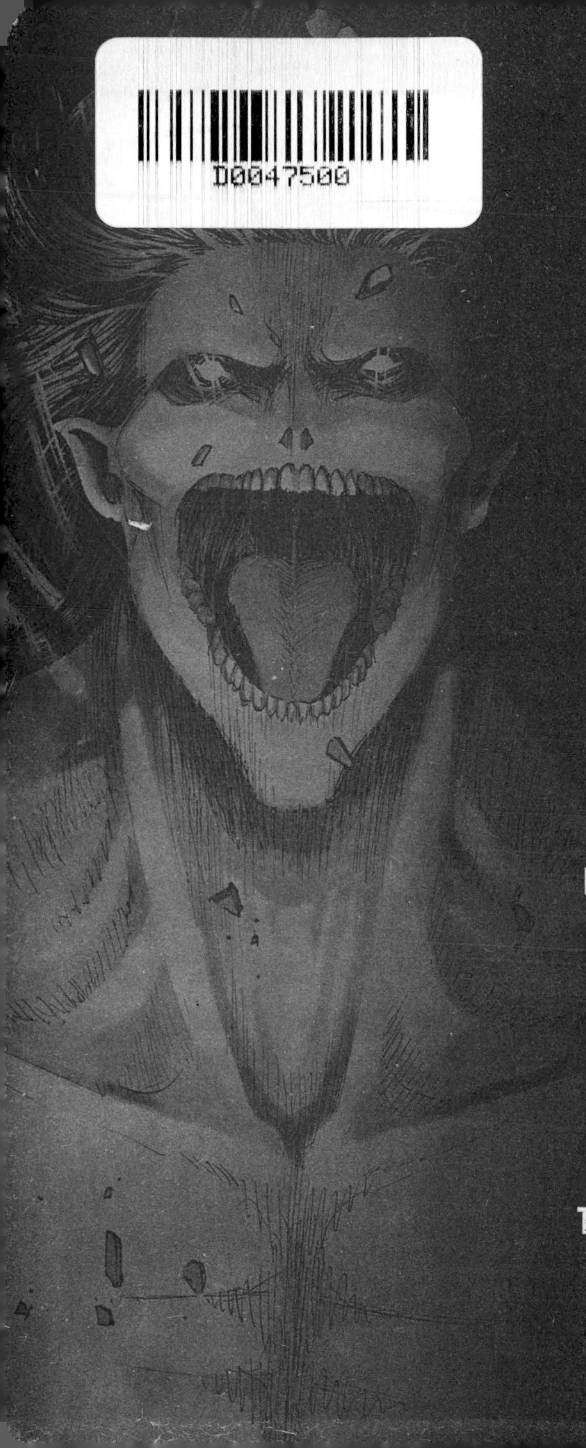

ATTACK ON TITAN 25

HAJIME ISAYAMA

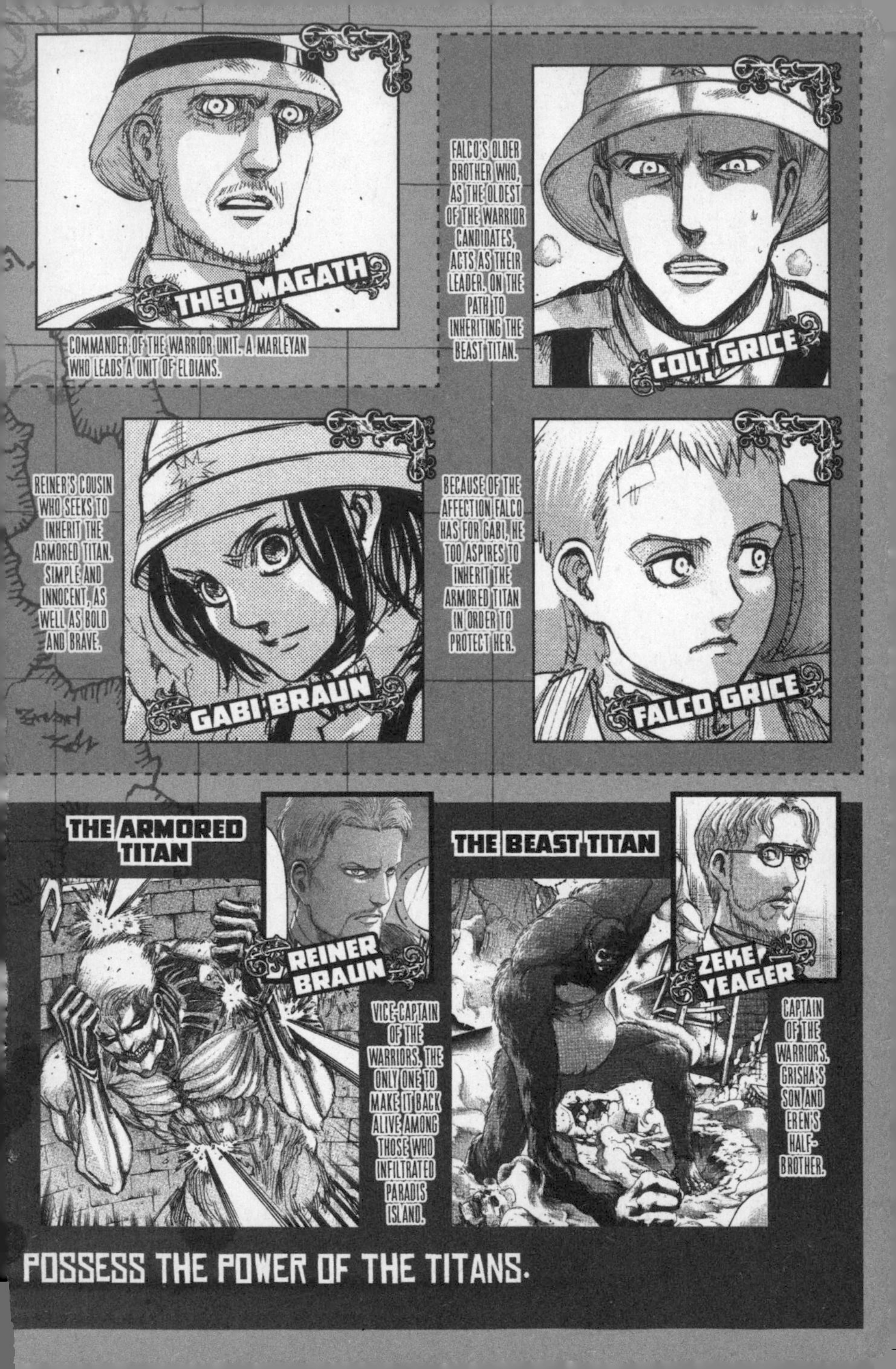
COLT GRICE
FALCO'S OLDER BROTHER WHO, AS THE OLDEST OF THE WARRIOR CANDIDATES, ACTS AS THEIR LEADER, ON THE PATH TO INHERITING THE BEAST TITAN.
THEO MAGATH
COMMANDER OF THE WARRIOR UNIT. A MARLEYAN WHO LEADS A UNIT OF ELDIANS.
FALCO GRICE
BECAUSE OF THE AFFECTION FALCO HAS FOR GABI, HE TOO ASPIRES TO INHERIT THE ARMORED TITAN IN ORDER TO PROTECT HER.
GABI BRAUN
REINER'S COUSIN WHO SEEKS TO INHERIT THE ARMORED TITAN. SIMPLE AND INNOCENT, AS WELL AS BOLD AND BRAVE.
THE BEAST TITAN
ZEKE YEAGER
CAPTAIN OF THE WARRIORS. GRISHA'S SON AND EREN'S HALF-BROTHER.
THE ARMORED TITAN
REINER BRAUN
VICE-CAPTAIN OF THE WARRIORS, THE ONLY ONE TO MAKE IT BACK ALIVE AMONG THOSE WHO INFILTRATED PARADIS ISLAND.
POSSESS THE POWER OF THE TITANS.

ATTACK ON TITAN CHARACTERS: MARLEY ARC

THE ELDIAN WARRIORS
THE MARLEYAN ARMY

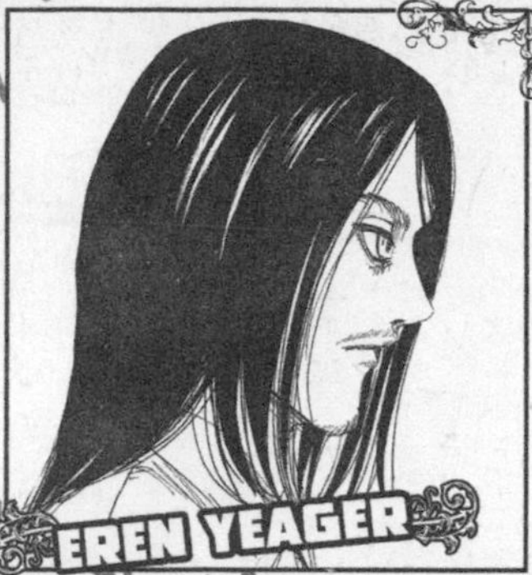

EREN YEAGER

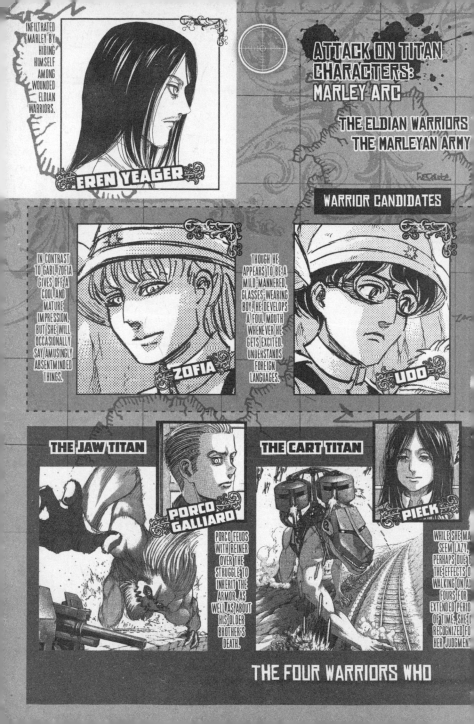

INFILTRATED MARLEY BY HIDING HIMSELF AMONG WOUNDED ELDIAN WARRIORS.

WARRIOR CANDIDATES

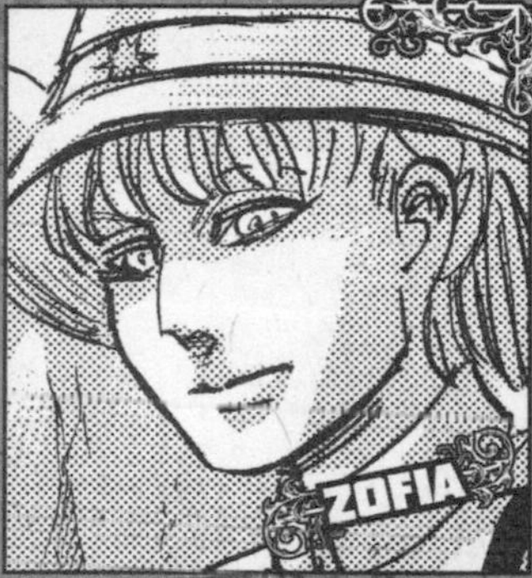

ZOFIA

IN CONTRAST TO GABI, ZOFIA GIVES OFF A COOL AND MATURE IMPRESSION, BUT SHE WILL OCCASIONALLY SAY AMUSINGLY ABSENTMINDED THINGS.

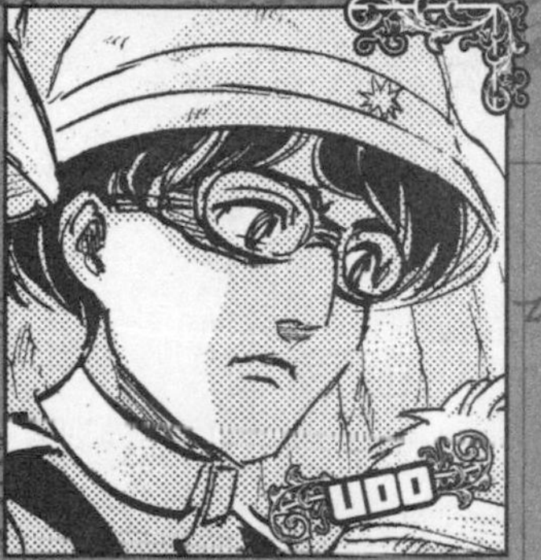

UDO

THOUGH HE APPEARS TO BE A MILD-MANNERED, GLASSES-WEARING BOY, HE DEVELOPS A FOUL MOUTH WHENEVER HE GETS EXCITED. UNDERSTANDS FOREIGN LANGUAGES.

THE JAW TITAN

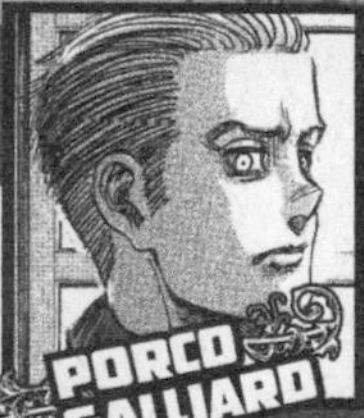

PORCO GALLIARD

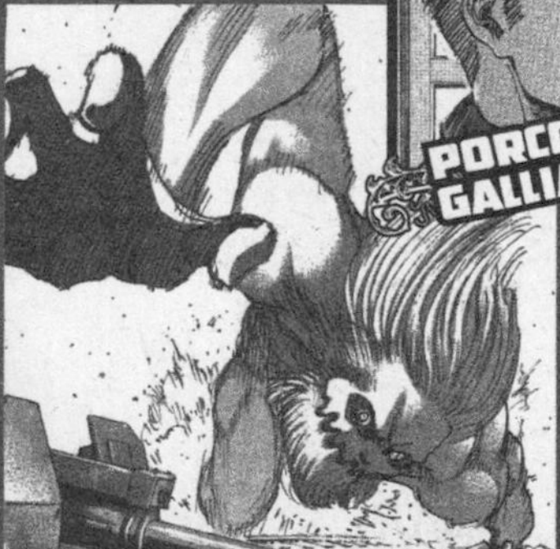

PORCO FEUDS WITH REINER OVER THE STRUGGLE TO INHERIT THE ARMOR, AS WELL AS ABOUT HIS OLDER BROTHER'S DEATH.

THE CART TITAN

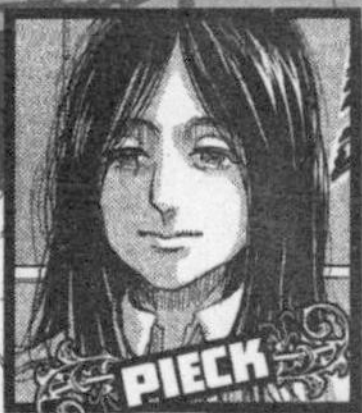

PIECK

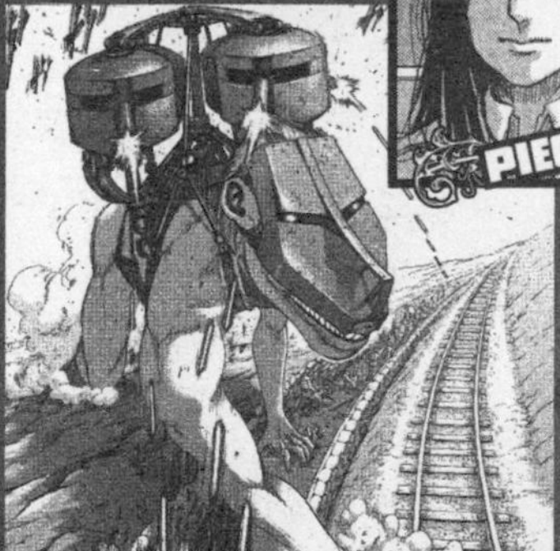

WHILE SHE MA SEEM LAZY, PERHAPS DUE T THE EFFECTS O WALKING ON A FOURS FOR EXTENDED PERIO OF TIME, SHE I RECOGNIZED FO HER JUDGMENT

THE FOUR WARRIORS WHO

ATTACK on TITAN

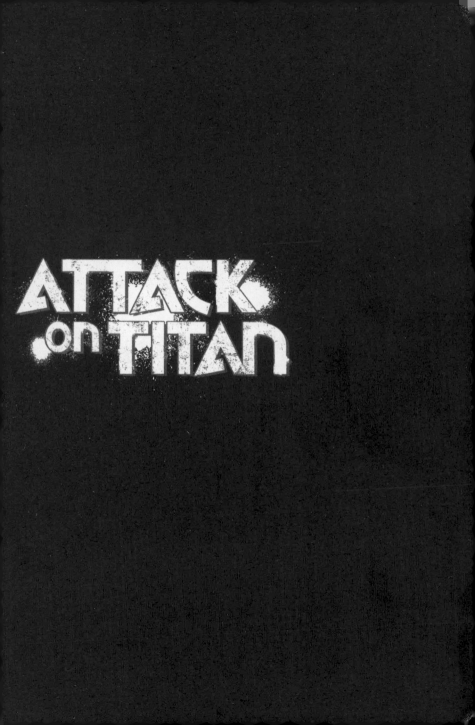

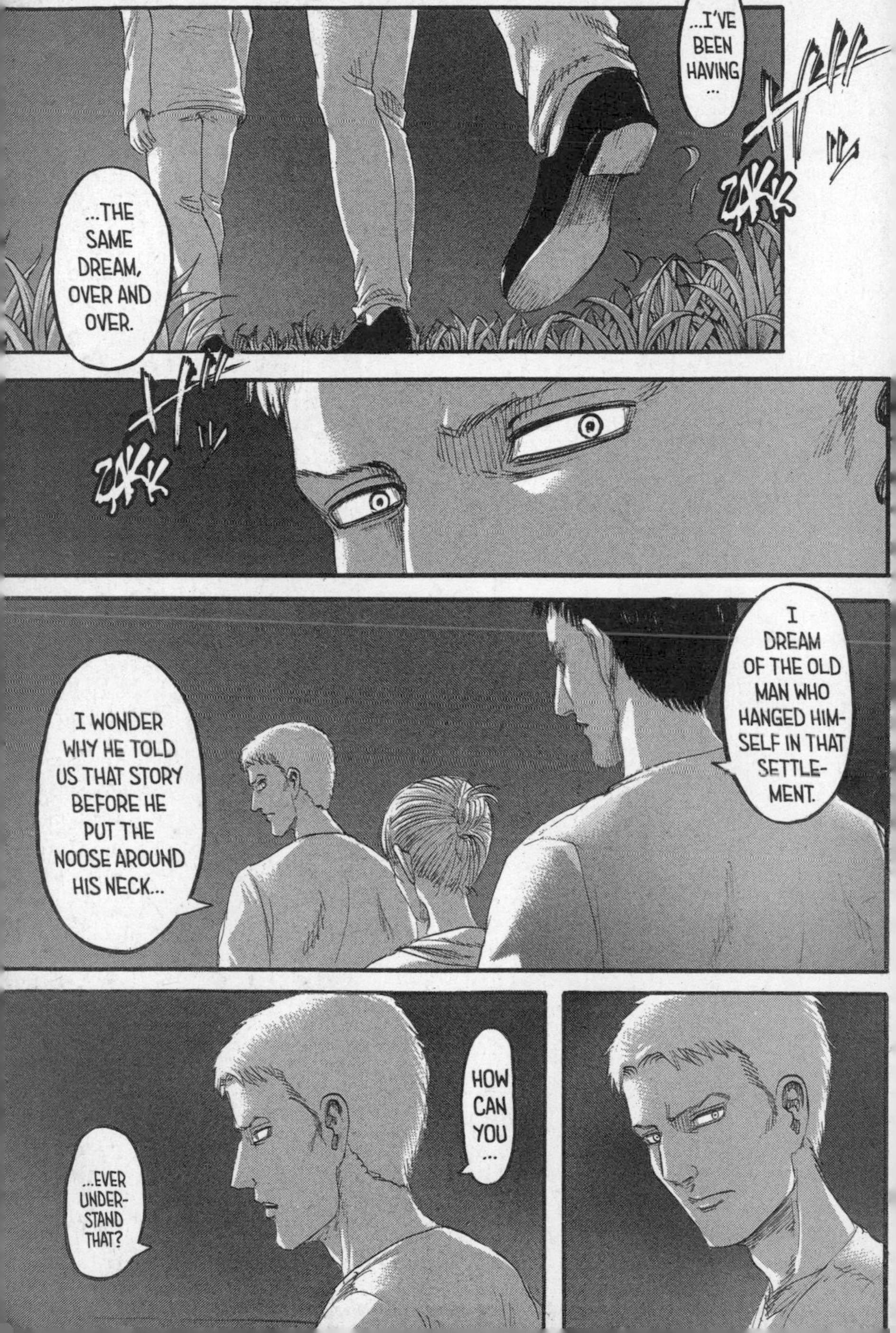
...I'VE BEEN HAVING...
ZAKK
...THE SAME DREAM, OVER AND OVER.
ZAKK
I DREAM OF THE OLD MAN WHO HANGED HIMSELF IN THAT SETTLEMENT.
I WONDER WHY HE TOLD US THAT STORY BEFORE HE PUT THE NOOSE AROUND HIS NECK...
HOW CAN YOU...
...EVER UNDERSTAND THAT?

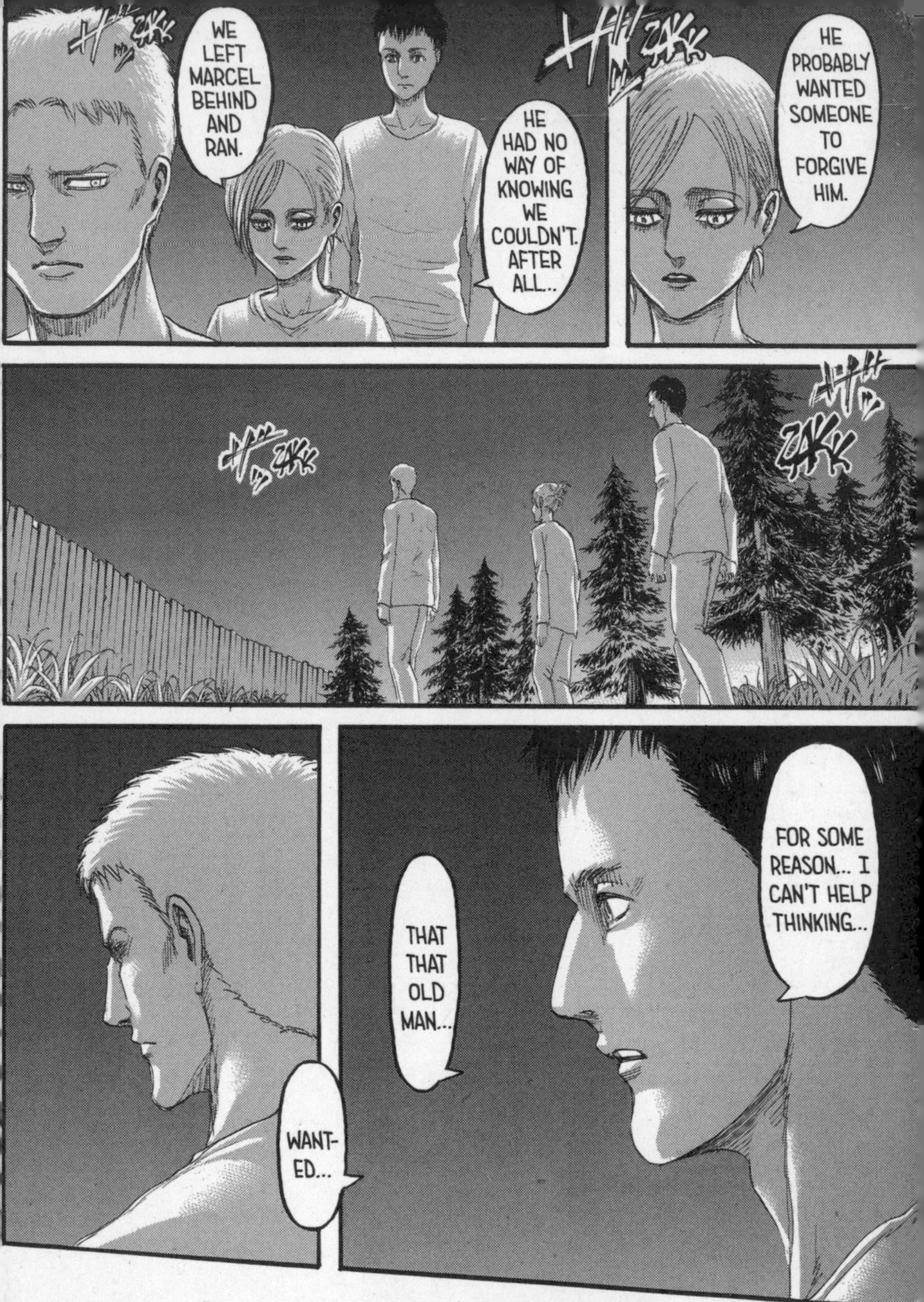
HE PROBABLY WANTED SOMEONE TO FORGIVE HIM.
HE HAD NO WAY OF KNOWING WE COULDN'T. AFTER ALL...
WE LEFT MARCEL BEHIND AND RAN.
FOR SOME REASON... I CAN'T HELP THINKING...
THAT THAT OLD MAN...
WANT-ED...

Episode 99: Guilty Shadow

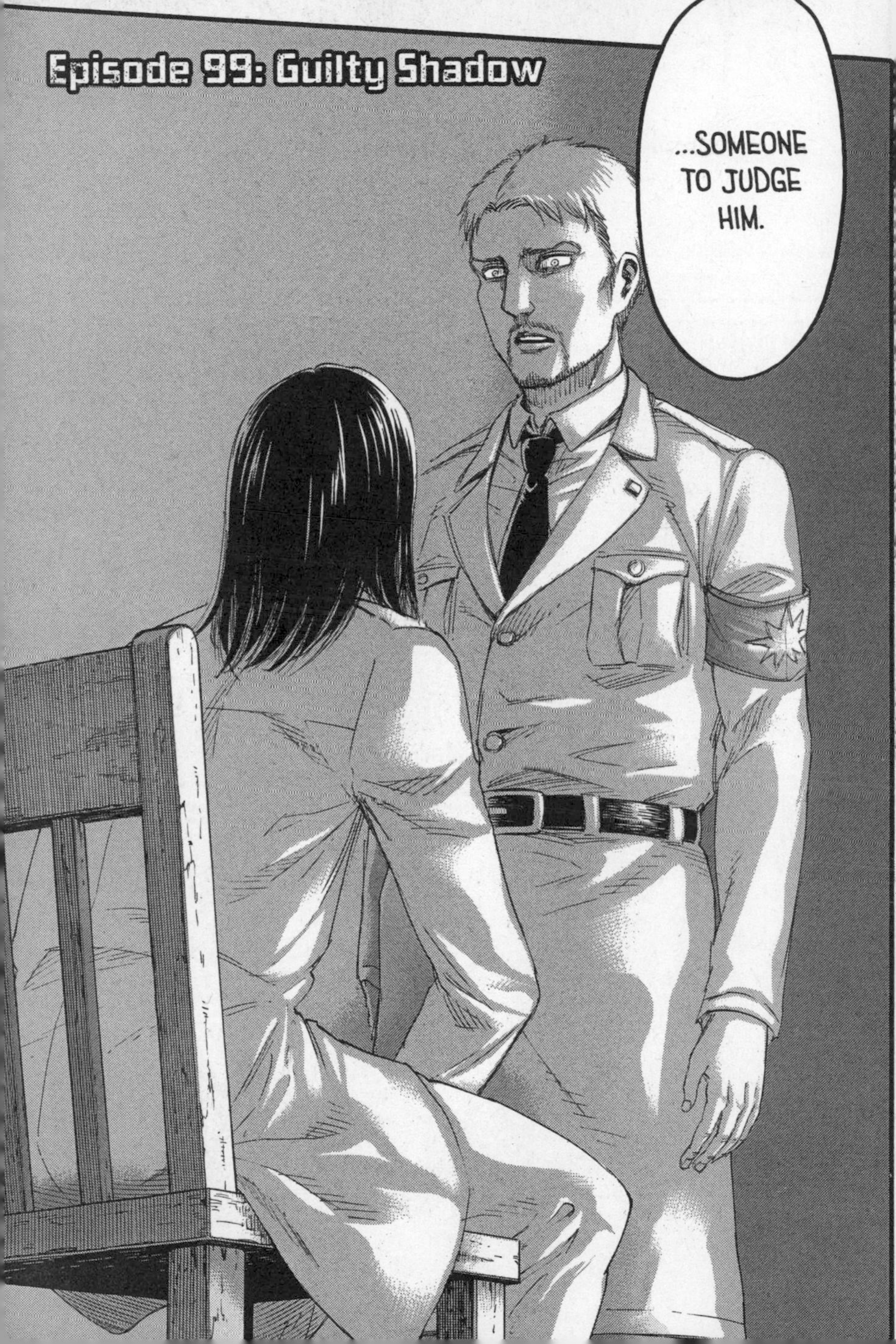
...SOMEONE TO JUDGE HIM.

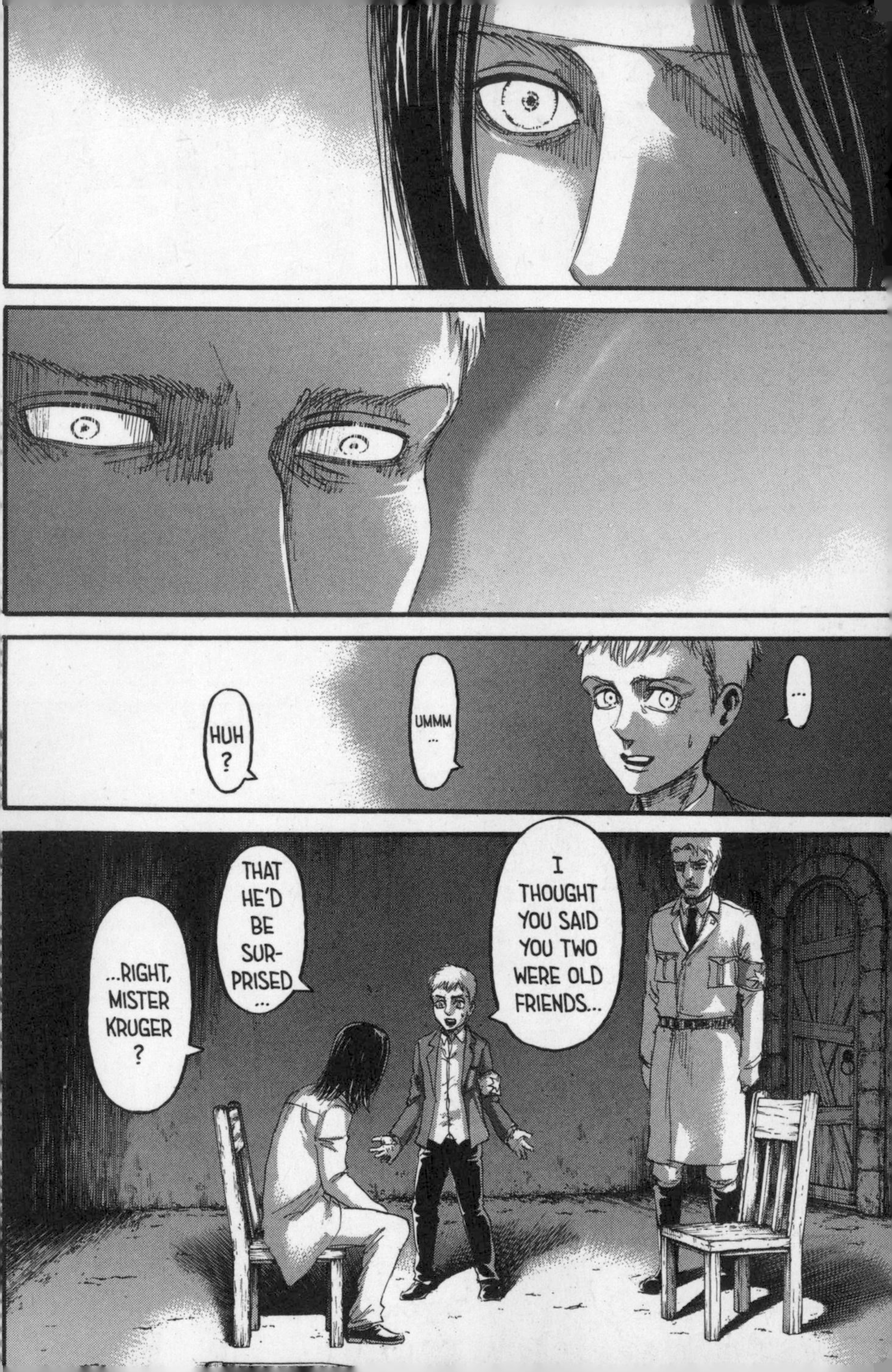
...
UMMM ...
HUH ?
I THOUGHT YOU SAID YOU TWO WERE OLD FRIENDS...
THAT HE'D BE SUR-PRISED ...
...RIGHT, MISTER KRUGER ?

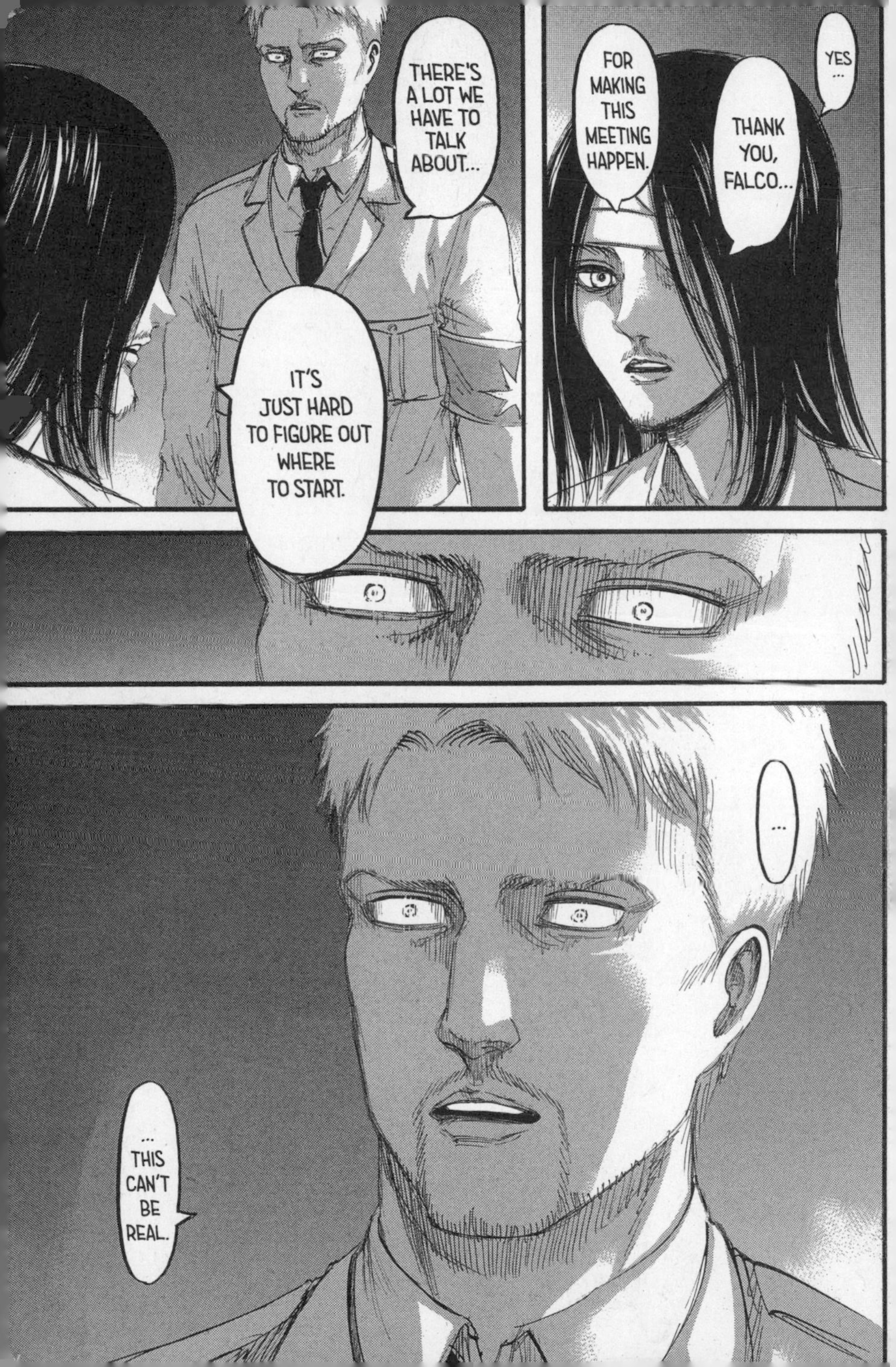
YES ...
THANK YOU, FALCO...
FOR MAKING THIS MEETING HAPPEN.
THERE'S A LOT WE HAVE TO TALK ABOUT...
IT'S JUST HARD TO FIGURE OUT WHERE TO START.
...
... THIS CAN'T BE REAL.

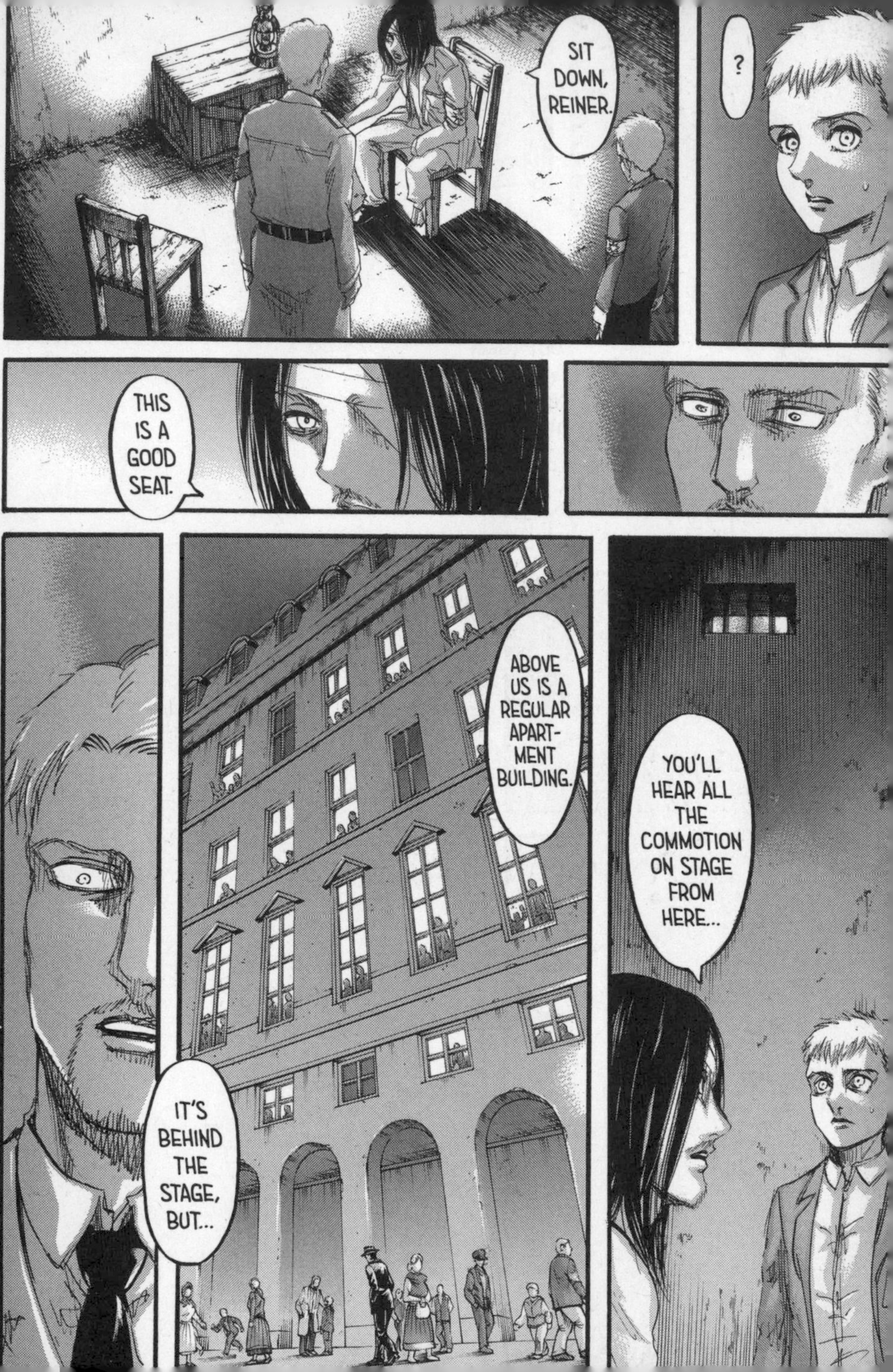
SIT DOWN, REINER.
?
THIS IS A GOOD SEAT.
IT'S BEHIND THE STAGE, BUT...
ABOVE US IS A REGULAR APARTMENT BUILDING.
YOU'LL HEAR ALL THE COMMOTION ON STAGE FROM HERE...

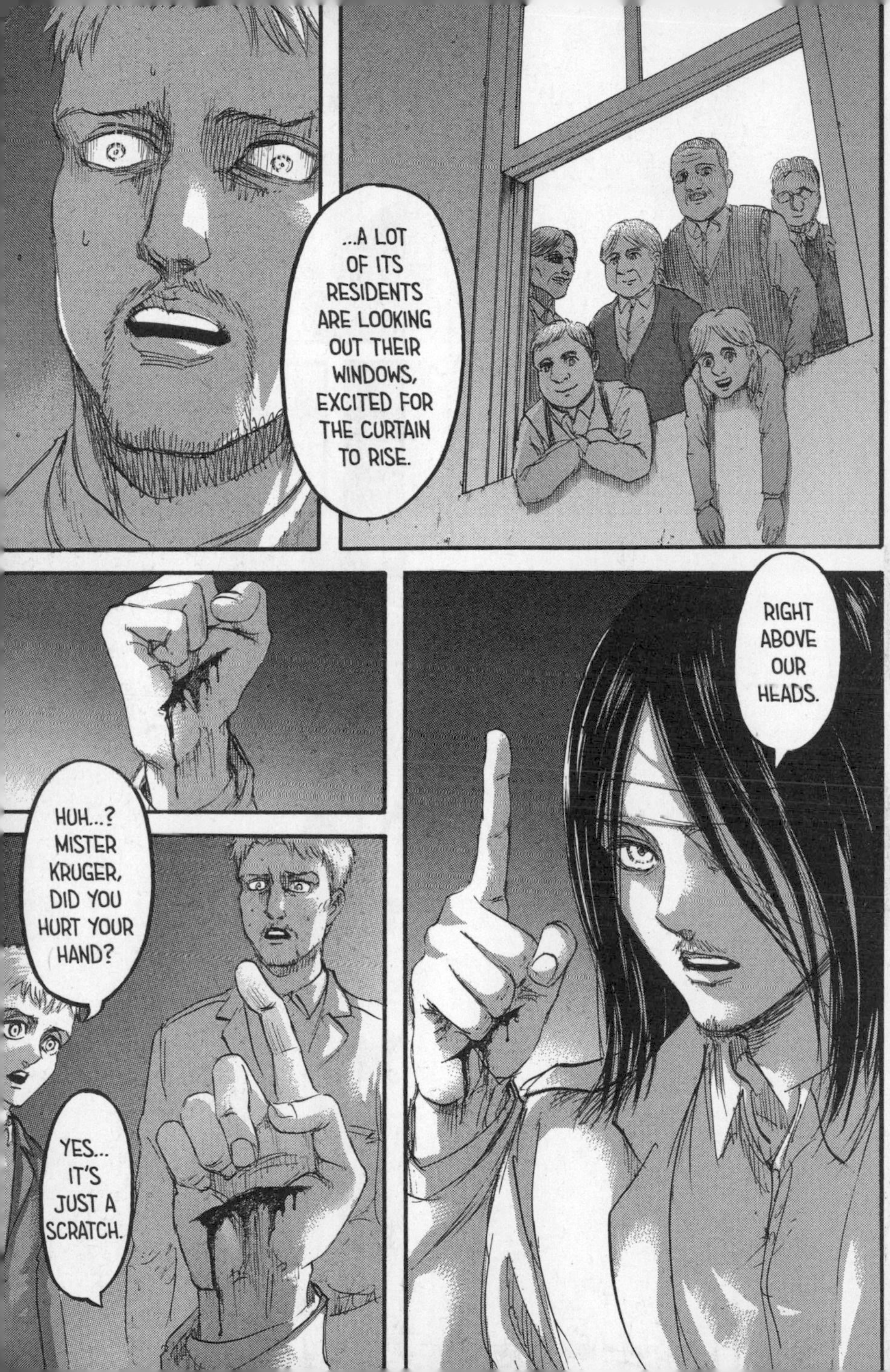
...A LOT OF ITS RESIDENTS ARE LOOKING OUT THEIR WINDOWS, EXCITED FOR THE CURTAIN TO RISE.
RIGHT ABOVE OUR HEADS.
HUH...? MISTER KRUGER, DID YOU HURT YOUR HAND?
YES... IT'S JUST A SCRATCH.

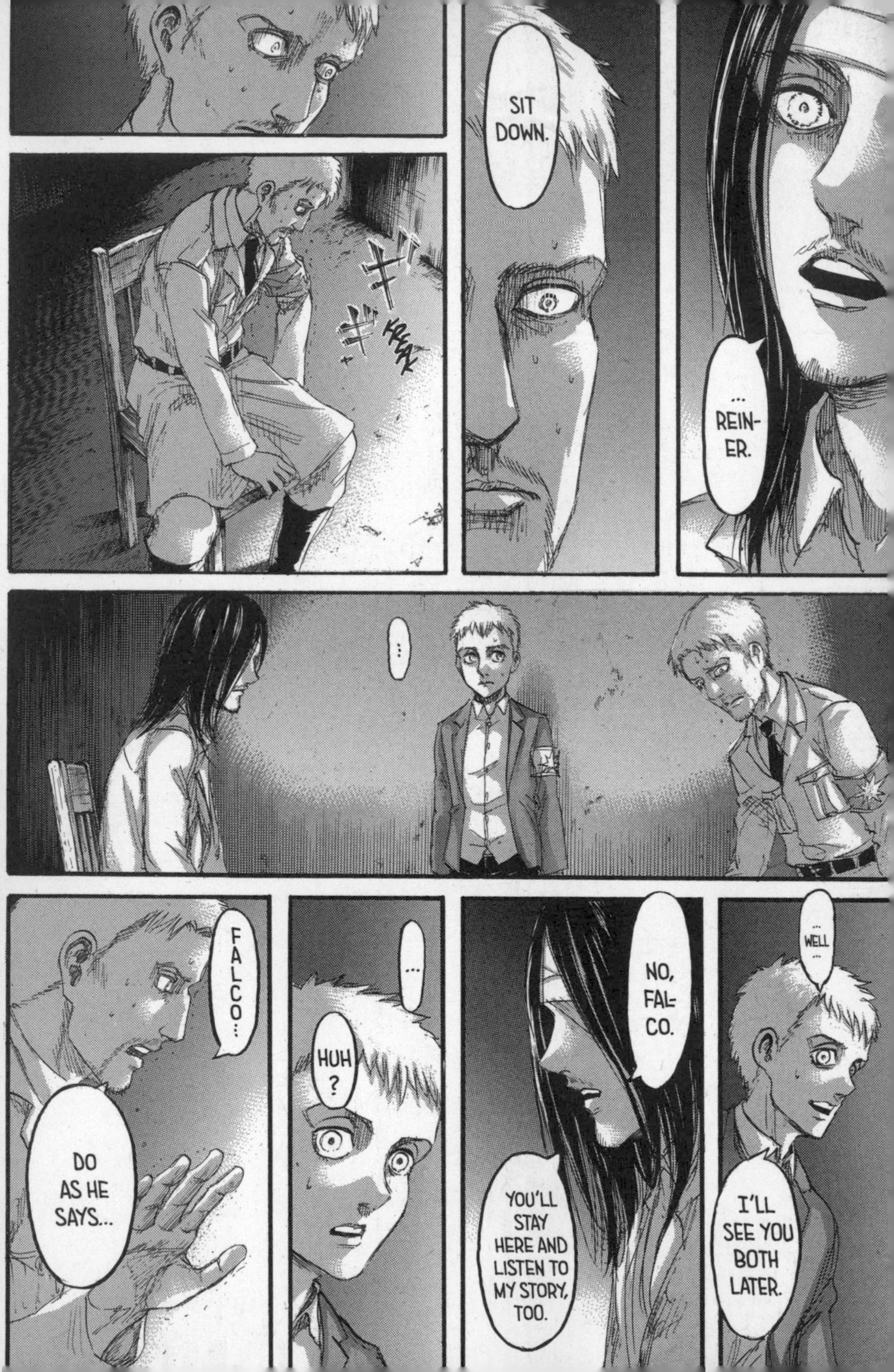
... REIN- ER.
SIT DOWN.
KREAK
...
... WELL ...
I'LL SEE YOU BOTH LATER.
NO, FAL- CO.
YOU'LL STAY HERE AND LISTEN TO MY STORY, TOO.
...
HUH ?
FALCO...
DO AS HE SAYS...

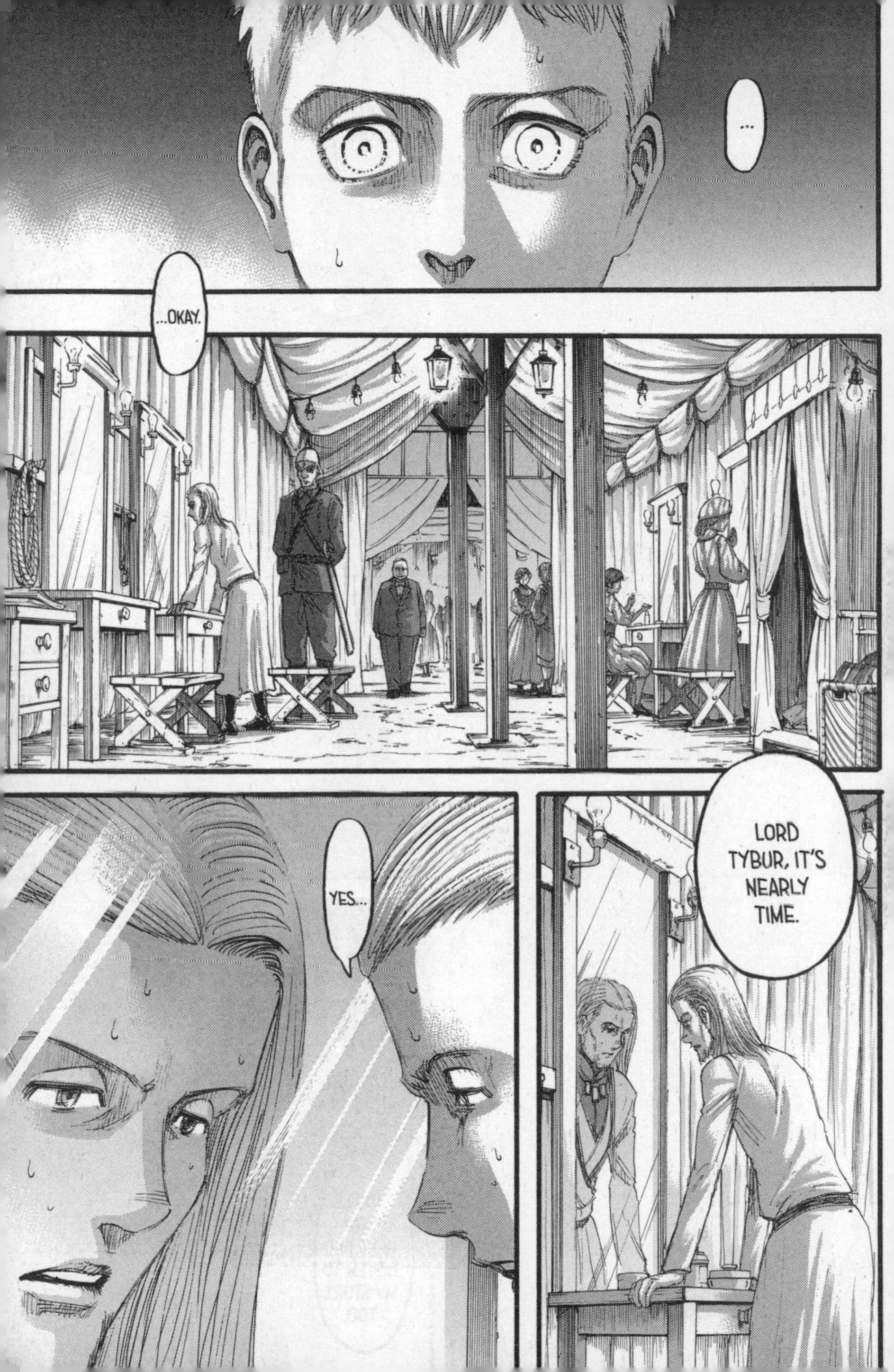
...
...OKAY.
LORD TYBUR, IT'S NEARLY TIME.
YES...

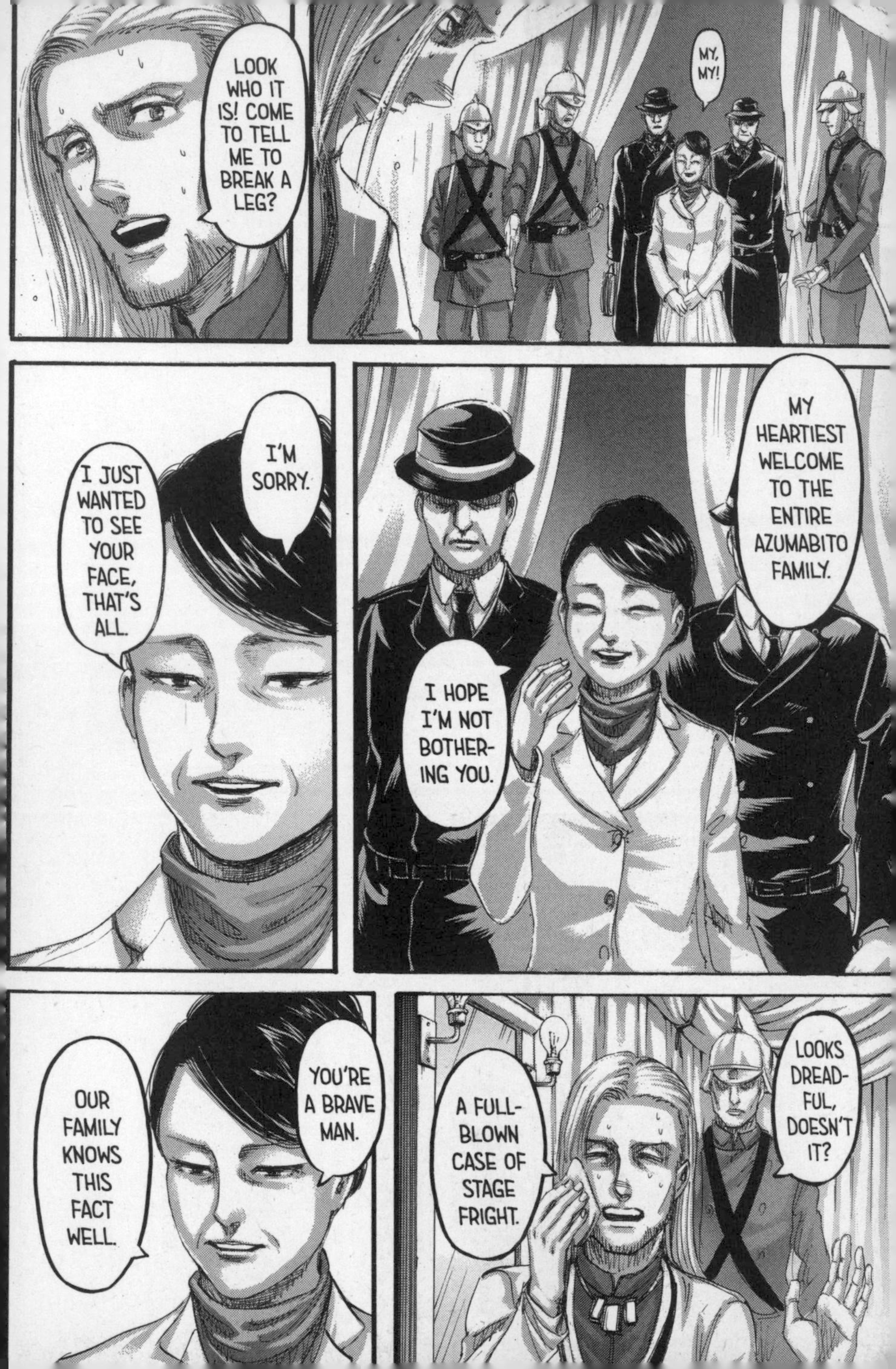
MY, MY!
LOOK WHO IT IS! COME TO TELL ME TO BREAK A LEG?
MY HEARTIEST WELCOME TO THE ENTIRE AZUMABITO FAMILY.
I HOPE I'M NOT BOTHERING YOU.
I'M SORRY.
I JUST WANTED TO SEE YOUR FACE, THAT'S ALL.
LOOKS DREADFUL, DOESN'T IT?
A FULL-BLOWN CASE OF STAGE FRIGHT.
YOU'RE A BRAVE MAN.
OUR FAMILY KNOWS THIS FACT WELL.

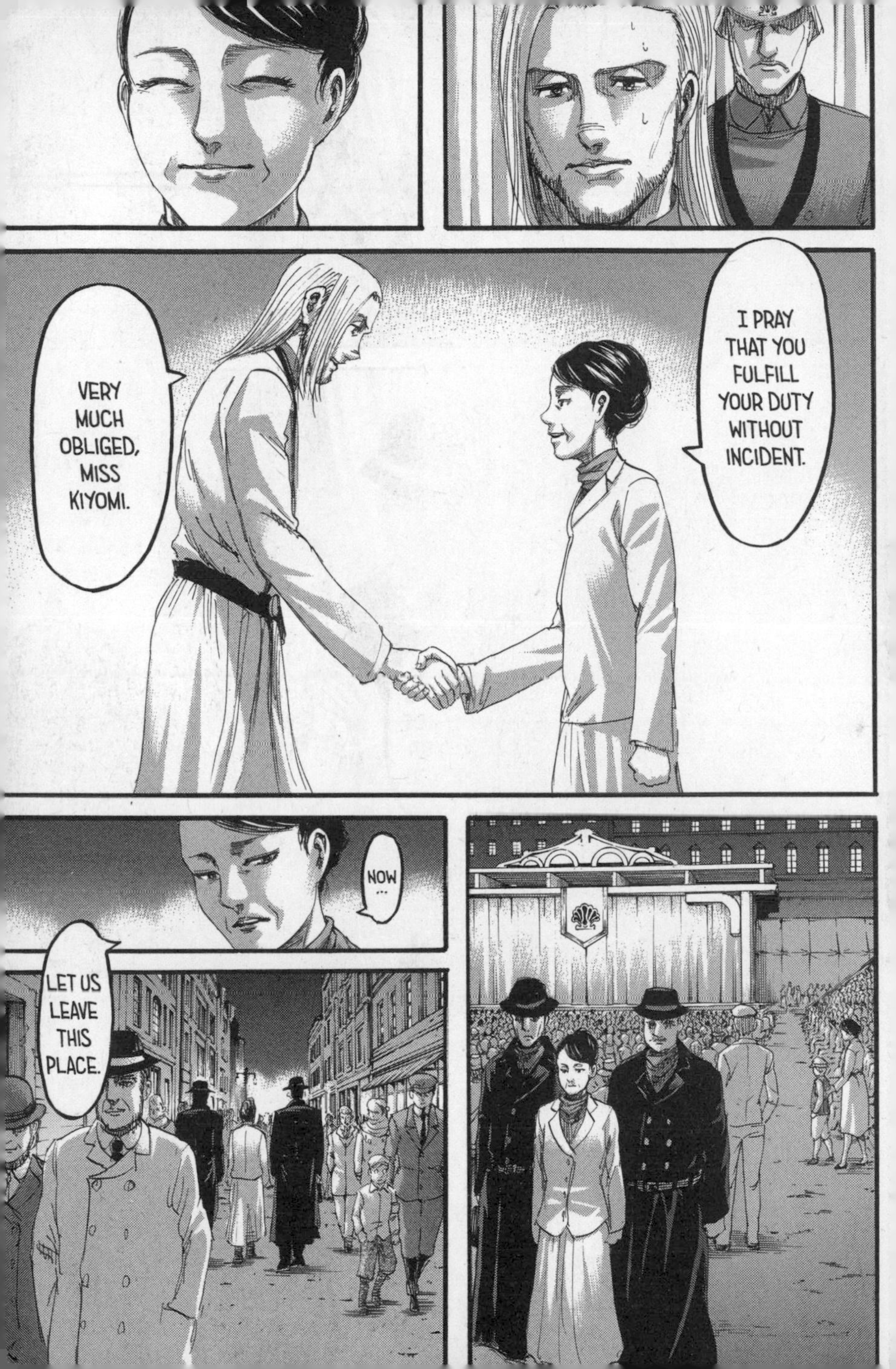
I PRAY THAT YOU FULFILL YOUR DUTY WITHOUT INCIDENT.
VERY MUCH OBLIGED, MISS KIYOMI.
NOW...
LET US LEAVE THIS PLACE.

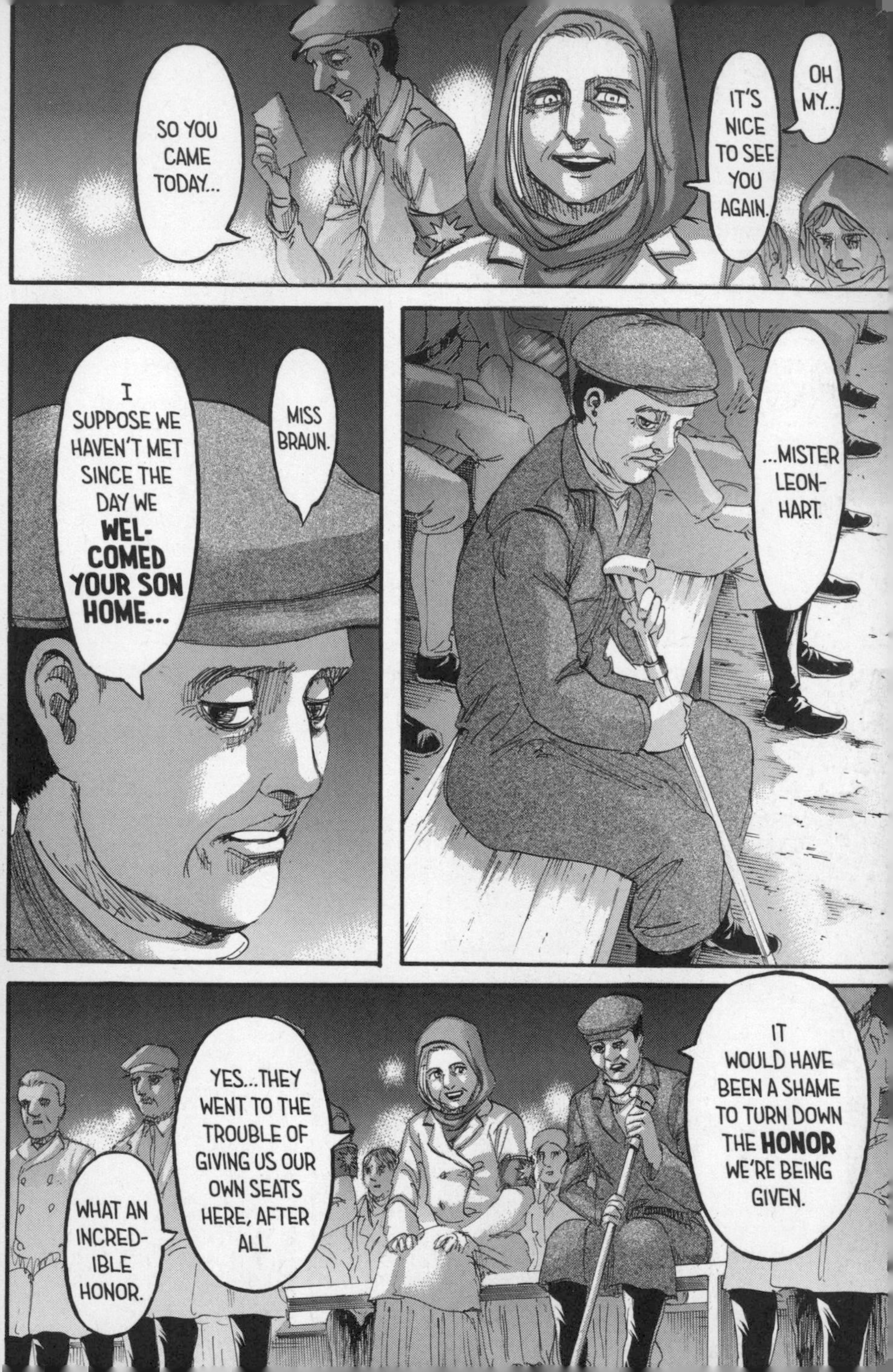
OH MY...
IT'S NICE TO SEE YOU AGAIN.
SO YOU CAME TODAY...
...MISTER LEON-HART.
MISS BRAUN.
I SUPPOSE WE HAVEN'T MET SINCE THE DAY WE **WEL-COMED YOUR SON HOME...**
IT WOULD HAVE BEEN A SHAME TO TURN DOWN THE **HONOR** WE'RE BEING GIVEN.
YES... THEY WENT TO THE TROUBLE OF GIVING US OUR OWN SEATS HERE, AFTER ALL.
WHAT AN INCRED-IBLE HONOR.

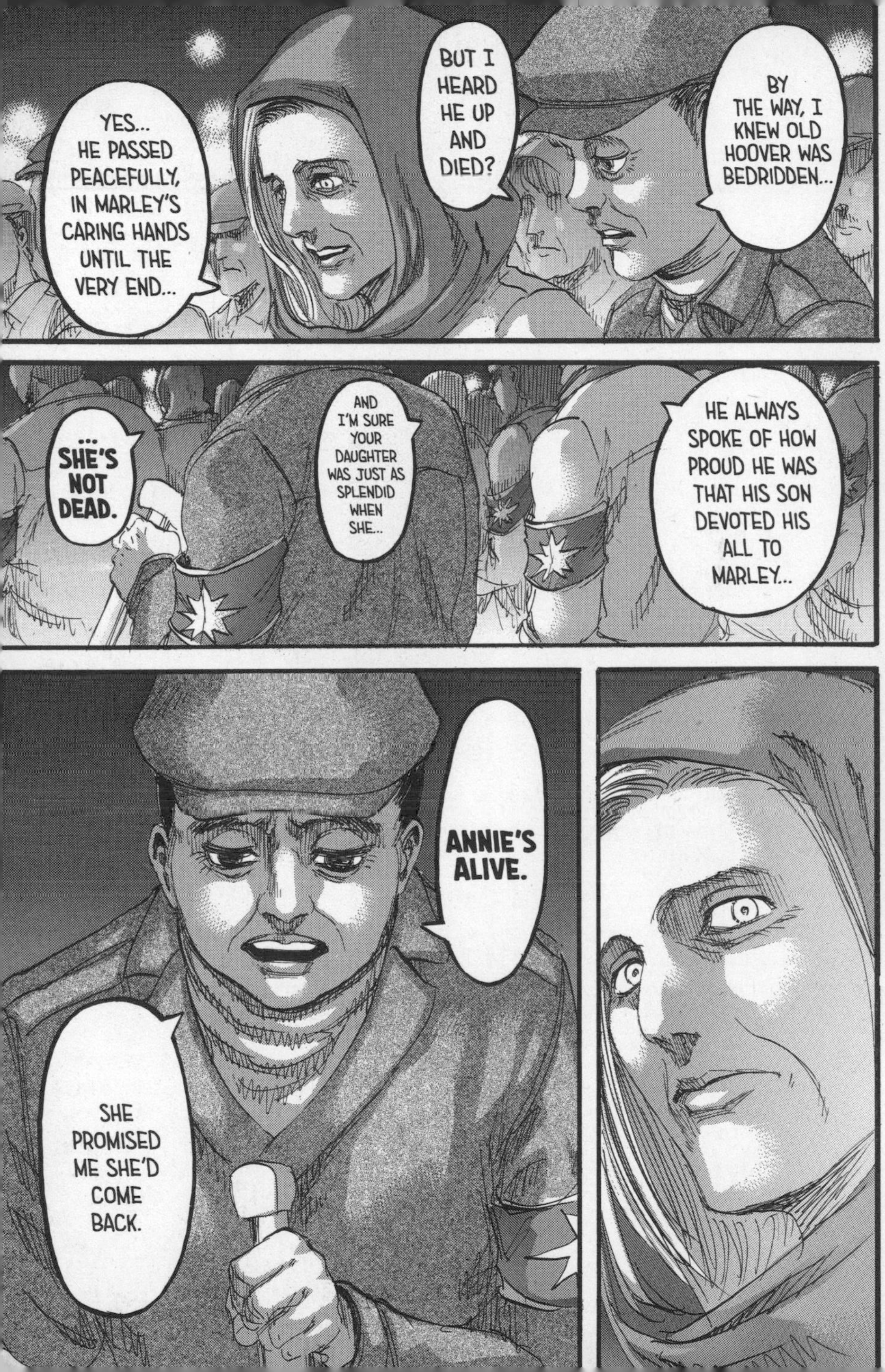
BY THE WAY, I KNEW OLD HOOVER WAS BEDRIDDEN...
BUT I HEARD HE UP AND DIED?
YES... HE PASSED PEACEFULLY, IN MARLEY'S CARING HANDS UNTIL THE VERY END...
HE ALWAYS SPOKE OF HOW PROUD HE WAS THAT HIS SON DEVOTED HIS ALL TO MARLEY...
AND I'M SURE YOUR DAUGHTER WAS JUST AS SPLENDID WHEN SHE...
...SHE'S NOT DEAD.
ANNIE'S ALIVE.
SHE PROMISED ME SHE'D COME BACK.

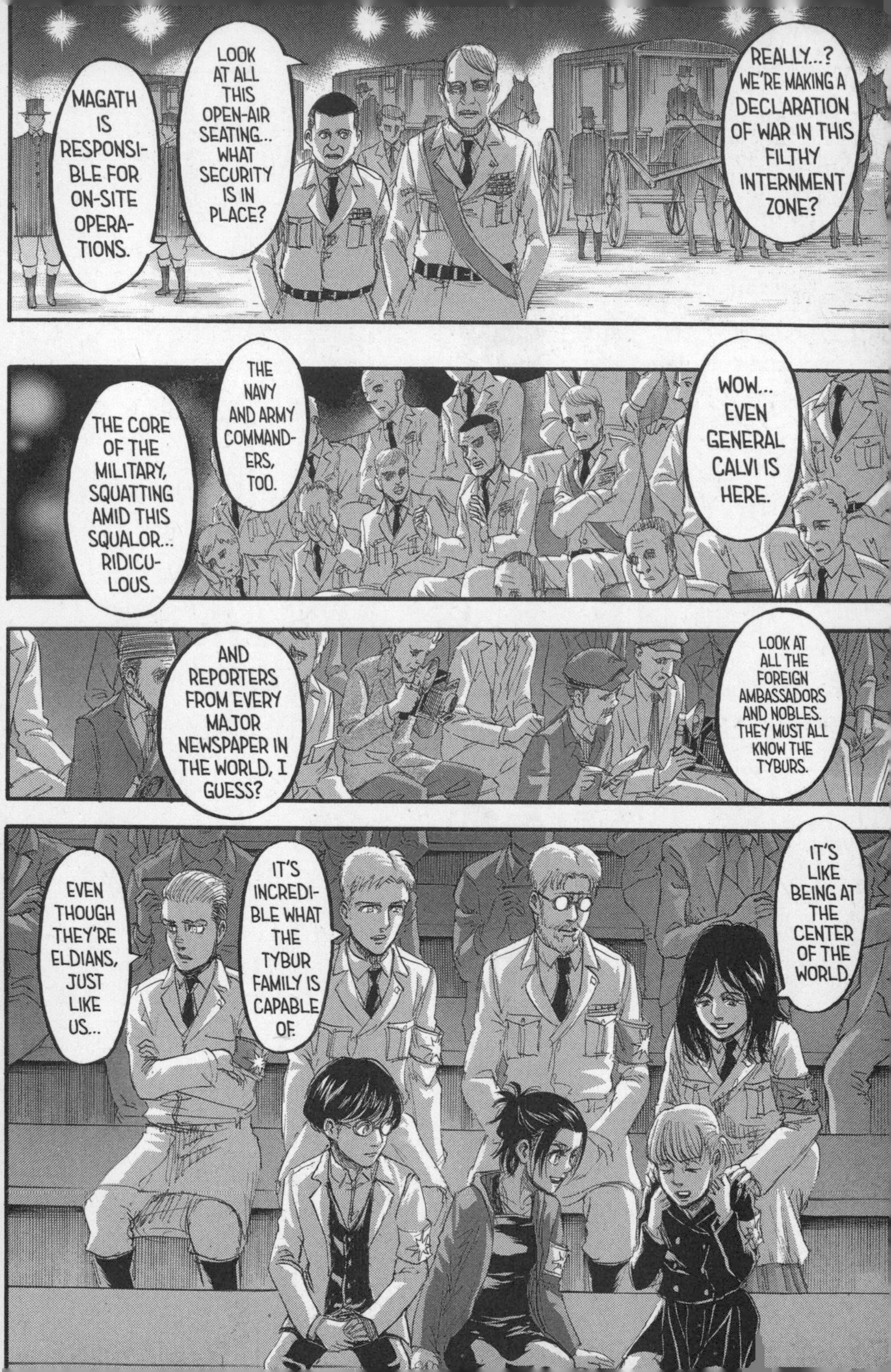
REALLY...? WE'RE MAKING A DECLARATION OF WAR IN THIS FILTHY INTERNMENT ZONE?
LOOK AT ALL THIS OPEN-AIR SEATING... WHAT SECURITY IS IN PLACE?
MAGATH IS RESPONSIBLE FOR ON-SITE OPERATIONS.
WOW... EVEN GENERAL CALVI IS HERE.
THE NAVY AND ARMY COMMANDERS, TOO.
THE CORE OF THE MILITARY, SQUATTING AMID THIS SQUALOR... RIDICULOUS.
LOOK AT ALL THE FOREIGN AMBASSADORS AND NOBLES. THEY MUST ALL KNOW THE TYBURS.
AND REPORTERS FROM EVERY MAJOR NEWSPAPER IN THE WORLD, I GUESS?
IT'S LIKE BEING AT THE CENTER OF THE WORLD.
IT'S INCREDIBLE WHAT THE TYBUR FAMILY IS CAPABLE OF.
EVEN THOUGH THEY'RE ELDIANS, JUST LIKE US...

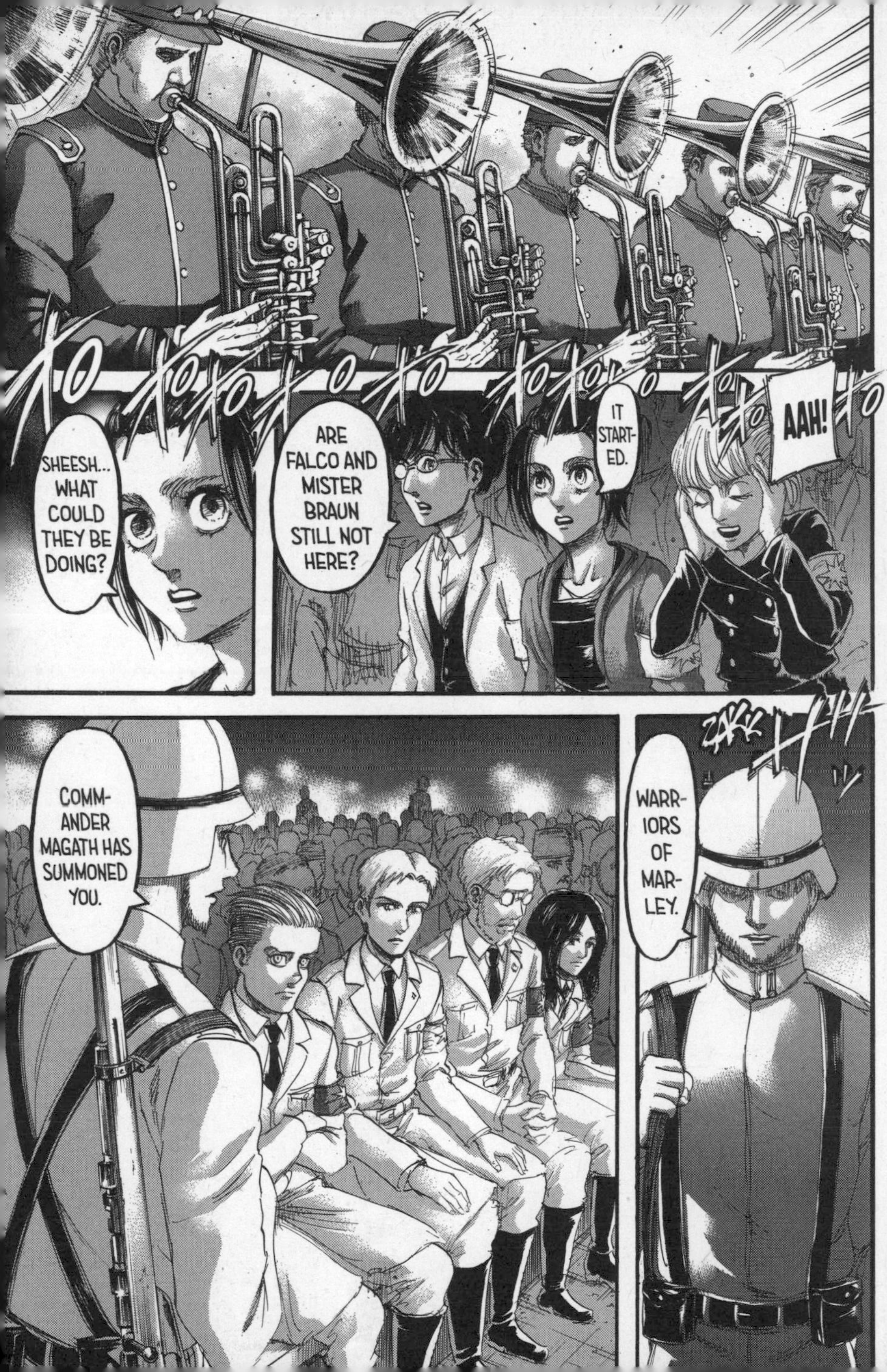
AAH!
IT START-ED.
ARE FALCO AND MISTER BRAUN STILL NOT HERE?
SHEESH... WHAT COULD THEY BE DOING?
WARR-IORS OF MAR-LEY.
COMM-ANDER MAGATH HAS SUMMONED YOU.

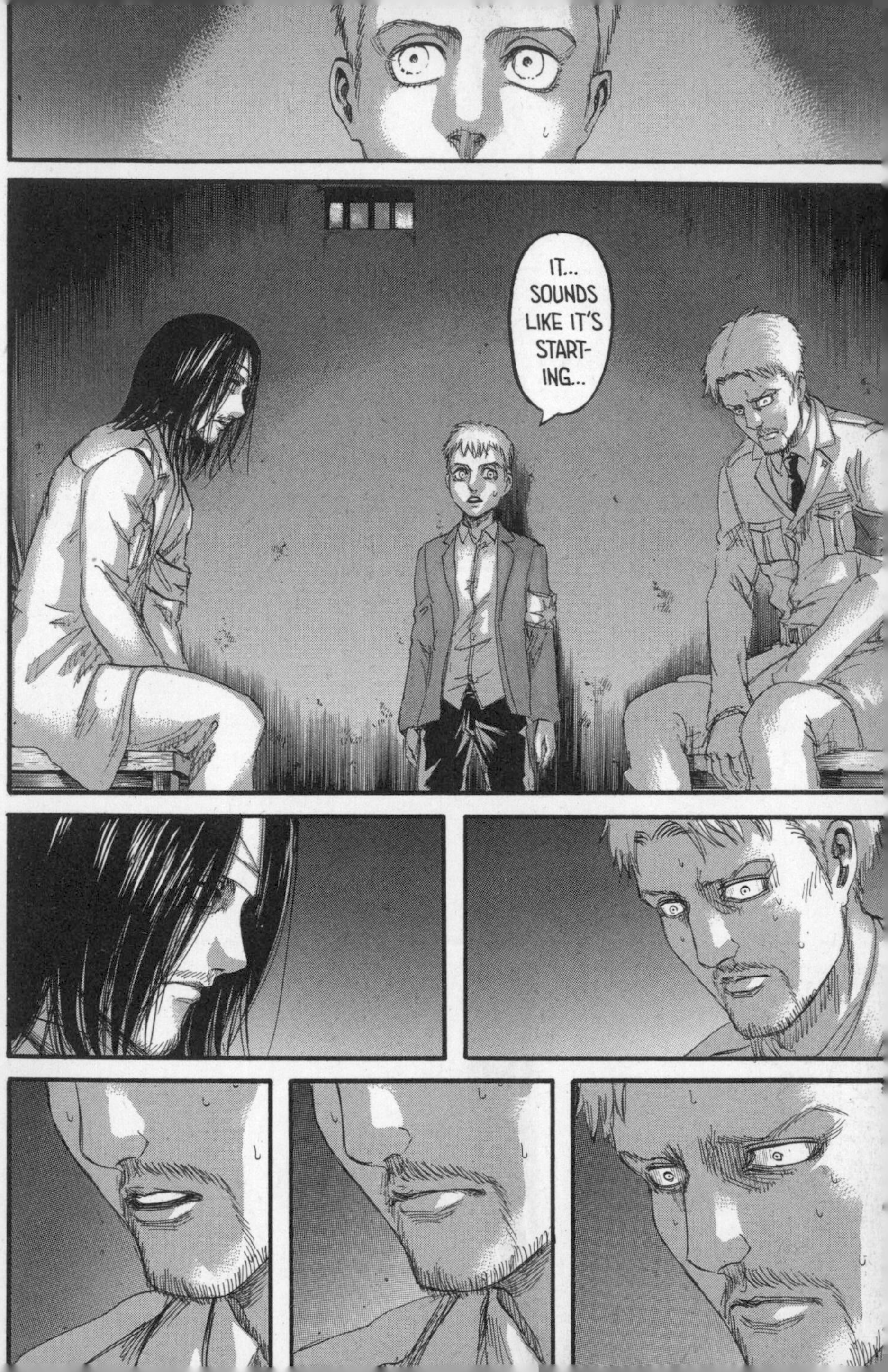
IT... SOUNDS LIKE IT'S START-ING...

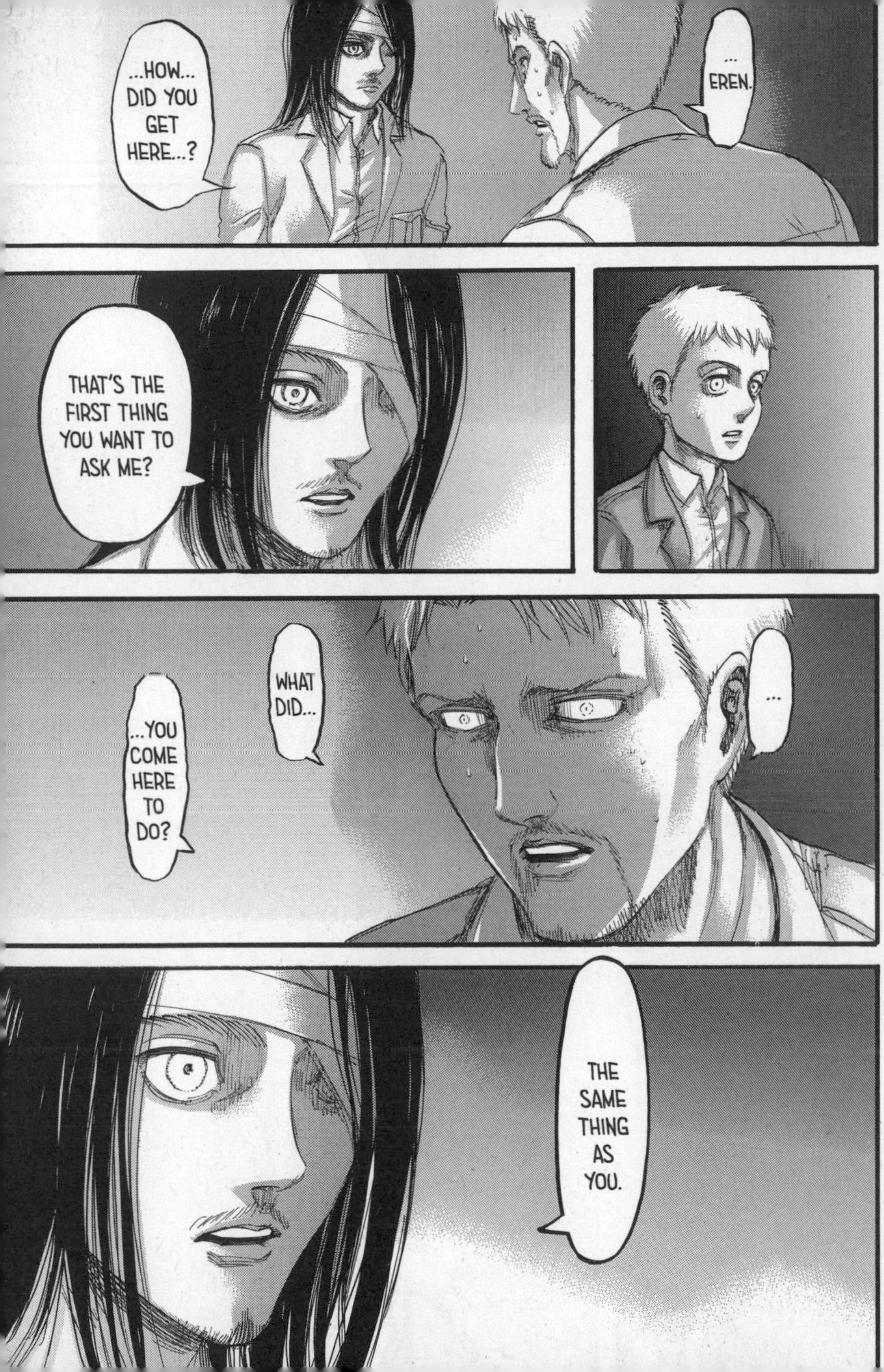
... EREN.
...HOW... DID YOU GET HERE...?
THAT'S THE FIRST THING YOU WANT TO ASK ME?
...
WHAT DID...
...YOU COME HERE TO DO?
THE SAME THING AS YOU.

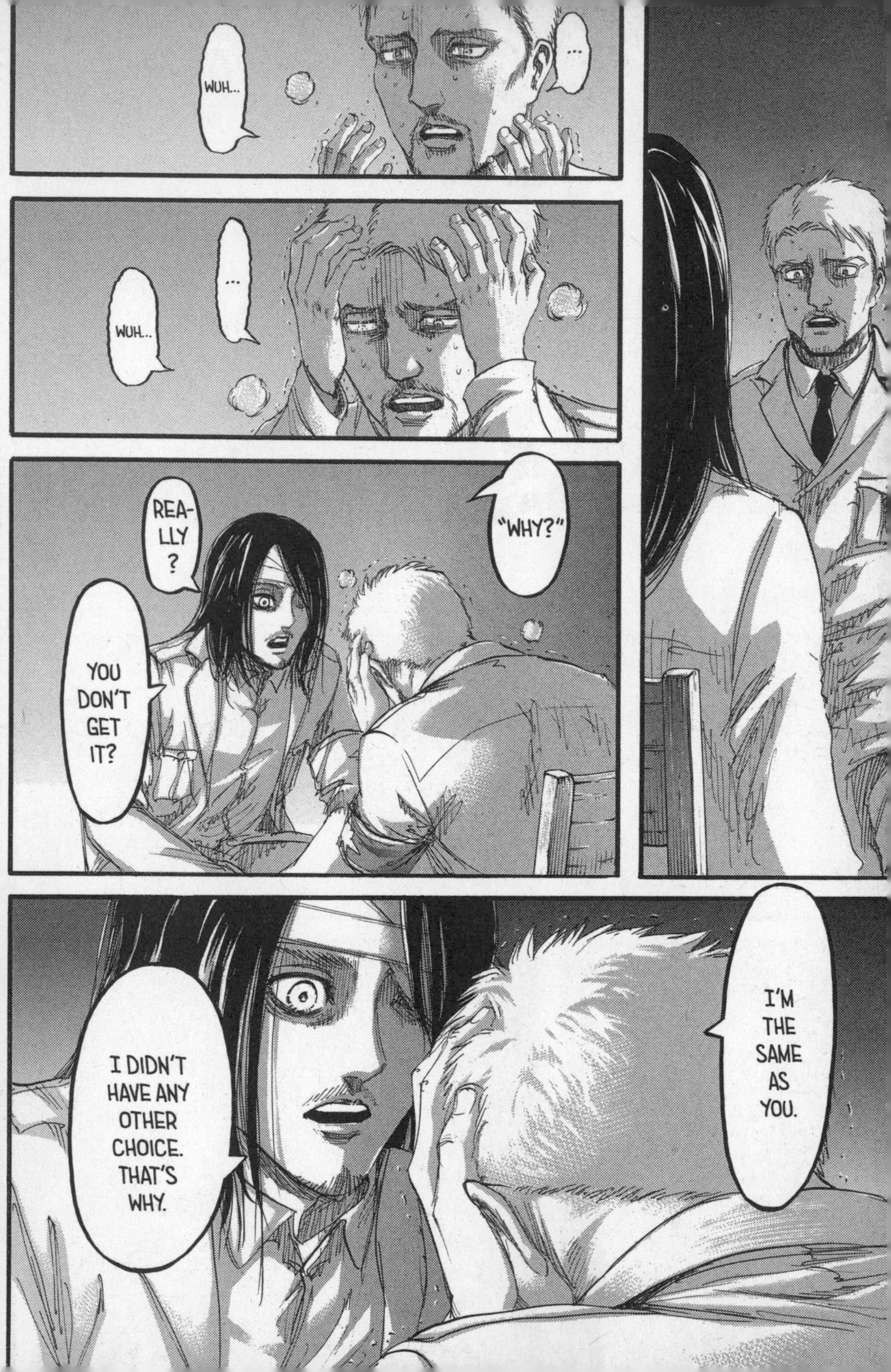
...
WUH...
...
WUH...
"WHY?"
REA-LLY?
YOU DON'T GET IT?
I'M THE SAME AS YOU.
I DIDN'T HAVE ANY OTHER CHOICE. THAT'S WHY.

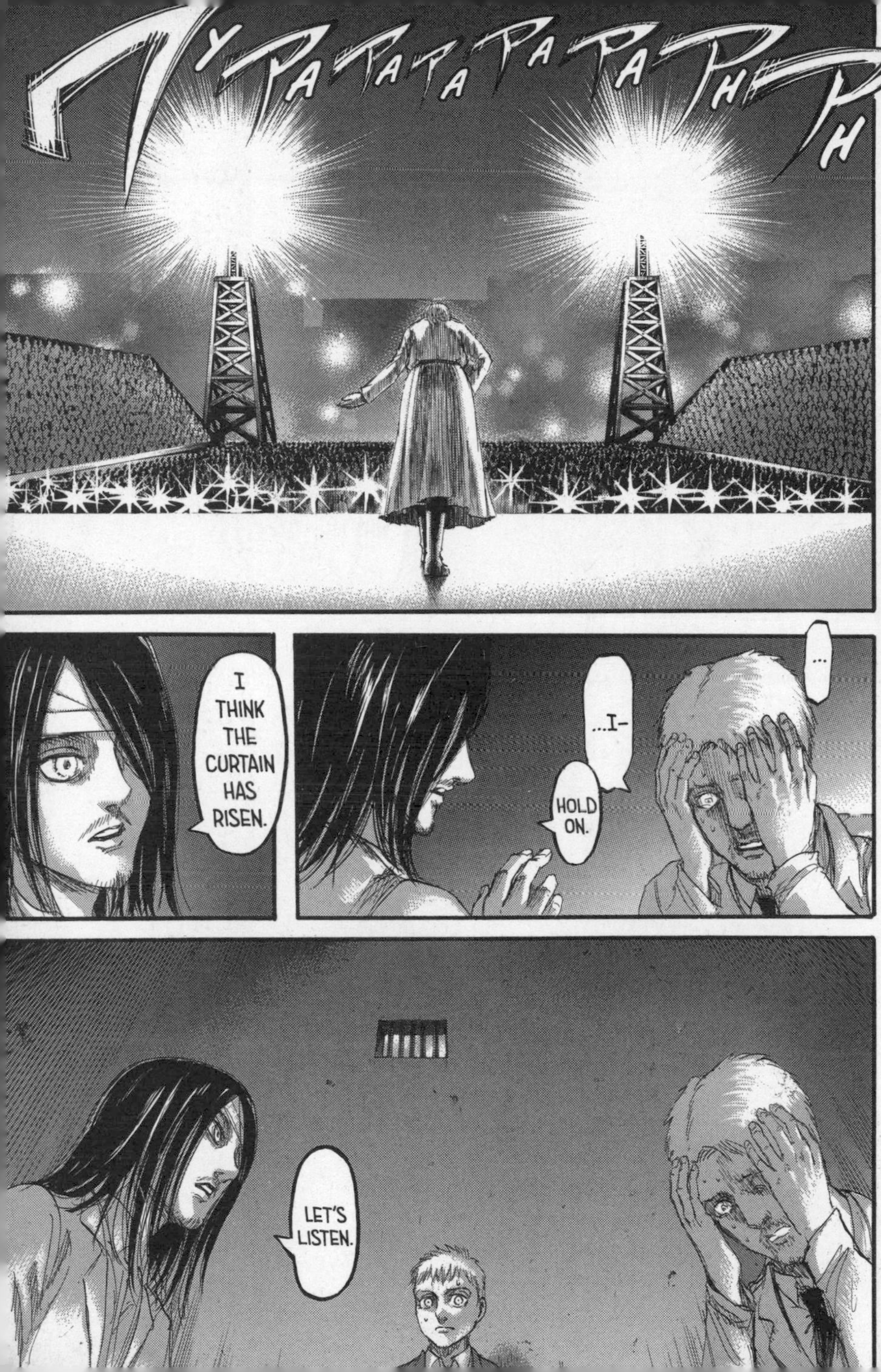
...
...I-
HOLD ON.
I THINK THE CURTAIN HAS RISEN.
LET'S LISTEN.

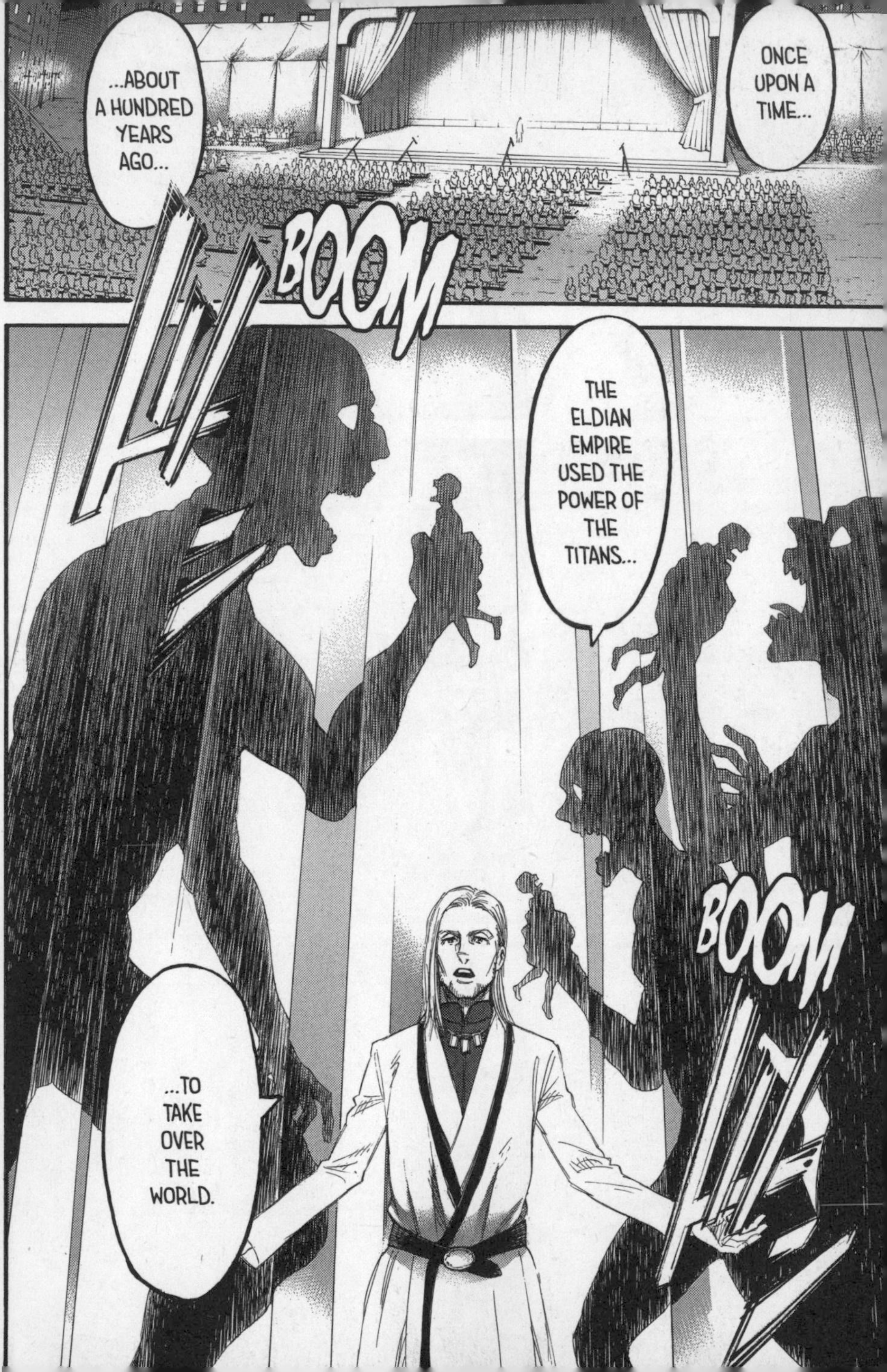
ONCE UPON A TIME...
...ABOUT A HUNDRED YEARS AGO...
BOOM
THE ELDIAN EMPIRE USED THE POWER OF THE TITANS...
BOOM
...TO TAKE OVER THE WORLD.

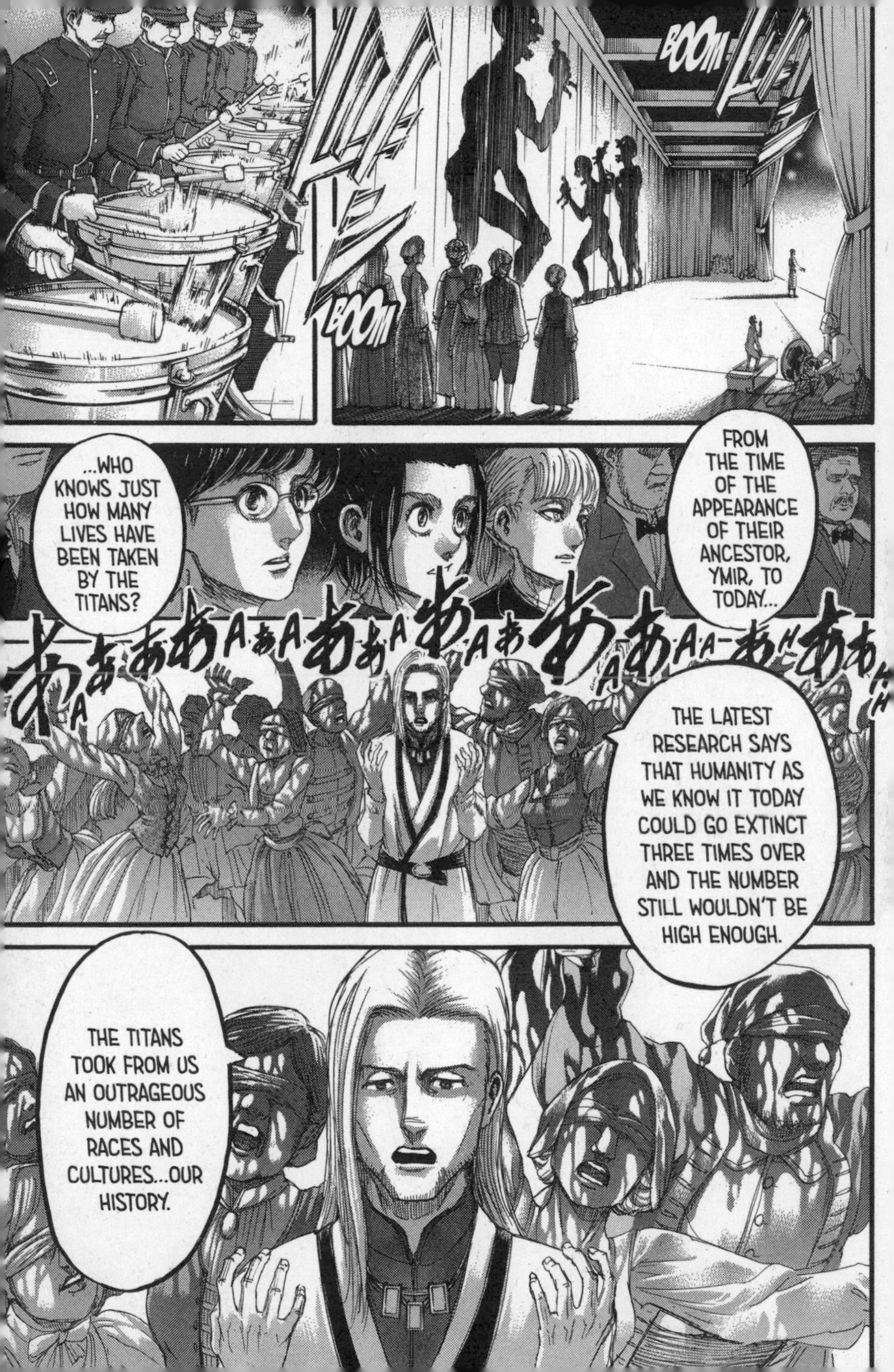
BOOM
BOOM
FROM THE TIME OF THE APPEARANCE OF THEIR ANCESTOR, YMIR, TO TODAY...
...WHO KNOWS JUST HOW MANY LIVES HAVE BEEN TAKEN BY THE TITANS?
THE LATEST RESEARCH SAYS THAT HUMANITY AS WE KNOW IT TODAY COULD GO EXTINCT THREE TIMES OVER AND THE NUMBER STILL WOULDN'T BE HIGH ENOUGH.
THE TITANS TOOK FROM US AN OUTRAGEOUS NUMBER OF RACES AND CULTURES...OUR HISTORY.

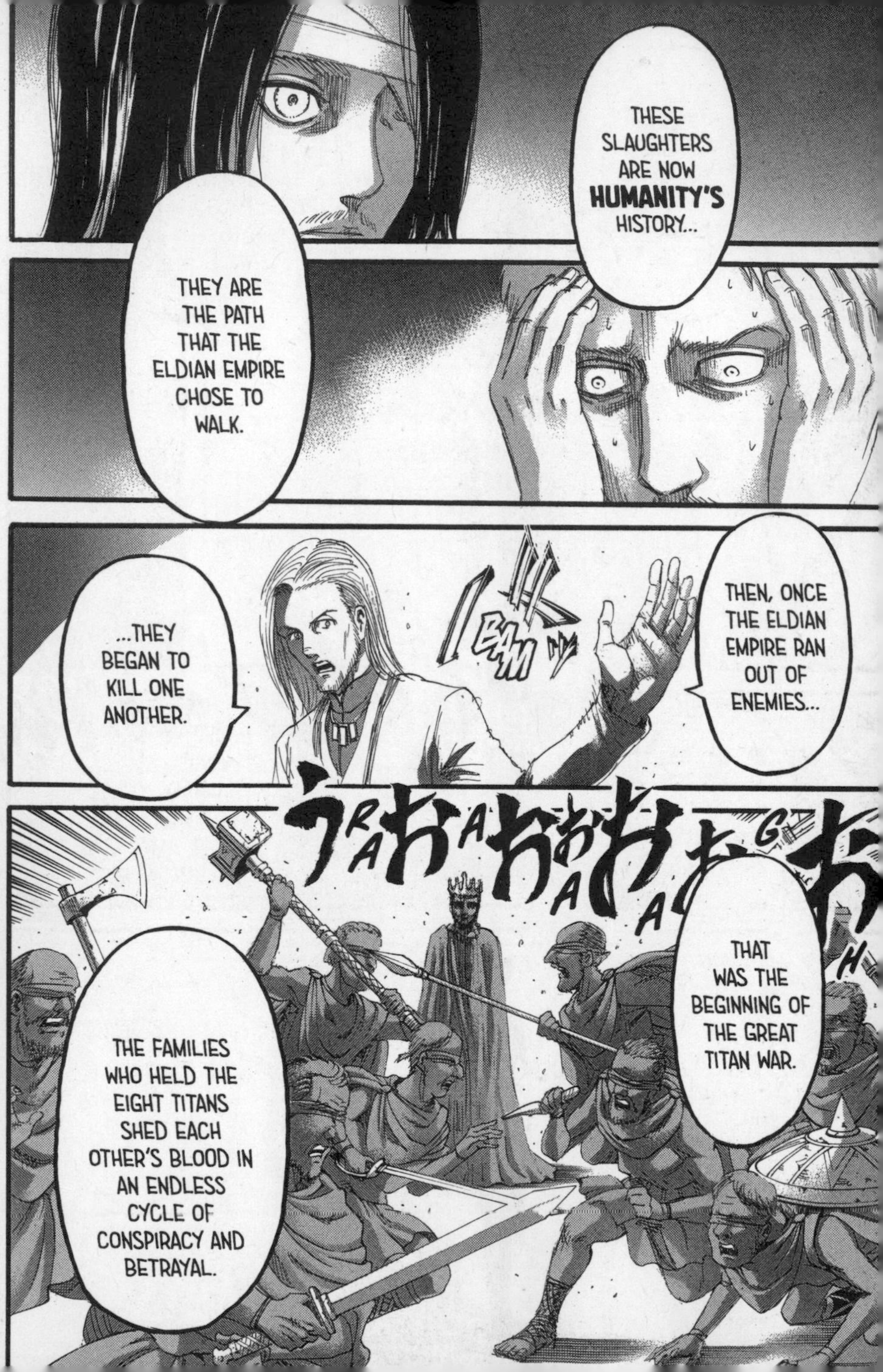
THESE SLAUGHTERS ARE NOW **HUMANITY'S** HISTORY...
THEY ARE THE PATH THAT THE ELDIAN EMPIRE CHOSE TO WALK.
THEN, ONCE THE ELDIAN EMPIRE RAN OUT OF ENEMIES...
BAM
...THEY BEGAN TO KILL ONE ANOTHER.
RAAAAAGH
THAT WAS THE BEGINNING OF THE GREAT TITAN WAR.
THE FAMILIES WHO HELD THE EIGHT TITANS SHED EACH OTHER'S BLOOD IN AN ENDLESS CYCLE OF CONSPIRACY AND BETRAYAL.

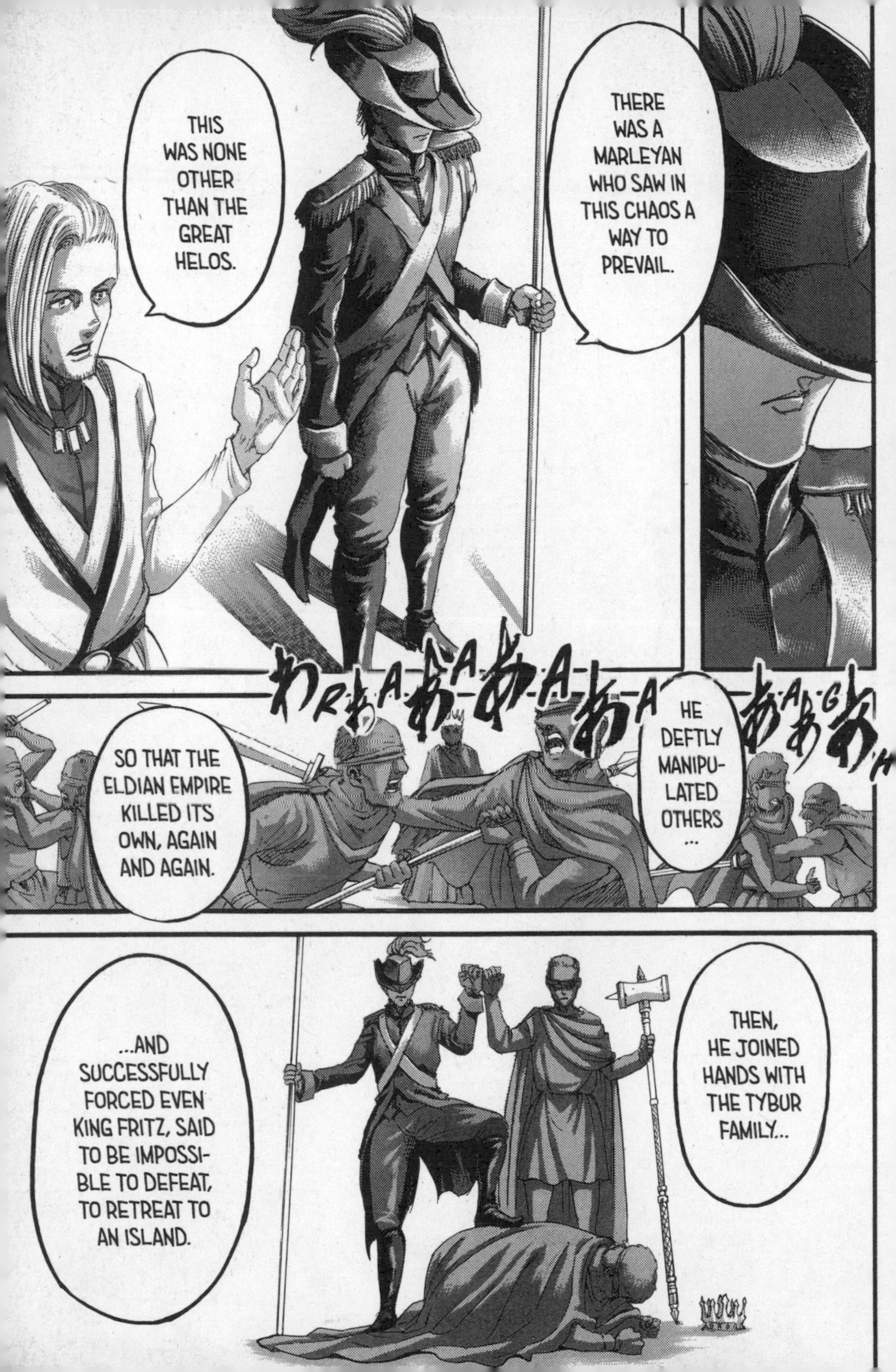
THERE WAS A MARLEYAN WHO SAW IN THIS CHAOS A WAY TO PREVAIL.
THIS WAS NONE OTHER THAN THE GREAT HELOS.
HE DEFTLY MANIPULATED OTHERS...
SO THAT THE ELDIAN EMPIRE KILLED ITS OWN, AGAIN AND AGAIN.
THEN, HE JOINED HANDS WITH THE TYBUR FAMILY...
...AND SUCCESSFULLY FORCED EVEN KING FRITZ, SAID TO BE IMPOSSIBLE TO DEFEAT, TO RETREAT TO AN ISLAND.

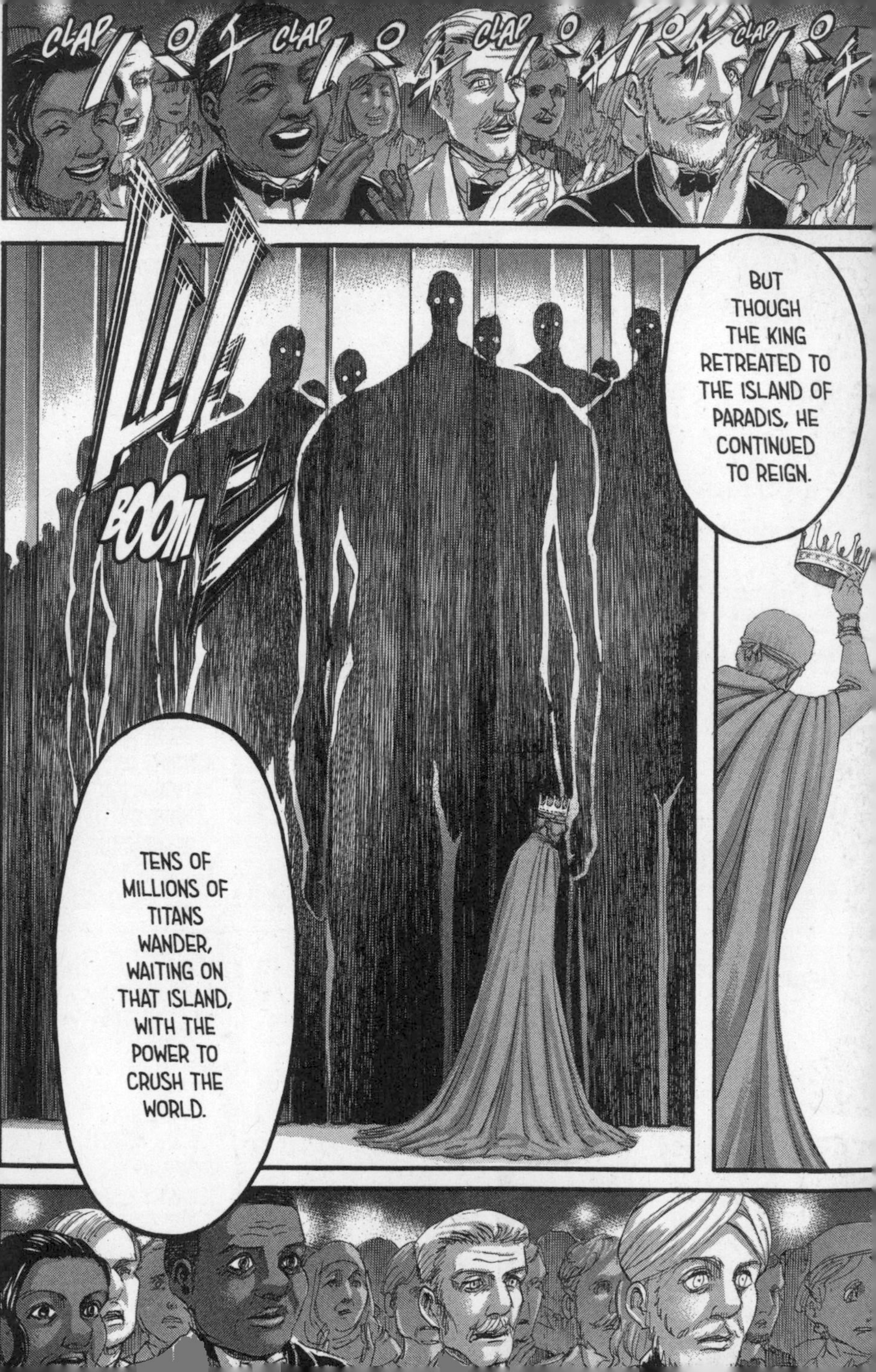
CLAP
CLAP
CLAP
CLAP
BUT THOUGH THE KING RETREATED TO THE ISLAND OF PARADIS, HE CONTINUED TO REIGN.
BOOM
TENS OF MILLIONS OF TITANS WANDER, WAITING ON THAT ISLAND, WITH THE POWER TO CRUSH THE WORLD.

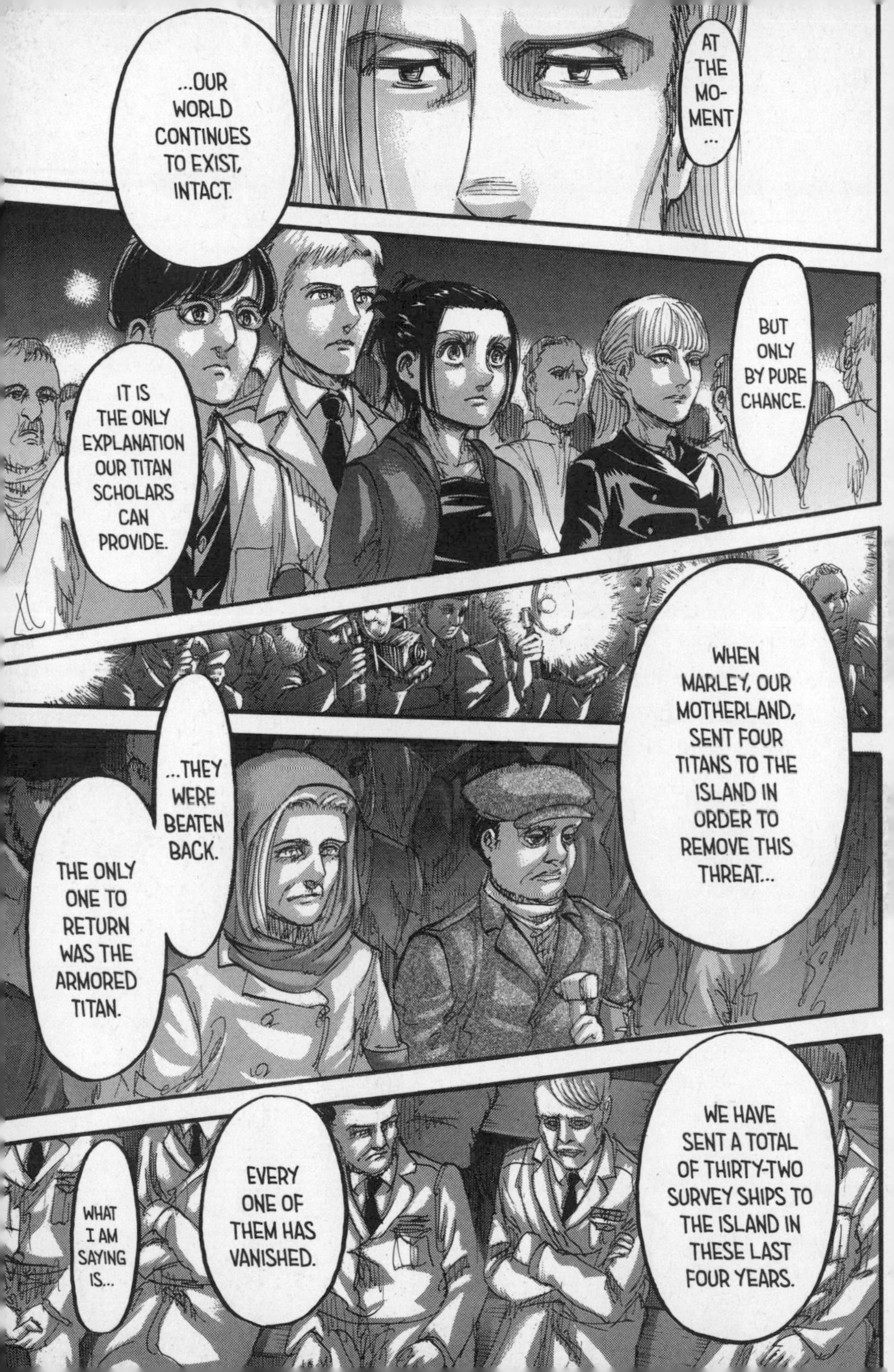
AT THE MO-MENT...
...OUR WORLD CONTINUES TO EXIST, INTACT.
BUT ONLY BY PURE CHANCE.
IT IS THE ONLY EXPLANATION OUR TITAN SCHOLARS CAN PROVIDE.
WHEN MARLEY, OUR MOTHERLAND, SENT FOUR TITANS TO THE ISLAND IN ORDER TO REMOVE THIS THREAT...
...THEY WERE BEATEN BACK.
THE ONLY ONE TO RETURN WAS THE ARMORED TITAN.
WE HAVE SENT A TOTAL OF THIRTY-TWO SURVEY SHIPS TO THE ISLAND IN THESE LAST FOUR YEARS.
EVERY ONE OF THEM HAS VANISHED.
WHAT I AM SAYING IS...

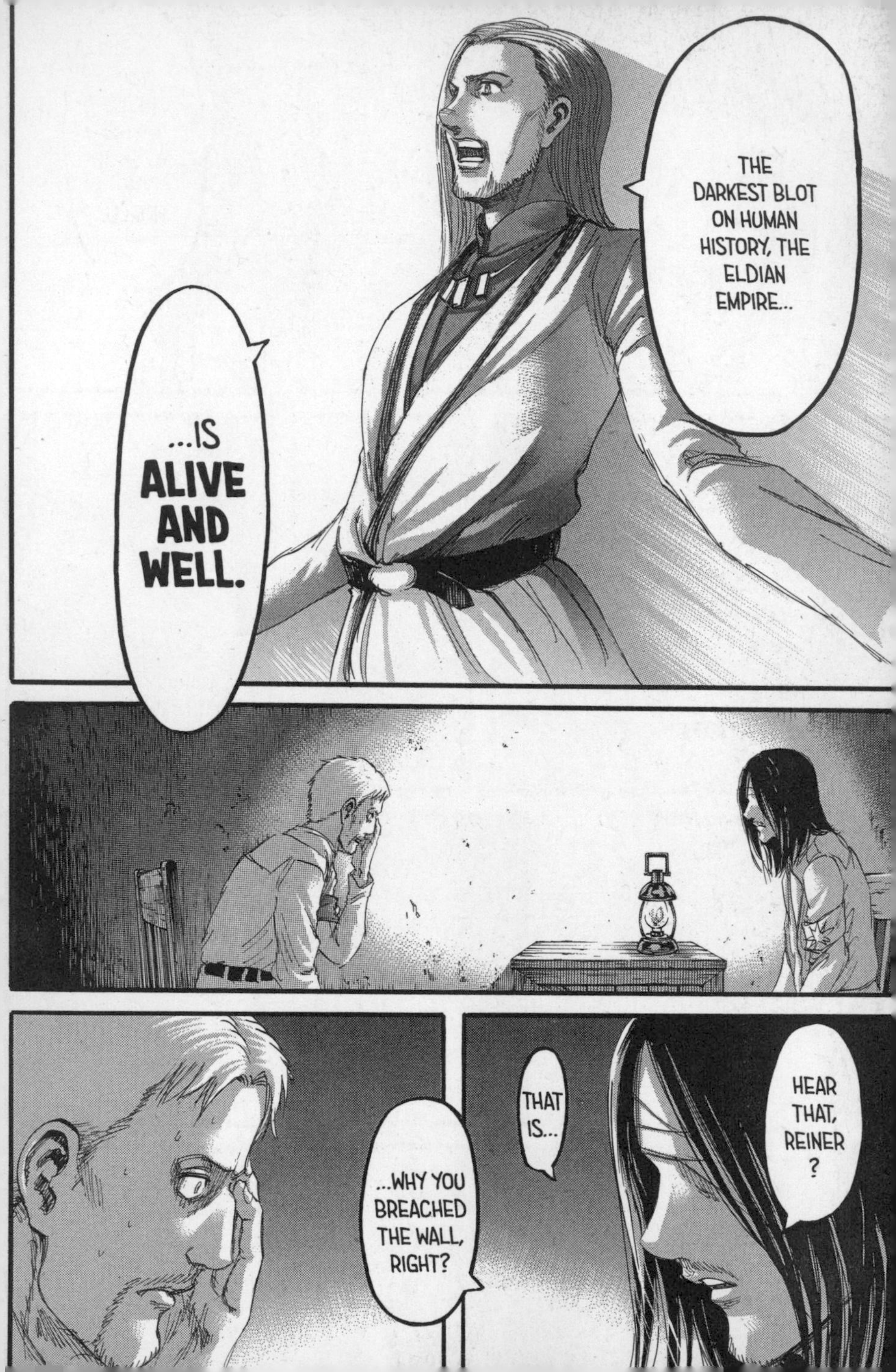
THE DARKEST BLOT ON HUMAN HISTORY, THE ELDIAN EMPIRE...
...IS ALIVE AND WELL.
HEAR THAT, REINER?
THAT IS...
...WHY YOU BREACHED THE WALL, RIGHT?

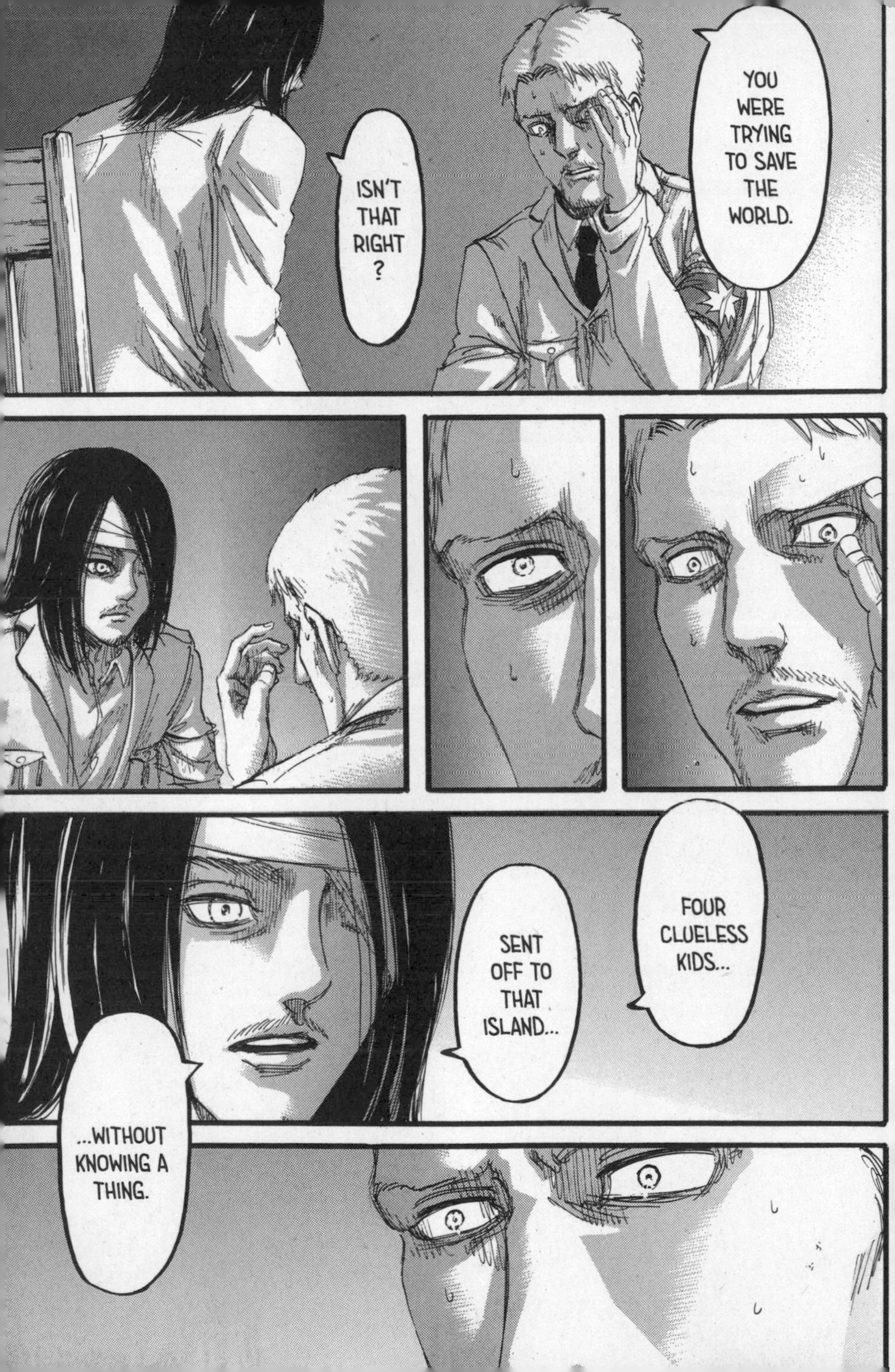
YOU WERE TRYING TO SAVE THE WORLD.
ISN'T THAT RIGHT ?
FOUR CLUELESS KIDS...
SENT OFF TO THAT ISLAND...
...WITHOUT KNOWING A THING.

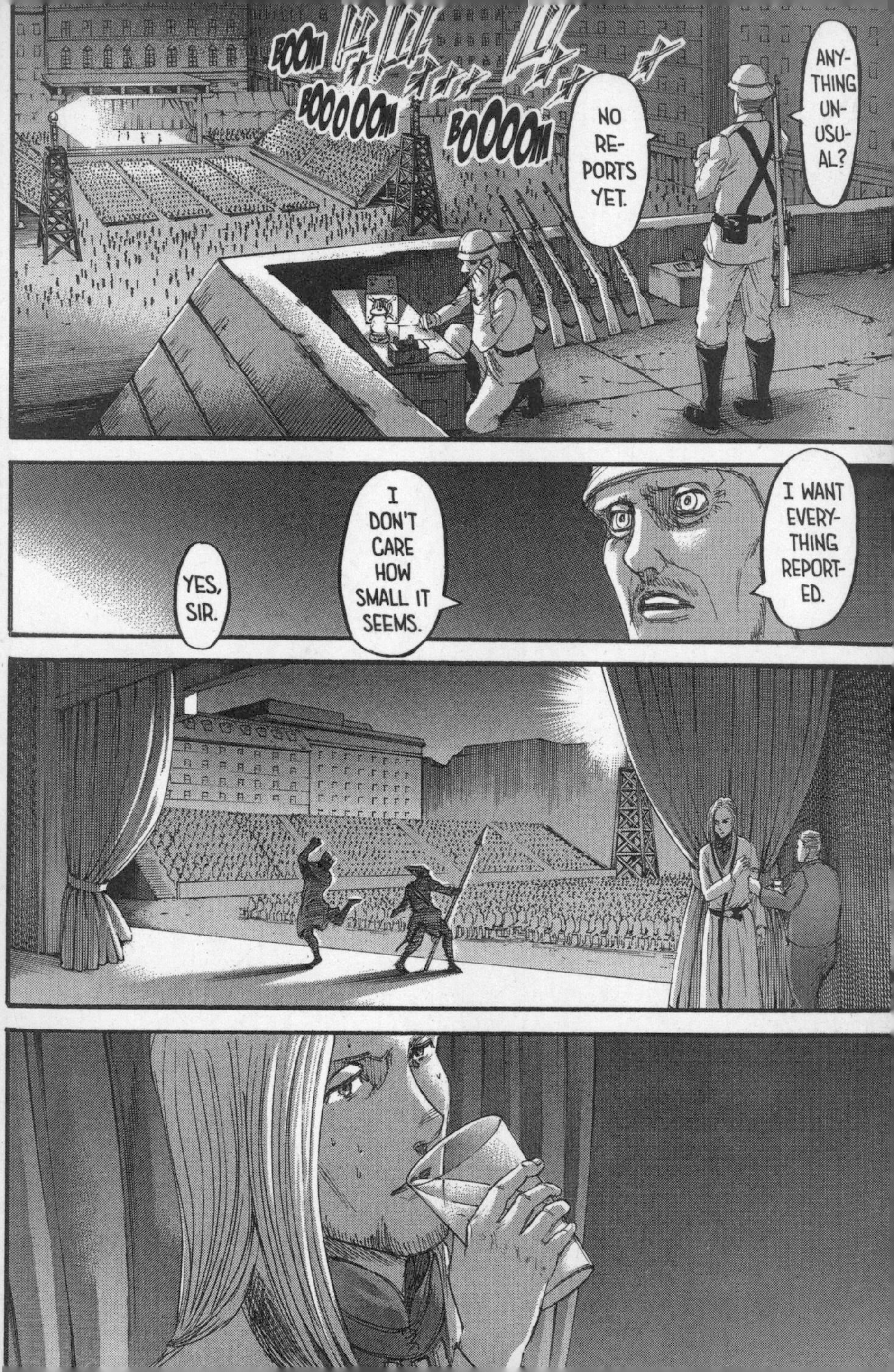
ANYTHING UNUSUAL?
NO REPORTS YET.
BOOM
BOOOOOM
BOOOOM
I WANT EVERYTHING REPORTED.
I DON'T CARE HOW SMALL IT SEEMS.
YES, SIR.

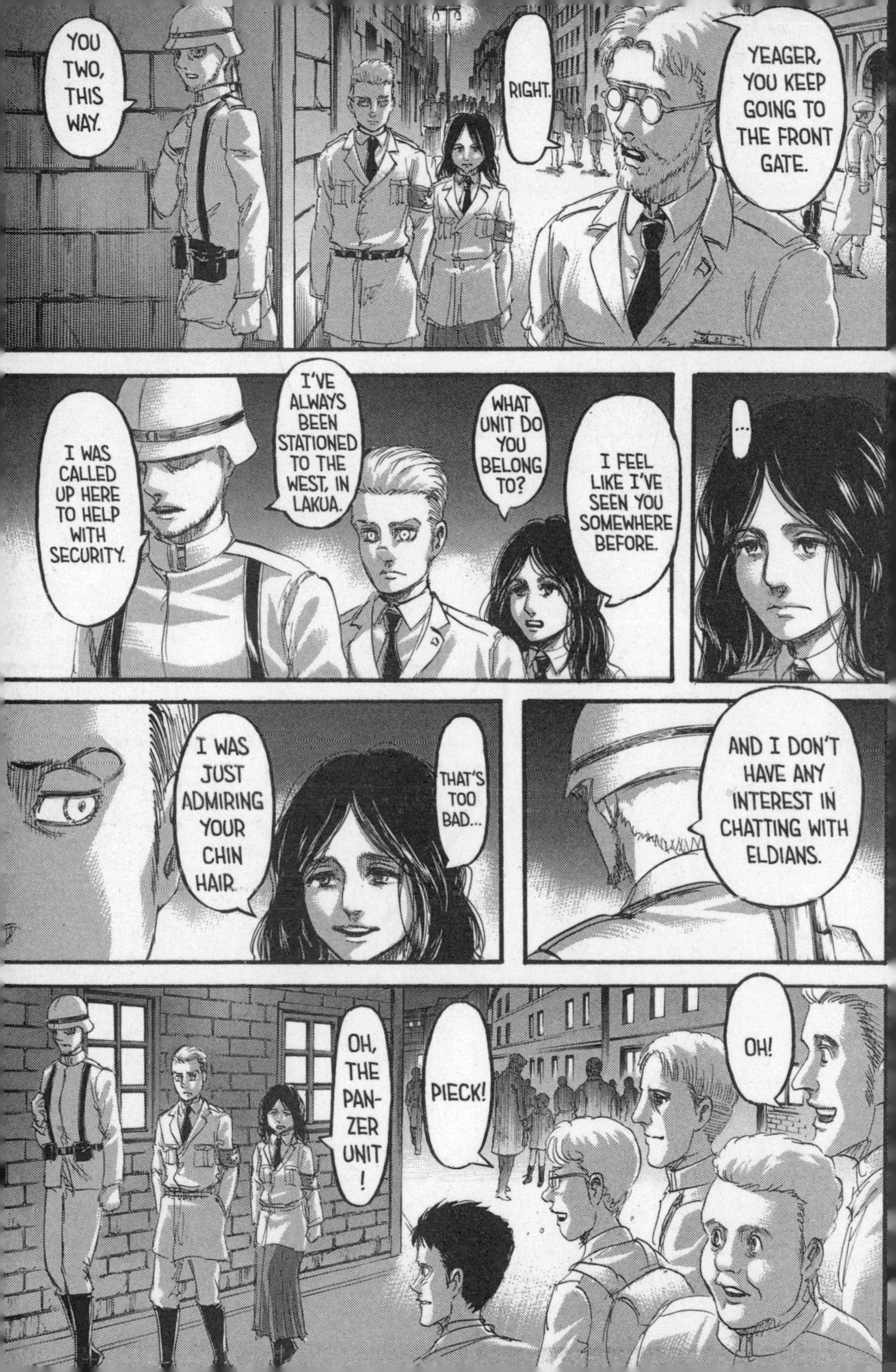

YEAGER, YOU KEEP GOING TO THE FRONT GATE.
RIGHT.
YOU TWO, THIS WAY.
...
I FEEL LIKE I'VE SEEN YOU SOMEWHERE BEFORE.
WHAT UNIT DO YOU BELONG TO?
I'VE ALWAYS BEEN STATIONED TO THE WEST, IN LAKUA.
I WAS CALLED UP HERE TO HELP WITH SECURITY.
AND I DON'T HAVE ANY INTEREST IN CHATTING WITH ELDIANS.
THAT'S TOO BAD...
I WAS JUST ADMIRING YOUR CHIN HAIR.
OH!
PIECK!
OH, THE PAN-ZER UNIT!

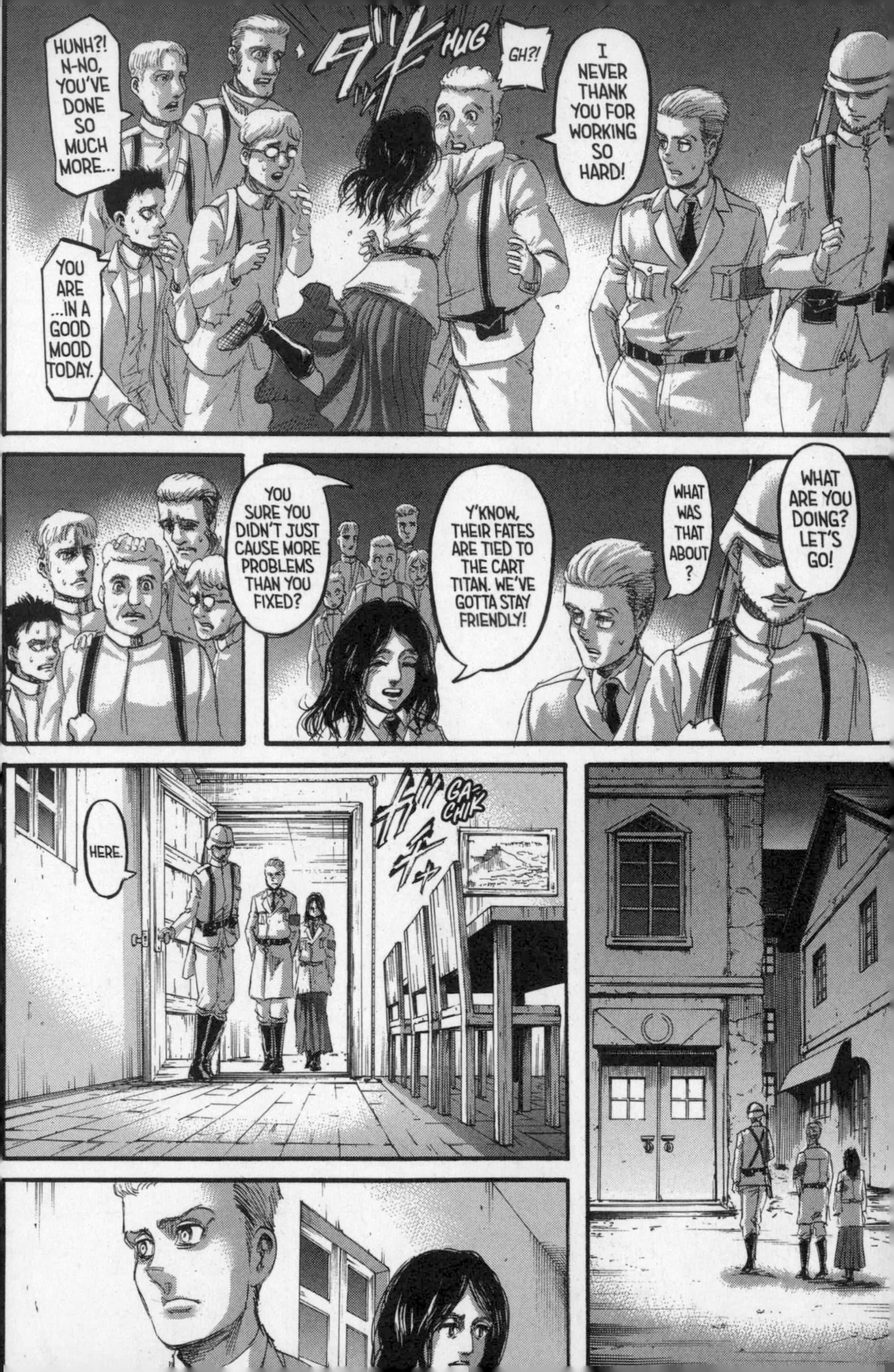
I NEVER THANK YOU FOR WORKING SO HARD!
GH?!
HUG
HUNH?! N-NO, YOU'VE DONE SO MUCH MORE...
YOU ARE ...IN A GOOD MOOD TODAY.
WHAT ARE YOU DOING? LET'S GO!
WHAT WAS THAT ABOUT?
Y'KNOW, THEIR FATES ARE TIED TO THE CART TITAN. WE'VE GOTTA STAY FRIENDLY!
YOU SURE YOU DIDN'T JUST CAUSE MORE PROBLEMS THAN YOU FIXED?
GA-CHIK
HERE.

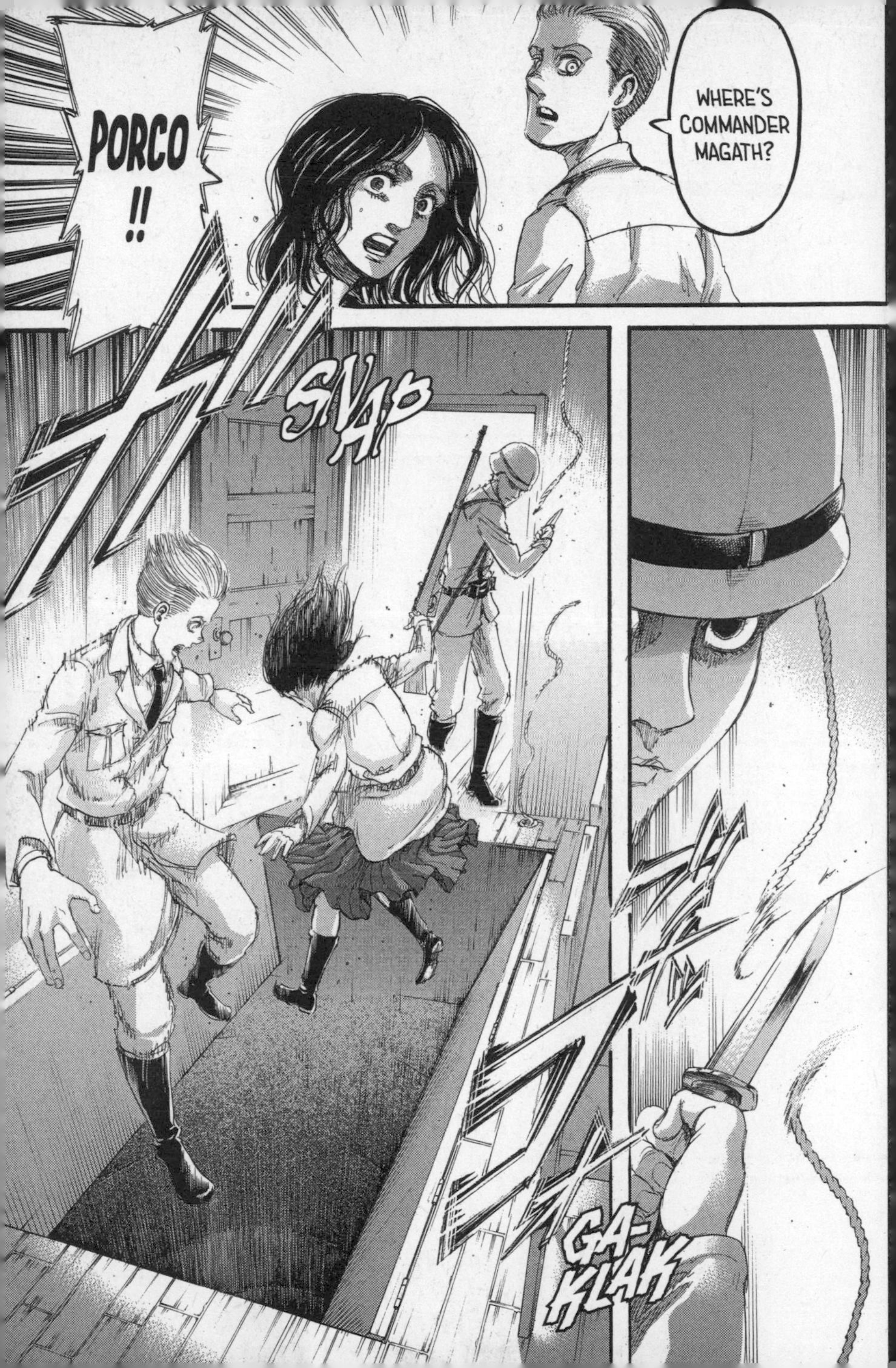
WHERE'S COMMANDER MAGATH?
PORCO !!
GA-KLAK
SNAP

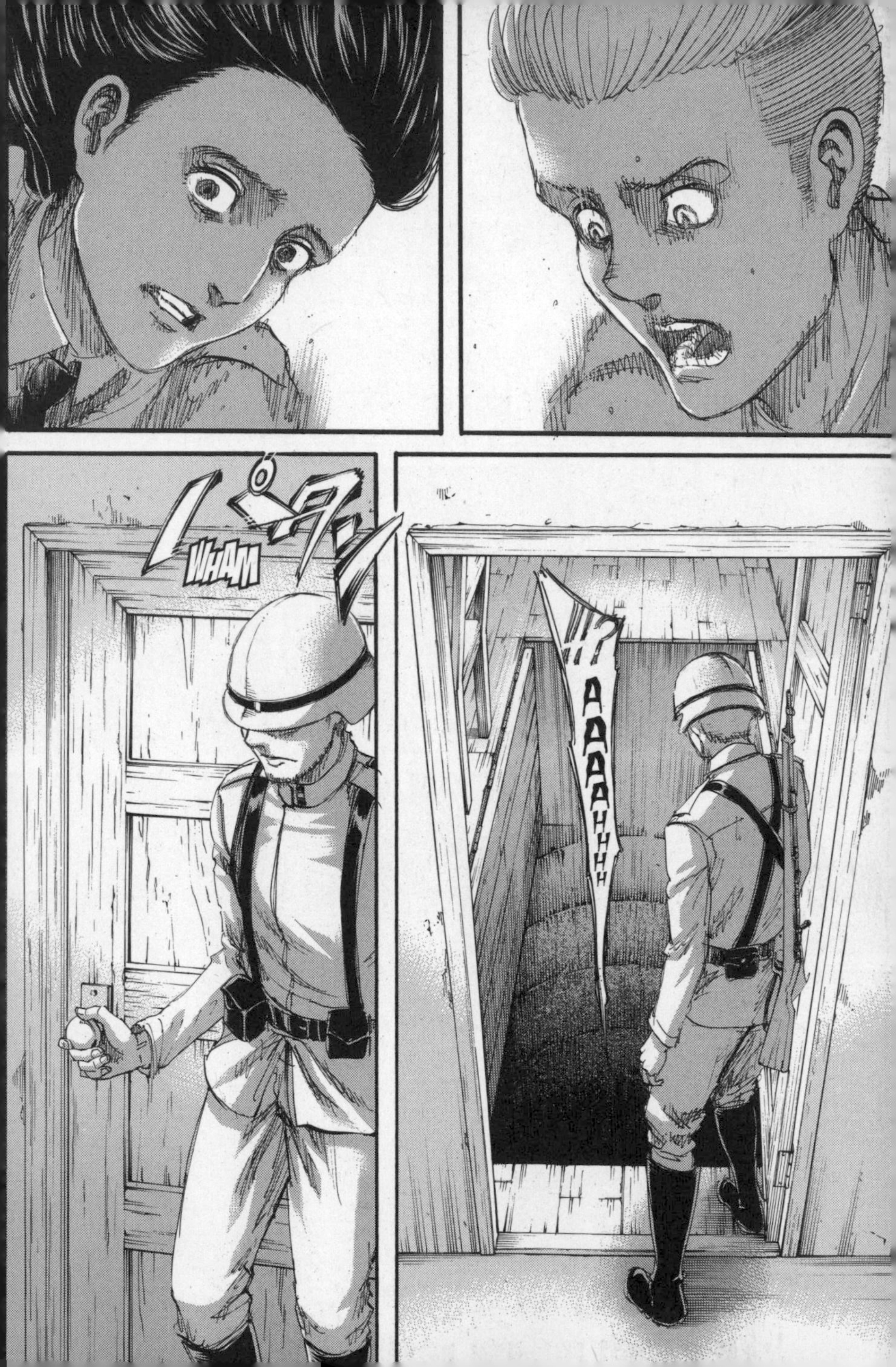
!!?
AAAAAAAHHHH
パタン
WHAM

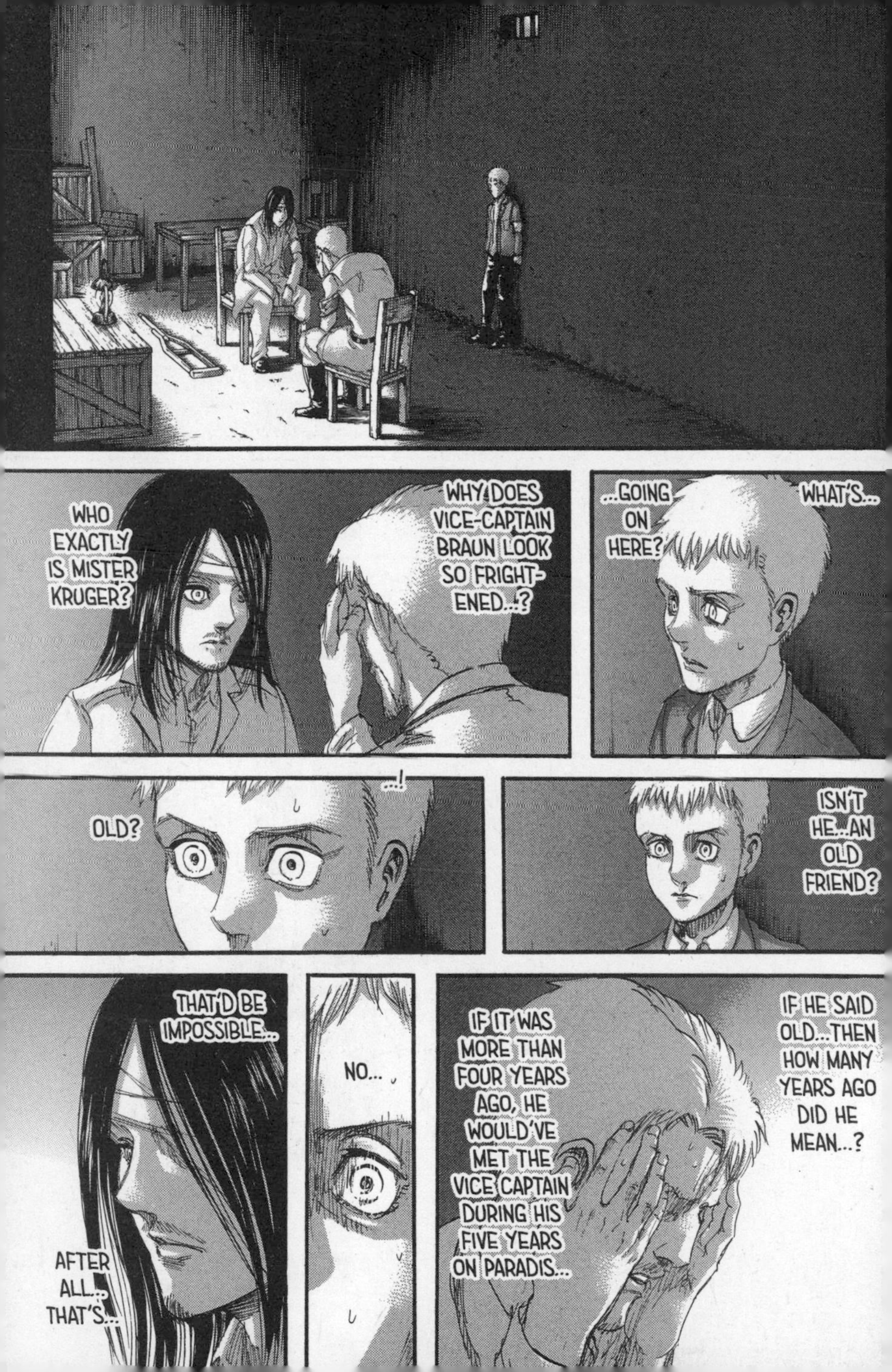
WHAT'S...
...GOING ON HERE?
WHY DOES VICE-CAPTAIN BRAUN LOOK SO FRIGHT-ENED...?
WHO EXACTLY IS MISTER KRUGER?
ISN'T HE...AN OLD FRIEND?
...!
OLD?
IF HE SAID OLD...THEN HOW MANY YEARS AGO DID HE MEAN...?
IF IT WAS MORE THAN FOUR YEARS AGO, HE WOULD'VE MET THE VICE CAPTAIN DURING HIS FIVE YEARS ON PARADIS...
NO...
THAT'D BE IMPOSSIBLE...
AFTER ALL... THAT'S...

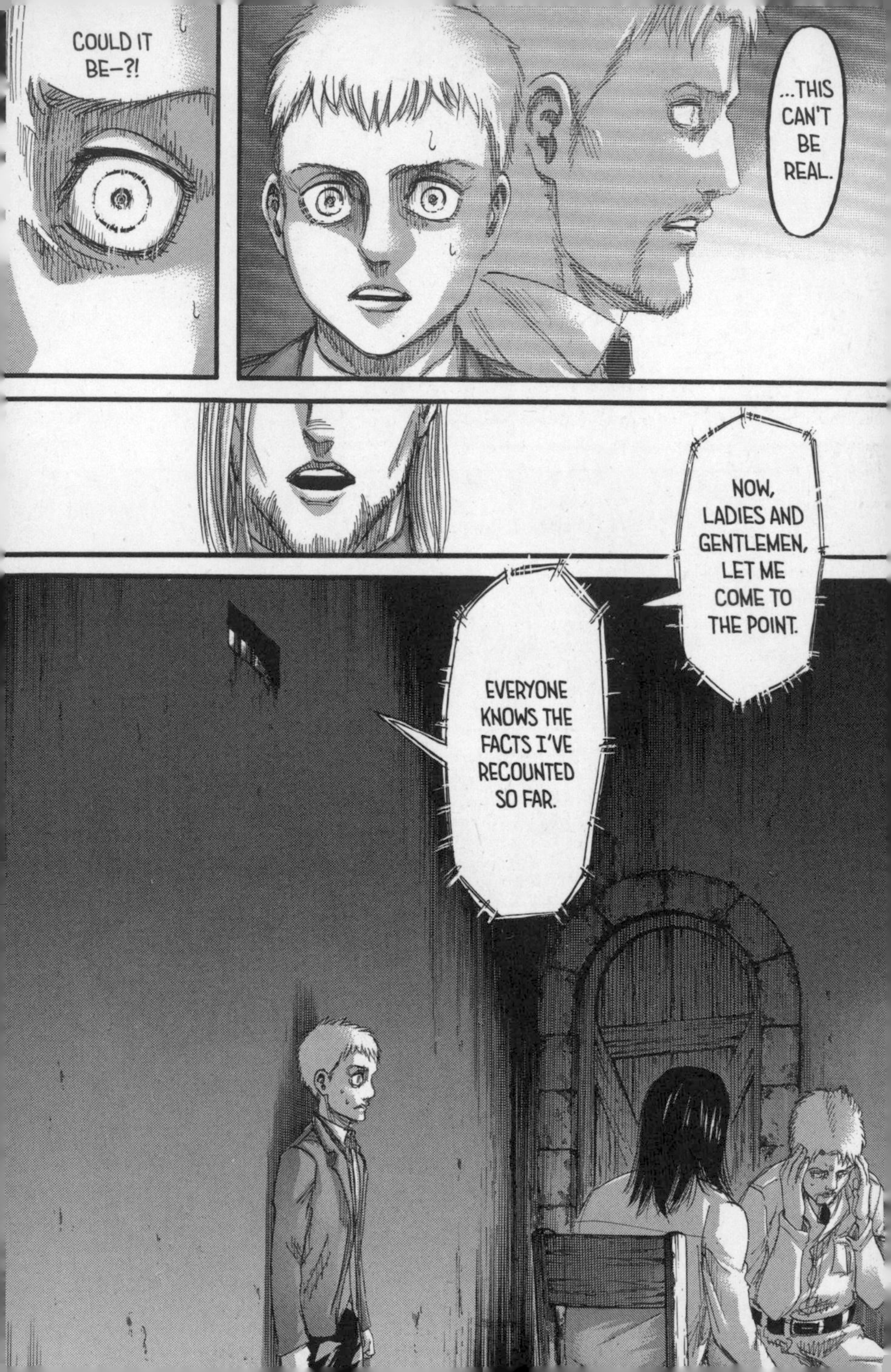
...THIS CAN'T BE REAL.
COULD IT BE–?!
NOW, LADIES AND GENTLEMEN, LET ME COME TO THE POINT.
EVERYONE KNOWS THE FACTS I'VE RECOUNTED SO FAR.

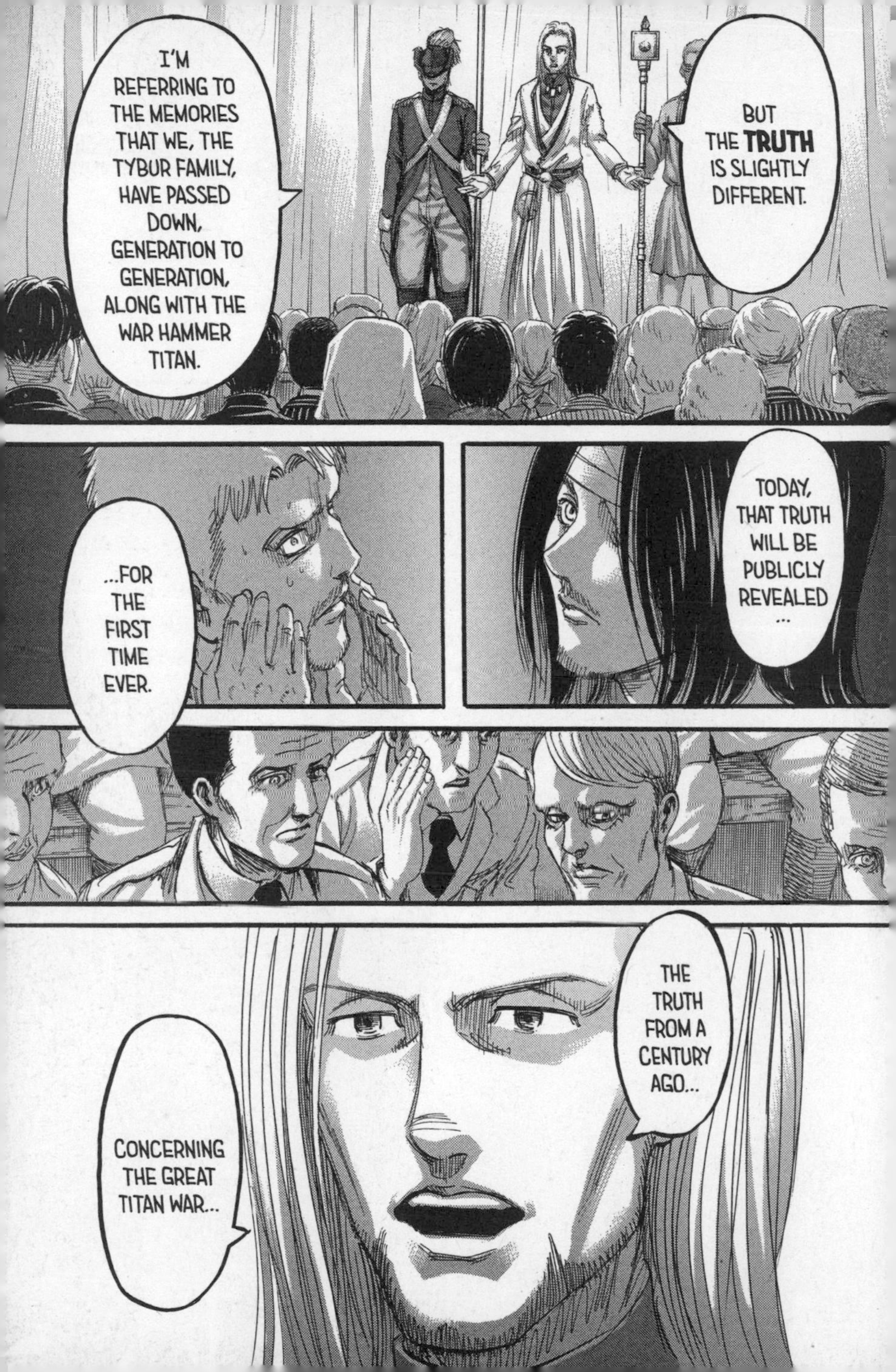
I'M REFERRING TO THE MEMORIES THAT WE, THE TYBUR FAMILY, HAVE PASSED DOWN, GENERATION TO GENERATION, ALONG WITH THE WAR HAMMER TITAN.
BUT THE **TRUTH** IS SLIGHTLY DIFFERENT.
TODAY, THAT TRUTH WILL BE PUBLICLY REVEALED ...
...FOR THE FIRST TIME EVER.
THE TRUTH FROM A CENTURY AGO...
CONCERNING THE GREAT TITAN WAR...

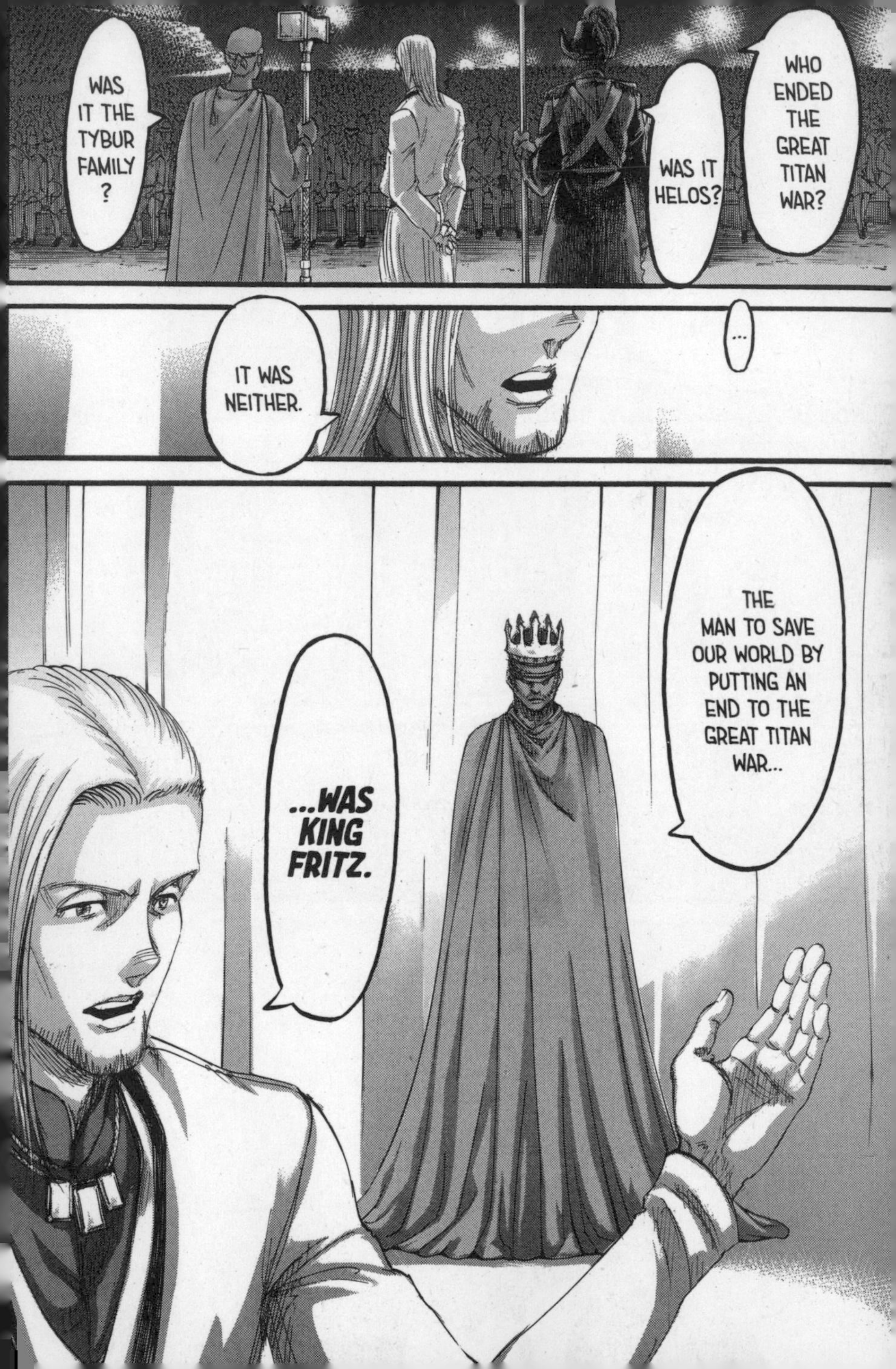
WHO ENDED THE GREAT TITAN WAR?
WAS IT HELOS?
WAS IT THE TYBUR FAMILY ?
...
IT WAS NEITHER.
THE MAN TO SAVE OUR WORLD BY PUTTING AN END TO THE GREAT TITAN WAR...
...WAS KING FRITZ.

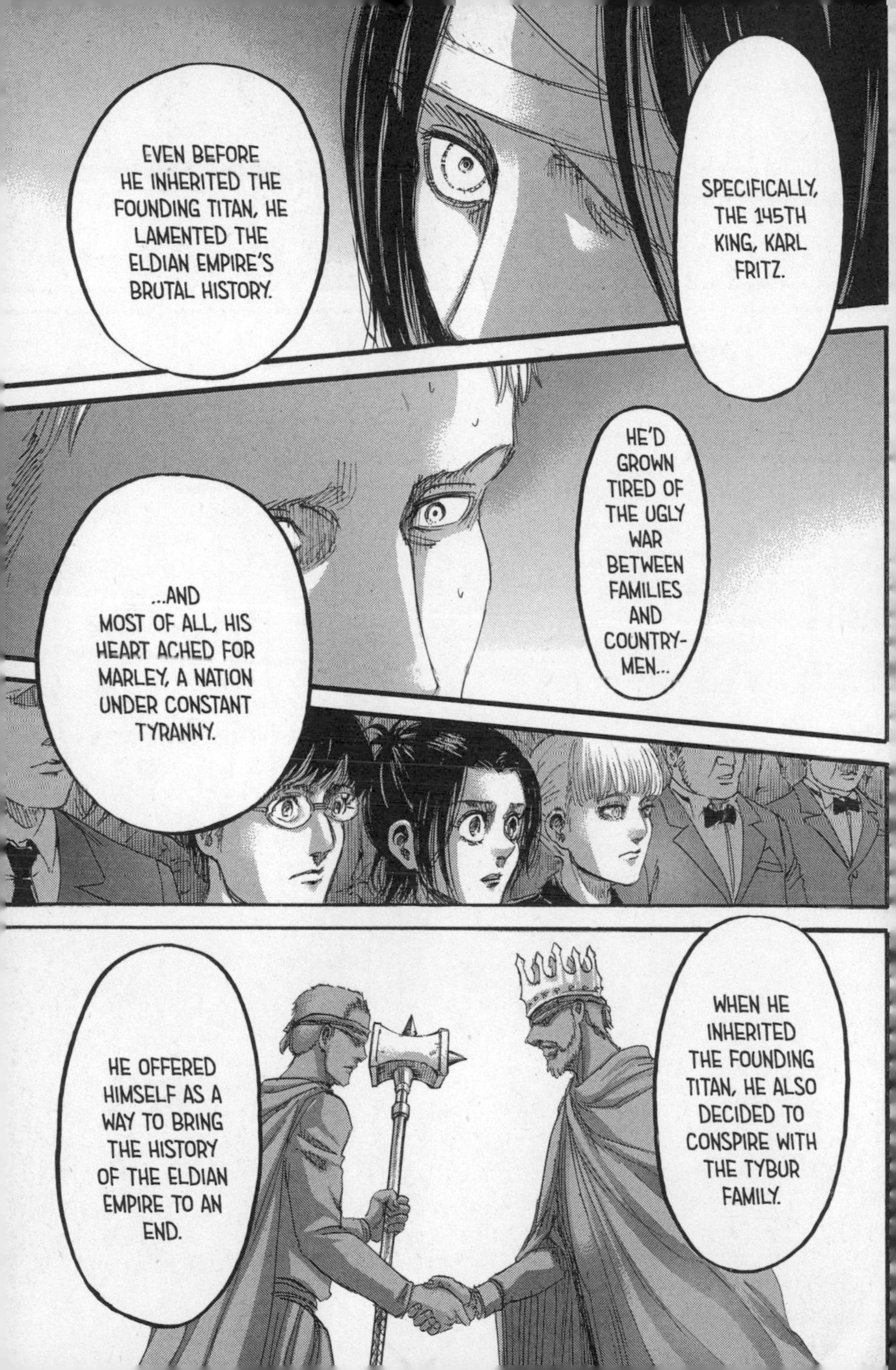
SPECIFICALLY, THE 145TH KING, KARL FRITZ.
EVEN BEFORE HE INHERITED THE FOUNDING TITAN, HE LAMENTED THE ELDIAN EMPIRE'S BRUTAL HISTORY.
HE'D GROWN TIRED OF THE UGLY WAR BETWEEN FAMILIES AND COUNTRY-MEN...
...AND MOST OF ALL, HIS HEART ACHED FOR MARLEY, A NATION UNDER CONSTANT TYRANNY.
WHEN HE INHERITED THE FOUNDING TITAN, HE ALSO DECIDED TO CONSPIRE WITH THE TYBUR FAMILY.
HE OFFERED HIMSELF AS A WAY TO BRING THE HISTORY OF THE ELDIAN EMPIRE TO AN END.

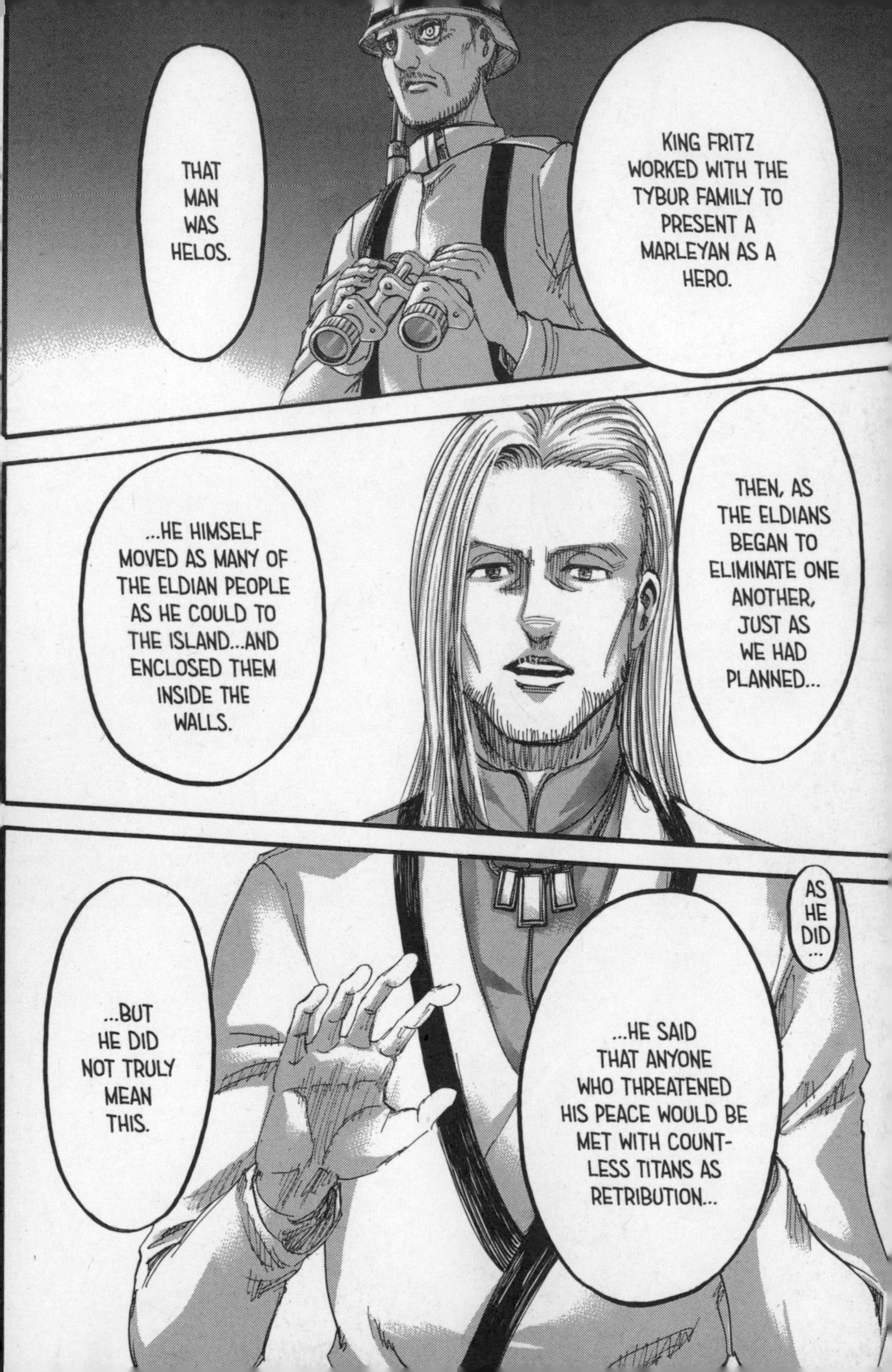
KING FRITZ WORKED WITH THE TYBUR FAMILY TO PRESENT A MARLEYAN AS A HERO.
THAT MAN WAS HELOS.
THEN, AS THE ELDIANS BEGAN TO ELIMINATE ONE ANOTHER, JUST AS WE HAD PLANNED...
...HE HIMSELF MOVED AS MANY OF THE ELDIAN PEOPLE AS HE COULD TO THE ISLAND...AND ENCLOSED THEM INSIDE THE WALLS.
AS HE DID...
...HE SAID THAT ANYONE WHO THREATENED HIS PEACE WOULD BE MET WITH COUNT-LESS TITANS AS RETRIBUTION...
...BUT HE DID NOT TRULY MEAN THIS.

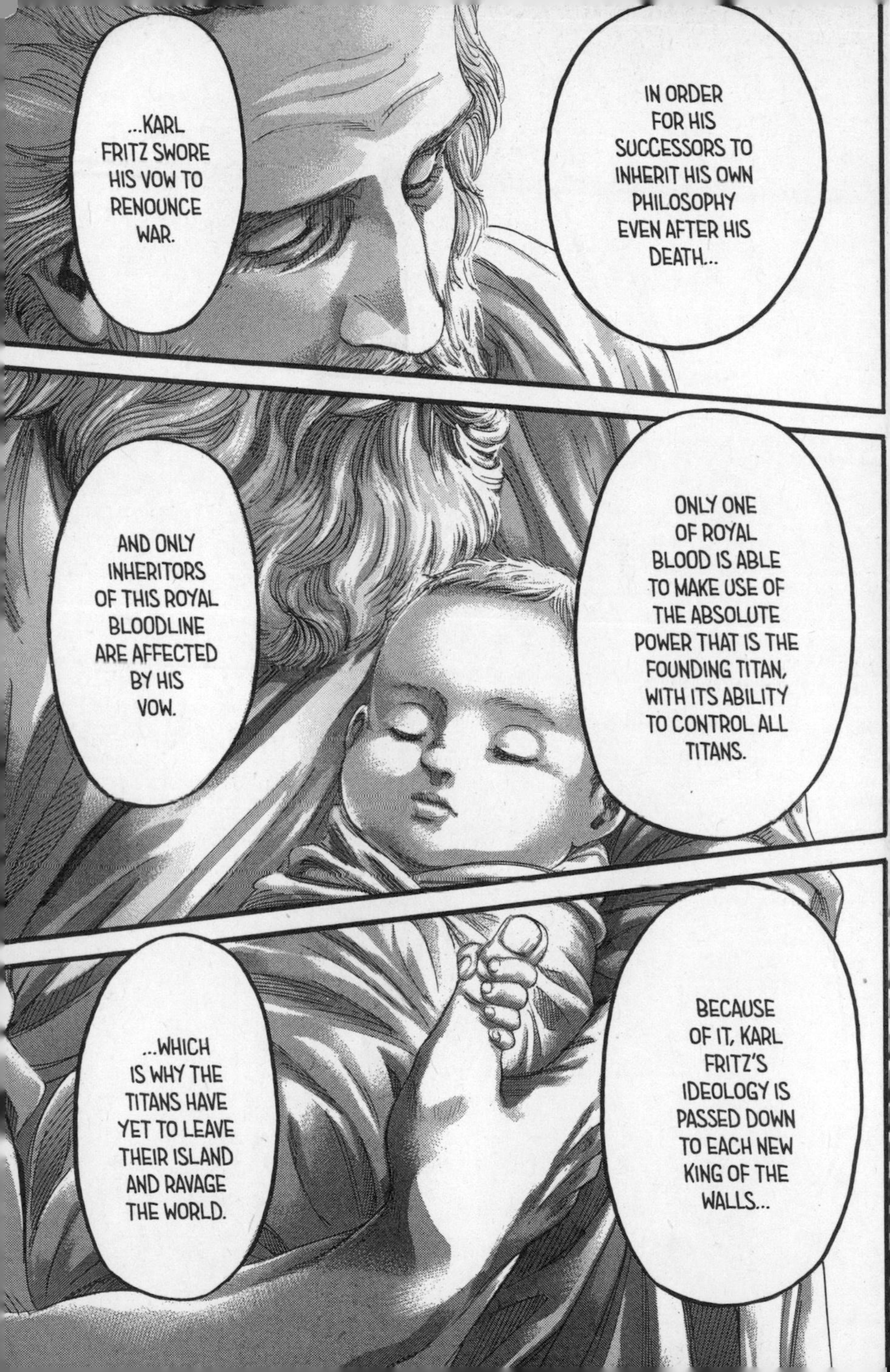
IN ORDER FOR HIS SUCCESSORS TO INHERIT HIS OWN PHILOSOPHY EVEN AFTER HIS DEATH...
...KARL FRITZ SWORE HIS VOW TO RENOUNCE WAR.
ONLY ONE OF ROYAL BLOOD IS ABLE TO MAKE USE OF THE ABSOLUTE POWER THAT IS THE FOUNDING TITAN, WITH ITS ABILITY TO CONTROL ALL TITANS.
AND ONLY INHERITORS OF THIS ROYAL BLOODLINE ARE AFFECTED BY HIS VOW.
BECAUSE OF IT, KARL FRITZ'S IDEOLOGY IS PASSED DOWN TO EACH NEW KING OF THE WALLS...
...WHICH IS WHY THE TITANS HAVE YET TO LEAVE THEIR ISLAND AND RAVAGE THE WORLD.

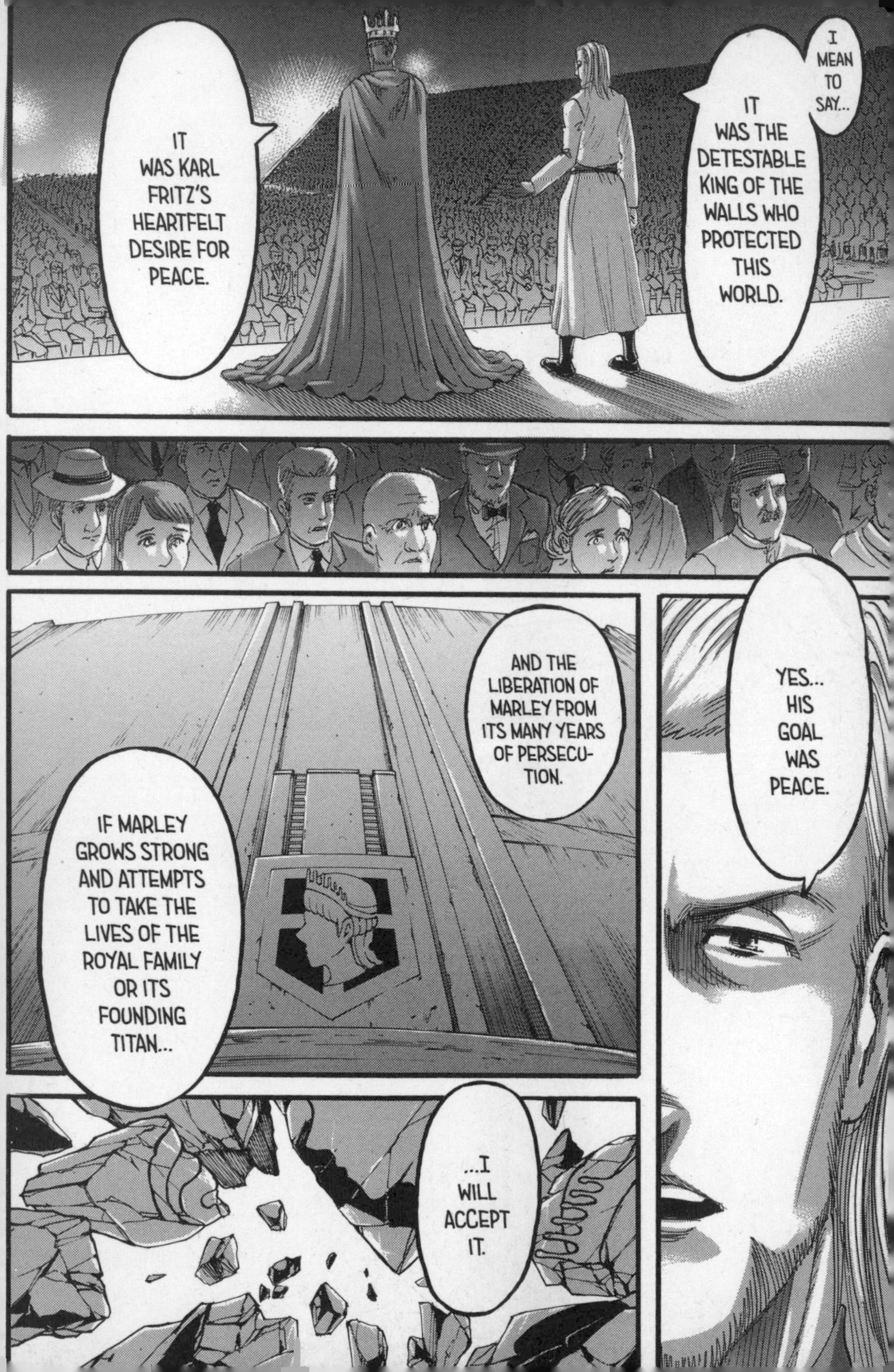
I MEAN TO SAY...
IT WAS THE DETESTABLE KING OF THE WALLS WHO PROTECTED THIS WORLD.
IT WAS KARL FRITZ'S HEARTFELT DESIRE FOR PEACE.
YES... HIS GOAL WAS PEACE.
AND THE LIBERATION OF MARLEY FROM ITS MANY YEARS OF PERSECU-TION.
IF MARLEY GROWS STRONG AND ATTEMPTS TO TAKE THE LIVES OF THE ROYAL FAMILY OR ITS FOUNDING TITAN...
...I WILL ACCEPT IT.

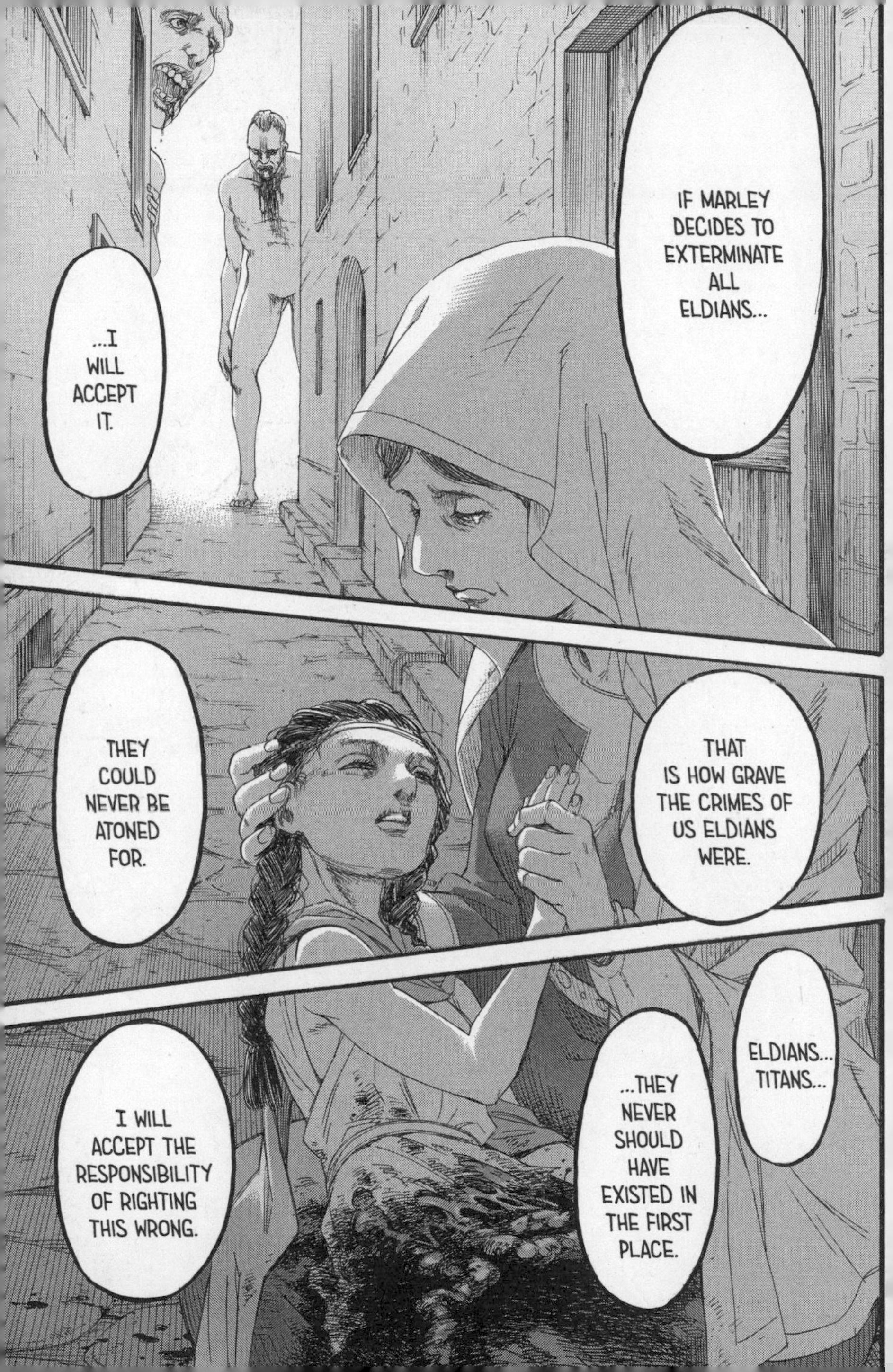
IF MARLEY DECIDES TO EXTERMINATE ALL ELDIANS...
...I WILL ACCEPT IT.
THAT IS HOW GRAVE THE CRIMES OF US ELDIANS WERE.
THEY COULD NEVER BE ATONED FOR.
ELDIANS... TITANS...
...THEY NEVER SHOULD HAVE EXISTED IN THE FIRST PLACE.
I WILL ACCEPT THE RESPONSIBILITY OF RIGHTING THIS WRONG.

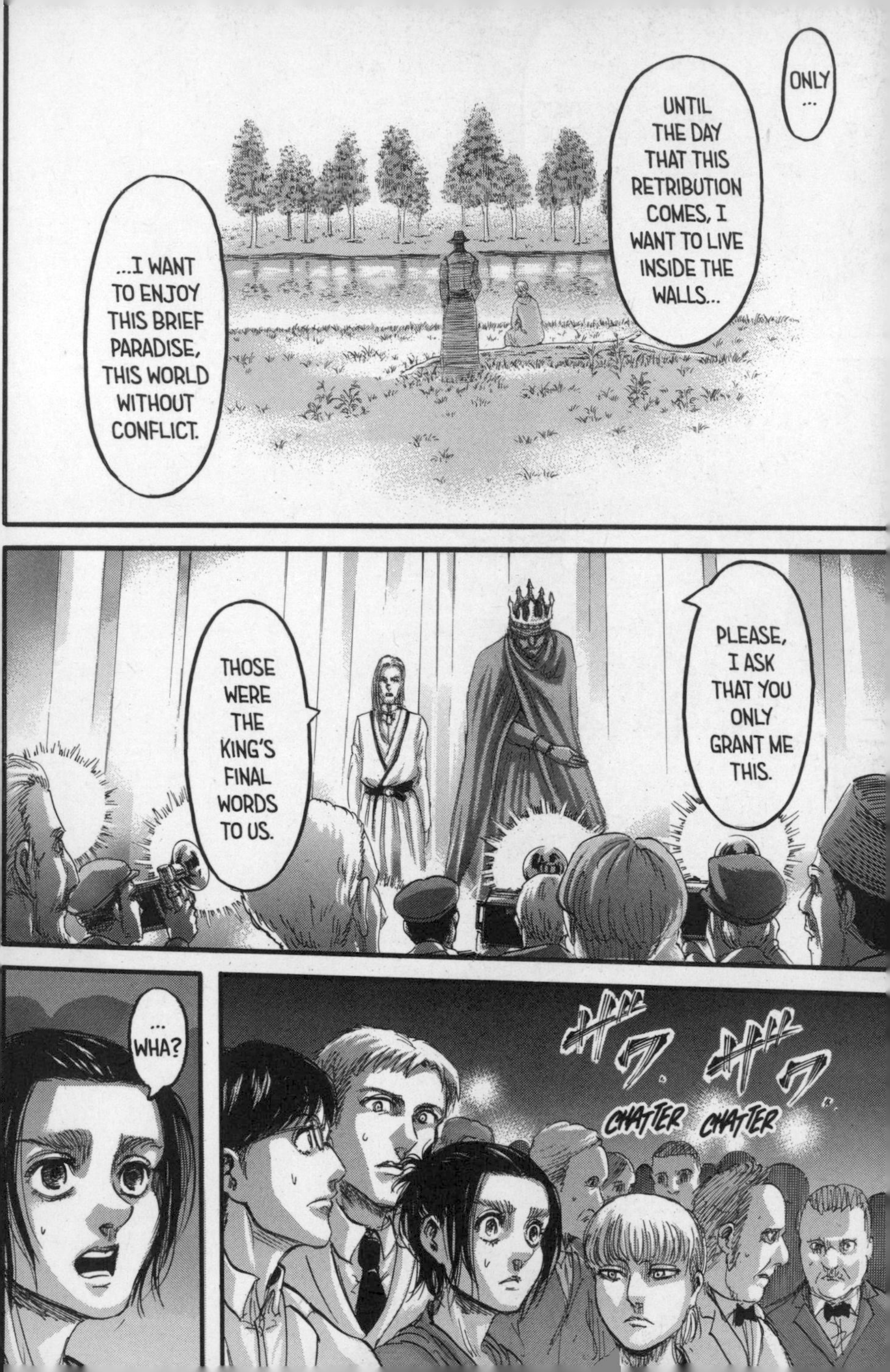
ONLY...
UNTIL THE DAY THAT THIS RETRIBUTION COMES, I WANT TO LIVE INSIDE THE WALLS...
...I WANT TO ENJOY THIS BRIEF PARADISE, THIS WORLD WITHOUT CONFLICT.
PLEASE, I ASK THAT YOU ONLY GRANT ME THIS.
THOSE WERE THE KING'S FINAL WORDS TO US.
ザワ ザワ
CHATTER CHATTER
... WHA?

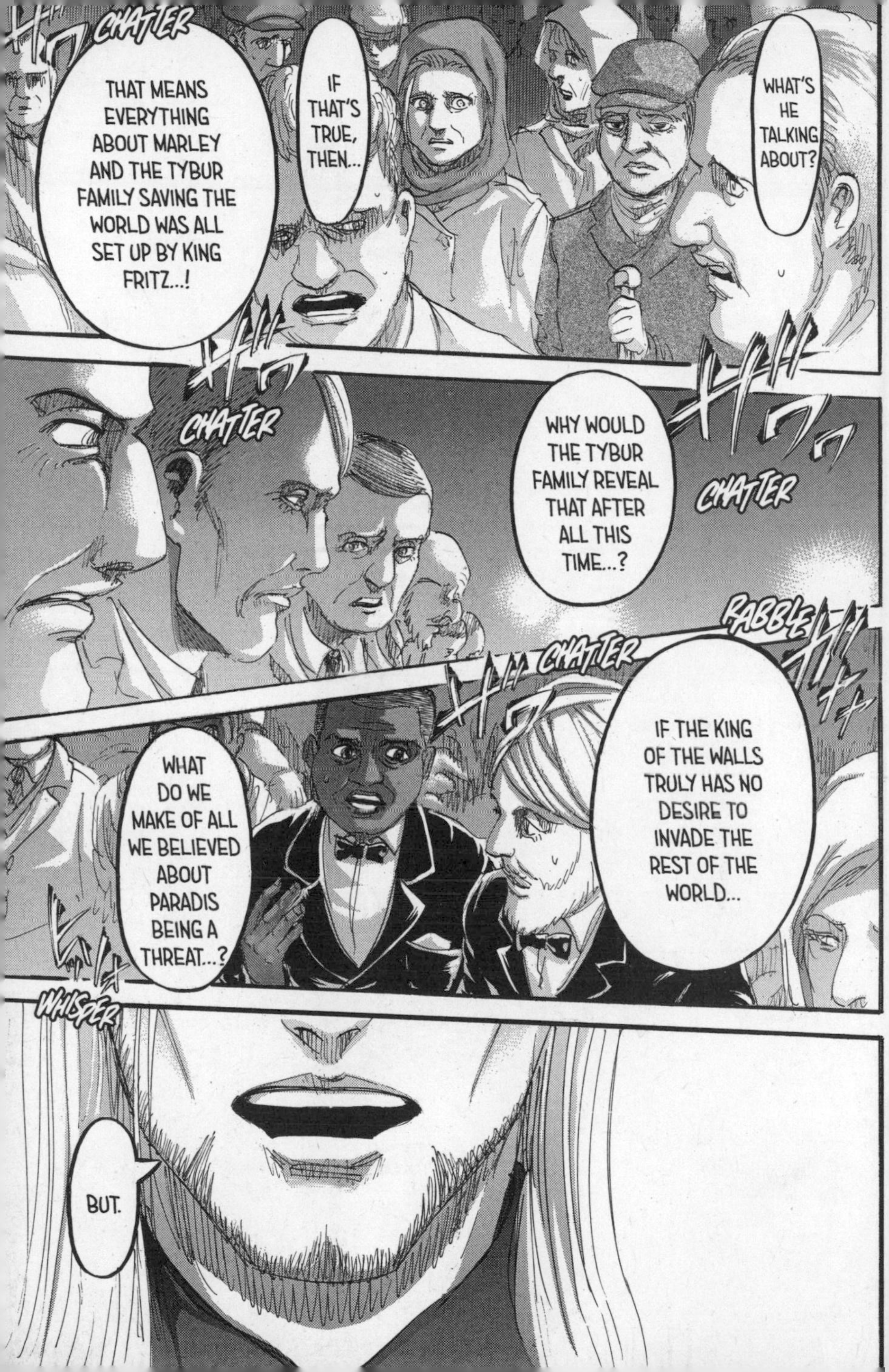
WHAT'S HE TALKING ABOUT?
IF THAT'S TRUE, THEN...
THAT MEANS EVERYTHING ABOUT MARLEY AND THE TYBUR FAMILY SAVING THE WORLD WAS ALL SET UP BY KING FRITZ...!
CHATTER
CHATTER
WHY WOULD THE TYBUR FAMILY REVEAL THAT AFTER ALL THIS TIME...?
CHATTER
RABBLE
IF THE KING OF THE WALLS TRULY HAS NO DESIRE TO INVADE THE REST OF THE WORLD...
CHATTER
WHAT DO WE MAKE OF ALL WE BELIEVED ABOUT PARADIS BEING A THREAT...?
WHISPER
BUT.

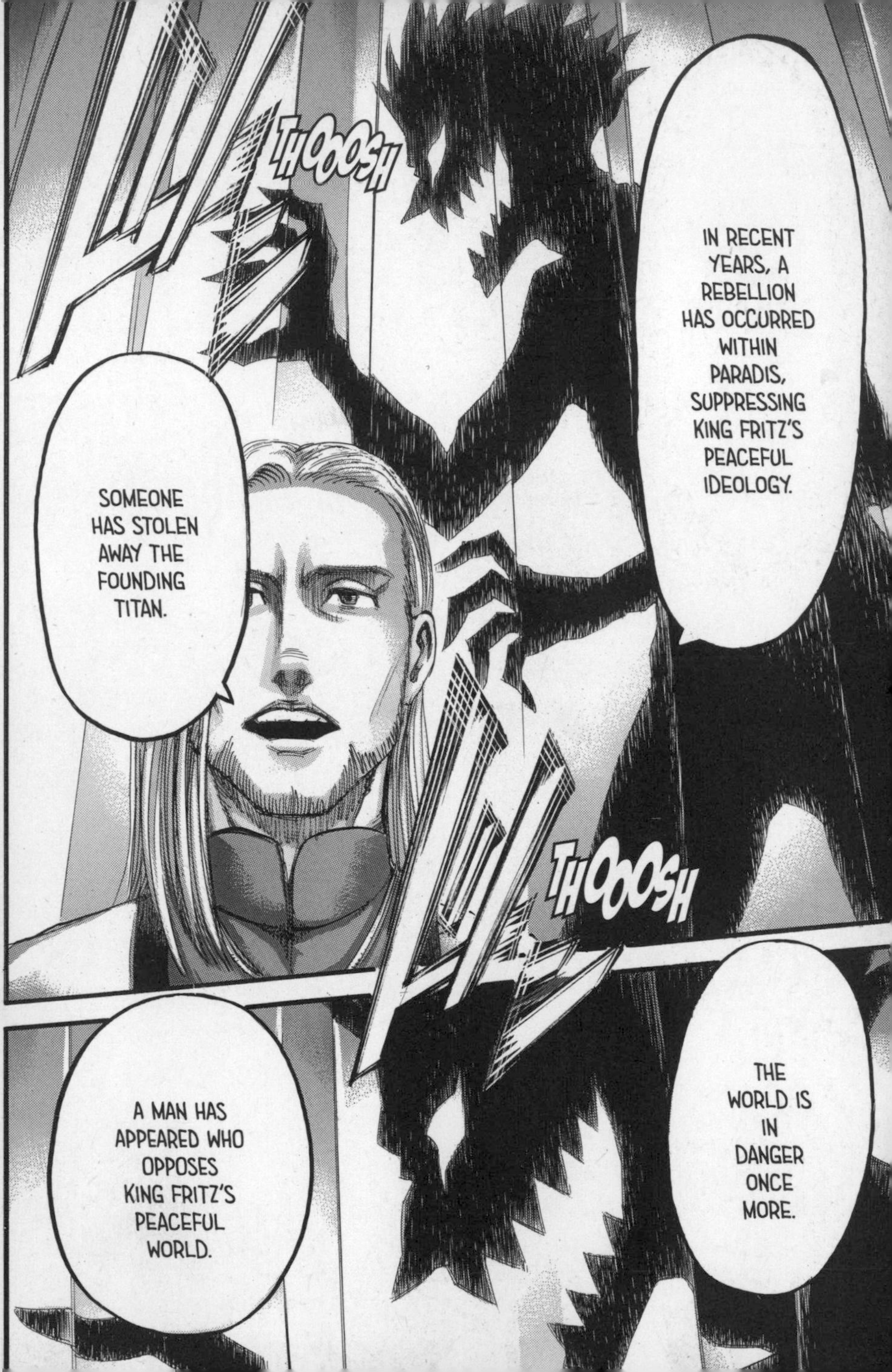
IN RECENT YEARS, A REBELLION HAS OCCURRED WITHIN PARADIS, SUPPRESSING KING FRITZ'S PEACEFUL IDEOLOGY.
THOOOSH
SOMEONE HAS STOLEN AWAY THE FOUNDING TITAN.
THOOOSH
THE WORLD IS IN DANGER ONCE MORE.
A MAN HAS APPEARED WHO OPPOSES KING FRITZ'S PEACEFUL WORLD.

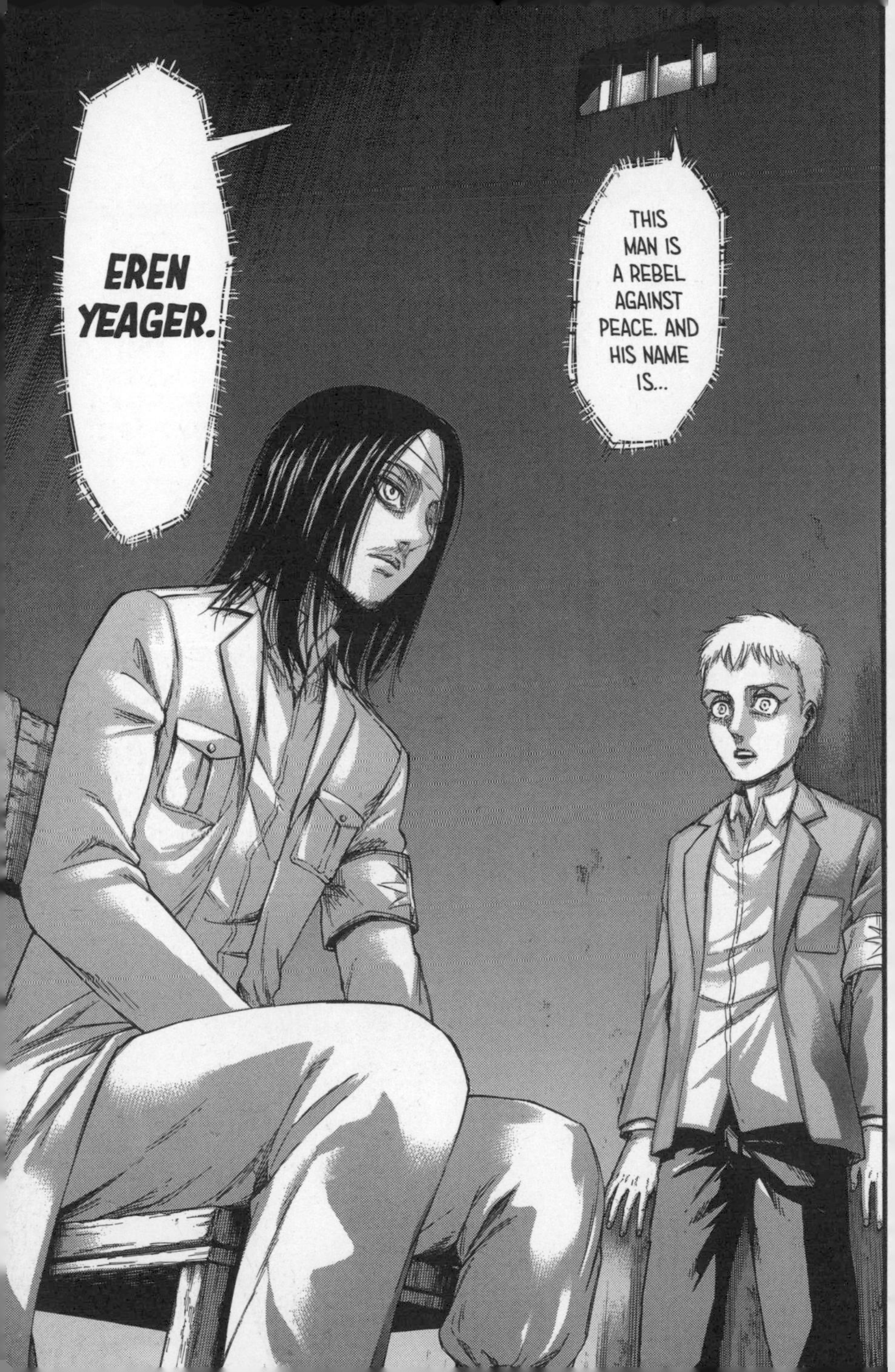
THIS MAN IS A REBEL AGAINST PEACE. AND HIS NAME IS...
EREN YEAGER.

ATTACK on TITAN

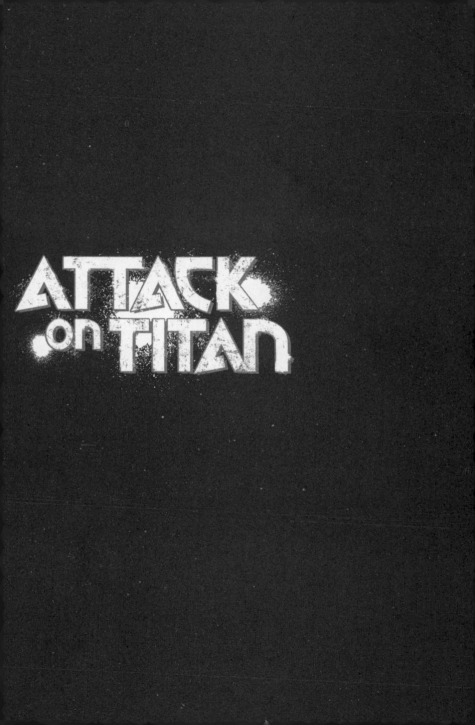

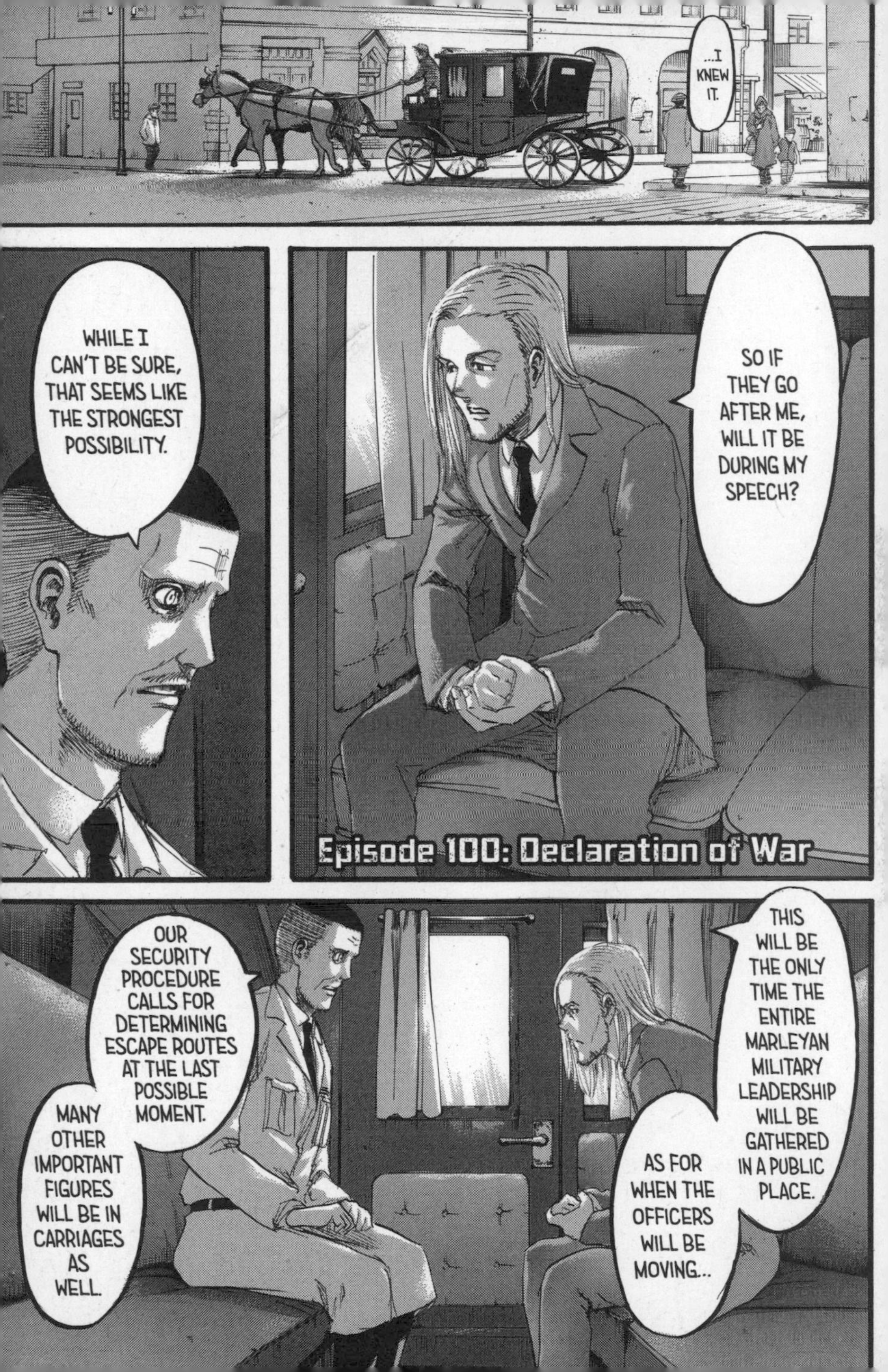
...I KNEW IT.
SO IF THEY GO AFTER ME, WILL IT BE DURING MY SPEECH?
Episode 100: Declaration of War
WHILE I CAN'T BE SURE, THAT SEEMS LIKE THE STRONGEST POSSIBILITY.
THIS WILL BE THE ONLY TIME THE ENTIRE MARLEYAN MILITARY LEADERSHIP WILL BE GATHERED IN A PUBLIC PLACE.
AS FOR WHEN THE OFFICERS WILL BE MOVING...
OUR SECURITY PROCEDURE CALLS FOR DETERMINING ESCAPE ROUTES AT THE LAST POSSIBLE MOMENT.
MANY OTHER IMPORTANT FIGURES WILL BE IN CARRIAGES AS WELL.

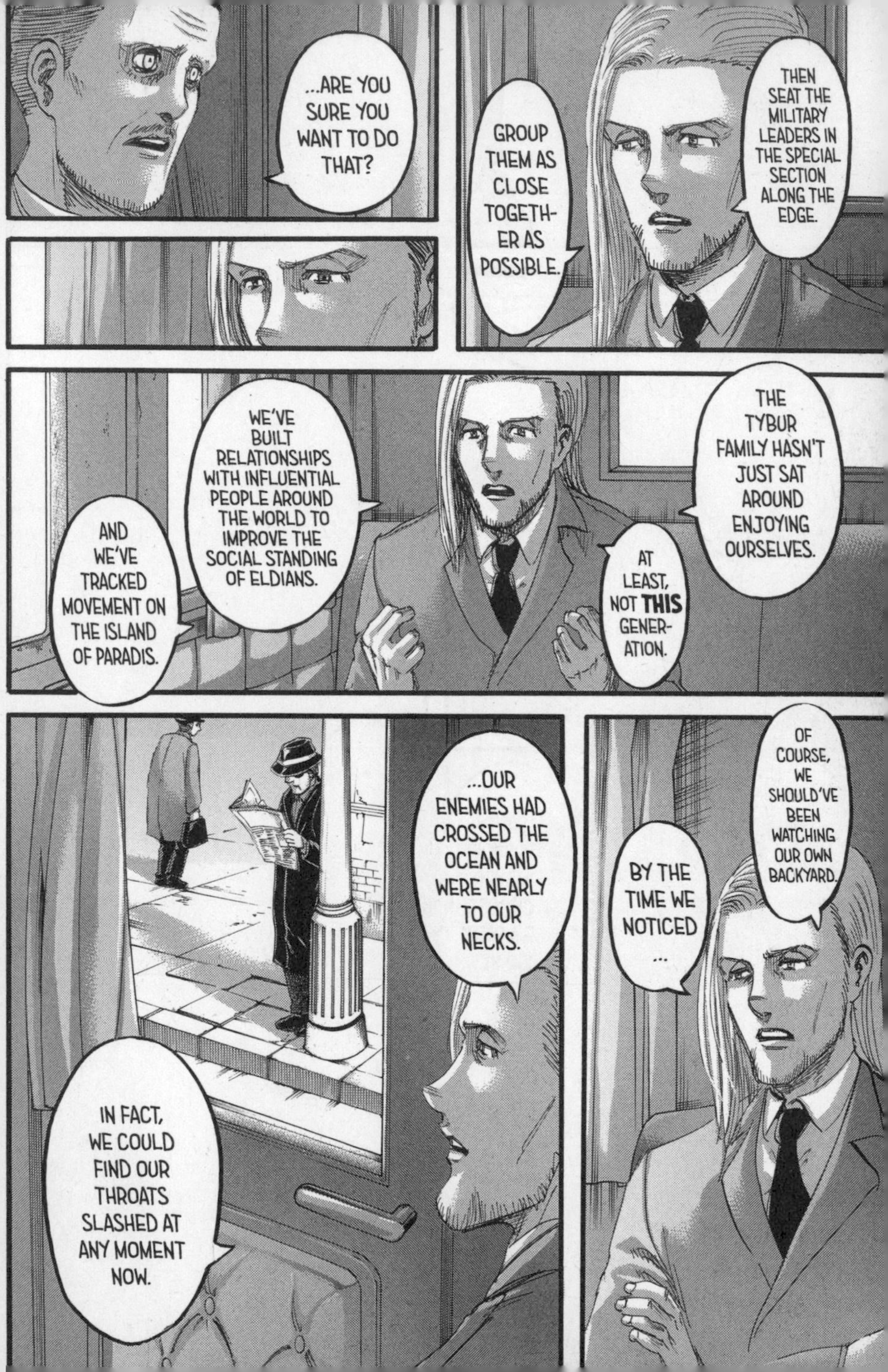
THEN SEAT THE MILITARY LEADERS IN THE SPECIAL SECTION ALONG THE EDGE.
GROUP THEM AS CLOSE TOGETHER AS POSSIBLE.
...ARE YOU SURE YOU WANT TO DO THAT?
THE TYBUR FAMILY HASN'T JUST SAT AROUND ENJOYING OURSELVES.
AT LEAST, NOT **THIS** GENERATION.
WE'VE BUILT RELATIONSHIPS WITH INFLUENTIAL PEOPLE AROUND THE WORLD TO IMPROVE THE SOCIAL STANDING OF ELDIANS.
AND WE'VE TRACKED MOVEMENT ON THE ISLAND OF PARADIS.
OF COURSE, WE SHOULD'VE BEEN WATCHING OUR OWN BACKYARD.
BY THE TIME WE NOTICED ...
...OUR ENEMIES HAD CROSSED THE OCEAN AND WERE NEARLY TO OUR NECKS.
IN FACT, WE COULD FIND OUR THROATS SLASHED AT ANY MOMENT NOW.

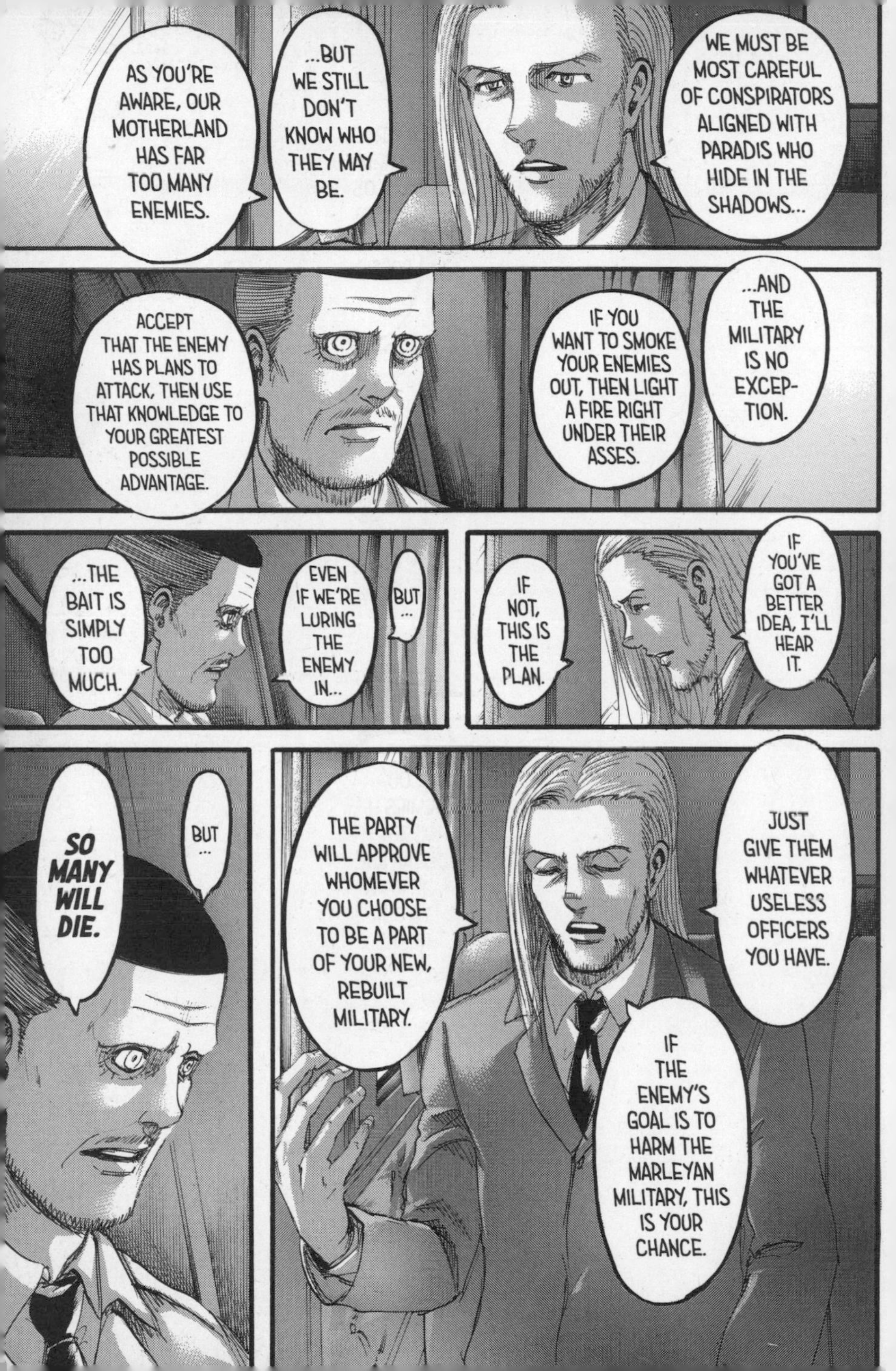
WE MUST BE MOST CAREFUL OF CONSPIRATORS ALIGNED WITH PARADIS WHO HIDE IN THE SHADOWS...
...BUT WE STILL DON'T KNOW WHO THEY MAY BE.
AS YOU'RE AWARE, OUR MOTHERLAND HAS FAR TOO MANY ENEMIES.
...AND THE MILITARY IS NO EXCEPTION.
IF YOU WANT TO SMOKE YOUR ENEMIES OUT, THEN LIGHT A FIRE RIGHT UNDER THEIR ASSES.
ACCEPT THAT THE ENEMY HAS PLANS TO ATTACK, THEN USE THAT KNOWLEDGE TO YOUR GREATEST POSSIBLE ADVANTAGE.
IF YOU'VE GOT A BETTER IDEA, I'LL HEAR IT.
IF NOT, THIS IS THE PLAN.
BUT...
EVEN IF WE'RE LURING THE ENEMY IN...
...THE BAIT IS SIMPLY TOO MUCH.
JUST GIVE THEM WHATEVER USELESS OFFICERS YOU HAVE.
IF THE ENEMY'S GOAL IS TO HARM THE MARLEYAN MILITARY, THIS IS YOUR CHANCE.
THE PARTY WILL APPROVE WHOMEVER YOU CHOOSE TO BE A PART OF YOUR NEW, REBUILT MILITARY.
BUT...
SO MANY WILL DIE.

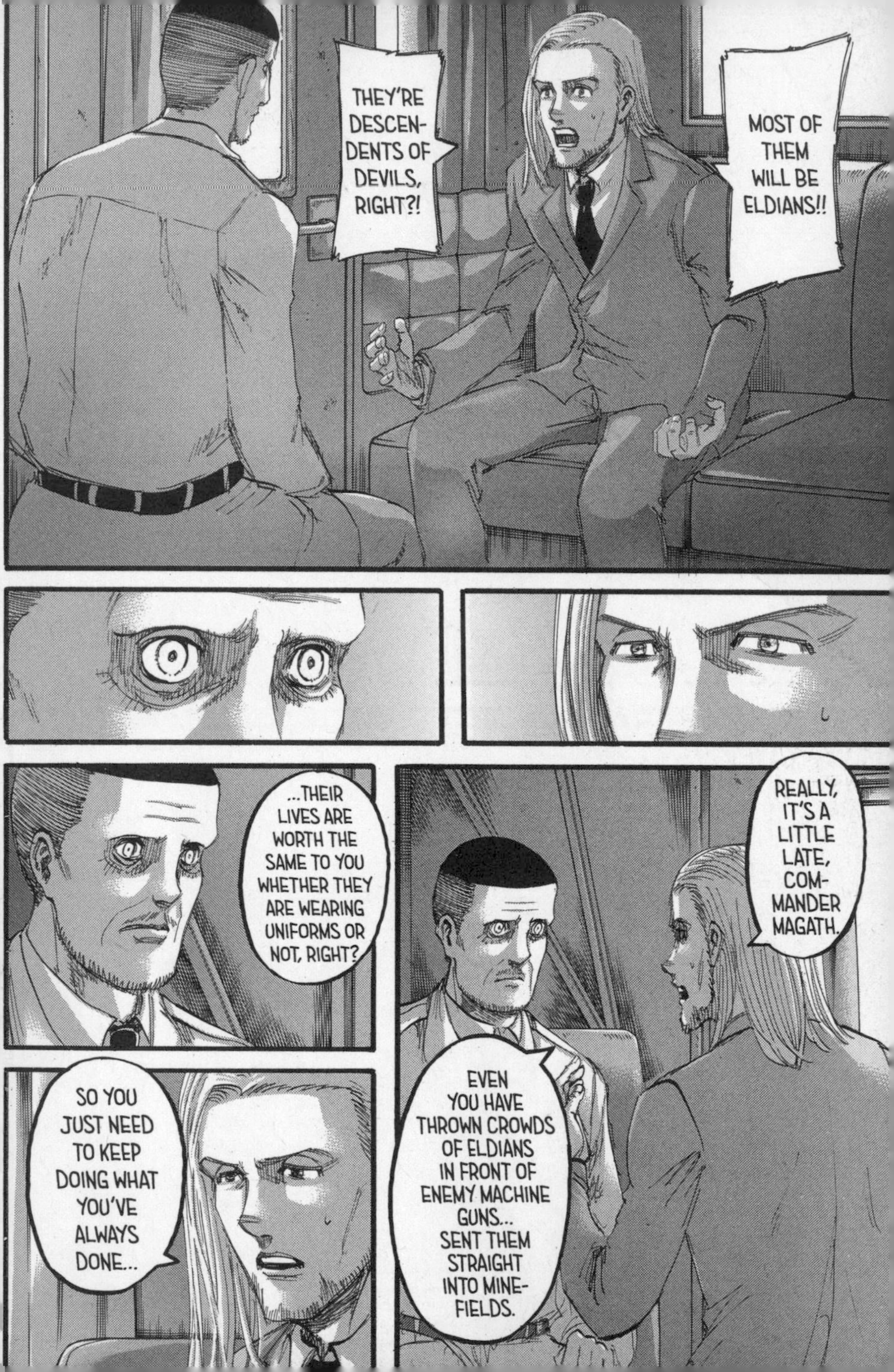
MOST OF THEM WILL BE ELDIANS!!
THEY'RE DESCEN-DENTS OF DEVILS, RIGHT?!
REALLY, IT'S A LITTLE LATE, COM-MANDER MAGATH.
EVEN YOU HAVE THROWN CROWDS OF ELDIANS IN FRONT OF ENEMY MACHINE GUNS... SENT THEM STRAIGHT INTO MINE-FIELDS.
...THEIR LIVES ARE WORTH THE SAME TO YOU WHETHER THEY ARE WEARING UNIFORMS OR NOT, RIGHT?
SO YOU JUST NEED TO KEEP DOING WHAT YOU'VE ALWAYS DONE...

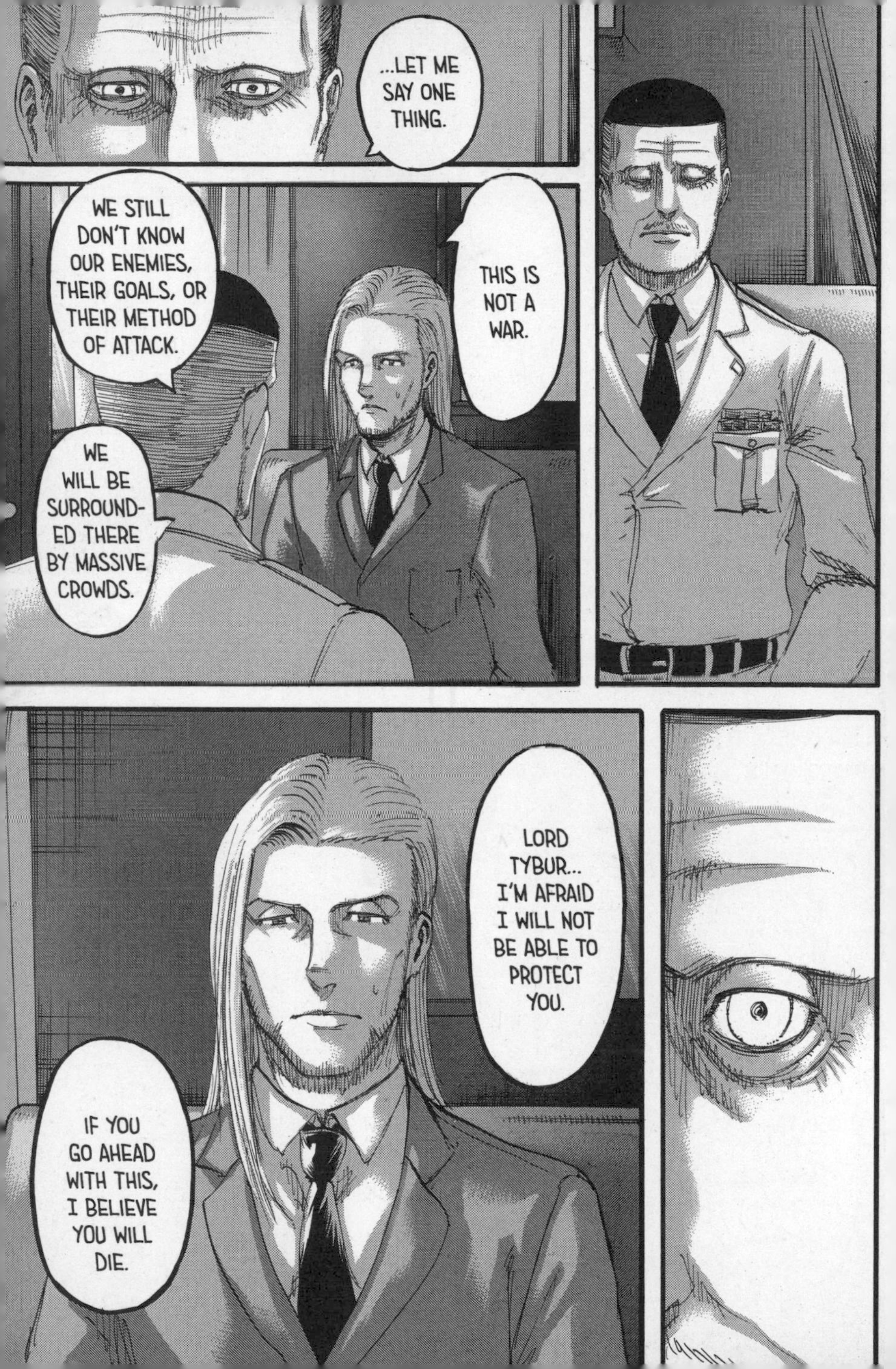
...LET ME SAY ONE THING.
THIS IS NOT A WAR.
WE STILL DON'T KNOW OUR ENEMIES, THEIR GOALS, OR THEIR METHOD OF ATTACK.
WE WILL BE SURROUND-ED THERE BY MASSIVE CROWDS.
LORD TYBUR... I'M AFRAID I WILL NOT BE ABLE TO PROTECT YOU.
IF YOU GO AHEAD WITH THIS, I BELIEVE YOU WILL DIE.

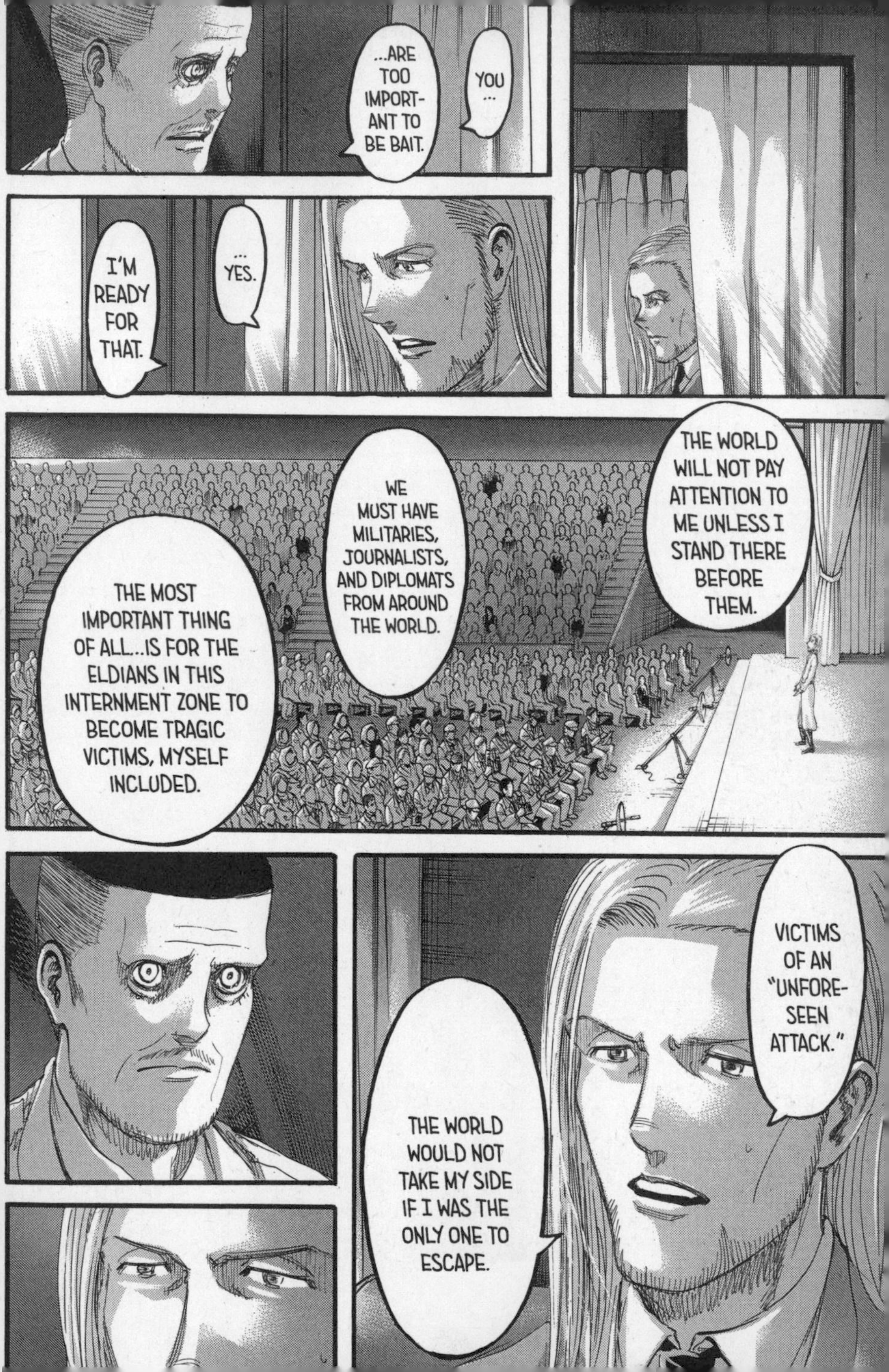
YOU ...
...ARE TOO IMPORTANT TO BE BAIT.
... YES.
I'M READY FOR THAT.
THE WORLD WILL NOT PAY ATTENTION TO ME UNLESS I STAND THERE BEFORE THEM.
WE MUST HAVE MILITARIES, JOURNALISTS, AND DIPLOMATS FROM AROUND THE WORLD.
THE MOST IMPORTANT THING OF ALL...IS FOR THE ELDIANS IN THIS INTERNMENT ZONE TO BECOME TRAGIC VICTIMS, MYSELF INCLUDED.
VICTIMS OF AN "UNFORESEEN ATTACK."
THE WORLD WOULD NOT TAKE MY SIDE IF I WAS THE ONLY ONE TO ESCAPE.

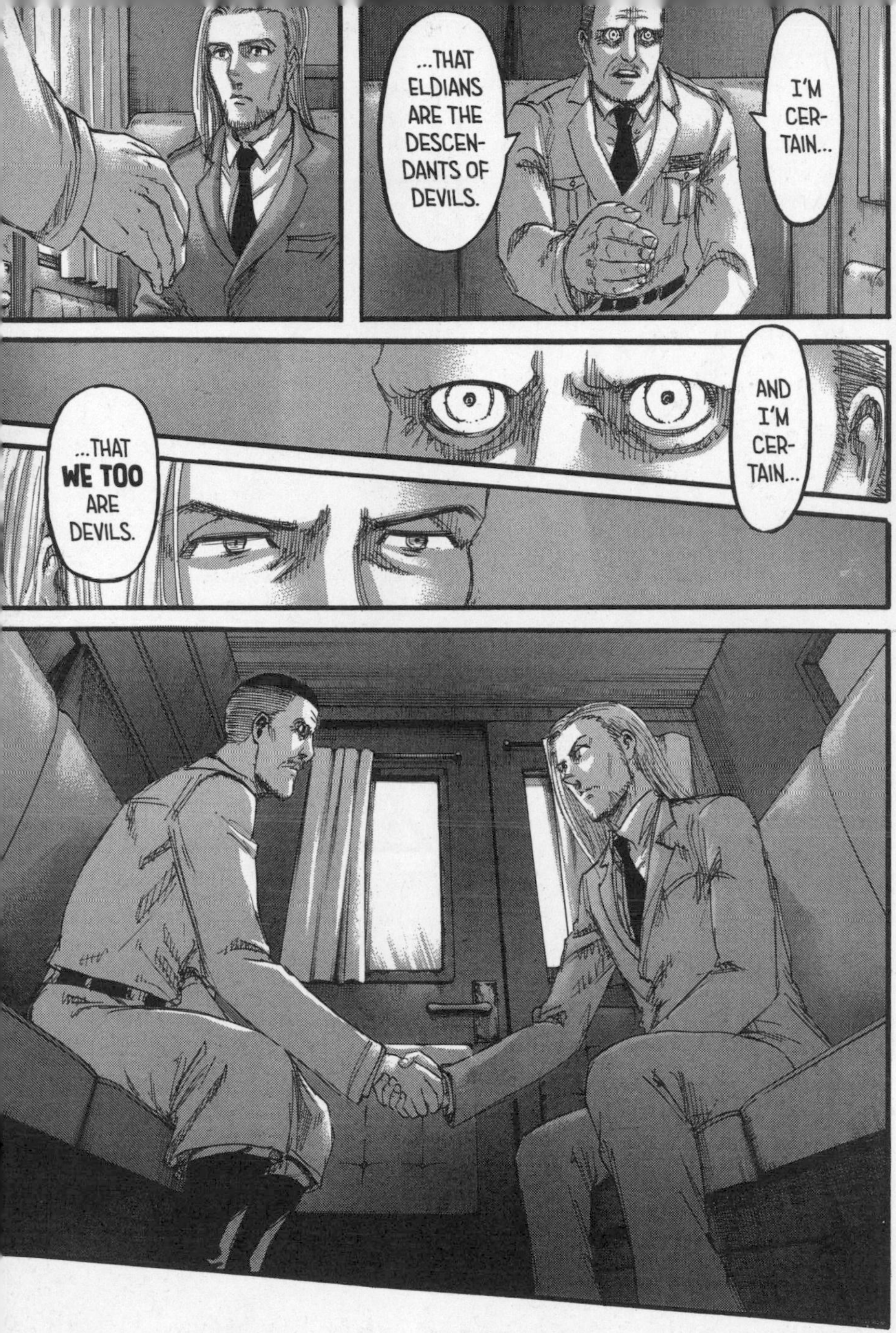
I'M CERTAIN...
...THAT ELDIANS ARE THE DESCENDANTS OF DEVILS.
AND I'M CERTAIN...
...THAT **WE TOO** ARE DEVILS.

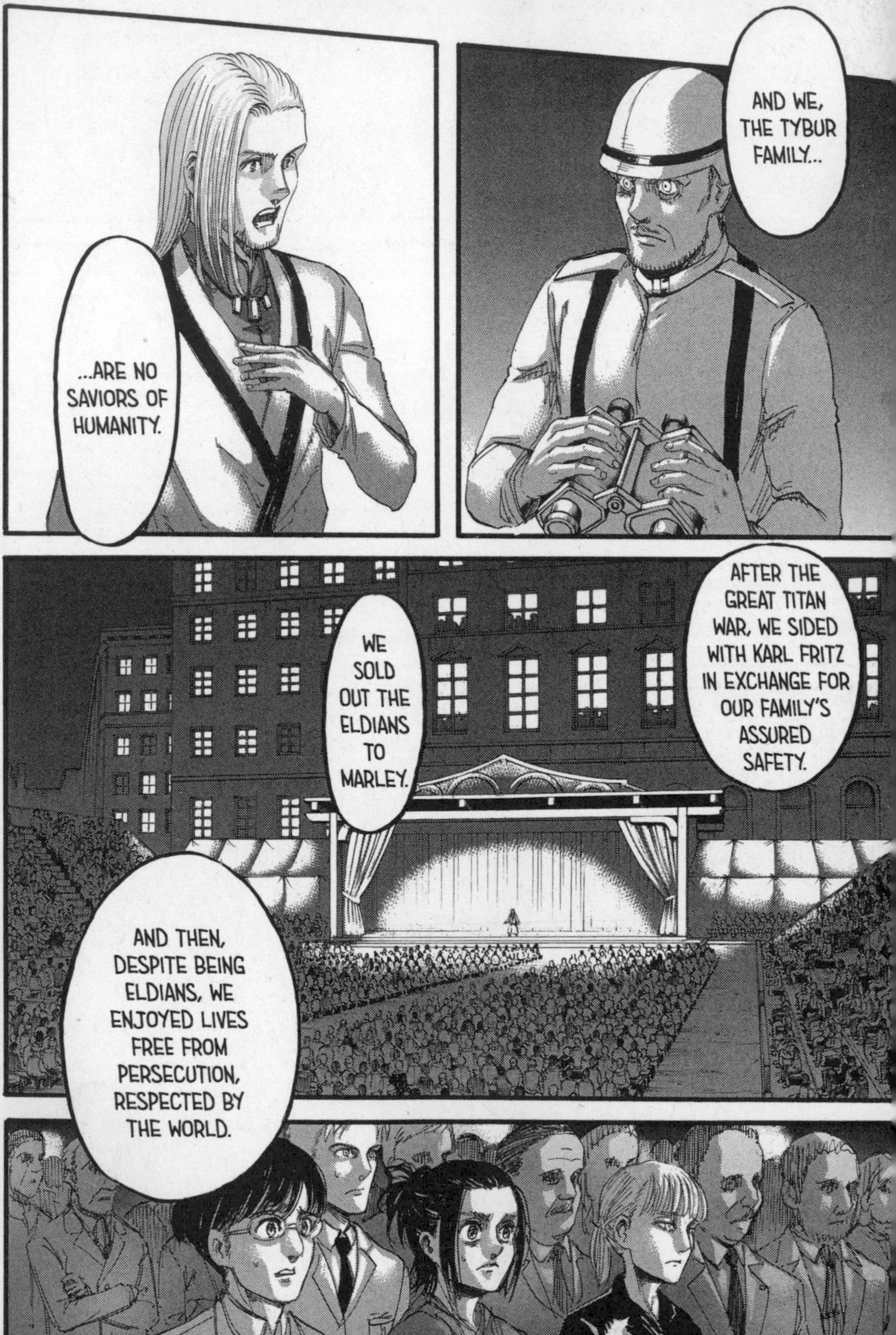
AND WE, THE TYBUR FAMILY...
...ARE NO SAVIORS OF HUMANITY.
AFTER THE GREAT TITAN WAR, WE SIDED WITH KARL FRITZ IN EXCHANGE FOR OUR FAMILY'S ASSURED SAFETY.
WE SOLD OUT THE ELDIANS TO MARLEY.
AND THEN, DESPITE BEING ELDIANS, WE ENJOYED LIVES FREE FROM PERSECUTION, RESPECTED BY THE WORLD.

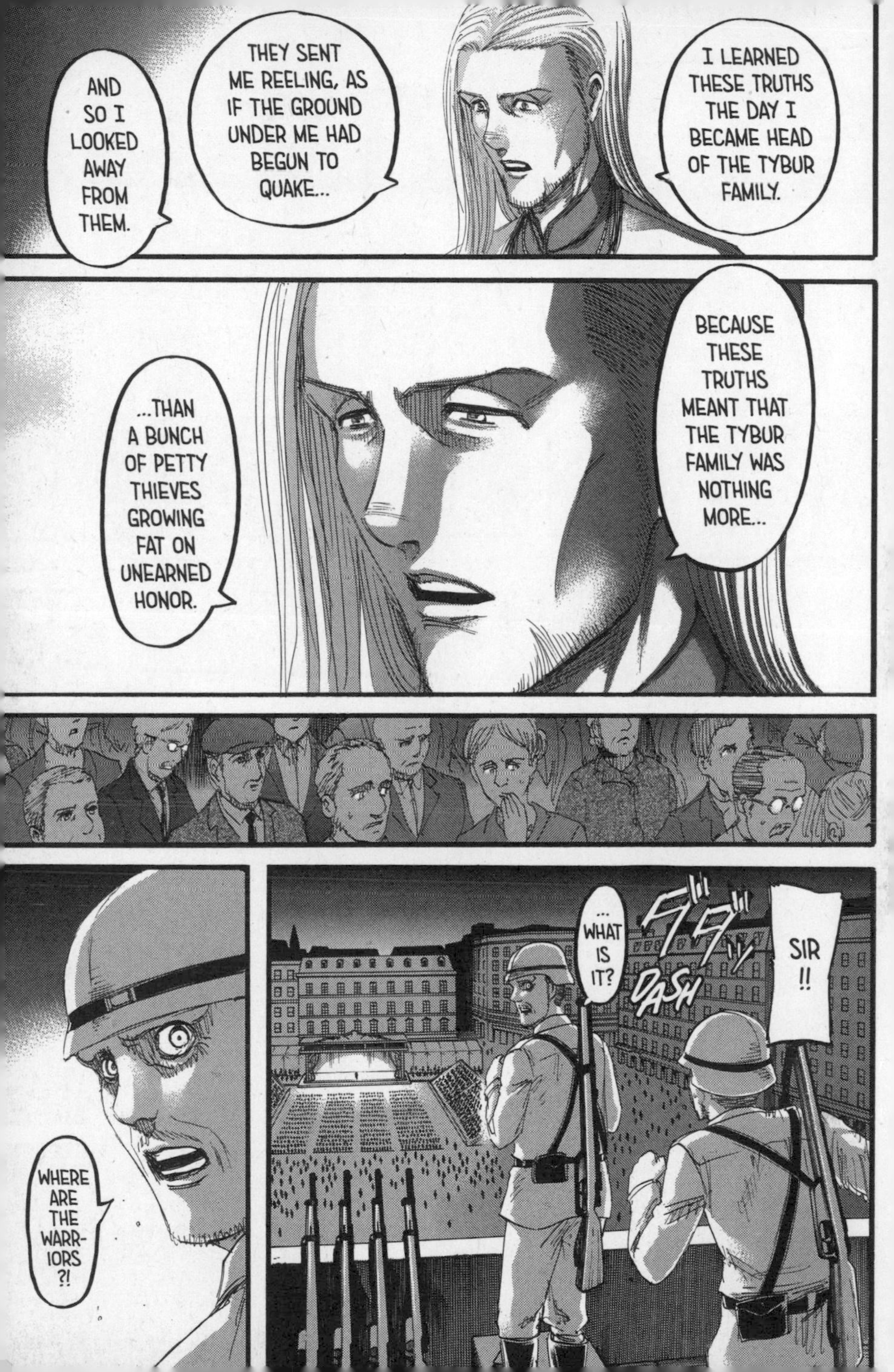
I LEARNED THESE TRUTHS THE DAY I BECAME HEAD OF THE TYBUR FAMILY.
THEY SENT ME REELING, AS IF THE GROUND UNDER ME HAD BEGUN TO QUAKE...
AND SO I LOOKED AWAY FROM THEM.
BECAUSE THESE TRUTHS MEANT THAT THE TYBUR FAMILY WAS NOTHING MORE...
...THAN A BUNCH OF PETTY THIEVES GROWING FAT ON UNEARNED HONOR.
SIR !!
DASH
...WHAT IS IT?
WHERE ARE THE WARRIORS?!

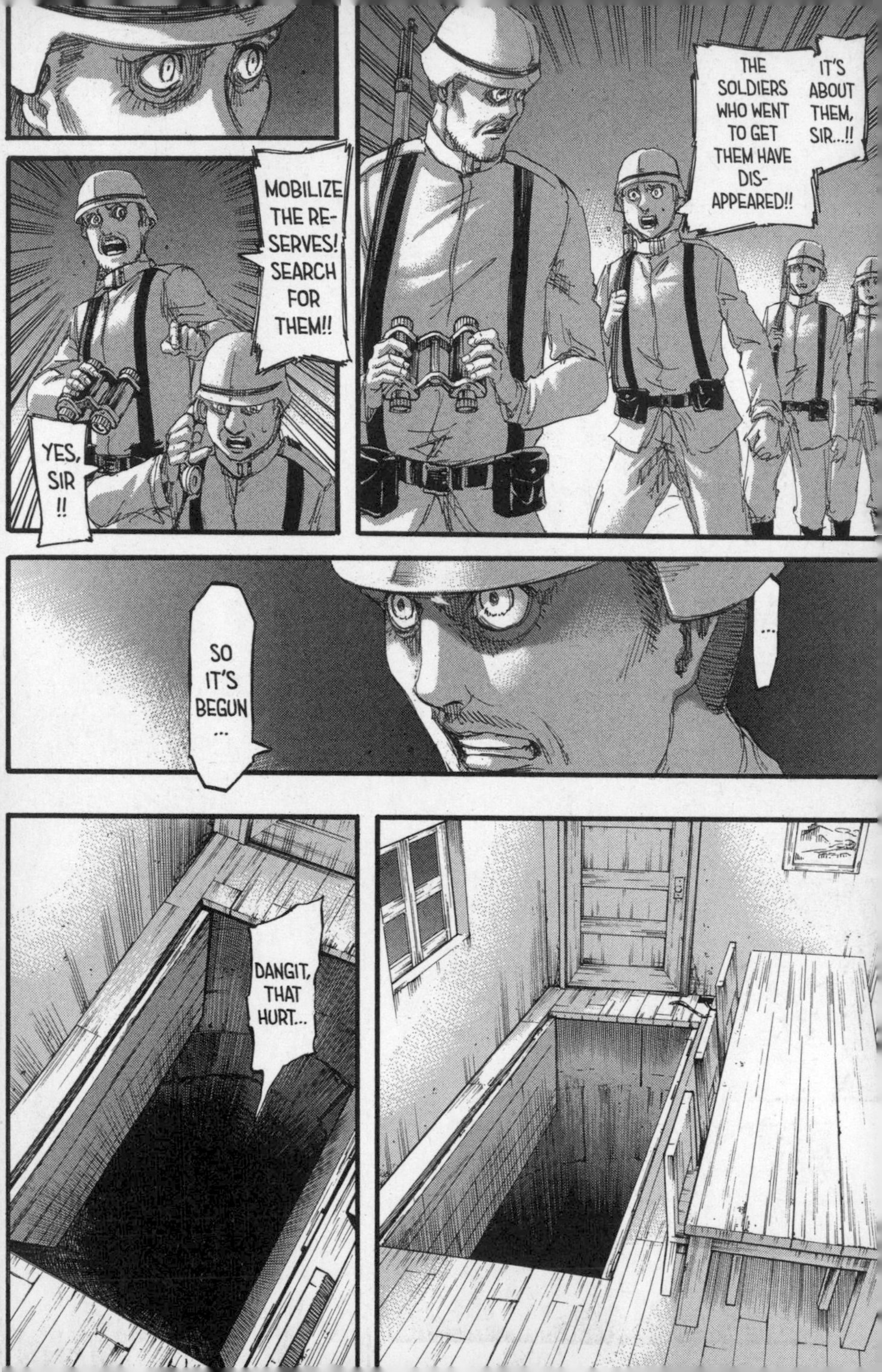
IT'S ABOUT THEM, SIR...!!
THE SOLDIERS WHO WENT TO GET THEM HAVE DIS-APPEARED!!
MOBILIZE THE RE-SERVES! SEARCH FOR THEM!!
YES, SIR!!
...
SO IT'S BEGUN...
DANGIT, THAT HURT...

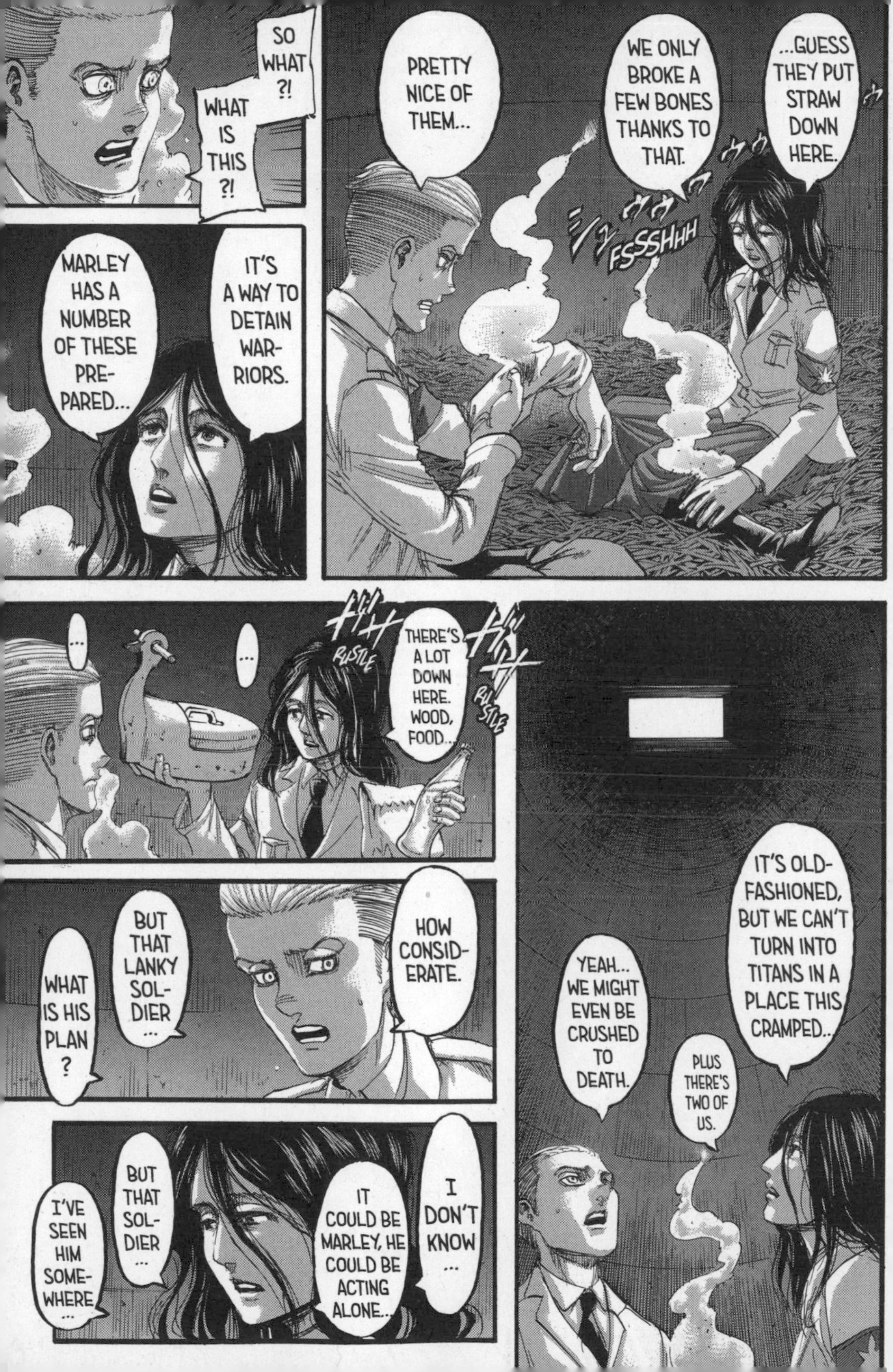
...GUESS THEY PUT STRAW DOWN HERE.
WE ONLY BROKE A FEW BONES THANKS TO THAT.
FSSSHHH
PRETTY NICE OF THEM...
SO WHAT ?!
WHAT IS THIS ?!
IT'S A WAY TO DETAIN WARRIORS.
MARLEY HAS A NUMBER OF THESE PREPARED...
IT'S OLD-FASHIONED, BUT WE CAN'T TURN INTO TITANS IN A PLACE THIS CRAMPED..
YEAH... WE MIGHT EVEN BE CRUSHED TO DEATH.
PLUS THERE'S TWO OF US.
RUSTLE
THERE'S A LOT DOWN HERE. WOOD, FOOD...
RUSTLE
...
...
HOW CONSIDERATE.
BUT THAT LANKY SOLDIER ...
WHAT IS HIS PLAN ?
I DON'T KNOW ...
IT COULD BE MARLEY, HE COULD BE ACTING ALONE..
BUT THAT SOLDIER ...
I'VE SEEN HIM SOMEWHERE ...

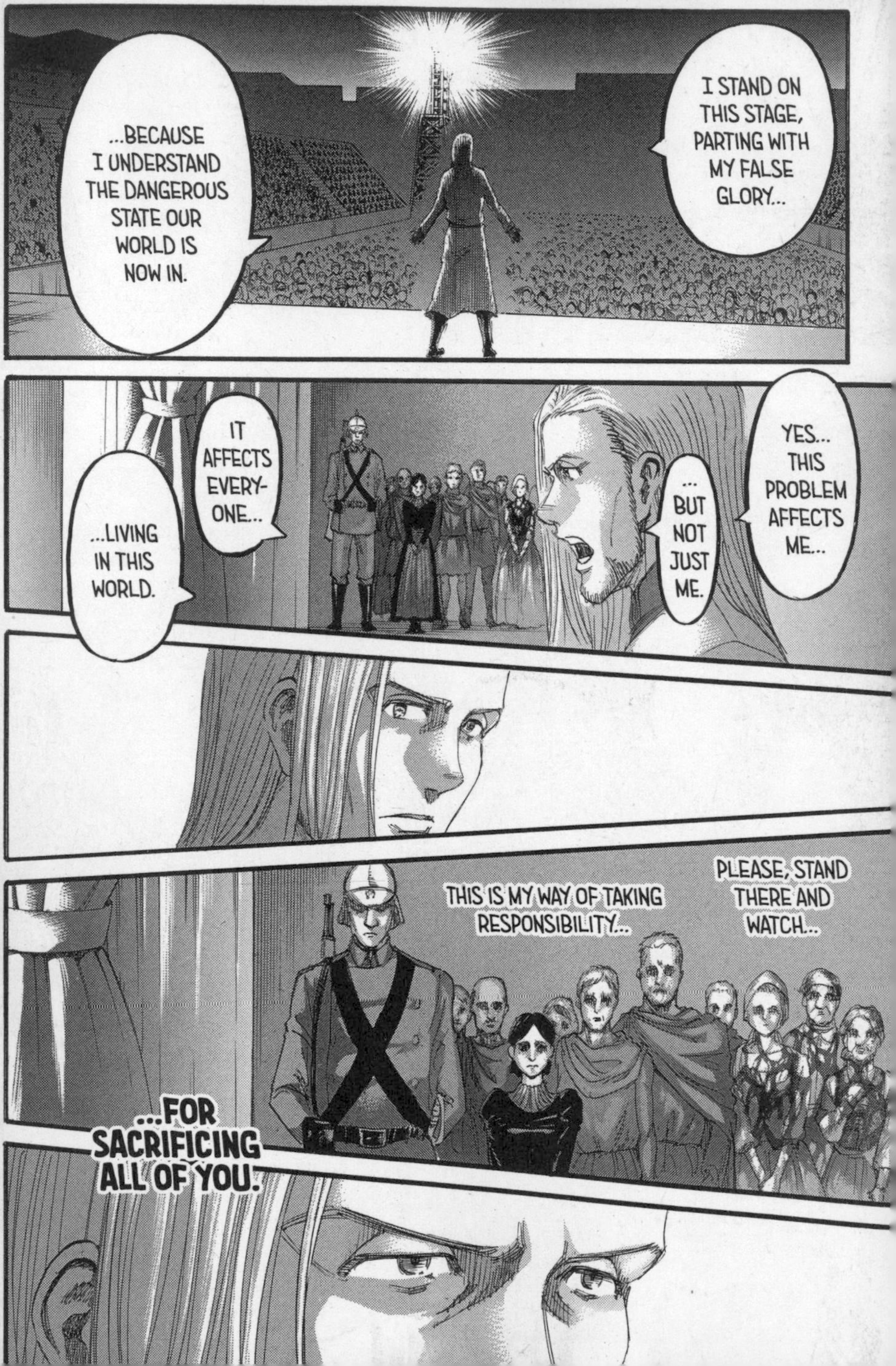
I STAND ON THIS STAGE, PARTING WITH MY FALSE GLORY...
...BECAUSE I UNDERSTAND THE DANGEROUS STATE OUR WORLD IS NOW IN.
YES... THIS PROBLEM AFFECTS ME...
... BUT NOT JUST ME.
IT AFFECTS EVERY-ONE...
...LIVING IN THIS WORLD.
PLEASE, STAND THERE AND WATCH...
THIS IS MY WAY OF TAKING RESPONSIBILITY...
...FOR SACRIFICING ALL OF YOU.

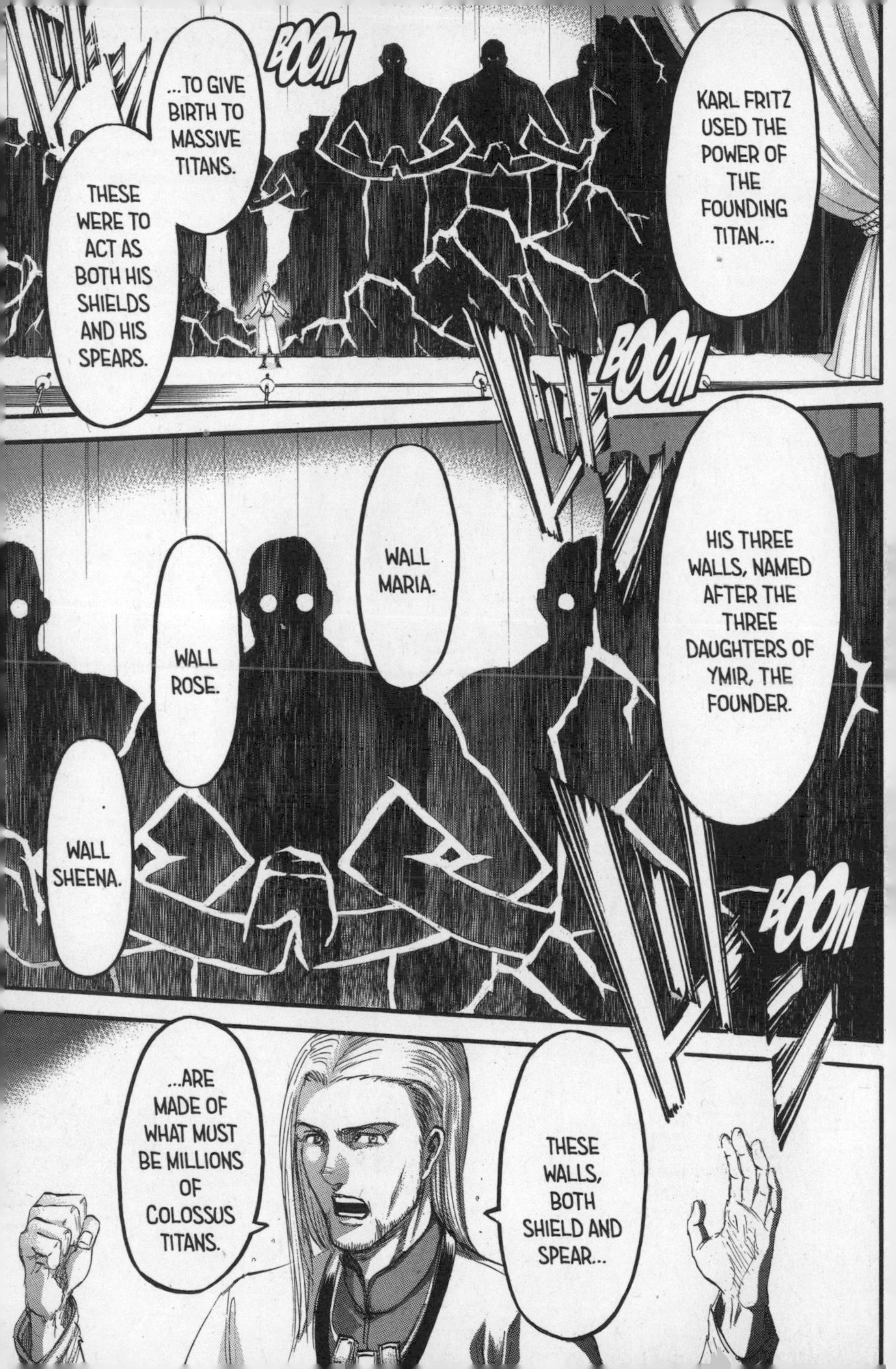
BOOM
KARL FRITZ USED THE POWER OF THE FOUNDING TITAN...
...TO GIVE BIRTH TO MASSIVE TITANS.
THESE WERE TO ACT AS BOTH HIS SHIELDS AND HIS SPEARS.
BOOM
HIS THREE WALLS, NAMED AFTER THE THREE DAUGHTERS OF YMIR, THE FOUNDER.
WALL MARIA.
WALL ROSE.
WALL SHEENA.
BOOM
THESE WALLS, BOTH SHIELD AND SPEAR...
...ARE MADE OF WHAT MUST BE MILLIONS OF COLOSSUS TITANS.

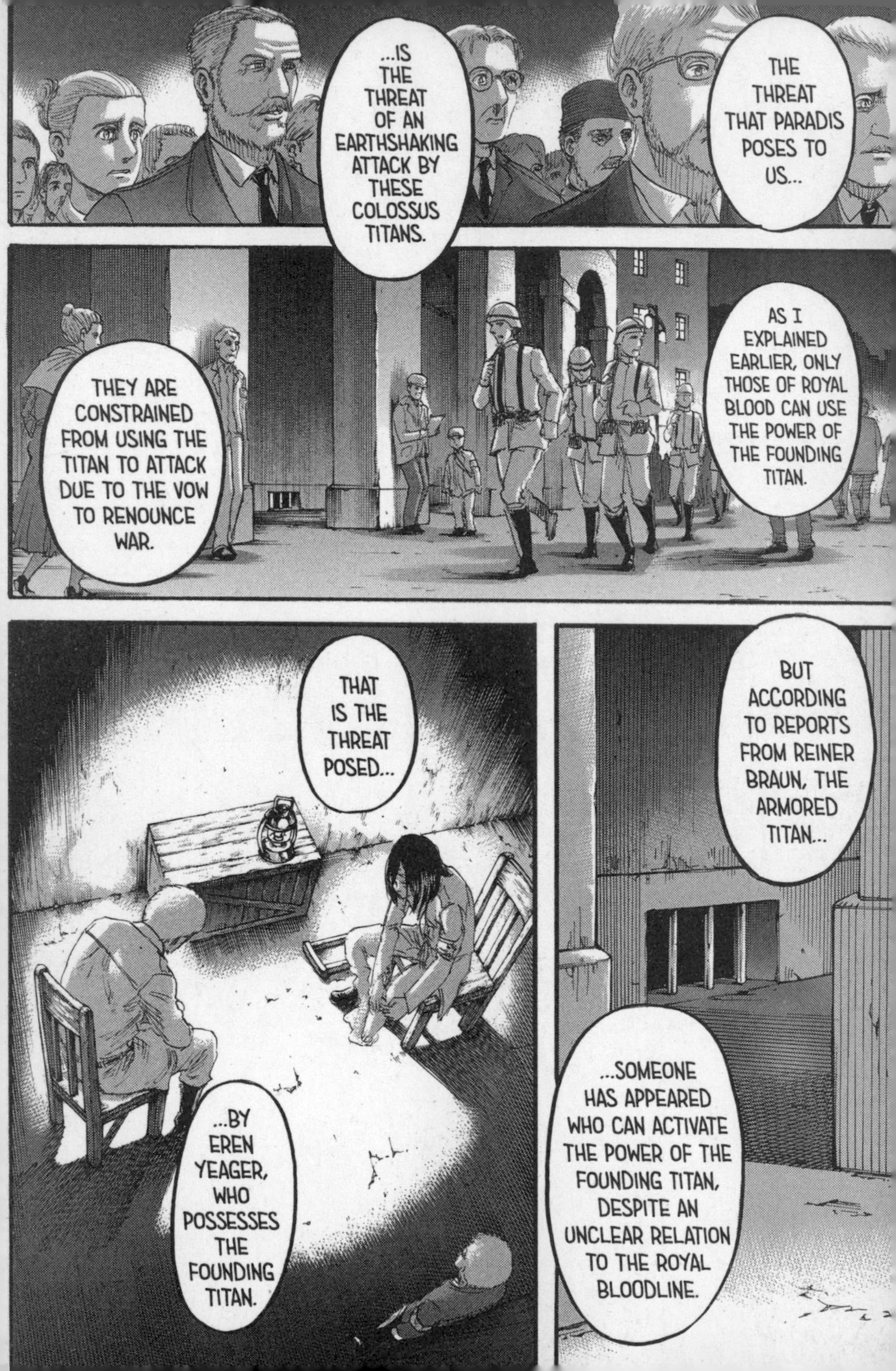
THE THREAT THAT PARADIS POSES TO US...
...IS THE THREAT OF AN EARTHSHAKING ATTACK BY THESE COLOSSUS TITANS.
AS I EXPLAINED EARLIER, ONLY THOSE OF ROYAL BLOOD CAN USE THE POWER OF THE FOUNDING TITAN.
THEY ARE CONSTRAINED FROM USING THE TITAN TO ATTACK DUE TO THE VOW TO RENOUNCE WAR.
BUT ACCORDING TO REPORTS FROM REINER BRAUN, THE ARMORED TITAN...
...SOMEONE HAS APPEARED WHO CAN ACTIVATE THE POWER OF THE FOUNDING TITAN, DESPITE AN UNCLEAR RELATION TO THE ROYAL BLOODLINE.
THAT IS THE THREAT POSED...
...BY EREN YEAGER, WHO POSSESSES THE FOUNDING TITAN.

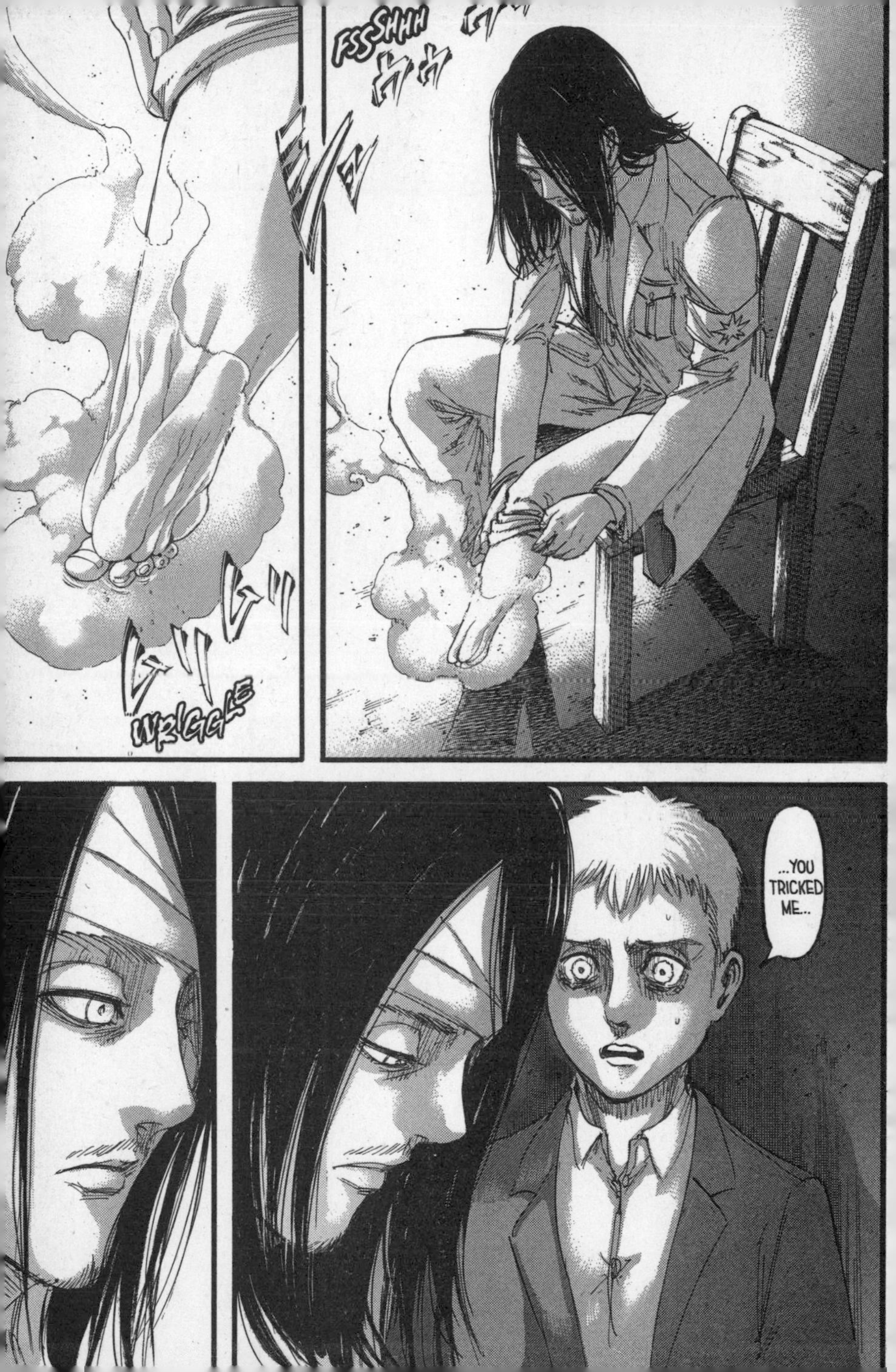
FSSHHH
WRIGGLE
...YOU TRICKED ME...

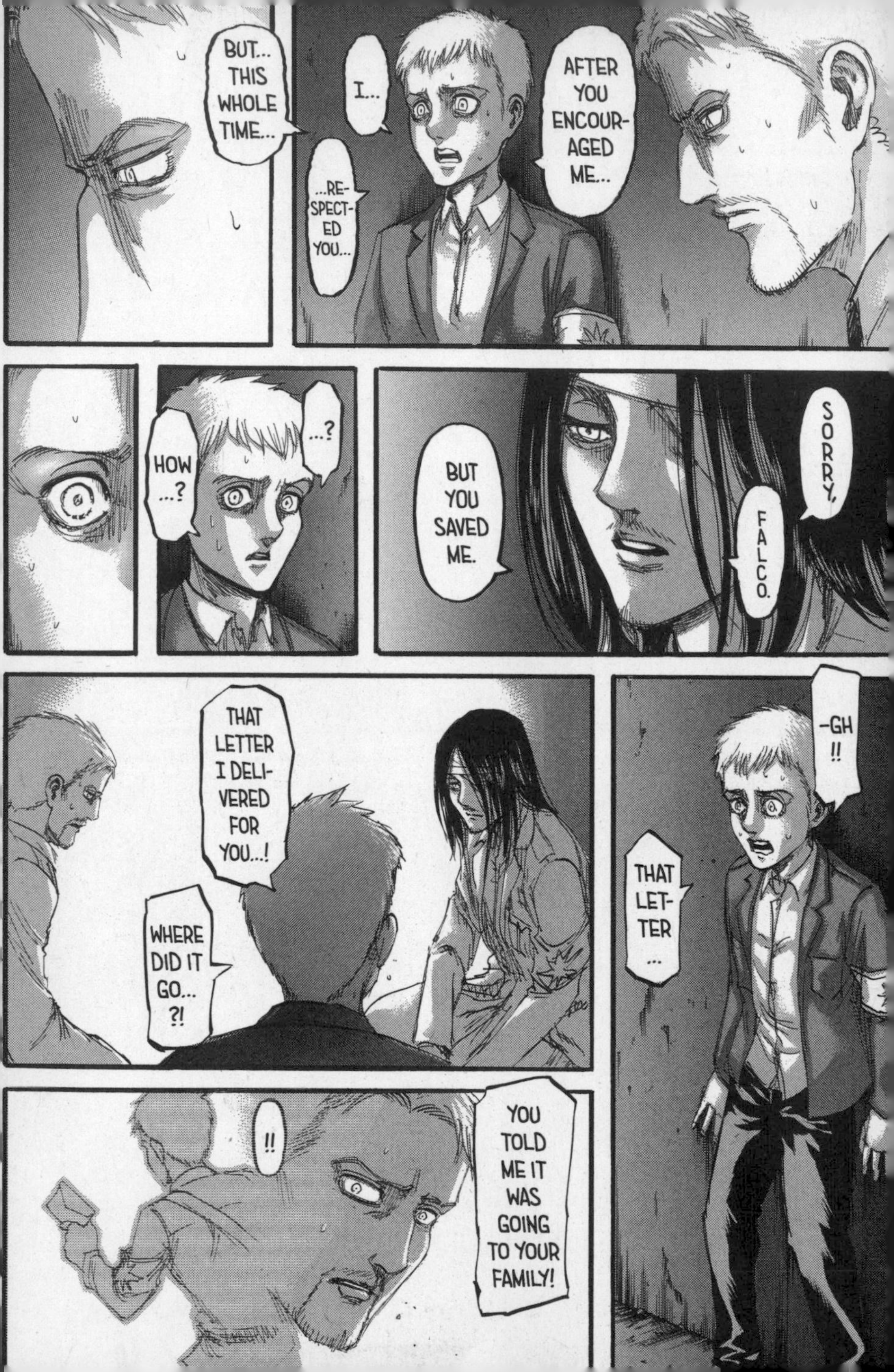

AFTER YOU ENCOURAGED ME...
I...
...RESPECTED YOU...
BUT... THIS WHOLE TIME...
SORRY, FALCO.
BUT YOU SAVED ME.
...?
HOW ...?
-GH !!
THAT LETTER ...
THAT LETTER I DELIVERED FOR YOU...!
WHERE DID IT GO... ?!
YOU TOLD ME IT WAS GOING TO YOUR FAMILY!
!!

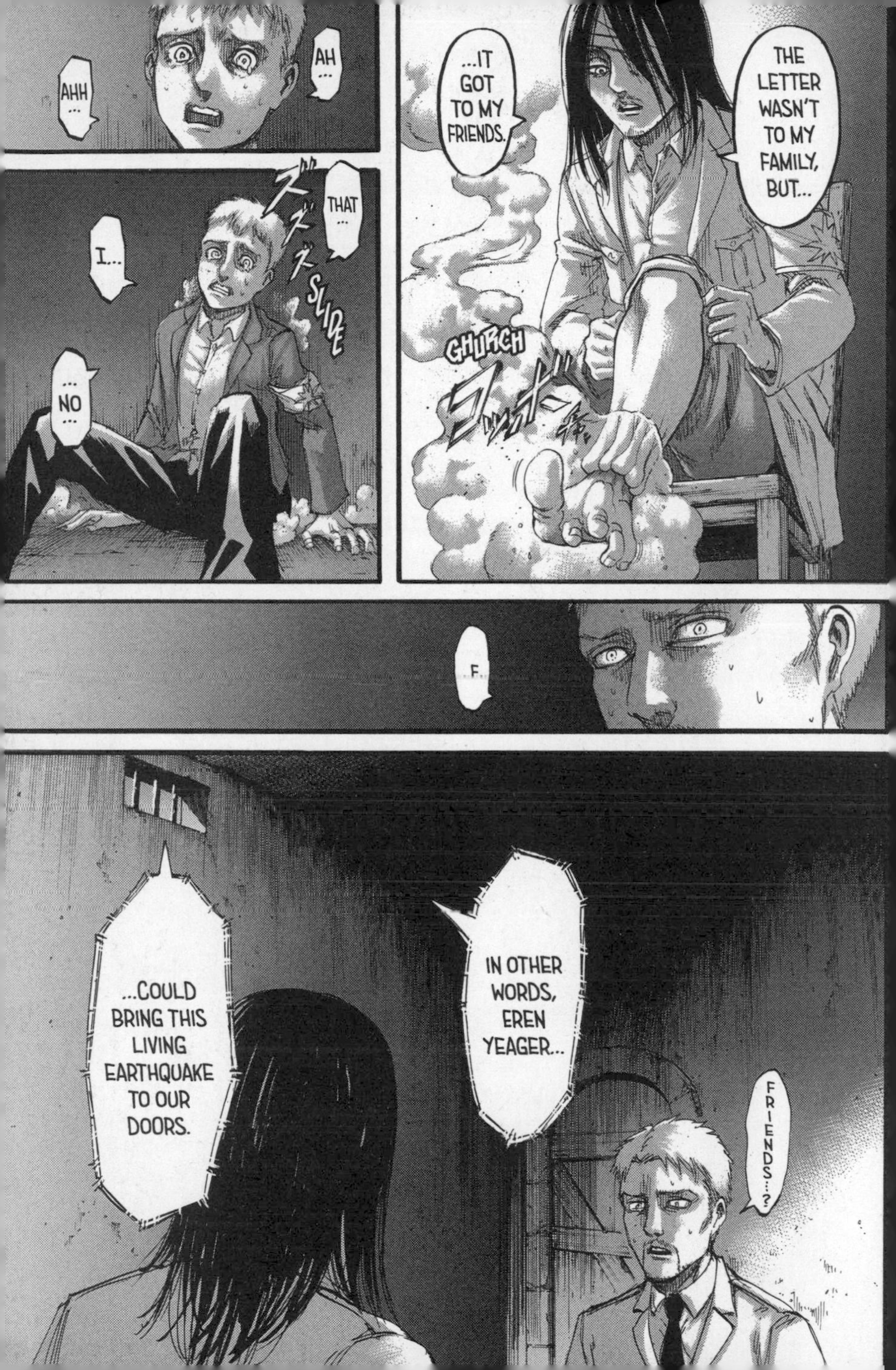
THE LETTER WASN'T TO MY FAMILY, BUT...
...IT GOT TO MY FRIENDS.
GHURCH
AH...
AHH...
THAT...
SLIDE
I...
...NO...
...F...
FRIENDS...?
IN OTHER WORDS, EREN YEAGER...
...COULD BRING THIS LIVING EARTHQUAKE TO OUR DOORS.

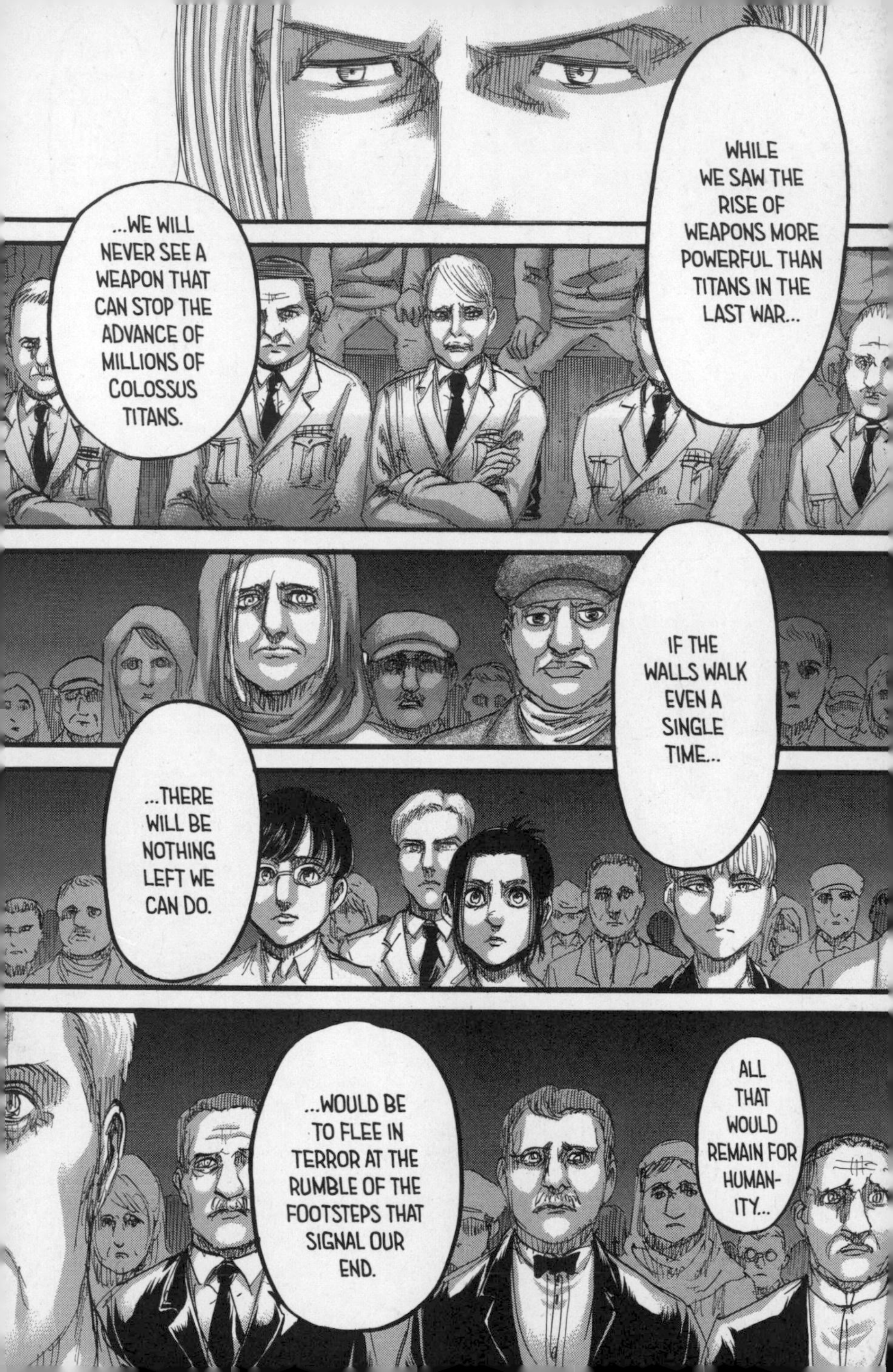
WHILE WE SAW THE RISE OF WEAPONS MORE POWERFUL THAN TITANS IN THE LAST WAR...
...WE WILL NEVER SEE A WEAPON THAT CAN STOP THE ADVANCE OF MILLIONS OF COLOSSUS TITANS.
IF THE WALLS WALK EVEN A SINGLE TIME...
...THERE WILL BE NOTHING LEFT WE CAN DO.
ALL THAT WOULD REMAIN FOR HUMAN-ITY...
...WOULD BE TO FLEE IN TERROR AT THE RUMBLE OF THE FOOTSTEPS THAT SIGNAL OUR END.

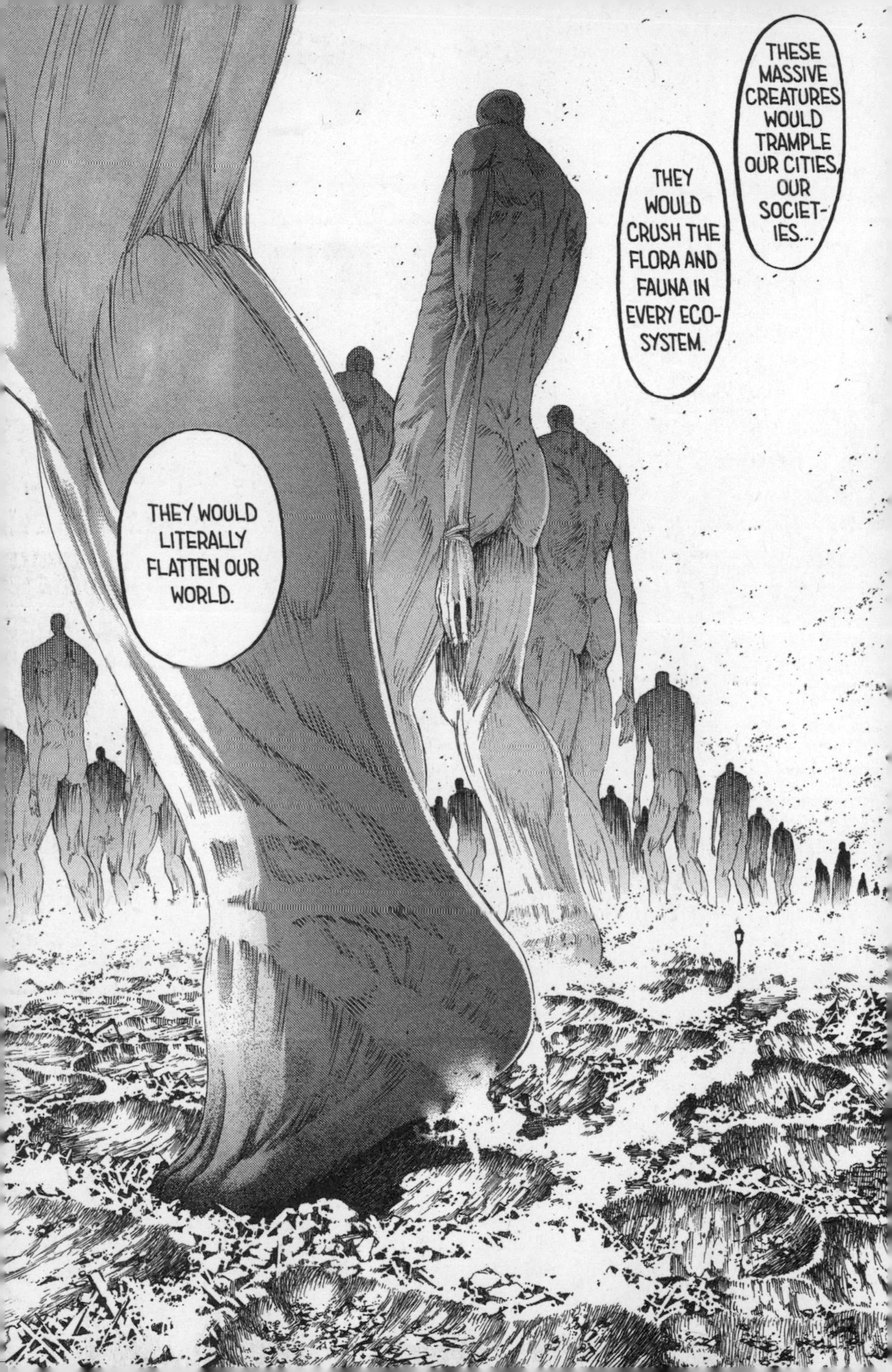
THESE MASSIVE CREATURES WOULD TRAMPLE OUR CITIES, OUR SOCIET-IES...
THEY WOULD CRUSH THE FLORA AND FAUNA IN EVERY ECO-SYSTEM.
THEY WOULD LITERALLY FLATTEN OUR WORLD.

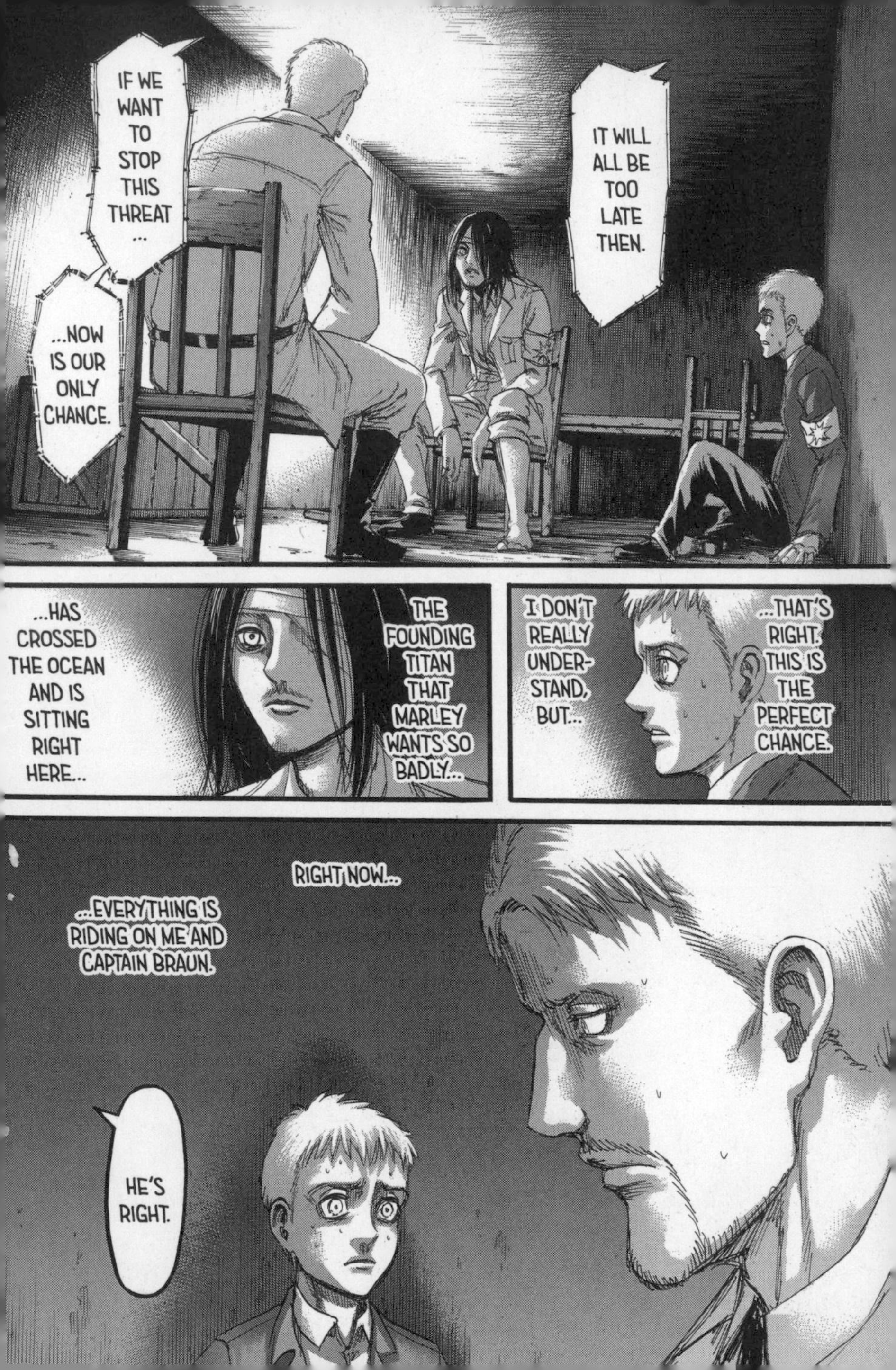
IT WILL ALL BE TOO LATE THEN.
IF WE WANT TO STOP THIS THREAT...
...NOW IS OUR ONLY CHANCE.
...THAT'S RIGHT. THIS IS THE PERFECT CHANCE.
I DON'T REALLY UNDERSTAND, BUT...
THE FOUNDING TITAN THAT MARLEY WANTS SO BADLY...
...HAS CROSSED THE OCEAN AND IS SITTING RIGHT HERE...
RIGHT NOW...
...EVERYTHING IS RIDING ON ME AND CAPTAIN BRAUN.
HE'S RIGHT.

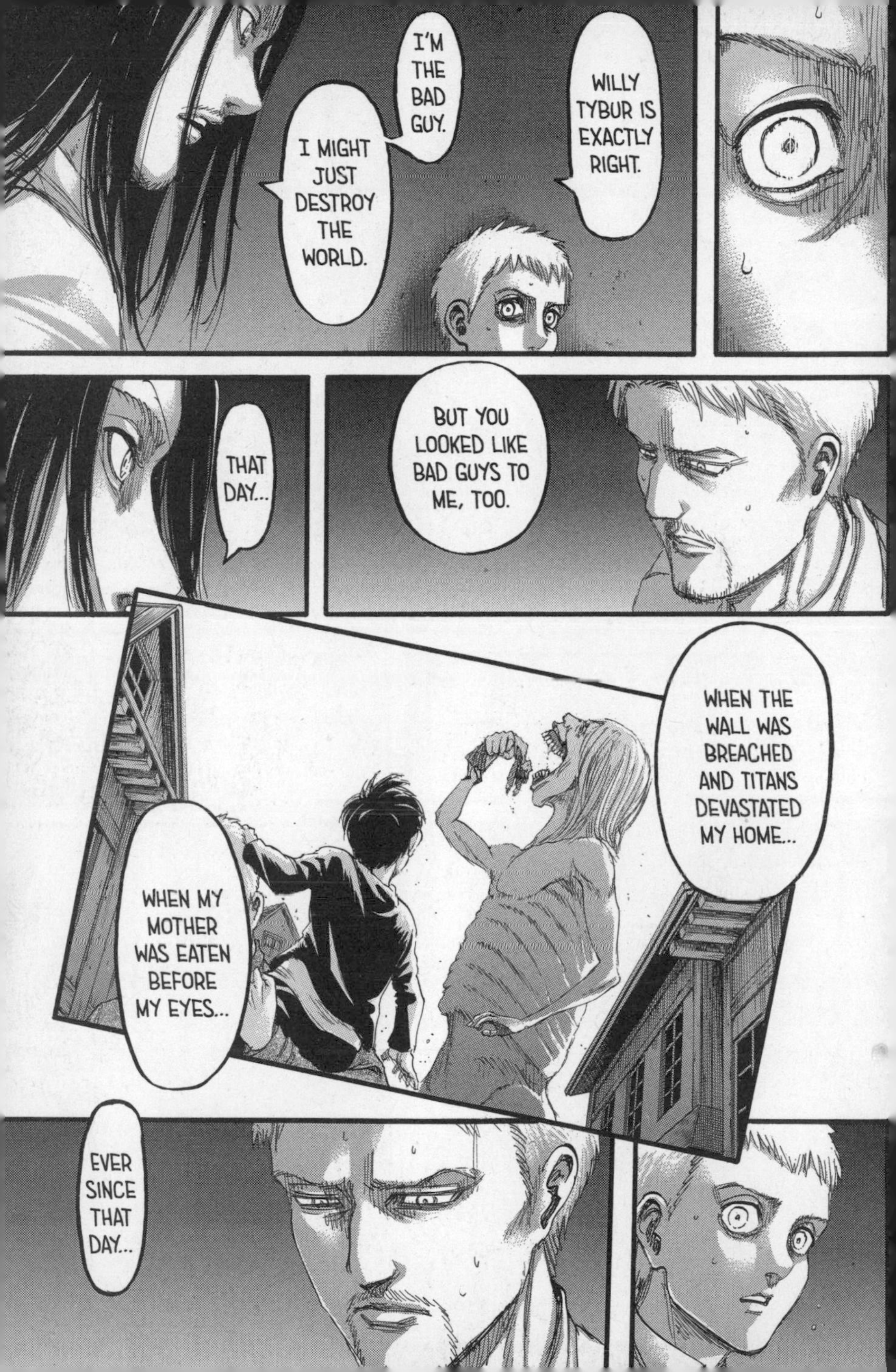
WILLY TYBUR IS EXACTLY RIGHT.
I'M THE BAD GUY.
I MIGHT JUST DESTROY THE WORLD.
BUT YOU LOOKED LIKE BAD GUYS TO ME, TOO.
THAT DAY...
WHEN THE WALL WAS BREACHED AND TITANS DEVASTATED MY HOME...
WHEN MY MOTHER WAS EATEN BEFORE MY EYES...
EVER SINCE THAT DAY...

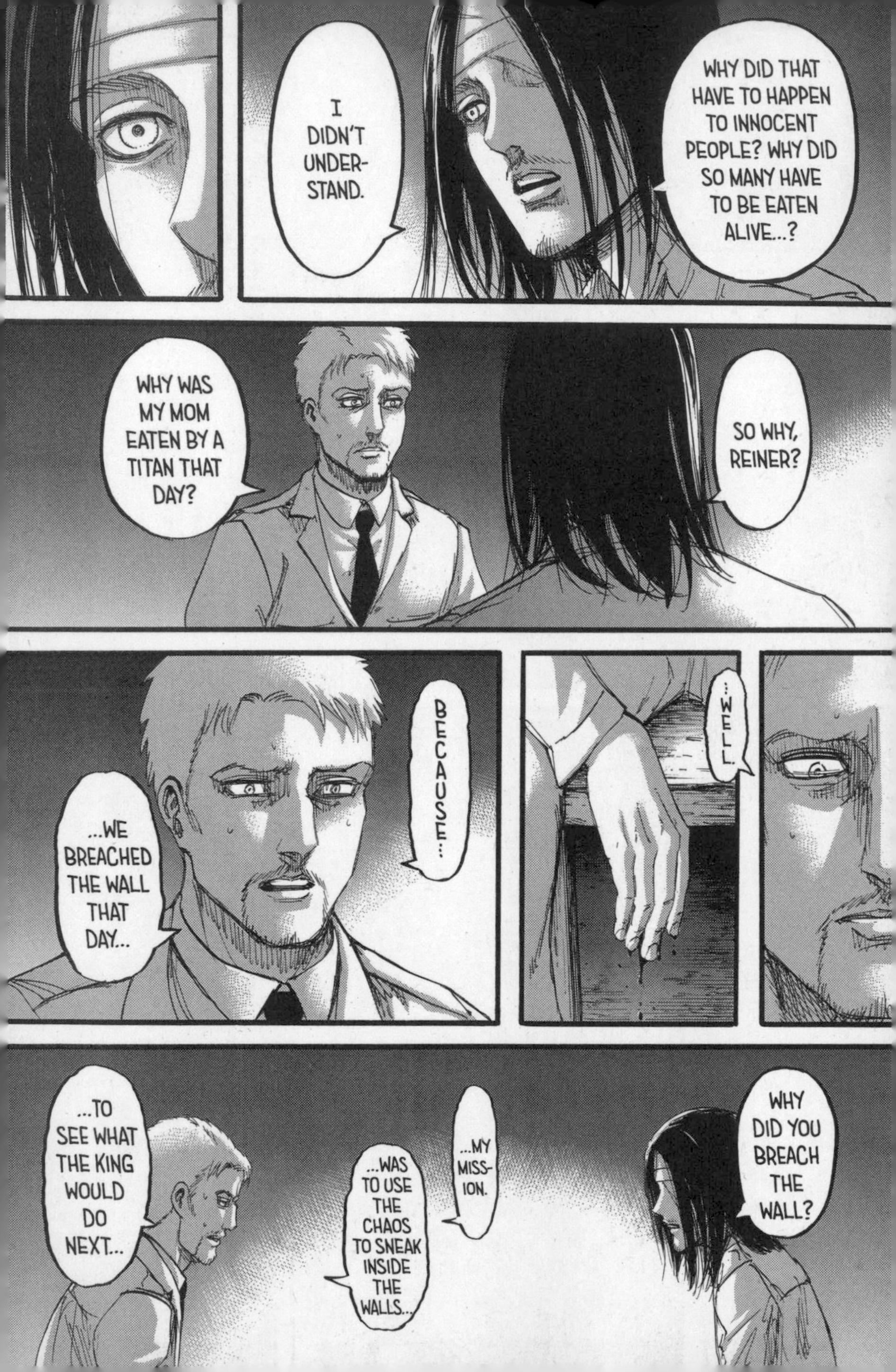
WHY DID THAT HAVE TO HAPPEN TO INNOCENT PEOPLE? WHY DID SO MANY HAVE TO BE EATEN ALIVE...?
I DIDN'T UNDER-STAND.
SO WHY, REINER?
WHY WAS MY MOM EATEN BY A TITAN THAT DAY?
...WELL.
BECAUSE...
...WE BREACHED THE WALL THAT DAY...
WHY DID YOU BREACH THE WALL?
...MY MISS-ION.
...WAS TO USE THE CHAOS TO SNEAK INSIDE THE WALLS...
...TO SEE WHAT THE KING WOULD DO NEXT...

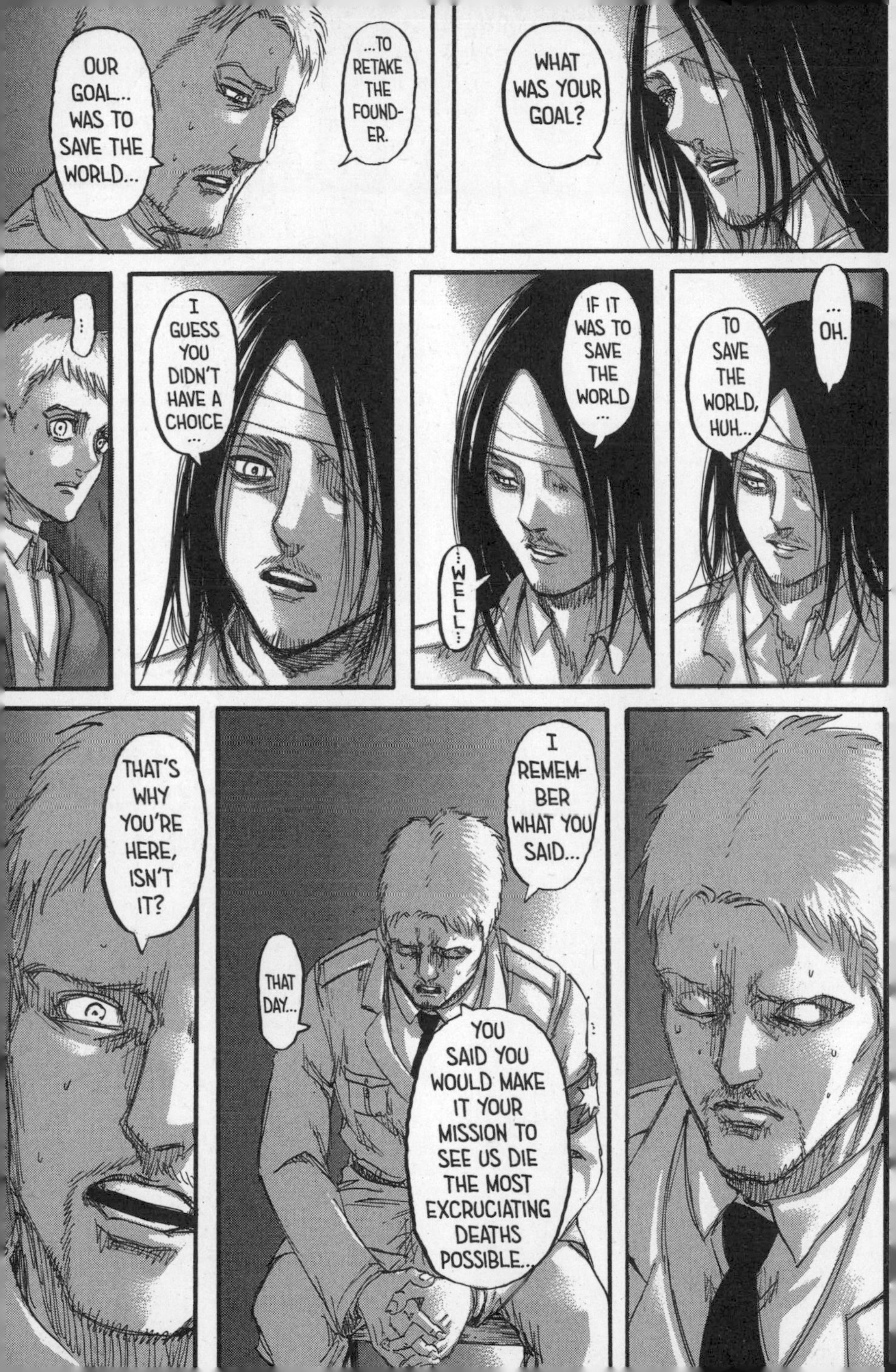
WHAT WAS YOUR GOAL?
...TO RETAKE THE FOUNDER.
OUR GOAL... WAS TO SAVE THE WORLD...
...OH.
TO SAVE THE WORLD, HUH...
IF IT WAS TO SAVE THE WORLD ...
...WELL...
I GUESS YOU DIDN'T HAVE A CHOICE ...
...!
I REMEMBER WHAT YOU SAID...
THAT DAY...
YOU SAID YOU WOULD MAKE IT YOUR MISSION TO SEE US DIE THE MOST EXCRUCIATING DEATHS POSSIBLE...
THAT'S WHY YOU'RE HERE, ISN'T IT?

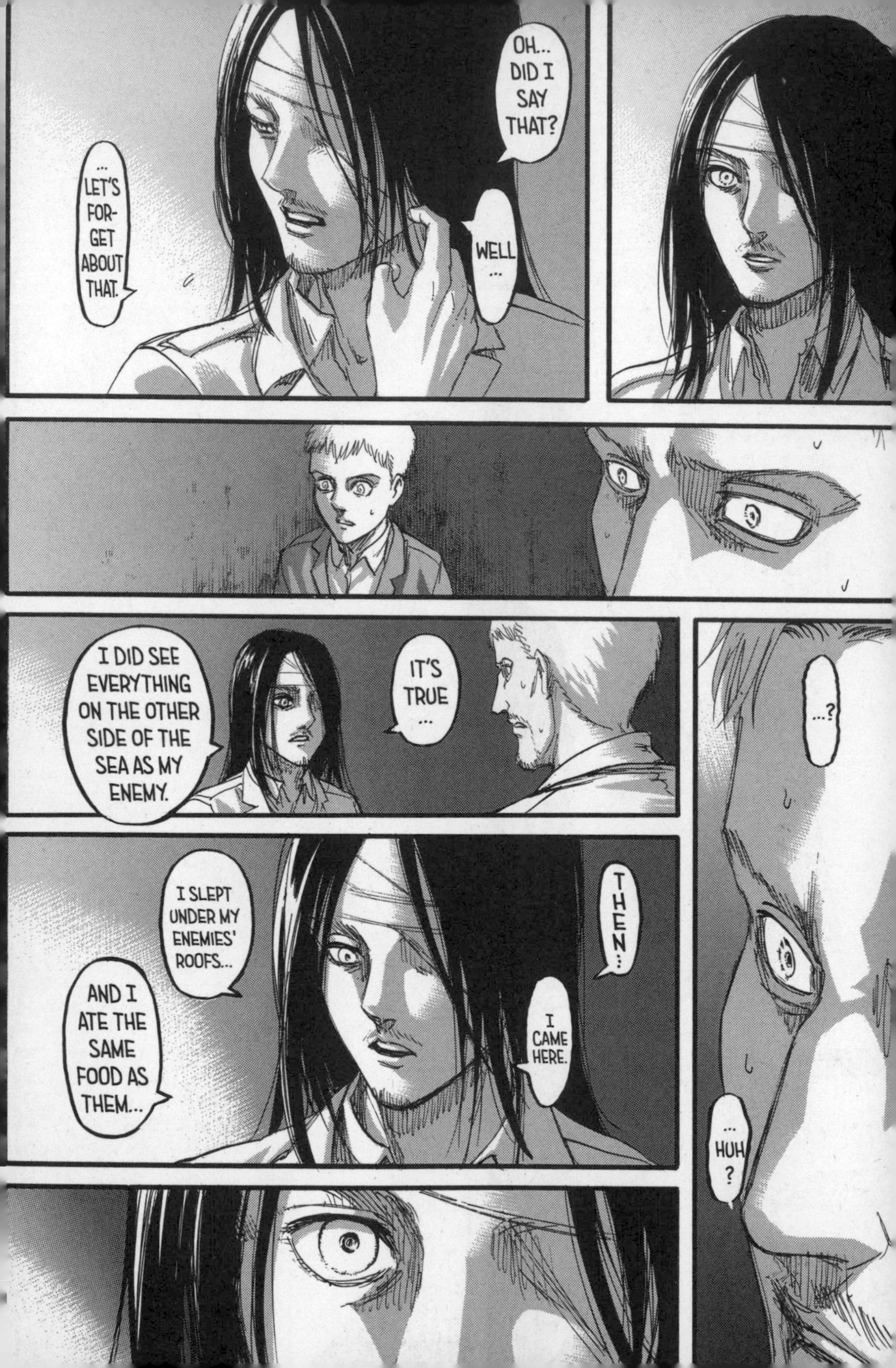
OH... DID I SAY THAT?
WELL...
...LET'S FOR-GET ABOUT THAT.
...?
...HUH?
IT'S TRUE...
I DID SEE EVERYTHING ON THE OTHER SIDE OF THE SEA AS MY ENEMY.
THEN...
I CAME HERE.
I SLEPT UNDER MY ENEMIES' ROOFS...
AND I ATE THE SAME FOOD AS THEM...

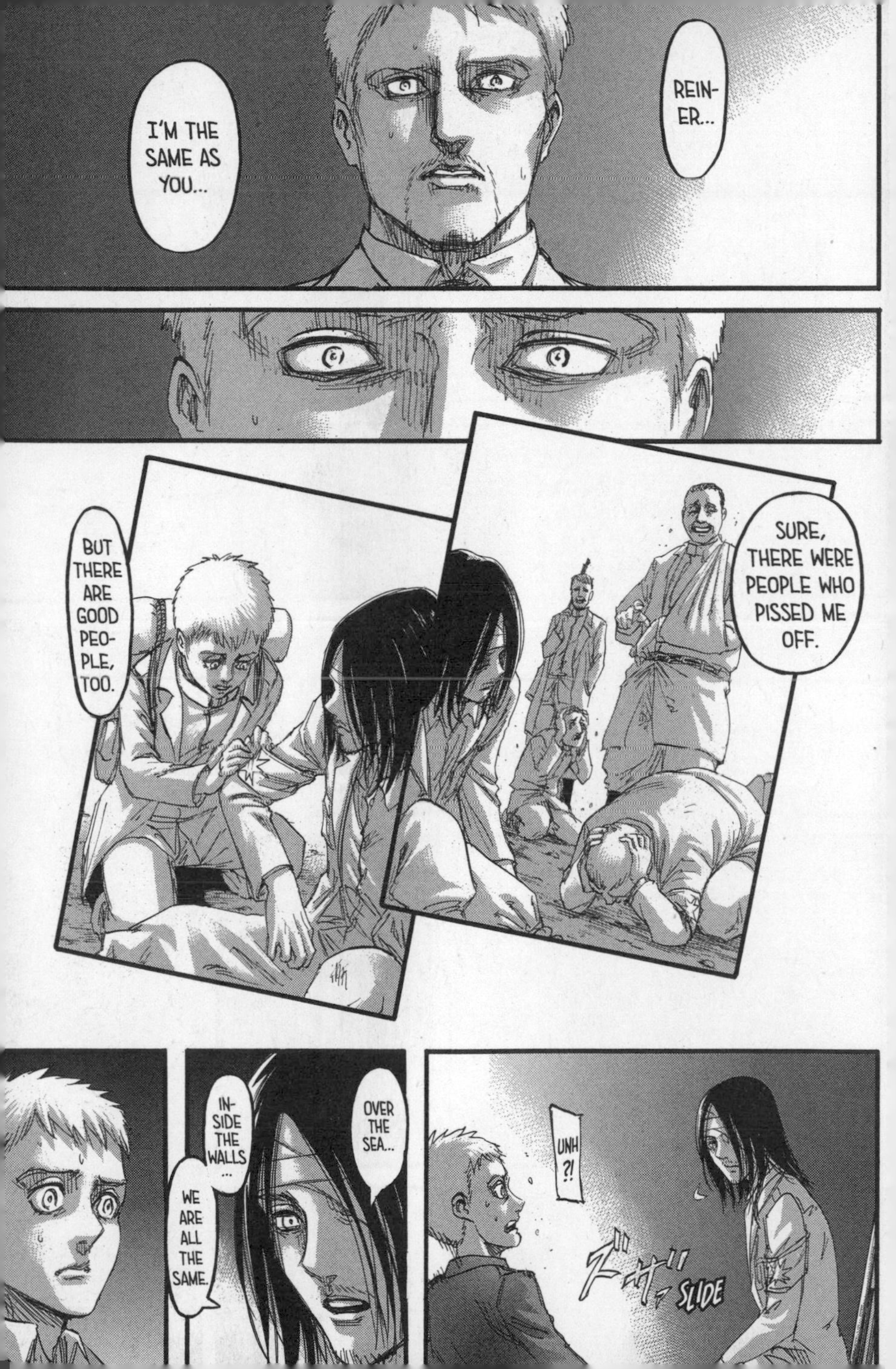
REIN-ER...
I'M THE SAME AS YOU...
SURE, THERE WERE PEOPLE WHO PISSED ME OFF.
BUT THERE ARE GOOD PEO-PLE, TOO.
UNH ?!
SLIDE
OVER THE SEA...
IN-SIDE THE WALLS ...
WE ARE ALL THE SAME.

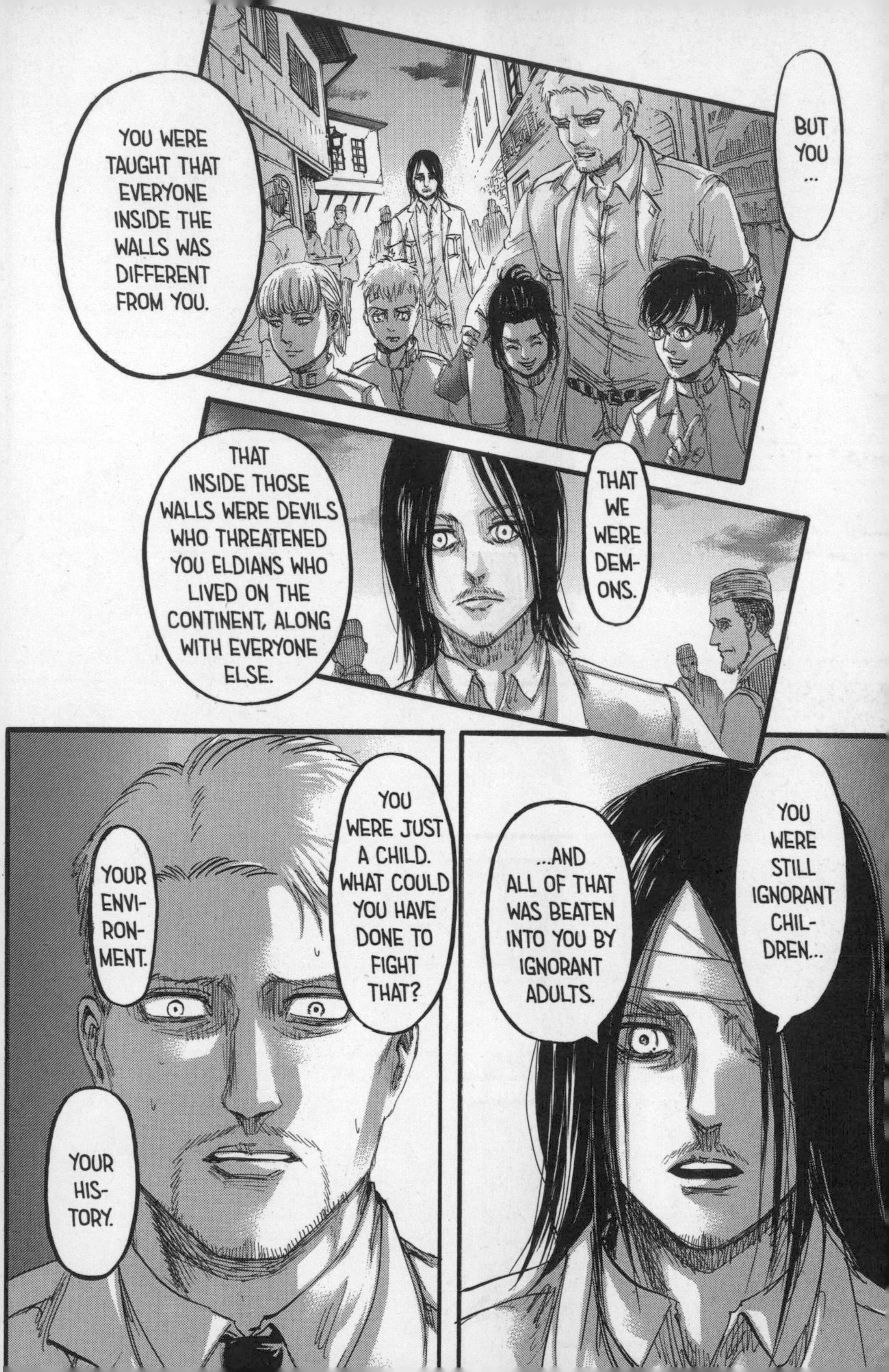
BUT YOU ...
YOU WERE TAUGHT THAT EVERYONE INSIDE THE WALLS WAS DIFFERENT FROM YOU.
THAT WE WERE DEM-ONS.
THAT INSIDE THOSE WALLS WERE DEVILS WHO THREATENED YOU ELDIANS WHO LIVED ON THE CONTINENT, ALONG WITH EVERYONE ELSE.
YOU WERE STILL IGNORANT CHIL-DREN...
...AND ALL OF THAT WAS BEATEN INTO YOU BY IGNORANT ADULTS.
YOU WERE JUST A CHILD. WHAT COULD YOU HAVE DONE TO FIGHT THAT?
YOUR ENVI-RON-MENT.
YOUR HIS-TORY.

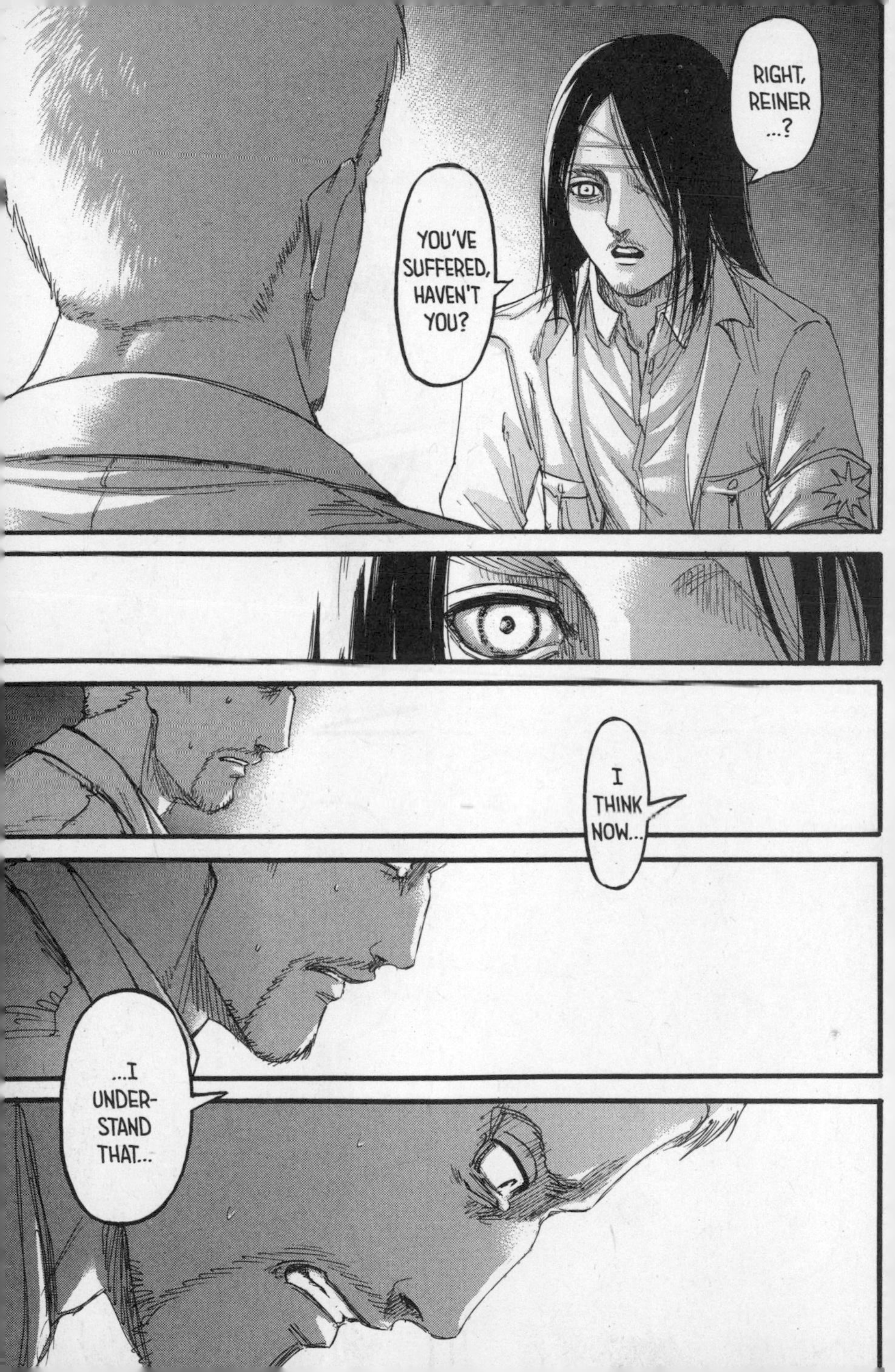
RIGHT, REINER ...?
YOU'VE SUFFERED, HAVEN'T YOU?
I THINK NOW...
...I UNDER-STAND THAT...

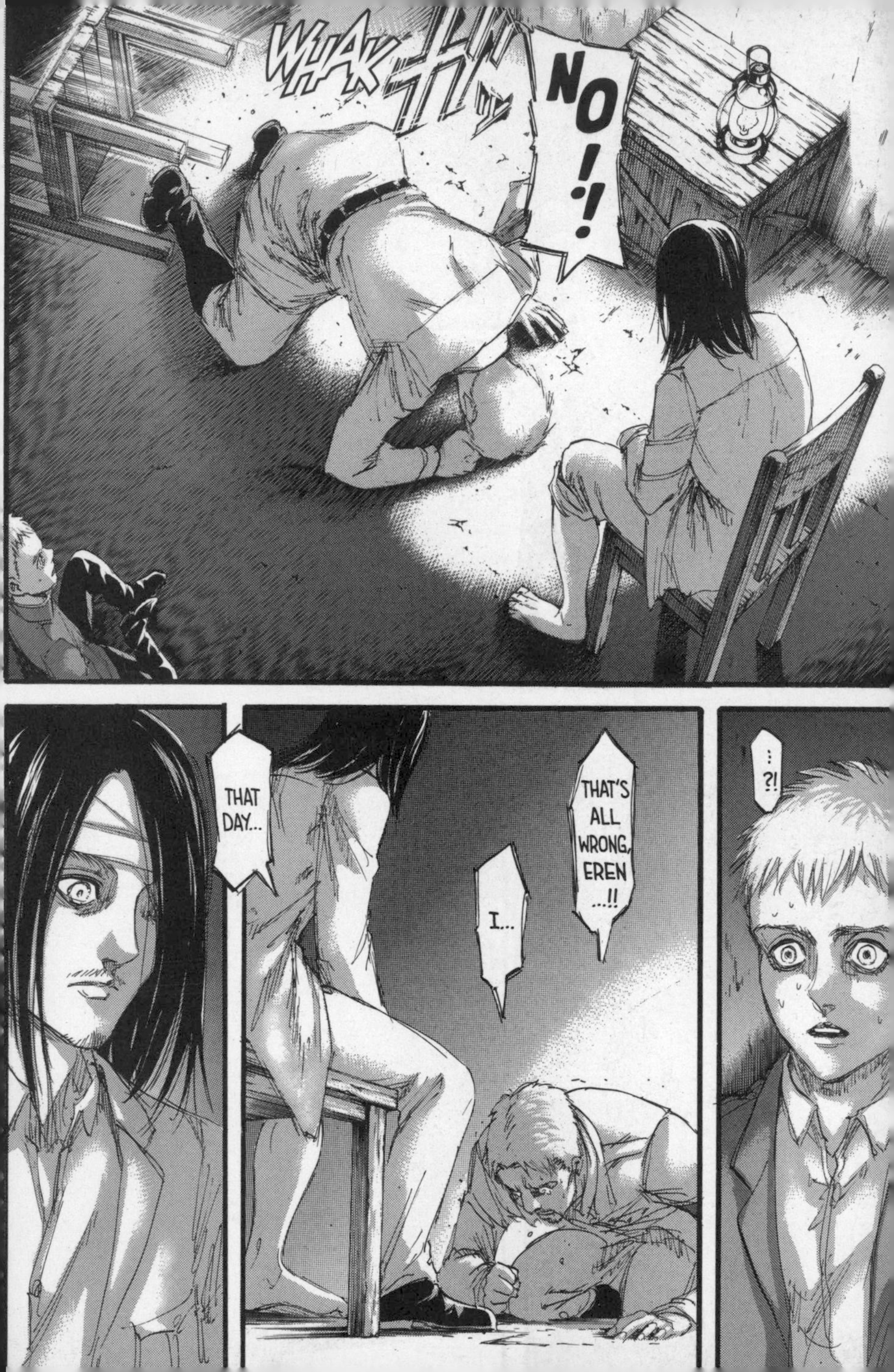
NO!!!
WHAK
...
?!
THAT'S ALL WRONG, EREN ...!!
I...
THAT DAY...

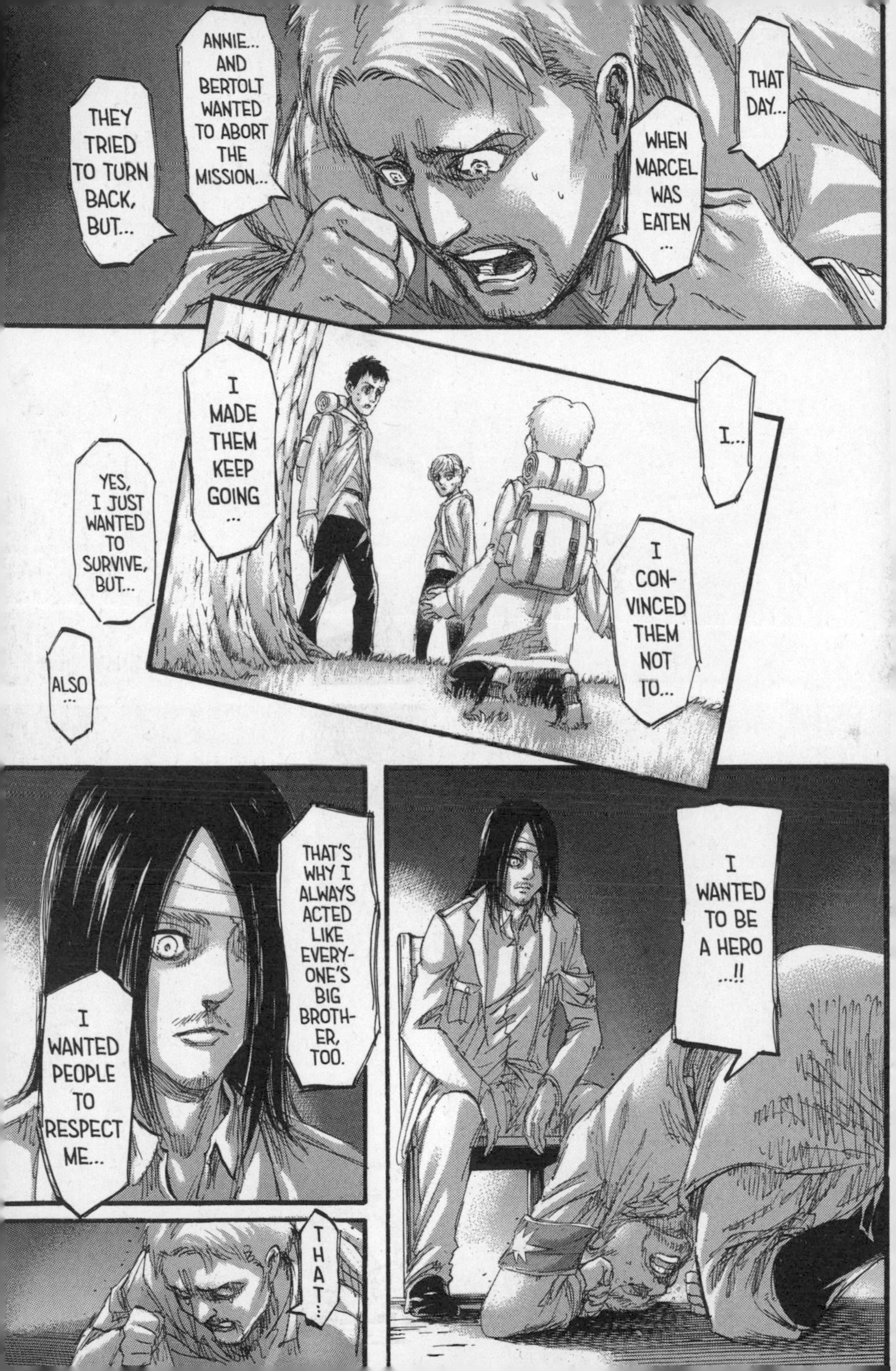
THAT DAY...
WHEN MARCEL WAS EATEN...
ANNIE... AND BERTOLT WANTED TO ABORT THE MISSION...
THEY TRIED TO TURN BACK, BUT...
I...
I CONVINCED THEM NOT TO...
I MADE THEM KEEP GOING...
YES, I JUST WANTED TO SURVIVE, BUT...
ALSO...
I WANTED TO BE A HERO...!!
THAT'S WHY I ALWAYS ACTED LIKE EVERYONE'S BIG BROTHER, TOO.
I WANTED PEOPLE TO RESPECT ME...
THAT...

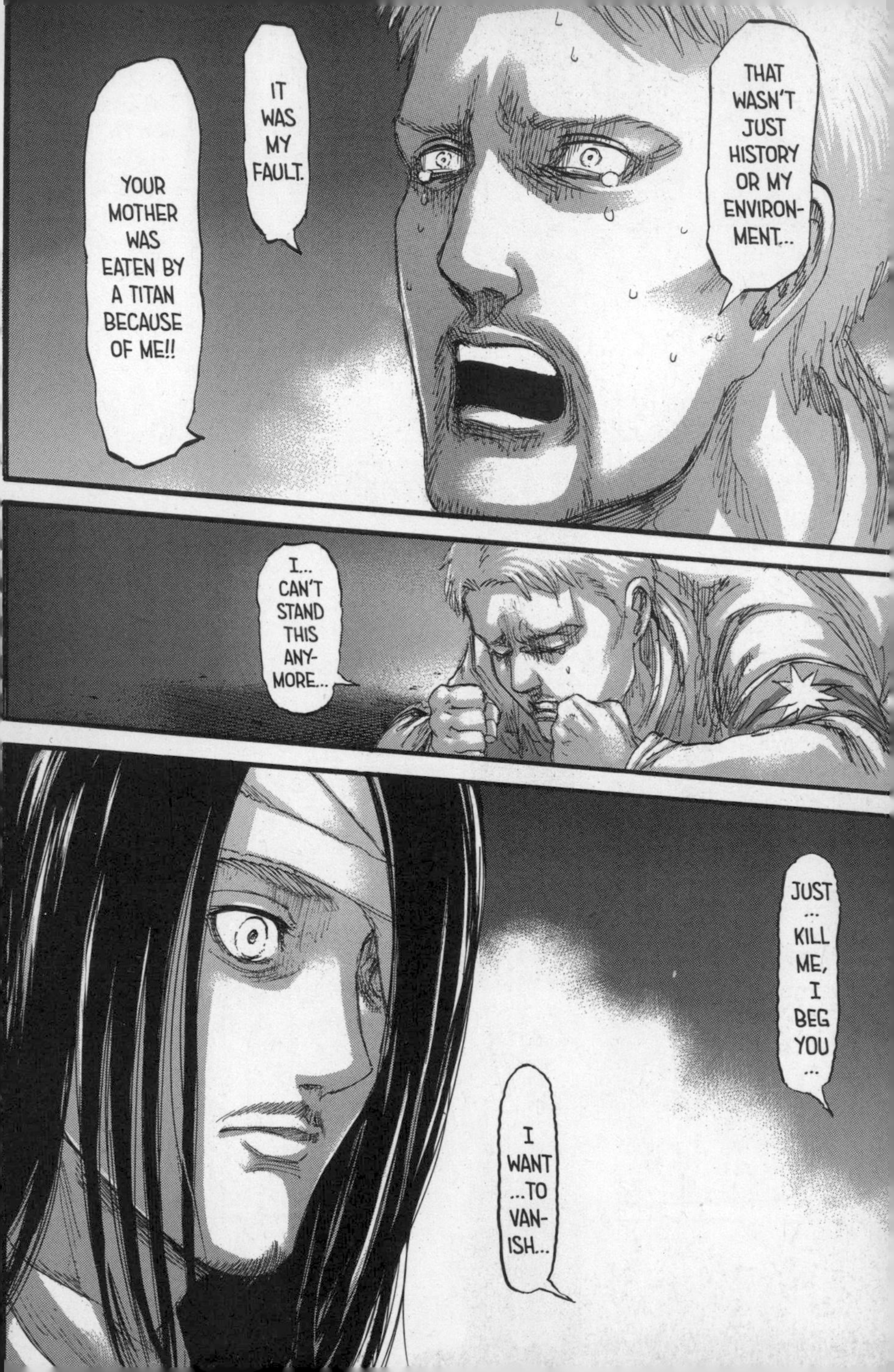
THAT WASN'T JUST HISTORY OR MY ENVIRONMENT...
IT WAS MY FAULT.
YOUR MOTHER WAS EATEN BY A TITAN BECAUSE OF ME!!
I... CAN'T STAND THIS ANYMORE...
JUST ... KILL ME, I BEG YOU ...
I WANT ...TO VANISH...

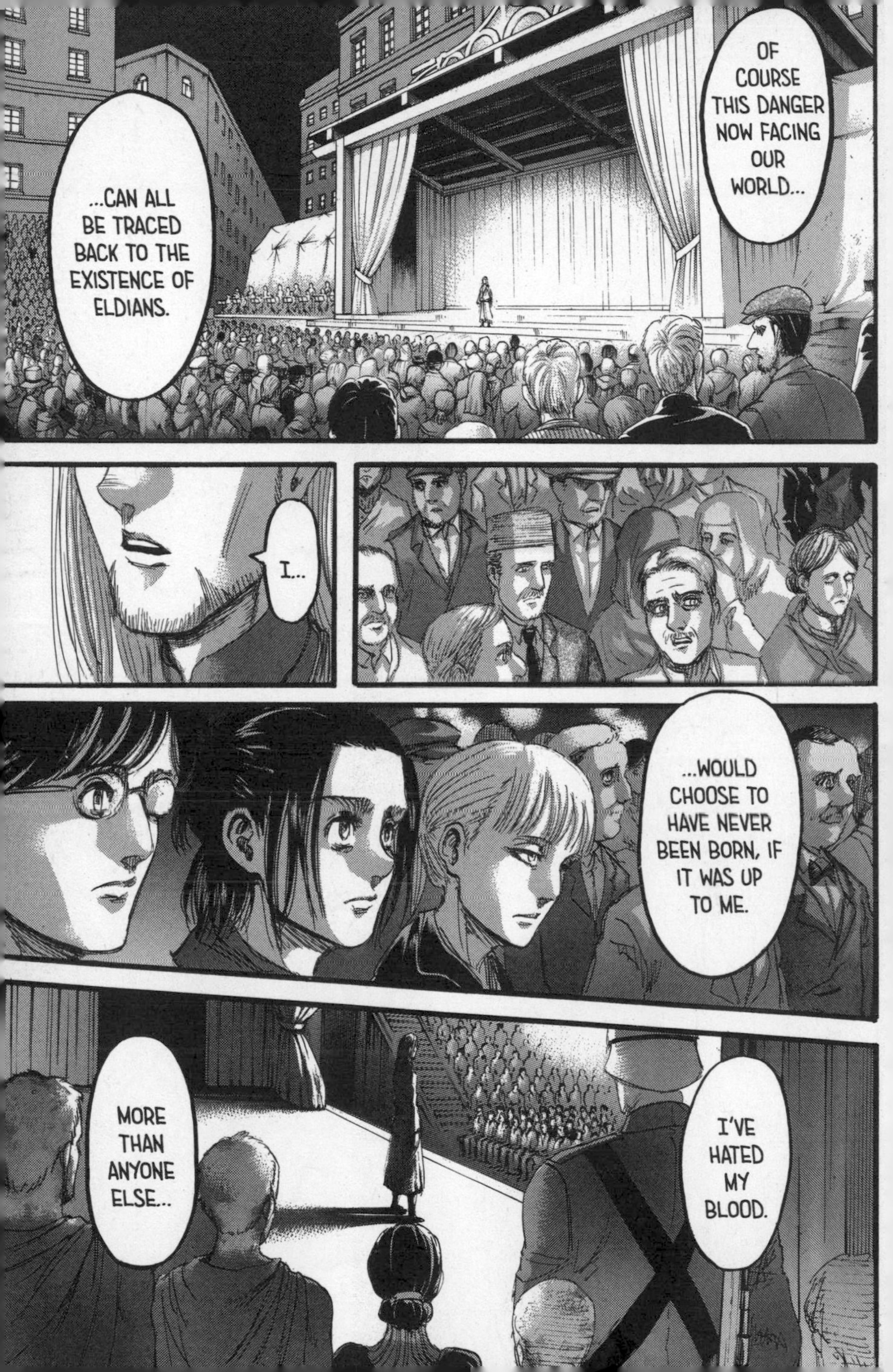

OF COURSE THIS DANGER NOW FACING OUR WORLD...
...CAN ALL BE TRACED BACK TO THE EXISTENCE OF ELDIANS.
I...
...WOULD CHOOSE TO HAVE NEVER BEEN BORN, IF IT WAS UP TO ME.
I'VE HATED MY BLOOD.
MORE THAN ANYONE ELSE...

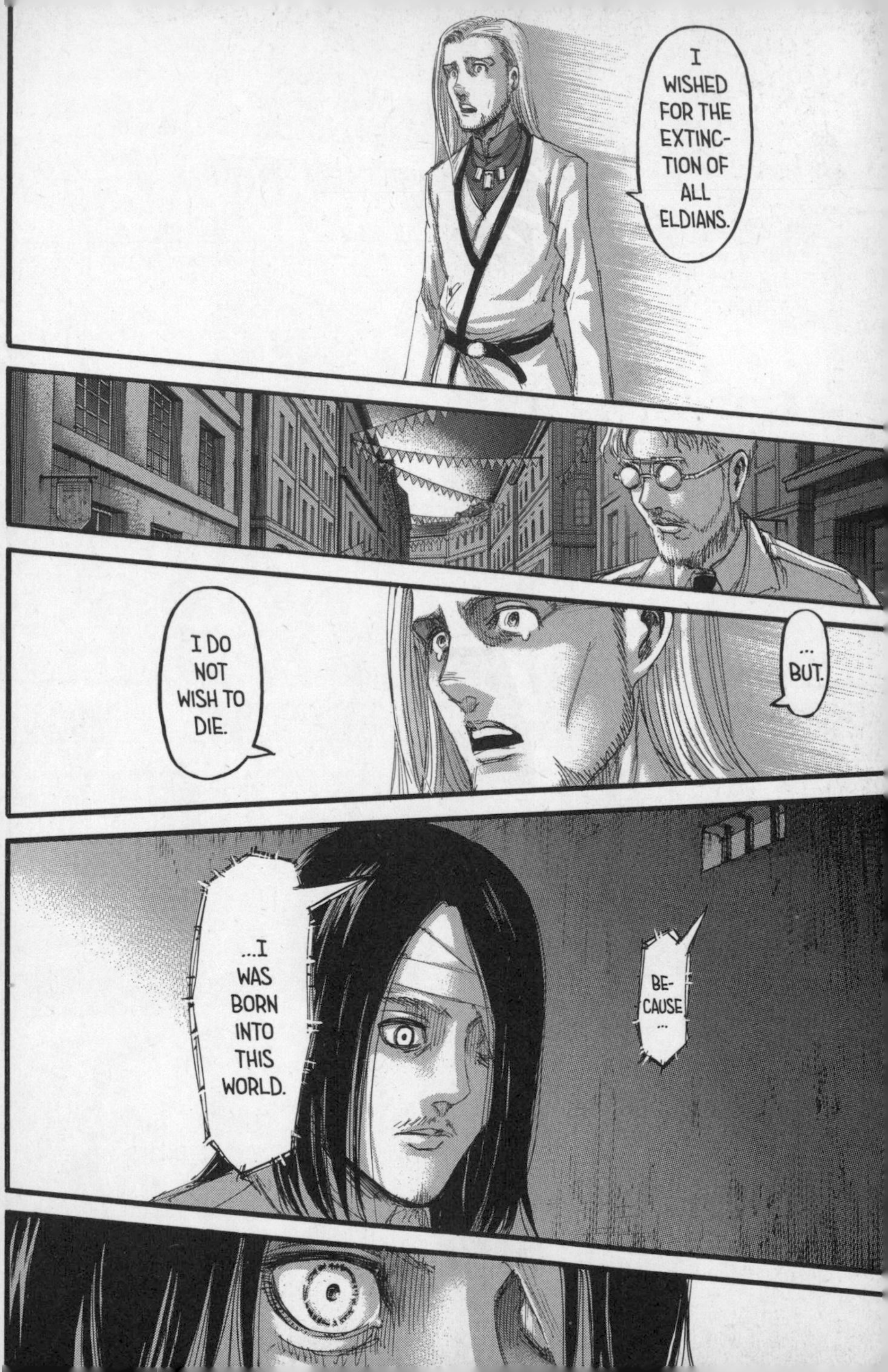
I WISHED FOR THE EXTINCTION OF ALL ELDIANS.
... BUT.
I DO NOT WISH TO DIE.
BE-CAUSE ...
...I WAS BORN INTO THIS WORLD.

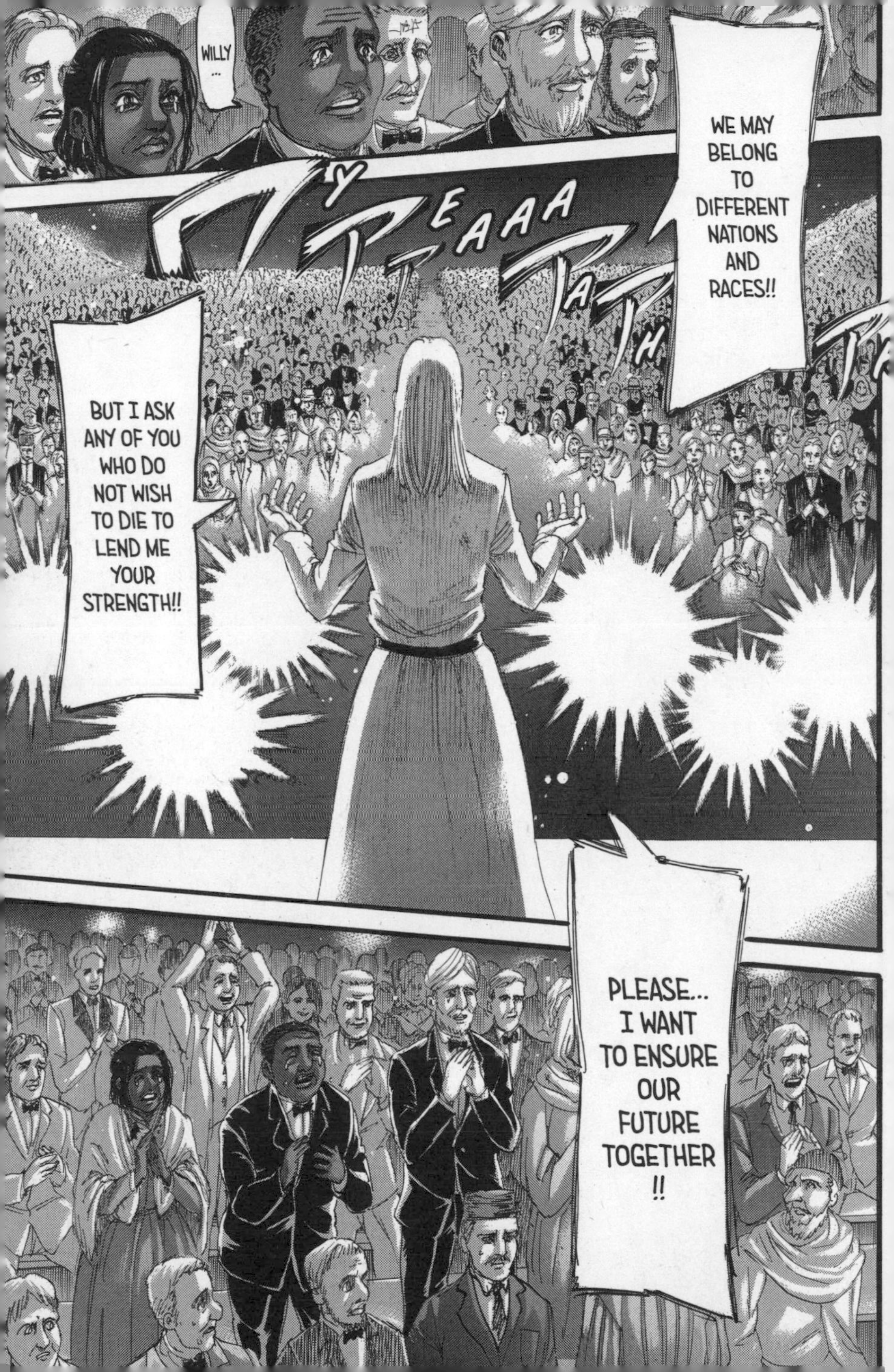
WE MAY BELONG TO DIFFERENT NATIONS AND RACES!!
WILLY ...
YEAAAAH
BUT I ASK ANY OF YOU WHO DO NOT WISH TO DIE TO LEND ME YOUR STRENGTH!!
PLEASE... I WANT TO ENSURE OUR FUTURE TOGETHER !!

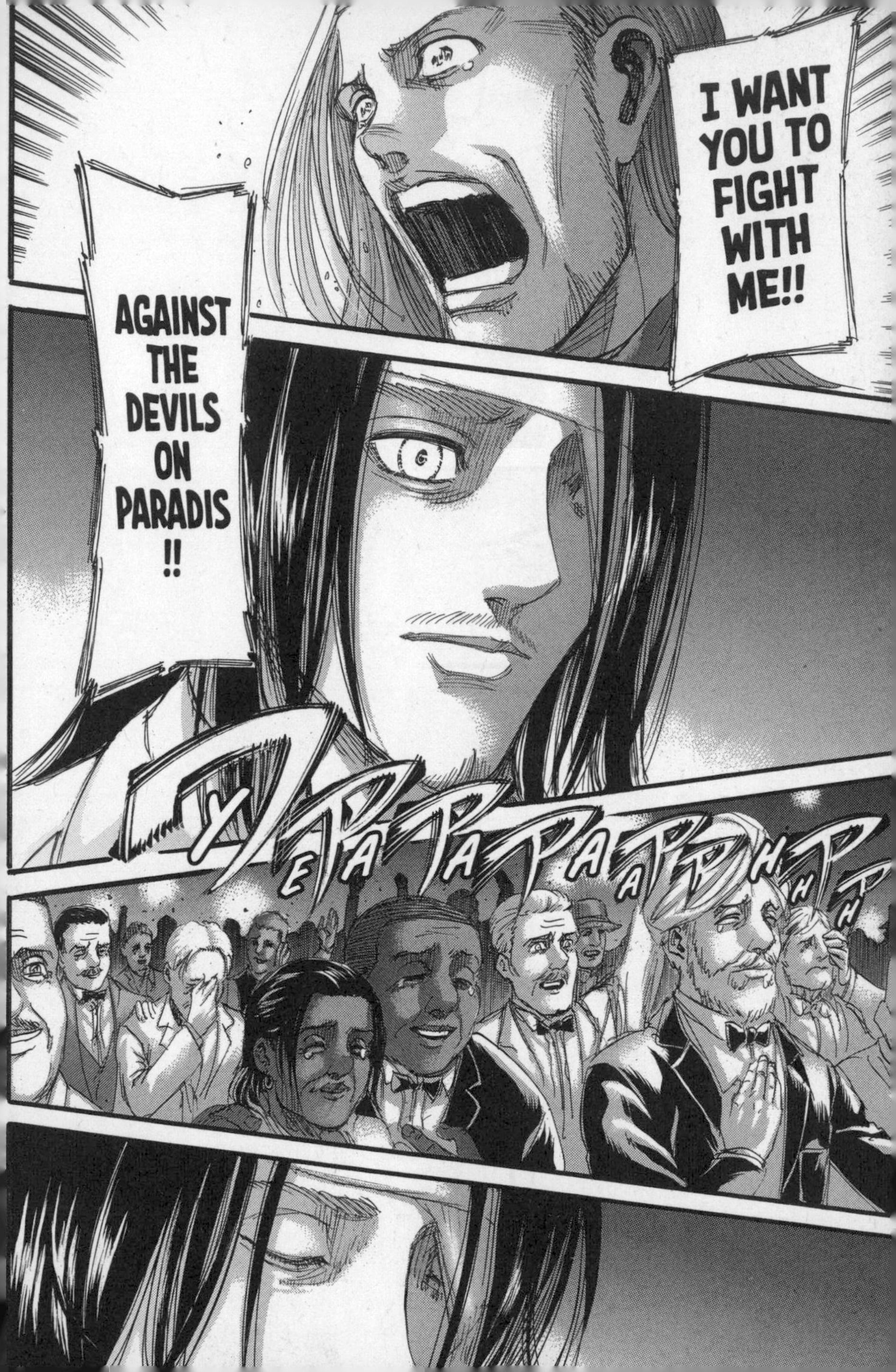
I WANT YOU TO FIGHT WITH ME!!
AGAINST THE DEVILS ON PARADIS!!

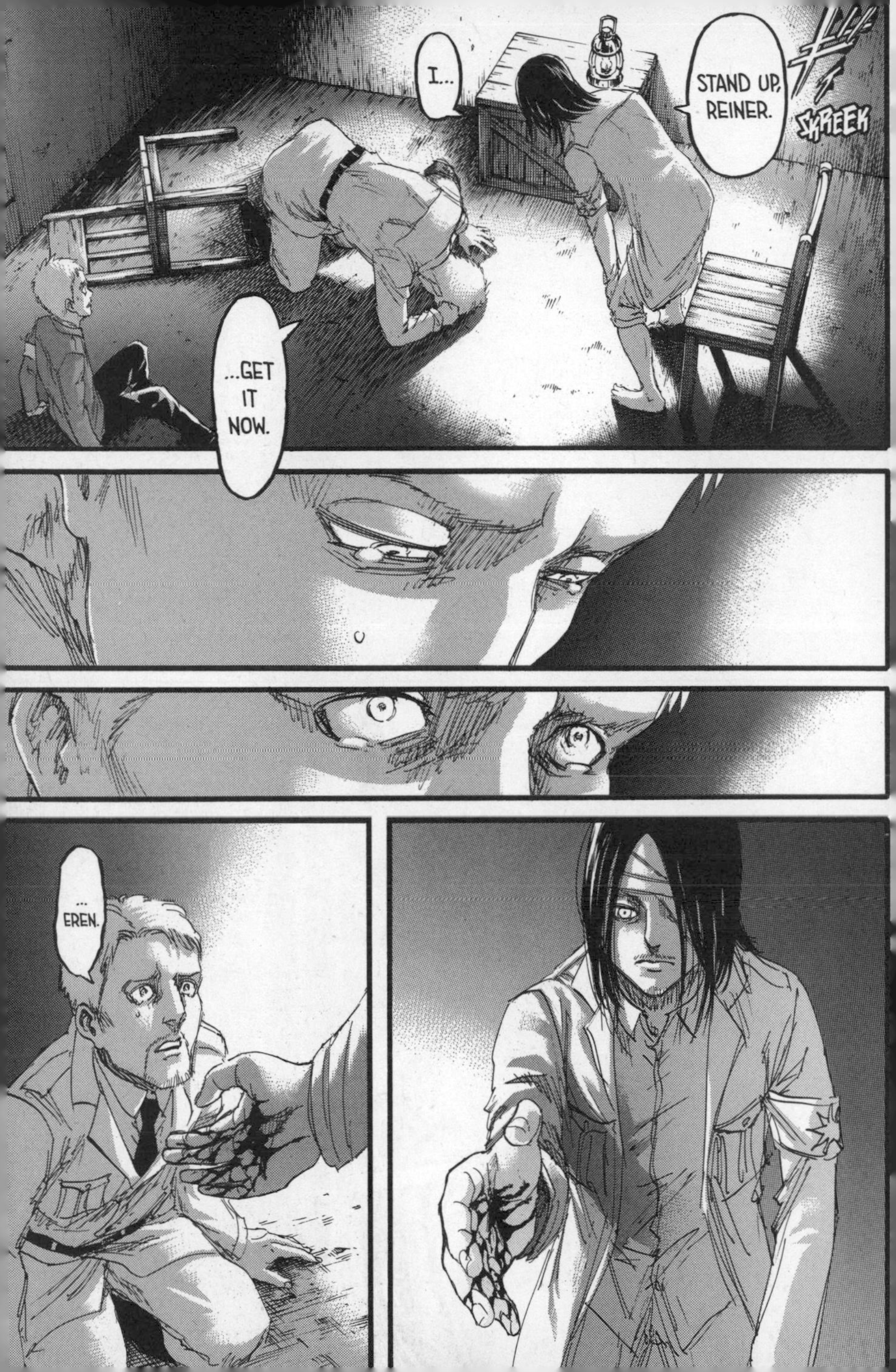
SKREEK
STAND UP, REINER.
I...
...GET IT NOW.
... EREN.

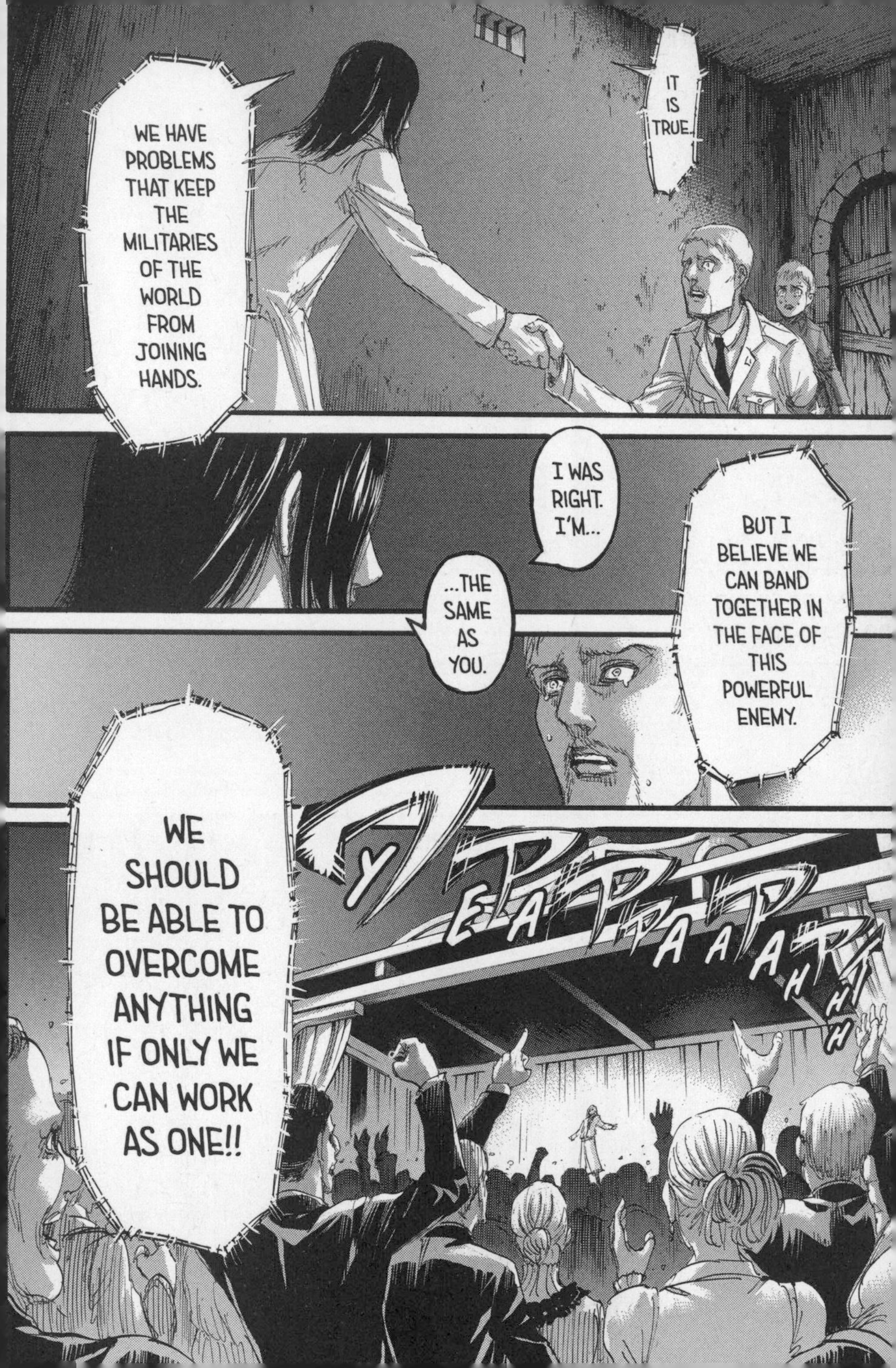
IT IS TRUE.
WE HAVE PROBLEMS THAT KEEP THE MILITARIES OF THE WORLD FROM JOINING HANDS.
BUT I BELIEVE WE CAN BAND TOGETHER IN THE FACE OF THIS POWERFUL ENEMY.
I WAS RIGHT. I'M...
...THE SAME AS YOU.
WE SHOULD BE ABLE TO OVERCOME ANYTHING IF ONLY WE CAN WORK AS ONE!!

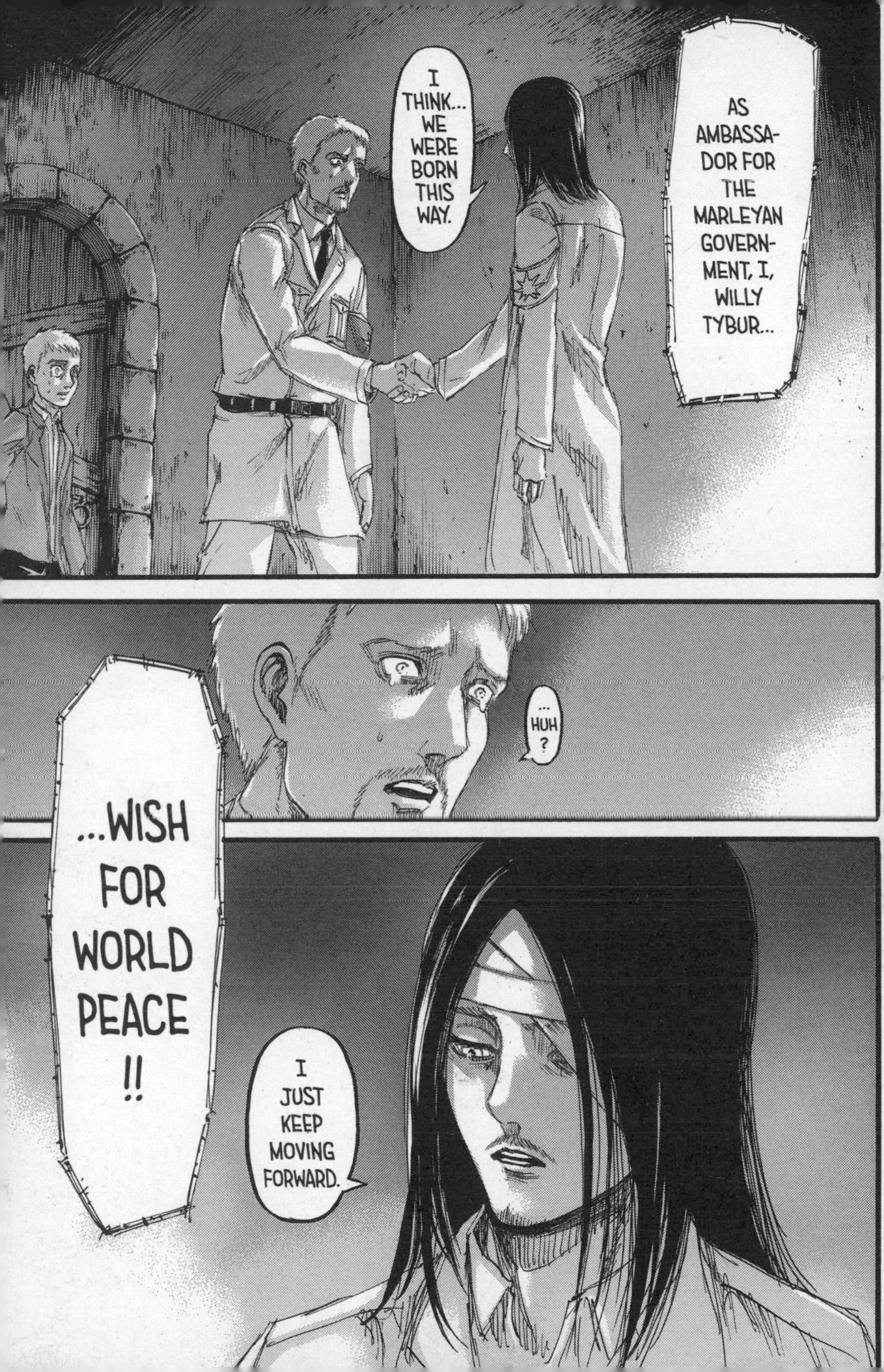
AS AMBASSADOR FOR THE MARLEYAN GOVERNMENT, I, WILLY TYBUR...
I THINK... WE WERE BORN THIS WAY.
...HUH?
...WISH FOR WORLD PEACE!!
I JUST KEEP MOVING FORWARD.

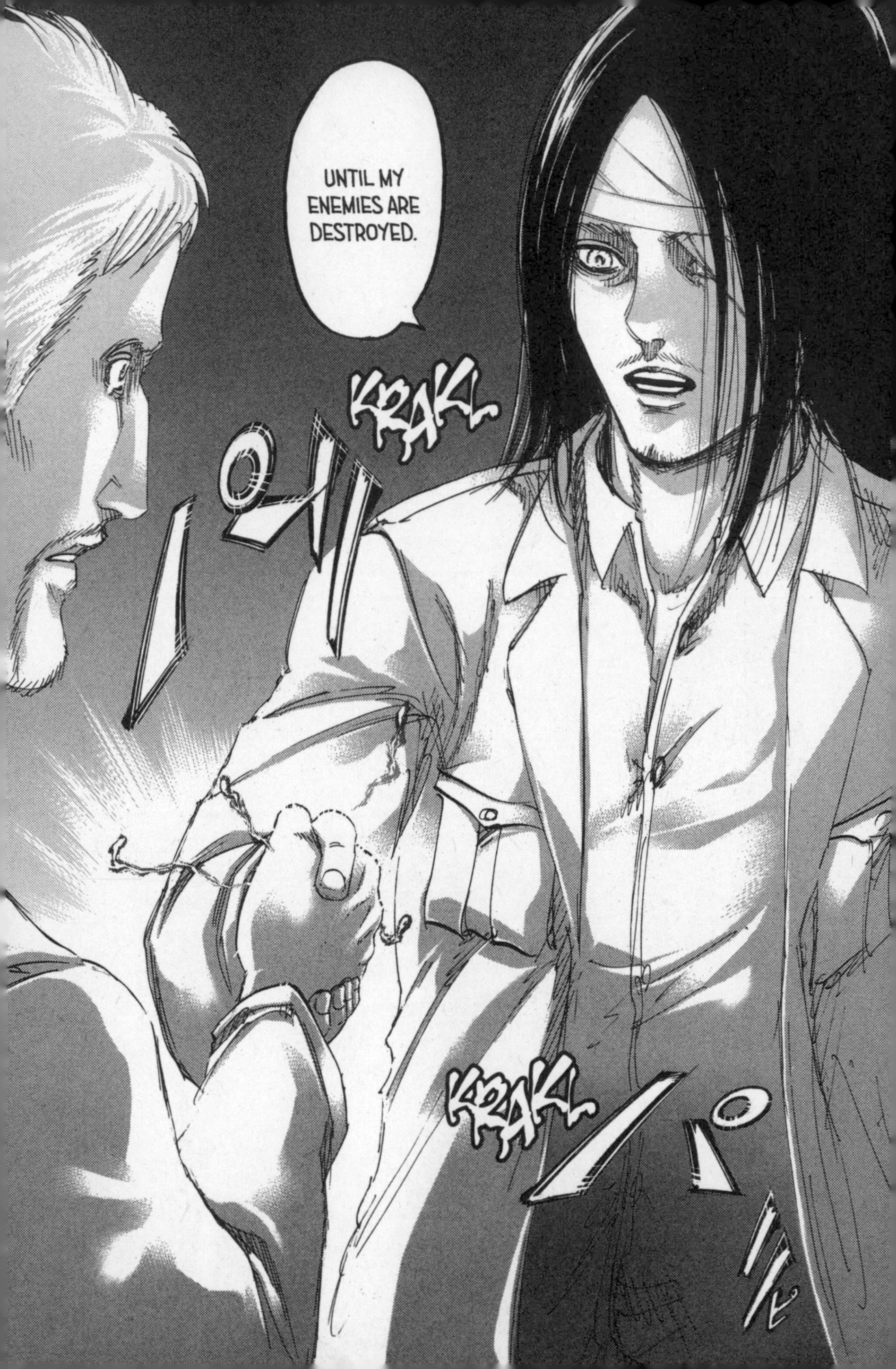
UNTIL MY ENEMIES ARE DESTROYED.
KRAKL
KRAKL

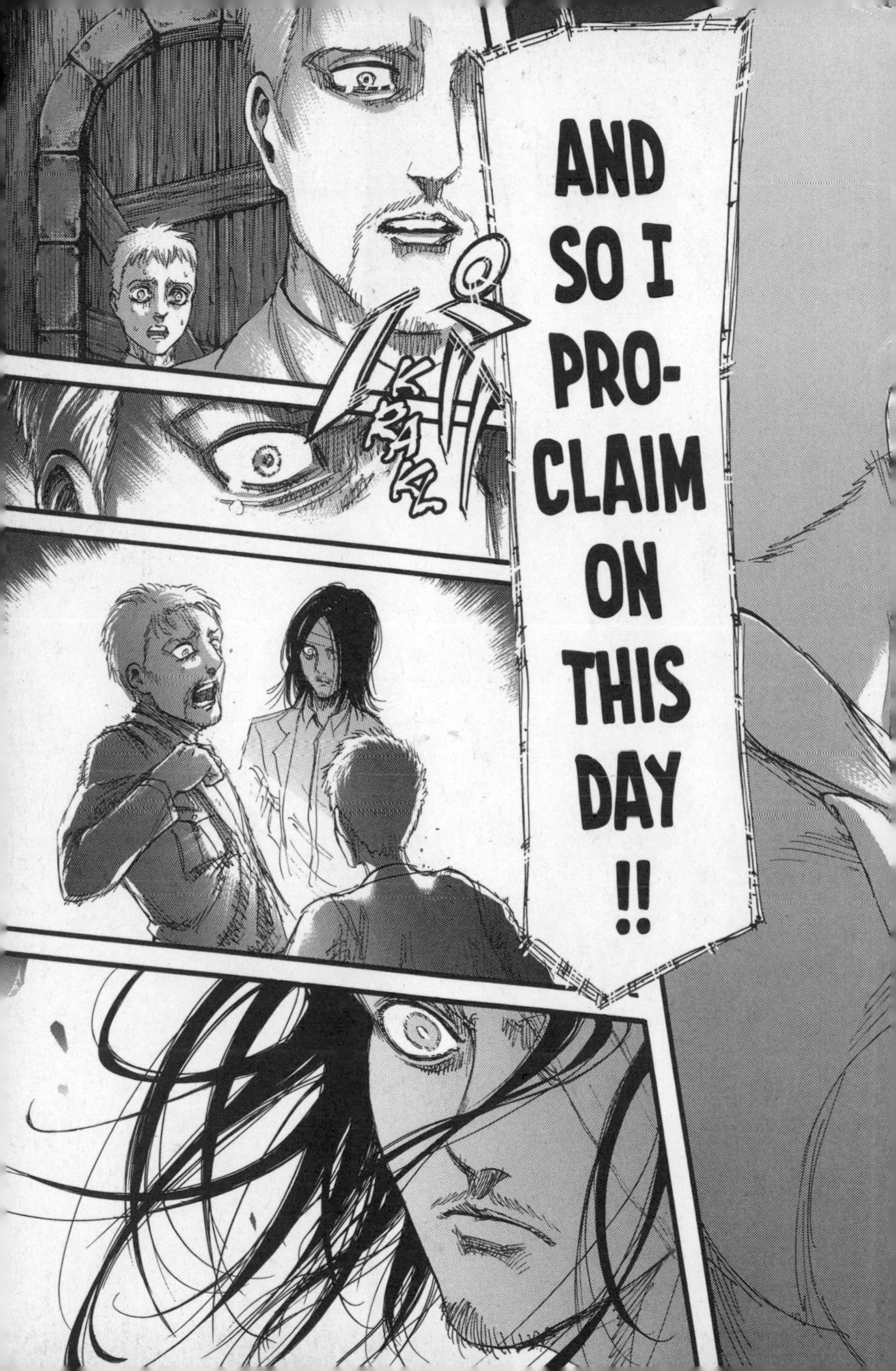
AND SO I PRO-CLAIM ON THIS DAY!!
KRAK

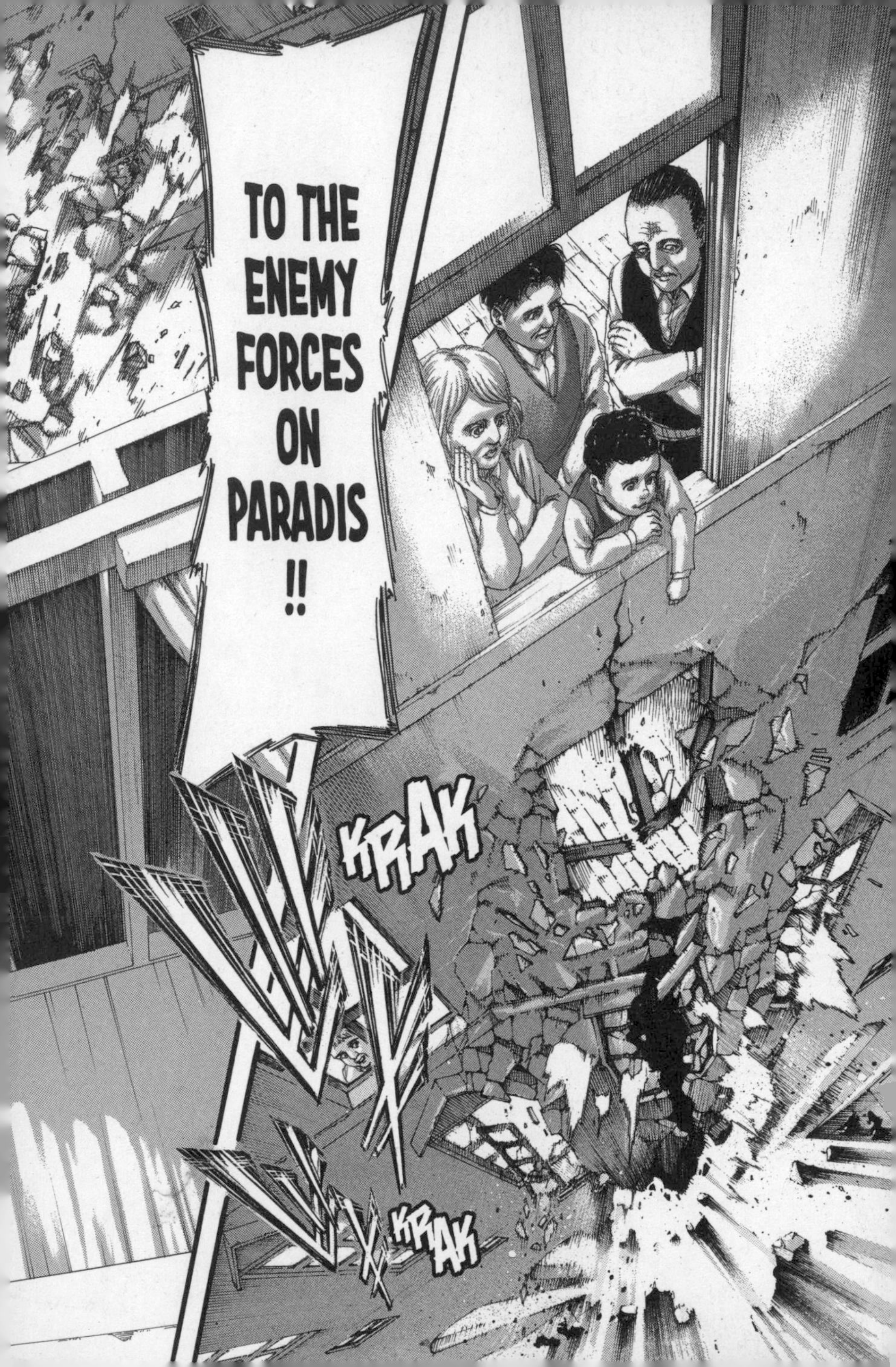
TO THE ENEMY FORCES ON PARADIS !!
KRAK
KRAK

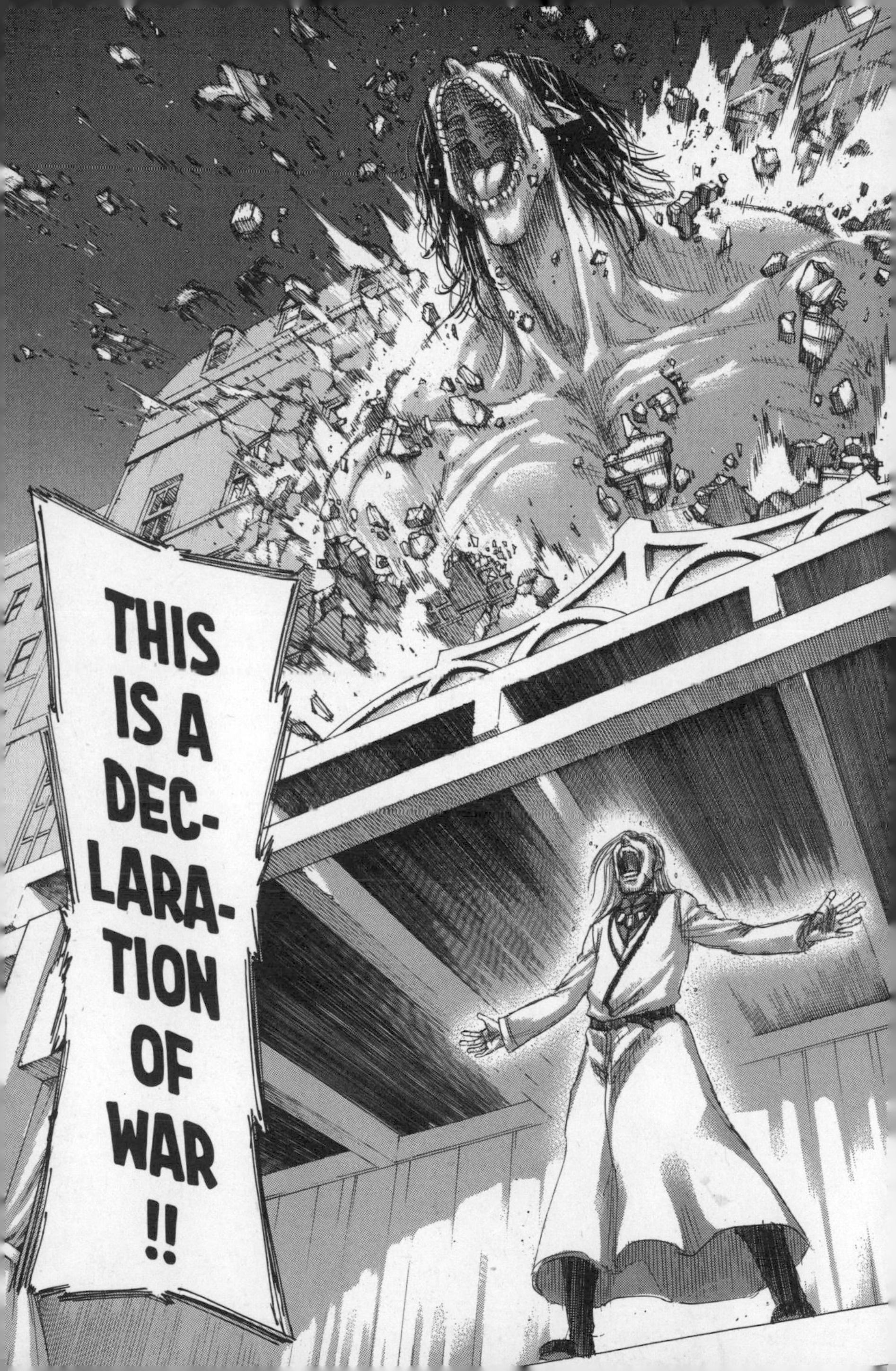
THIS IS A DEC-LARA-TION OF WAR!!

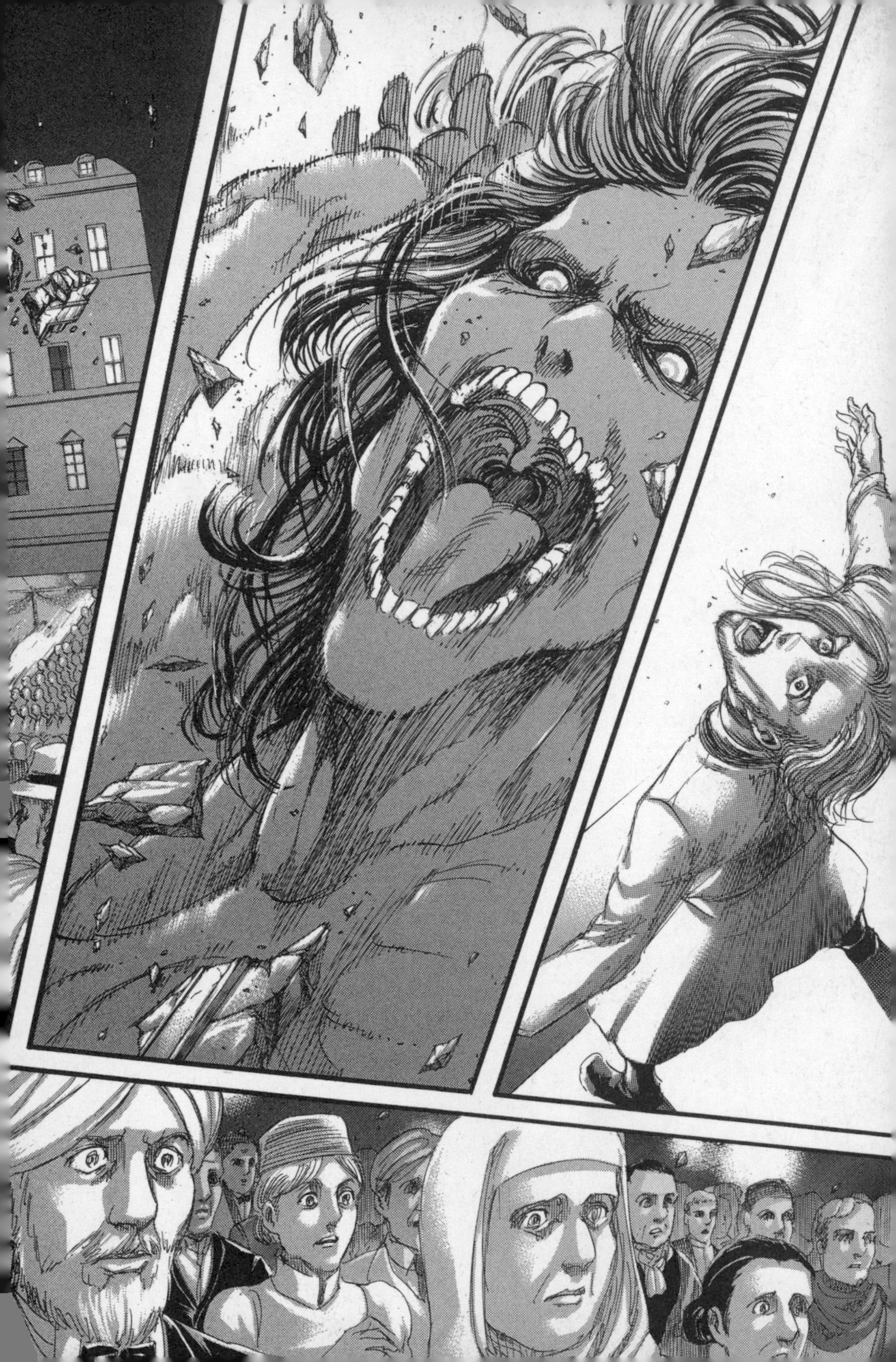

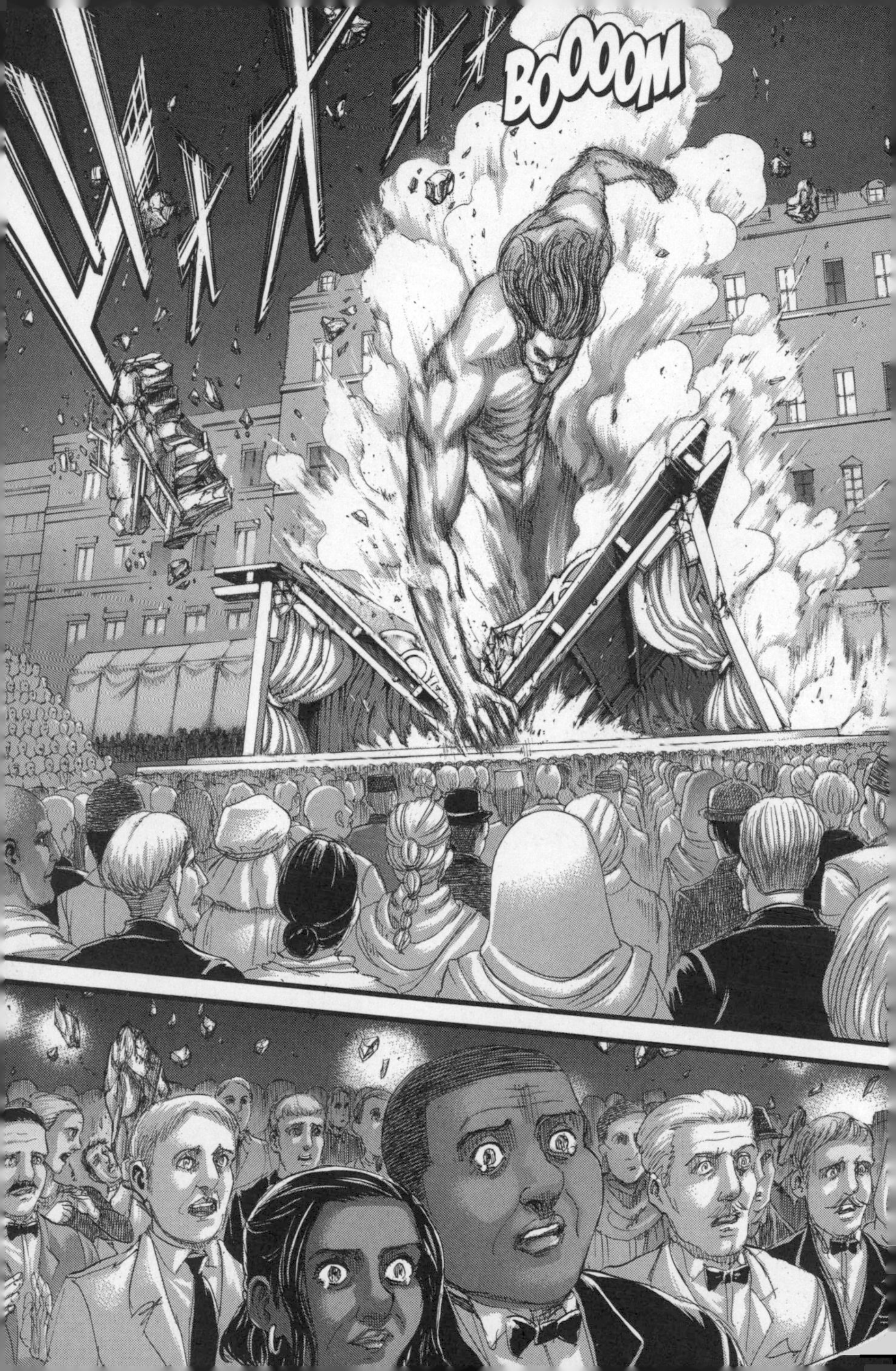
BOOOOM

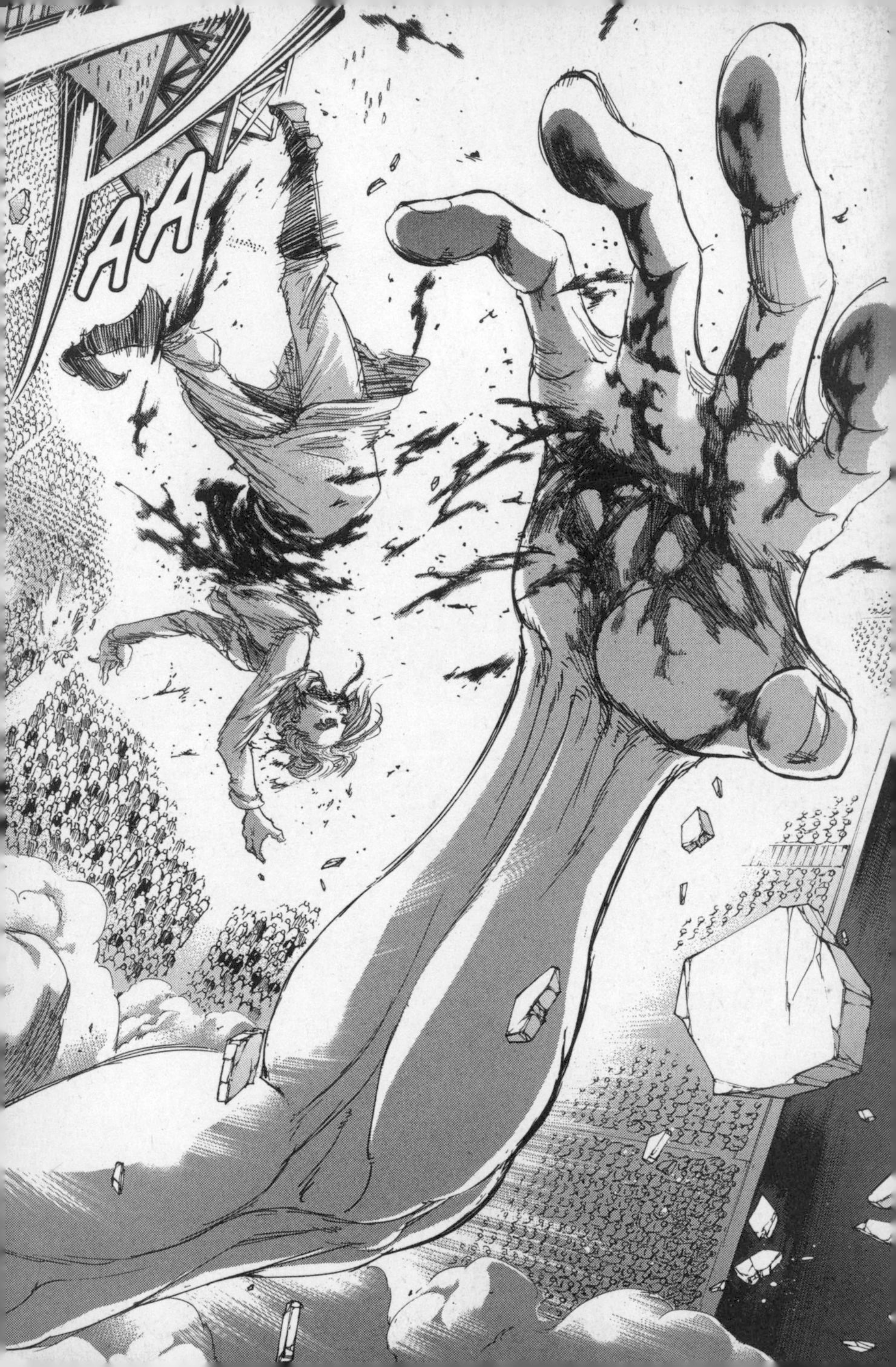
AA

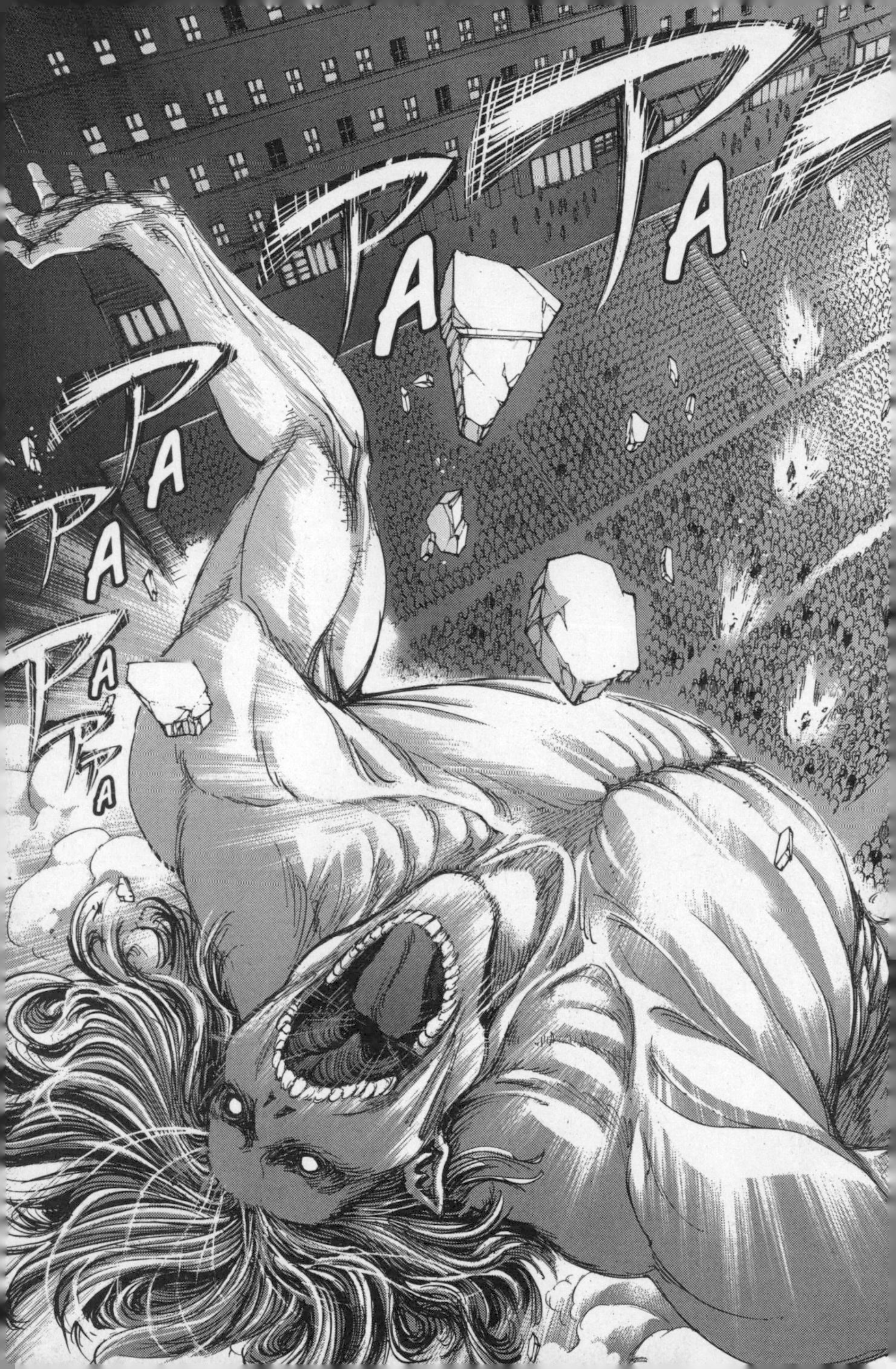
A
A
A
A
A
A
A

ATTACK on TITAN

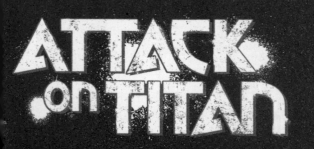

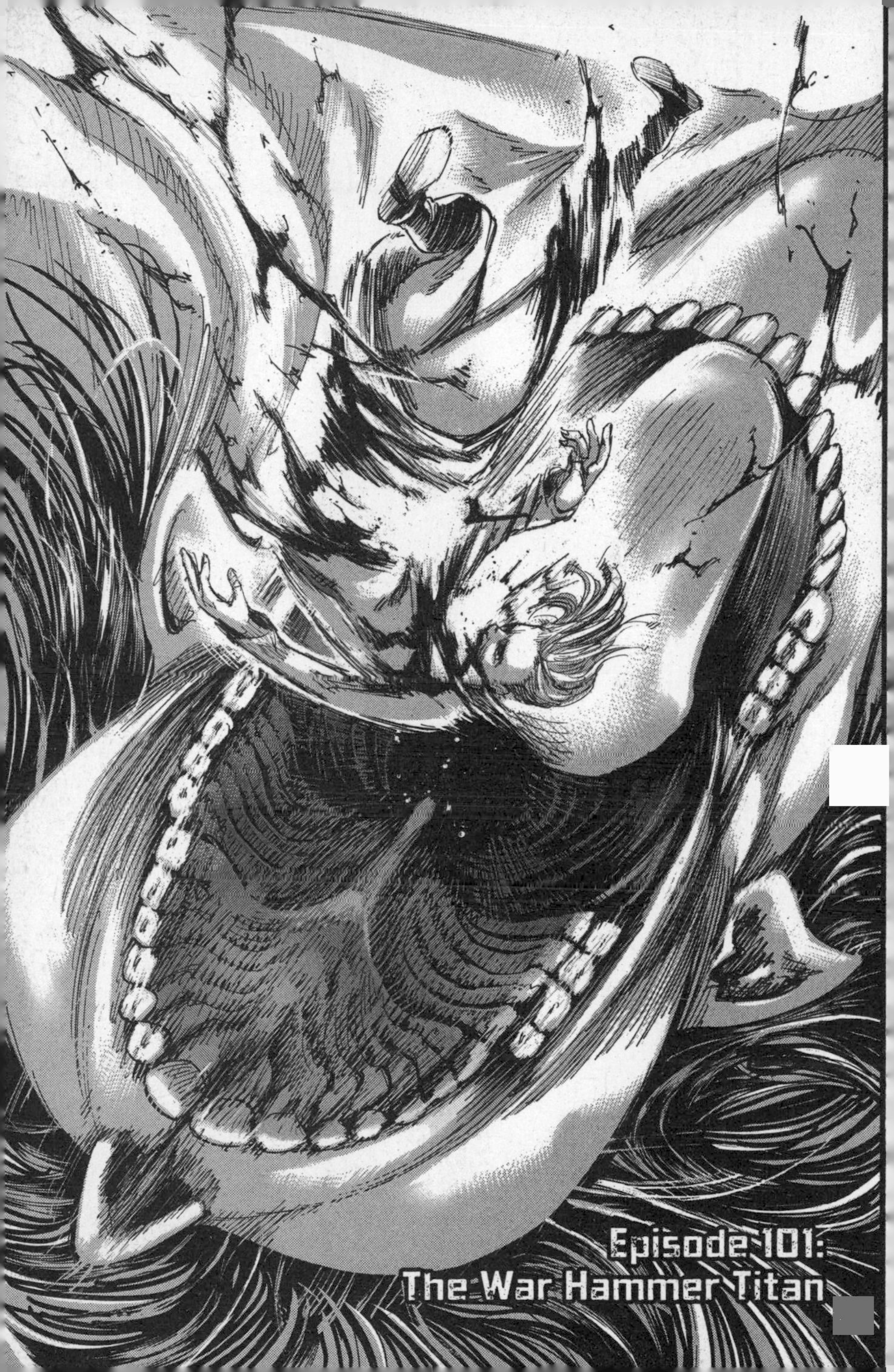
Episode 101:
The War Hammer Titan

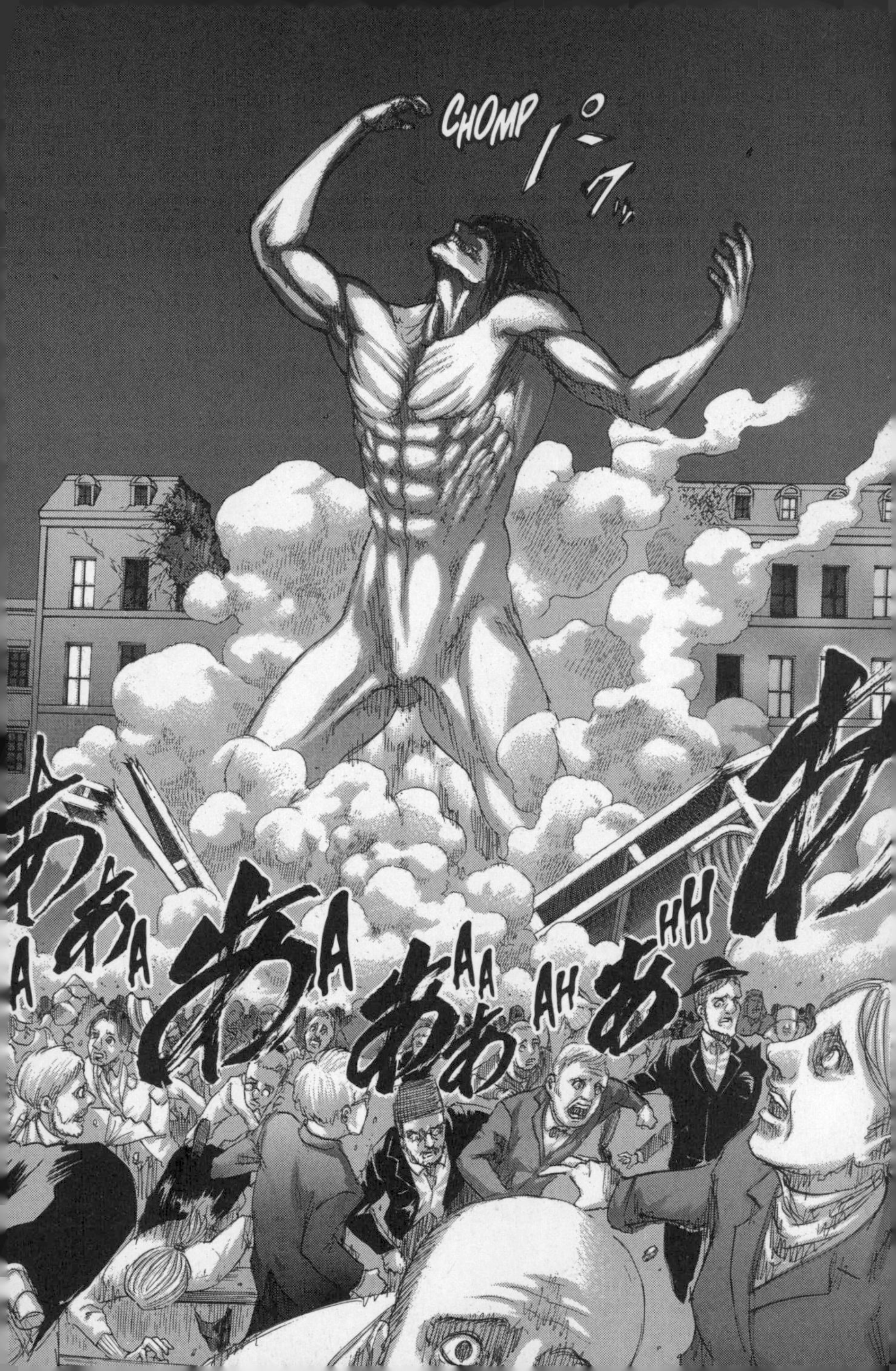
CHOMP
パクッ
AAAAAAAHHH

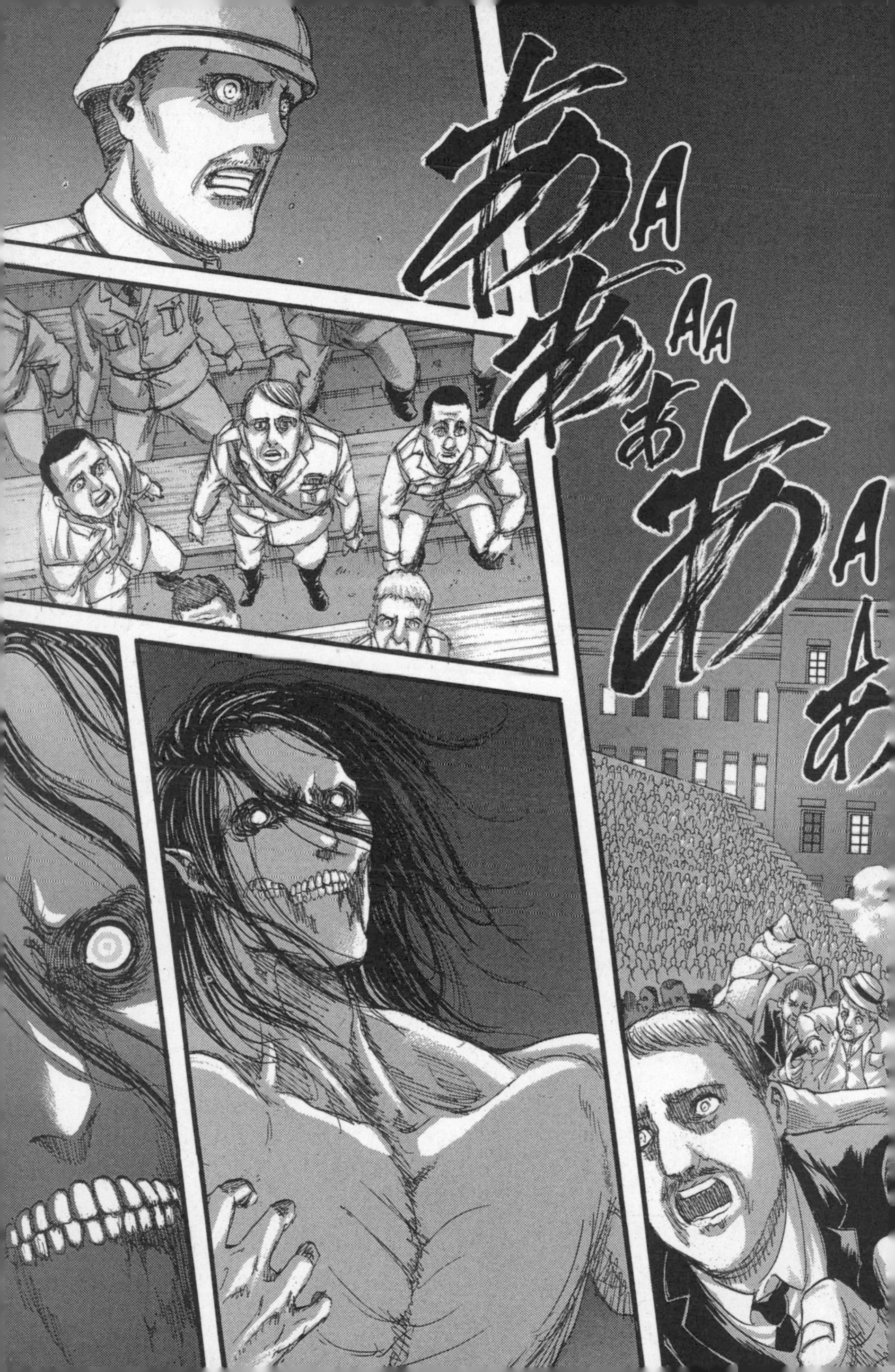
あああああ
A
AA
A
A
A

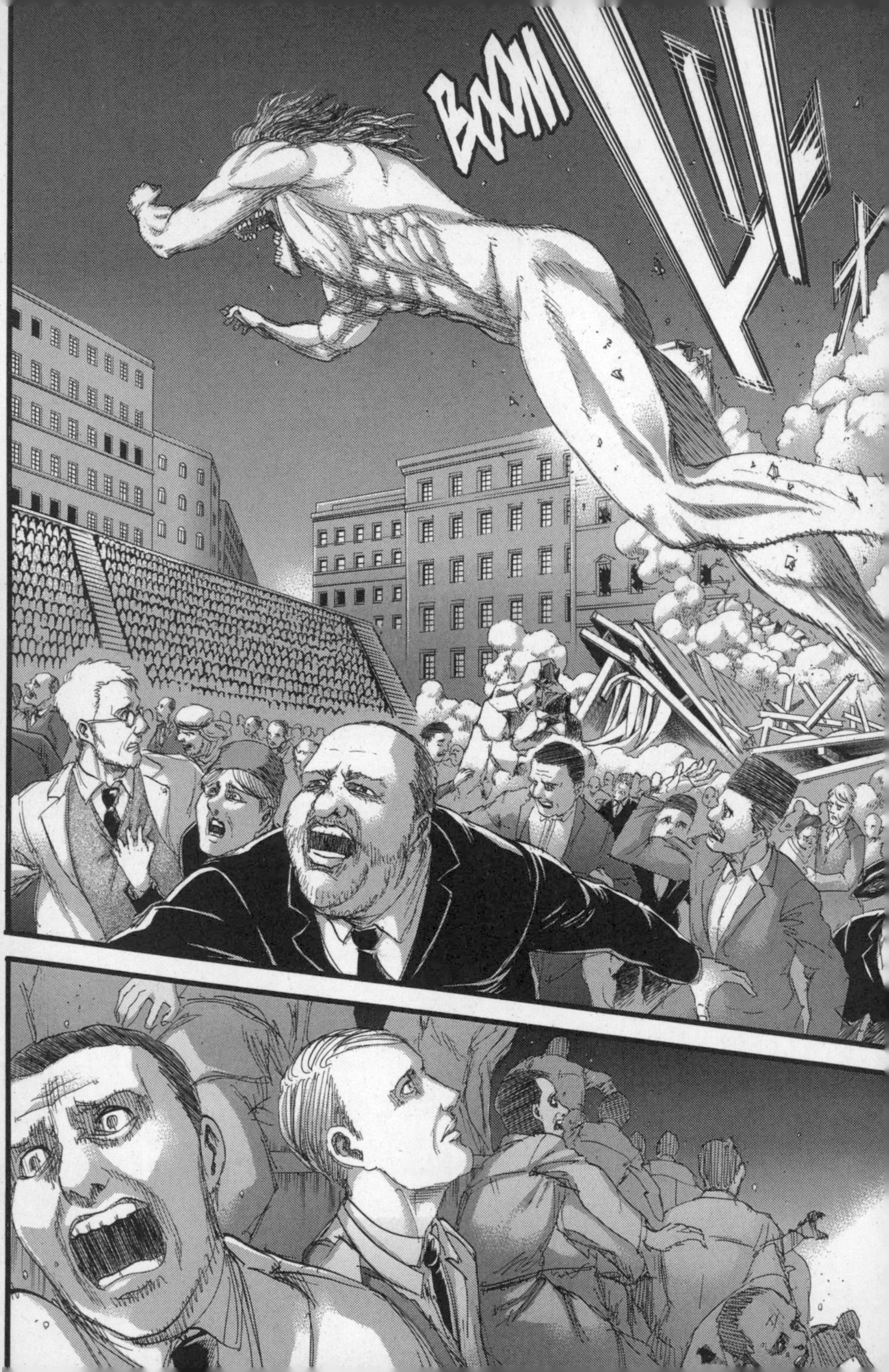
BOOM

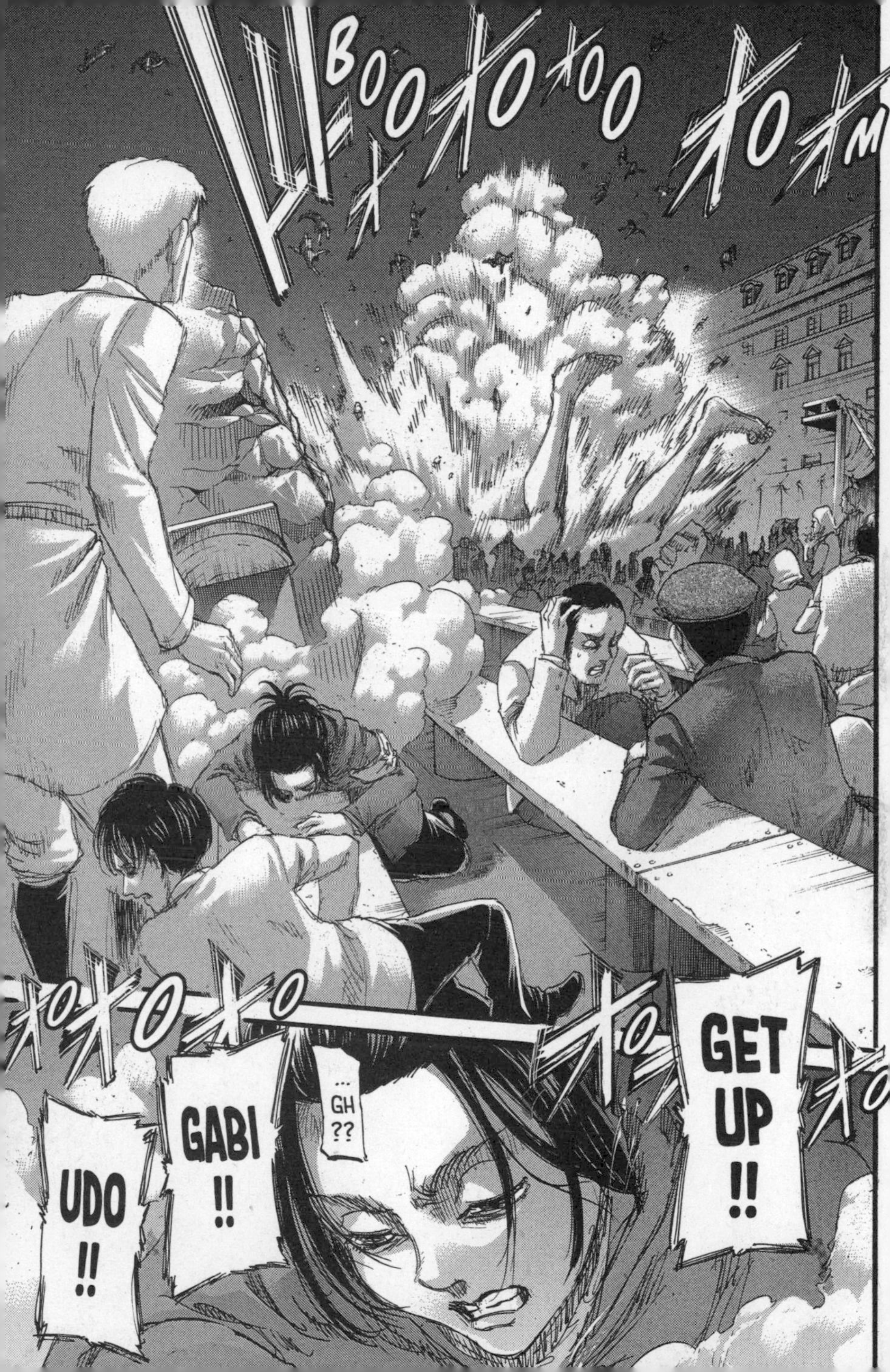
GET UP!!
...GH??
GABI!!
UDO!!

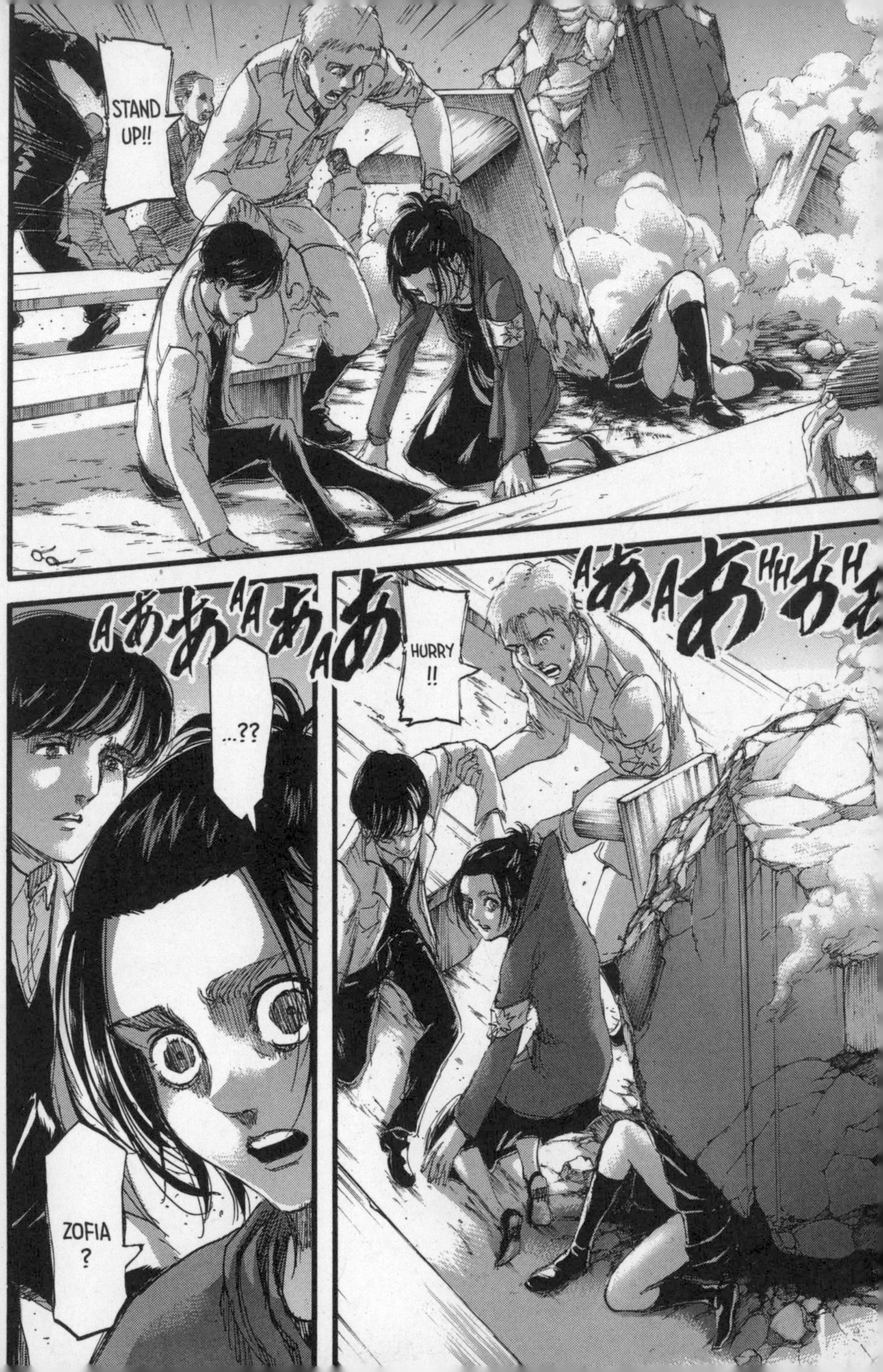
STAND UP!!
HURRY !!
...??
ZOFIA ?

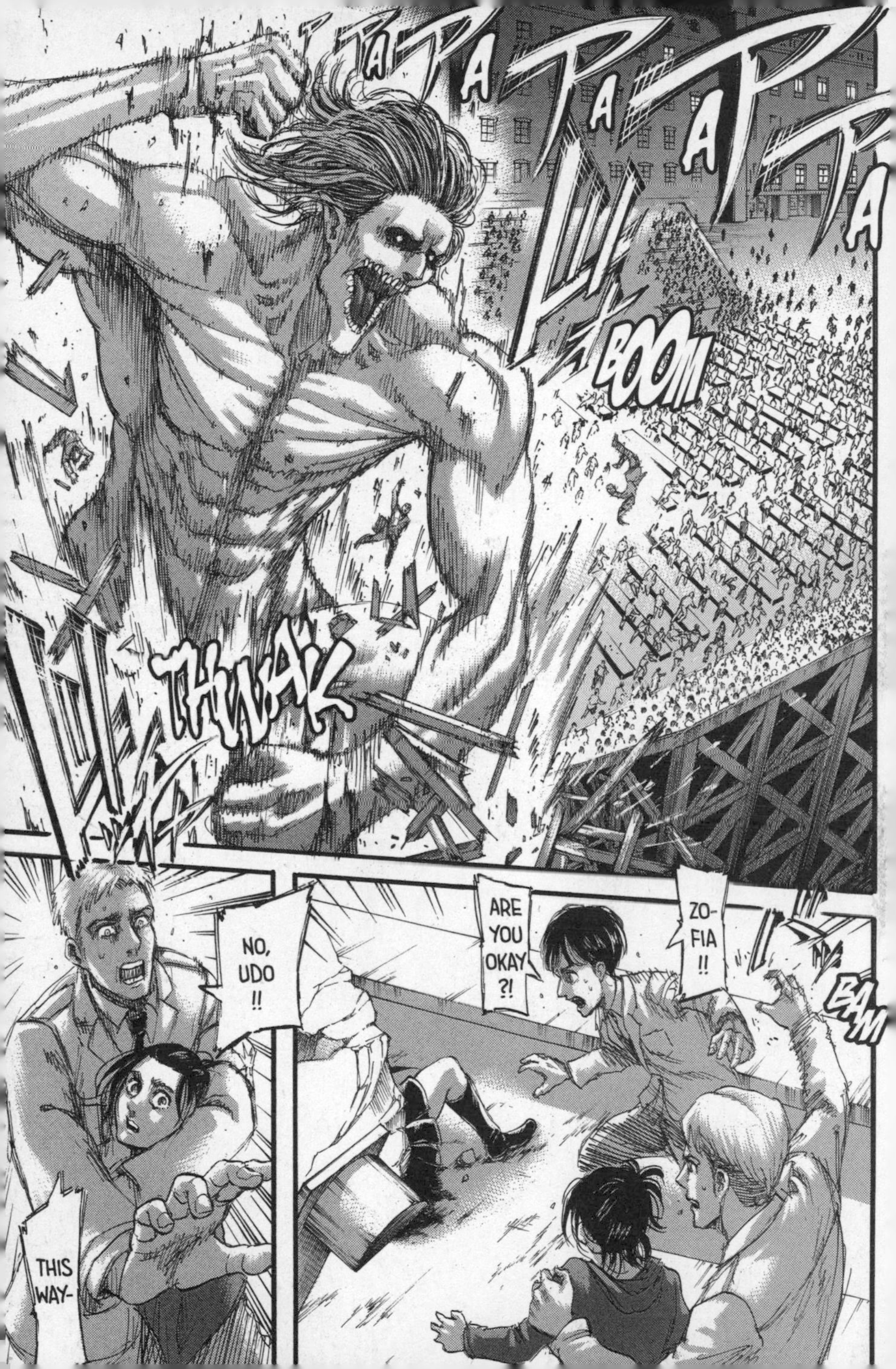
PA PA PA PA PA
BOOM
THWAK
BAM
ZO-FIA!!
ARE YOU OKAY?!
NO, UDO!!
THIS WAY-

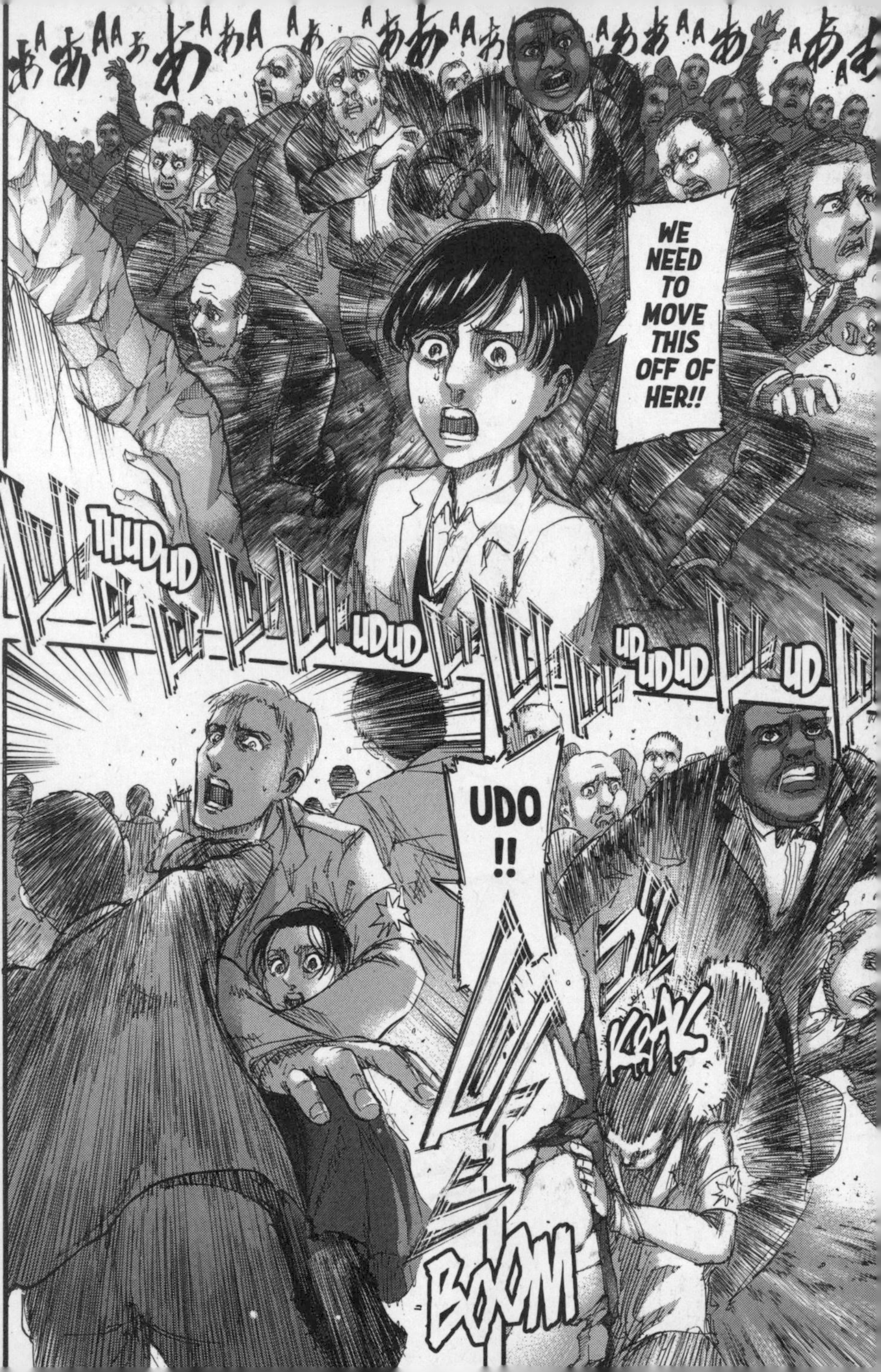
WE NEED TO MOVE THIS OFF OF HER!!
THUDUD
UDUD
UD UDUD
UD
UDO!!
KRAK
BOOM

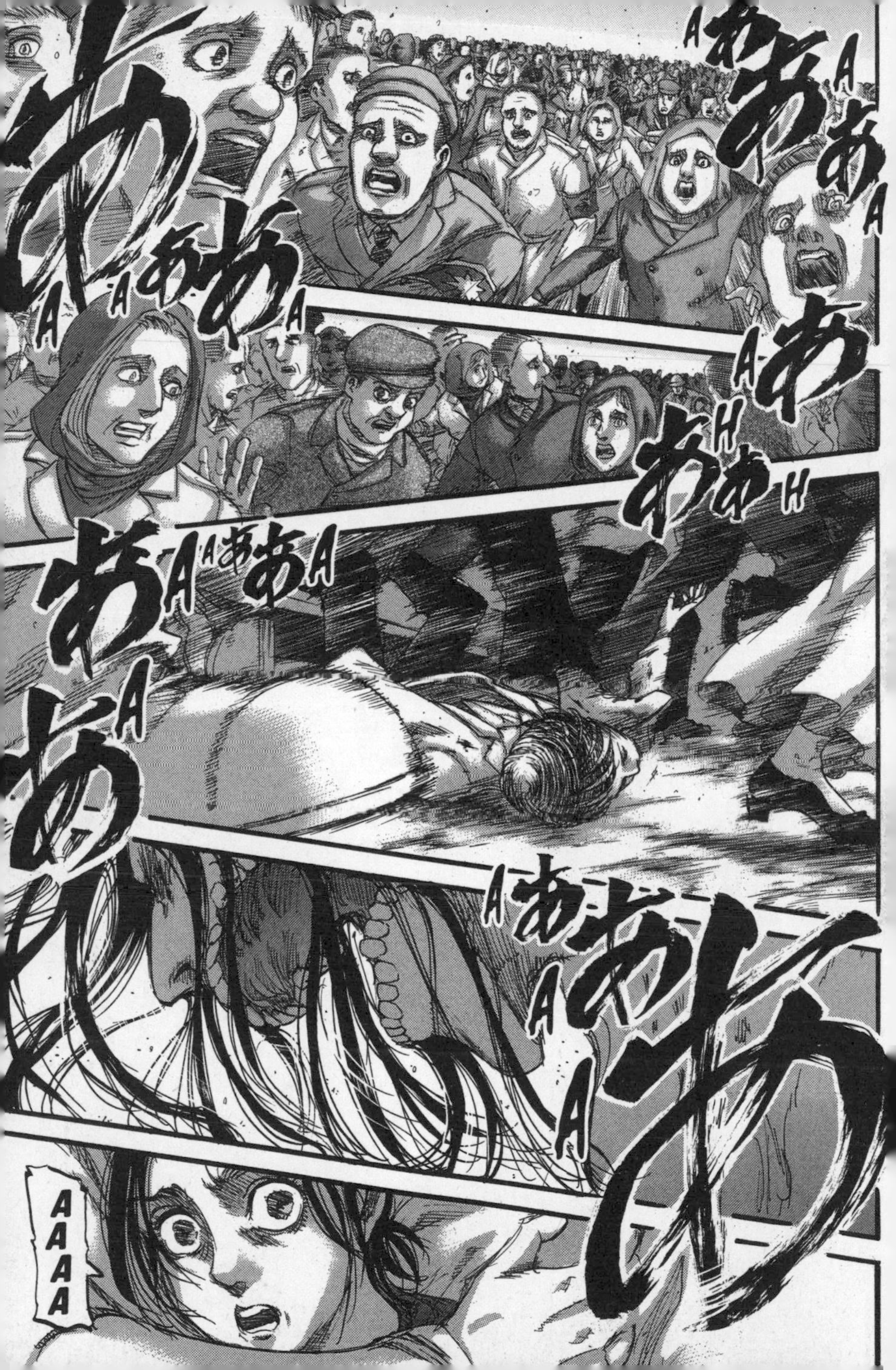
AAAA

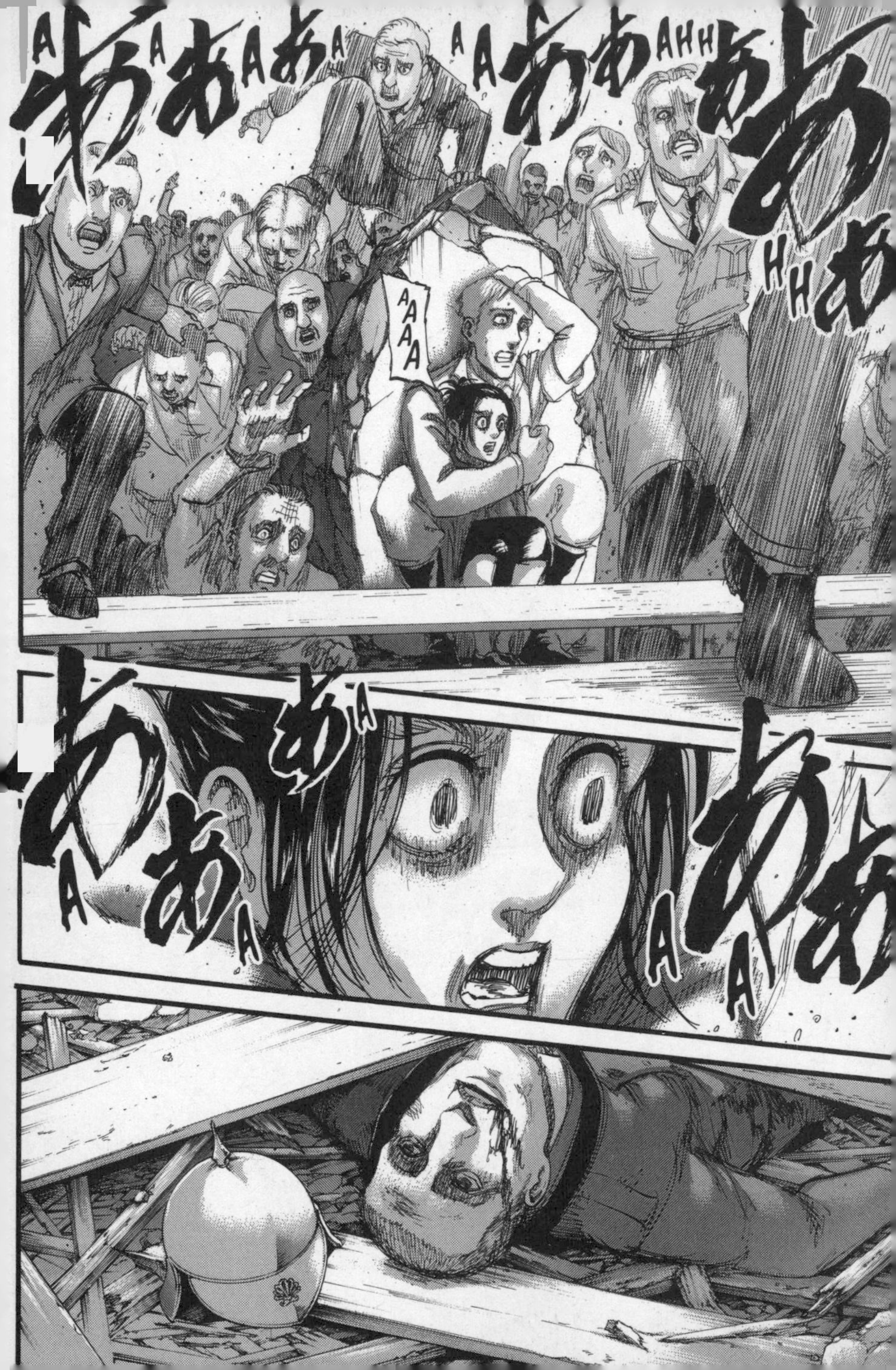
あああ
AHH
H H H
ああ
A A
ああああ
A A A A
AAAA
あああ
A A
ああ
A A
ああ
A A A

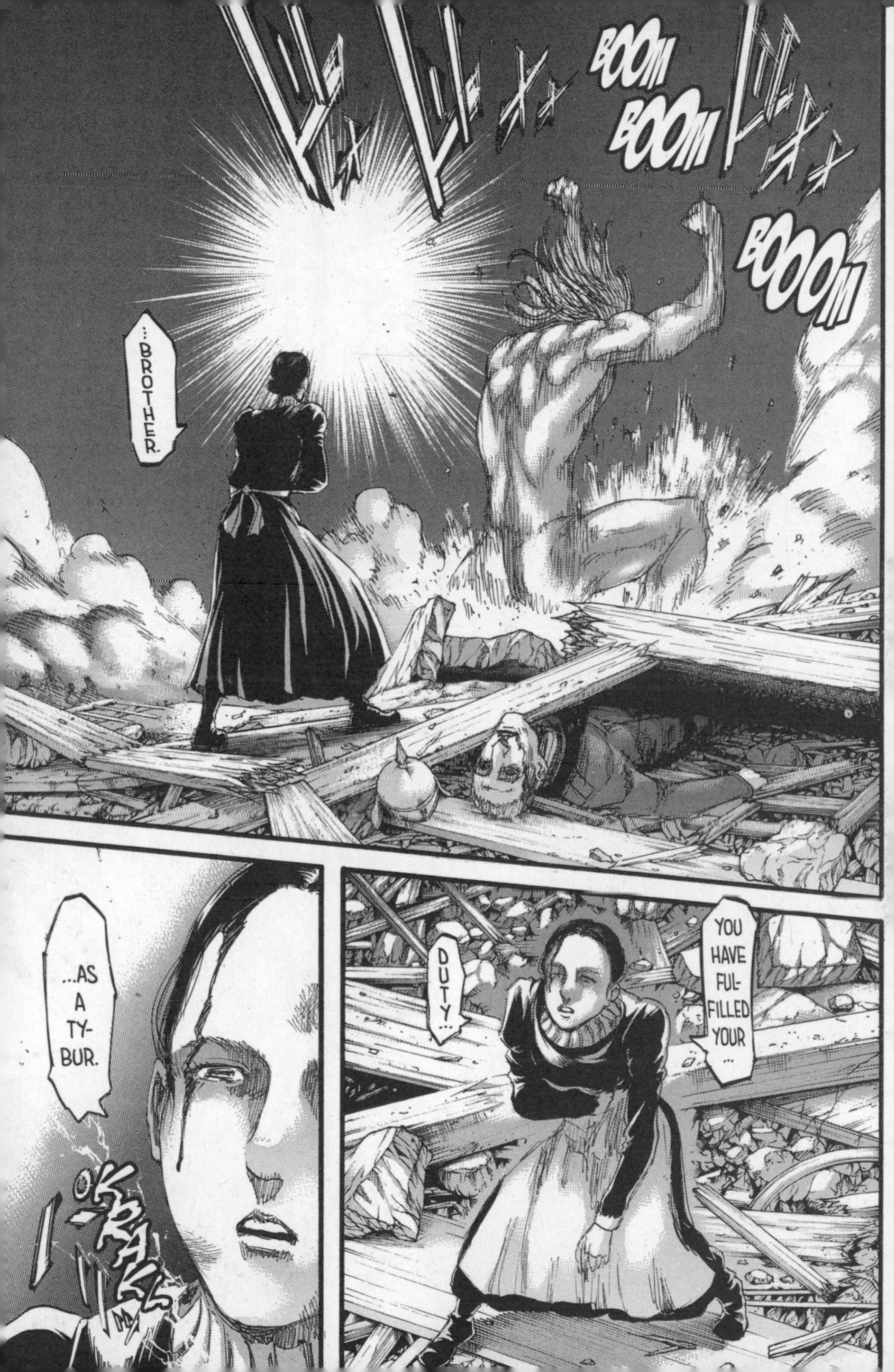
BOOM
BOOM
BOOOM
...BROTHER.
YOU HAVE FUL-FILLED YOUR ...
DUTY...
...AS A TY-BUR.
KRAKK

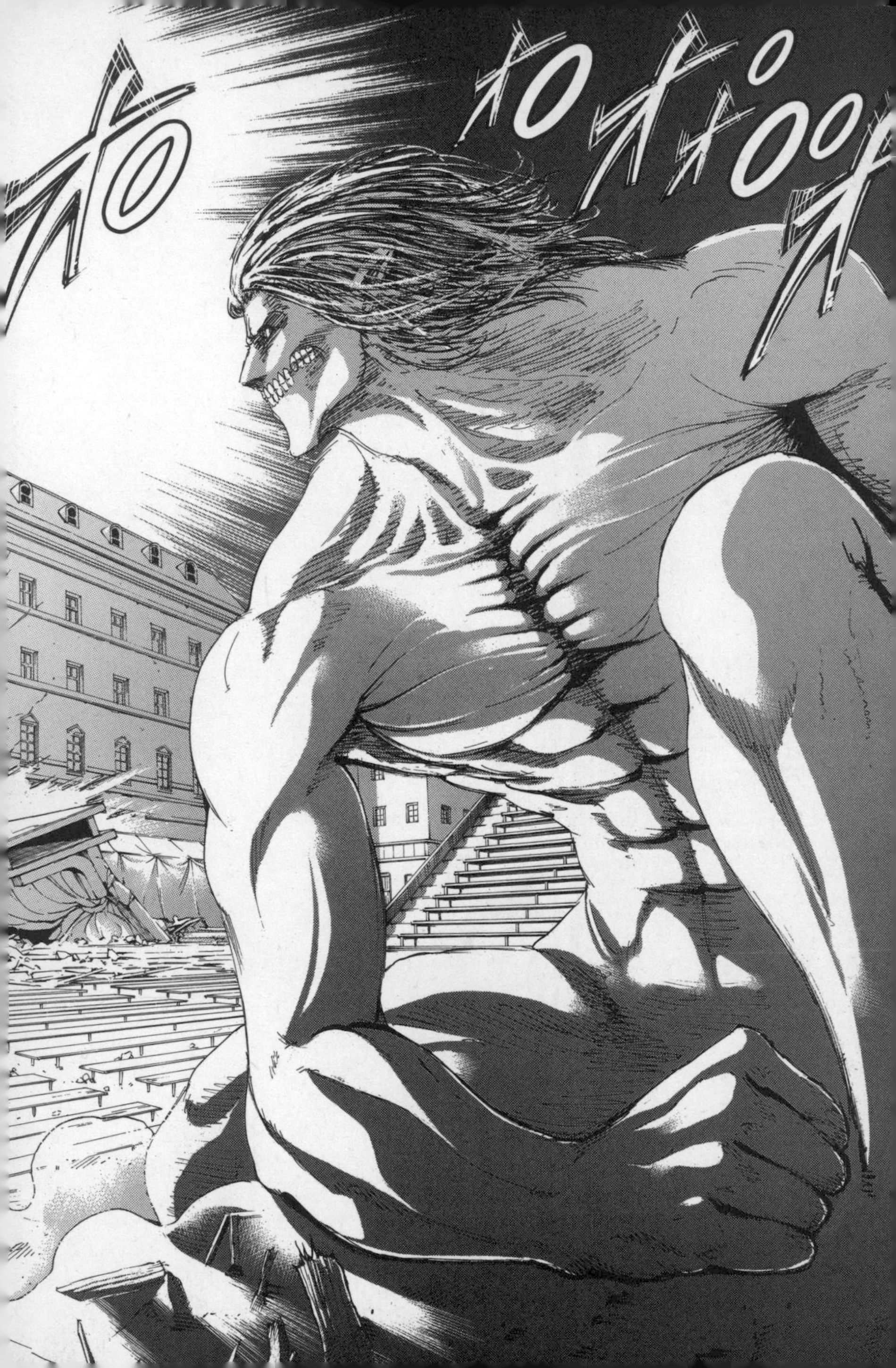

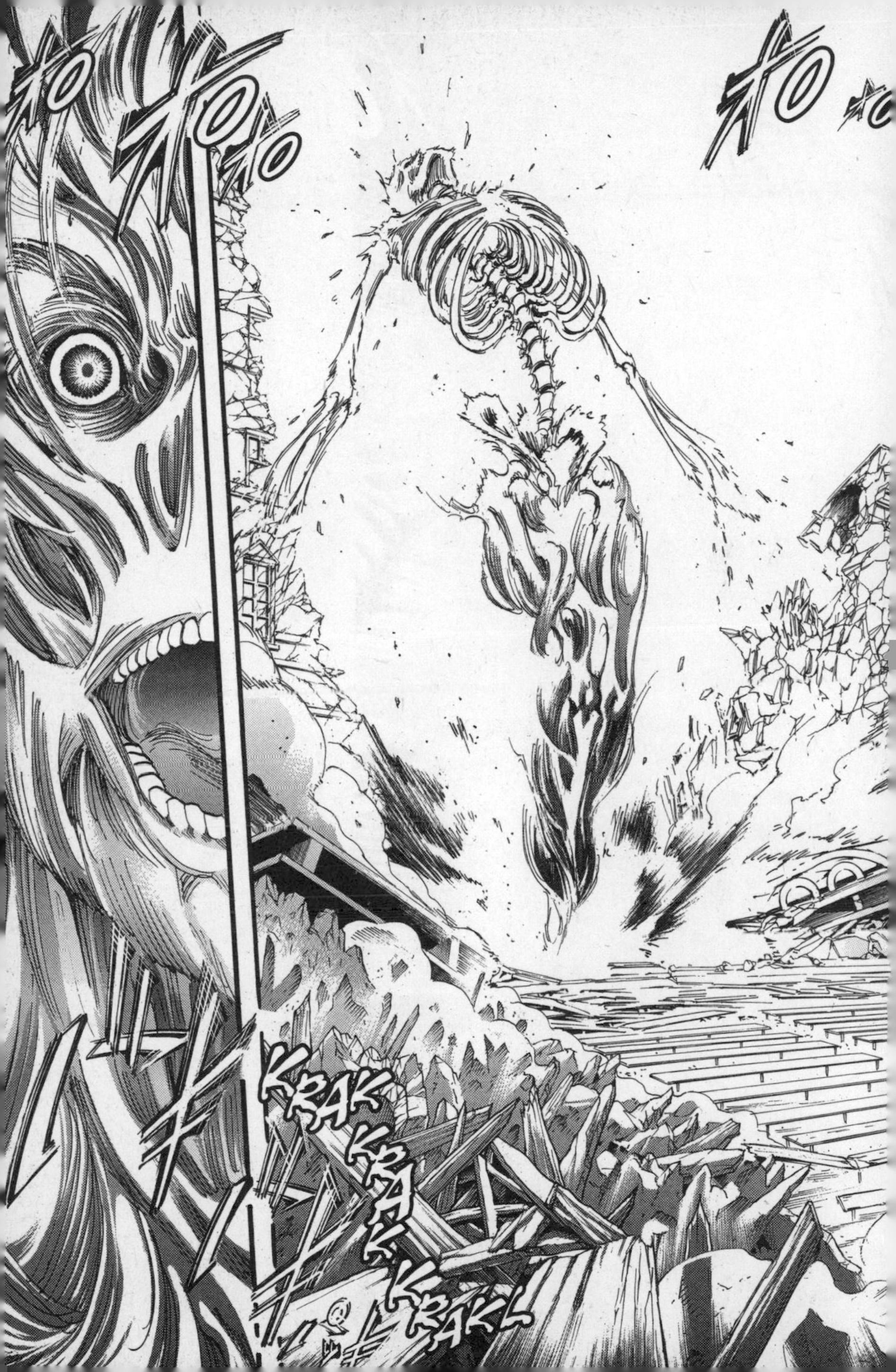
KRAK KRAK KRAKL

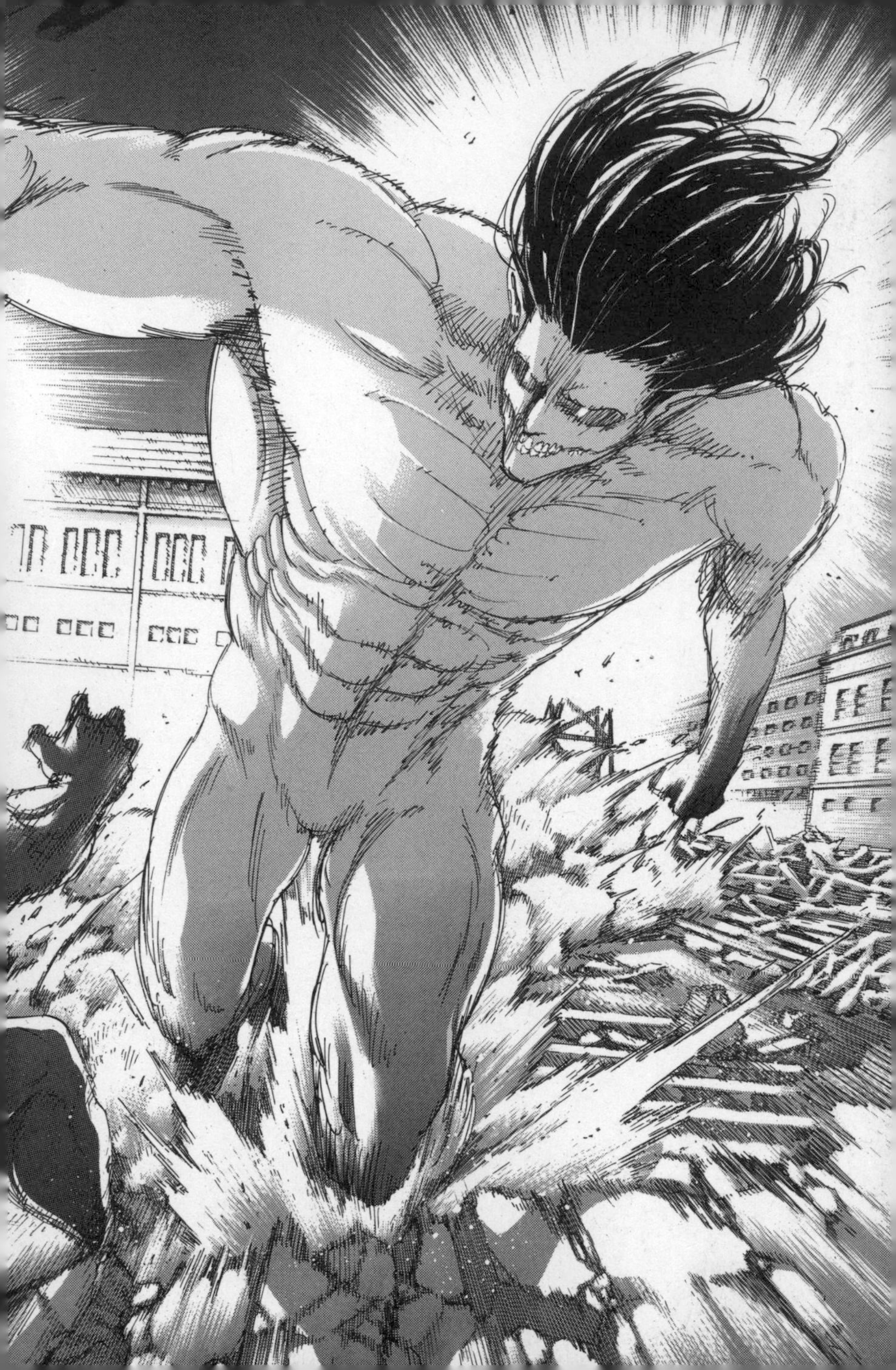

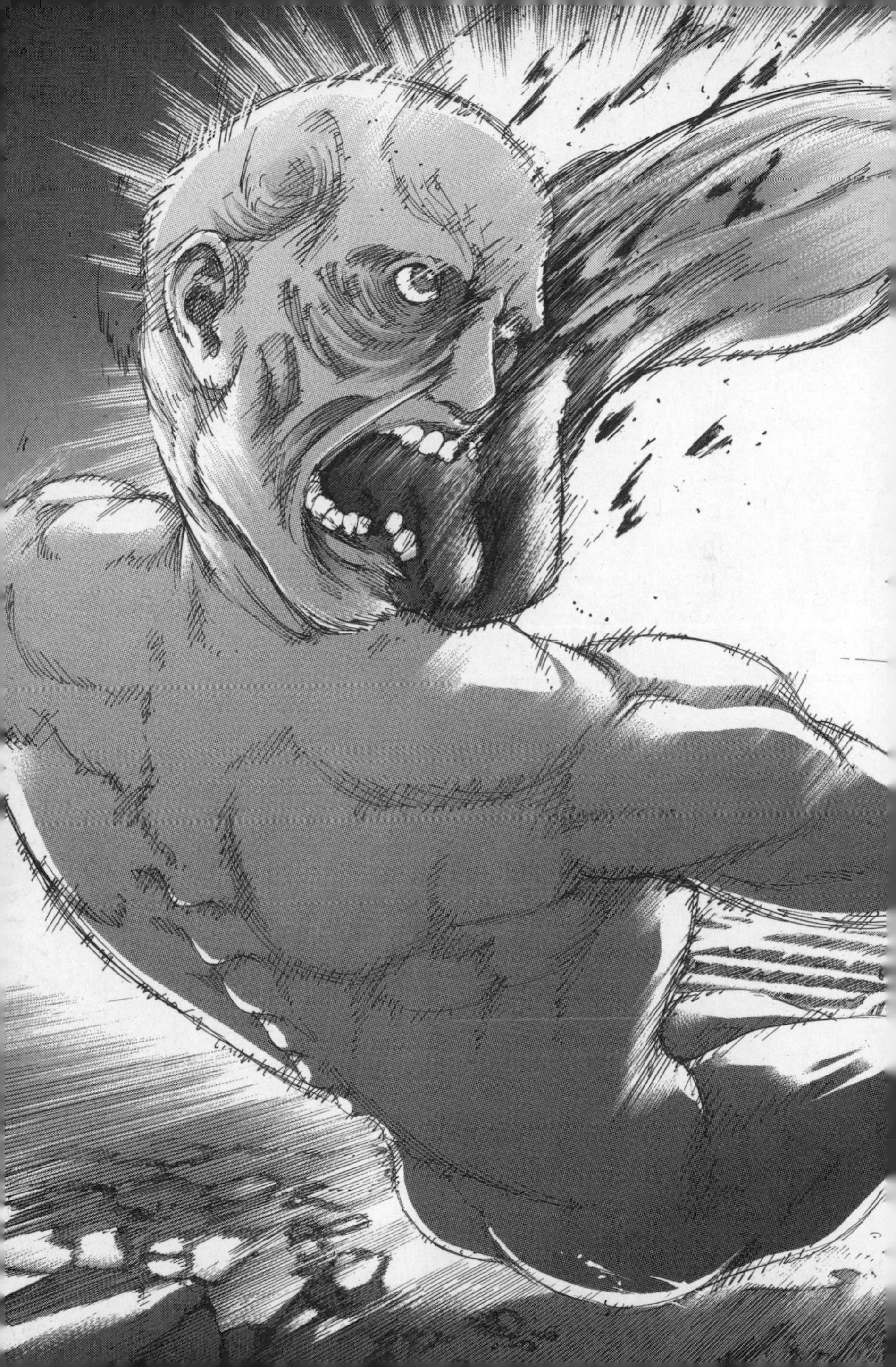

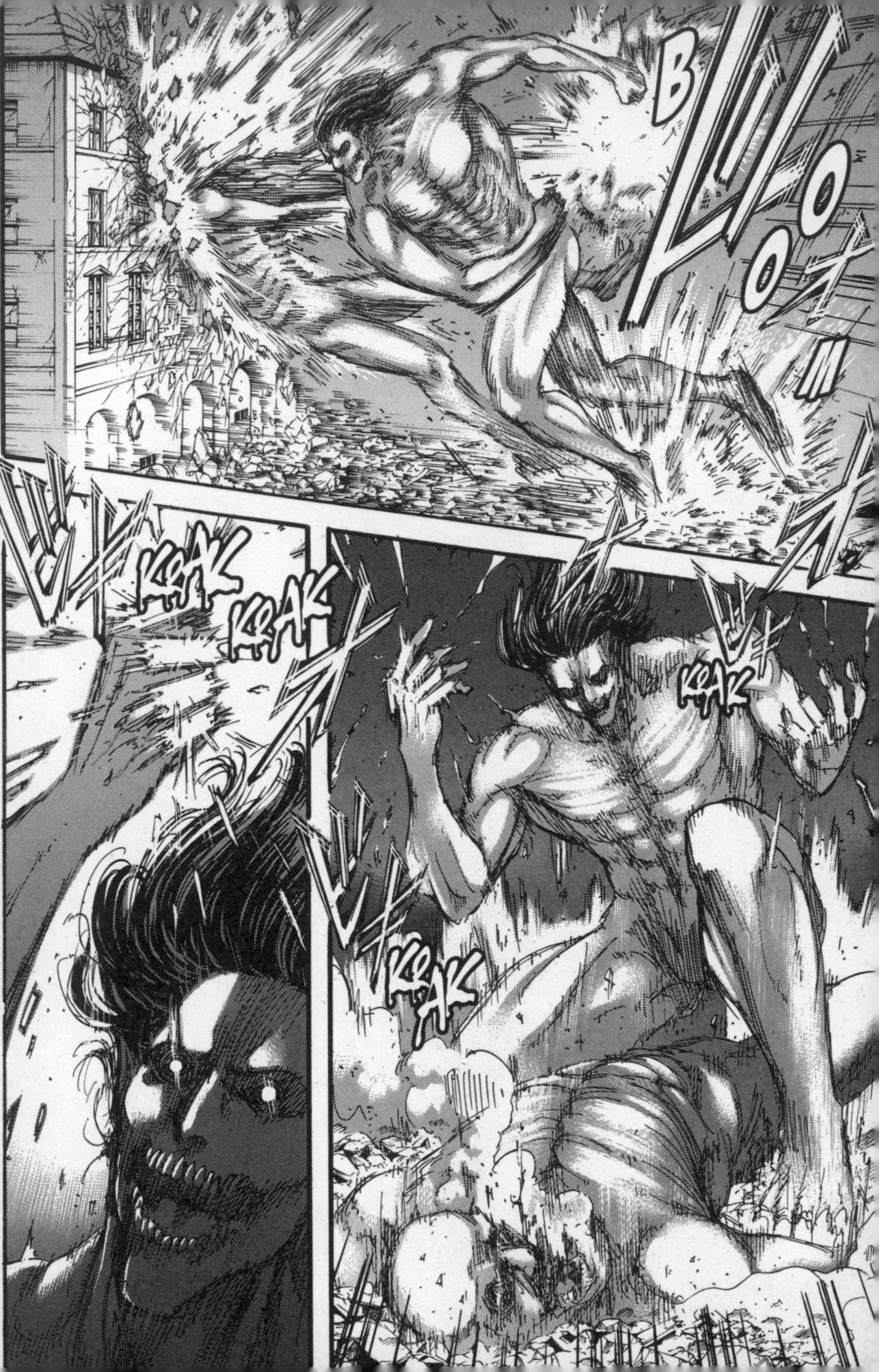
KRAK
KRAK
KRAK
KRAK

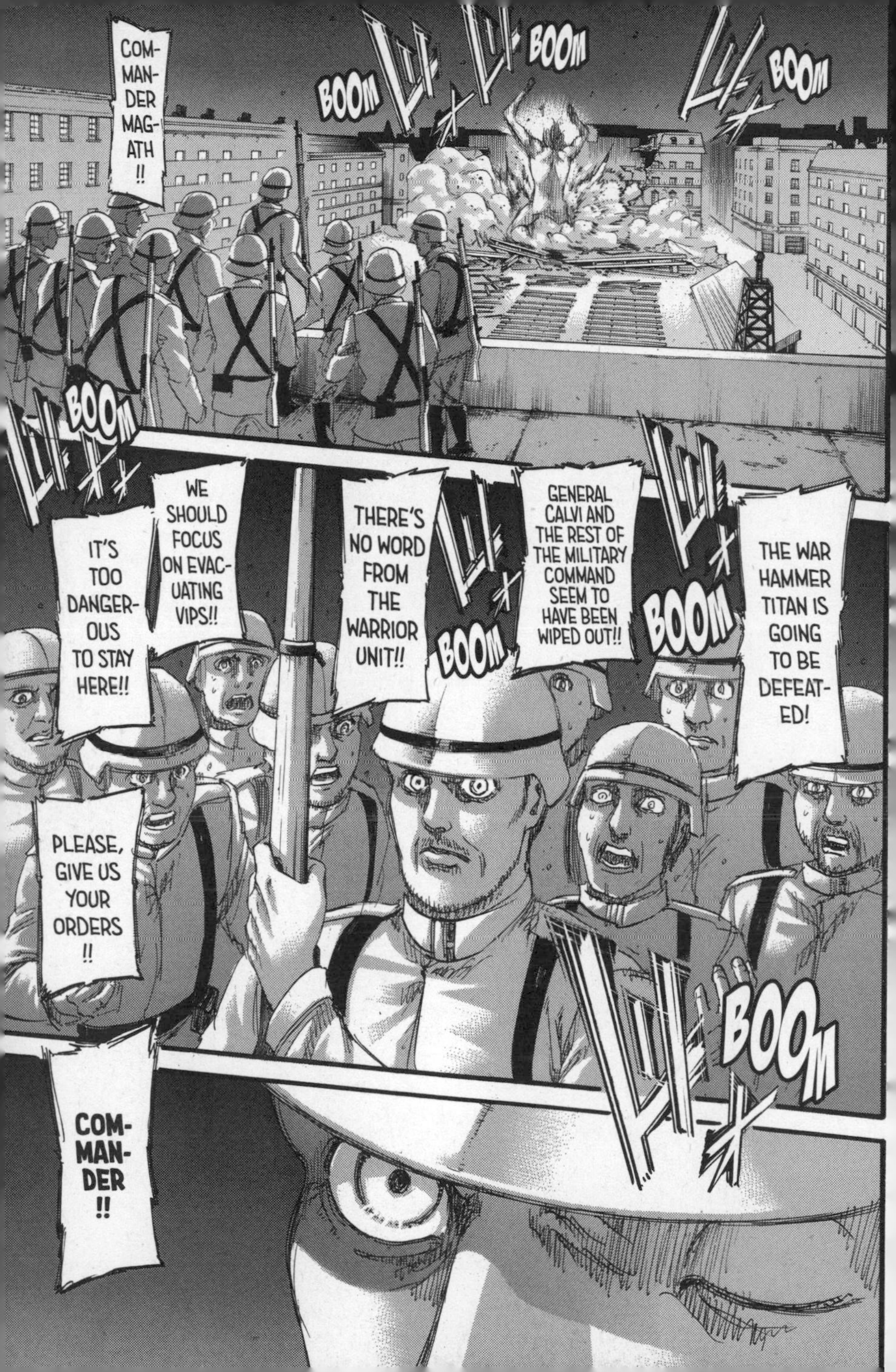

BOOM
BOOM
BOOM
COMMANDER MAGATH!!
BOOM
THE WAR HAMMER TITAN IS GOING TO BE DEFEATED!
BOOM
GENERAL CALVI AND THE REST OF THE MILITARY COMMAND SEEM TO HAVE BEEN WIPED OUT!!
BOOM
THERE'S NO WORD FROM THE WARRIOR UNIT!!
WE SHOULD FOCUS ON EVACUATING VIPS!!
IT'S TOO DANGEROUS TO STAY HERE!!
PLEASE, GIVE US YOUR ORDERS!!
BOOM
COMMANDER!!

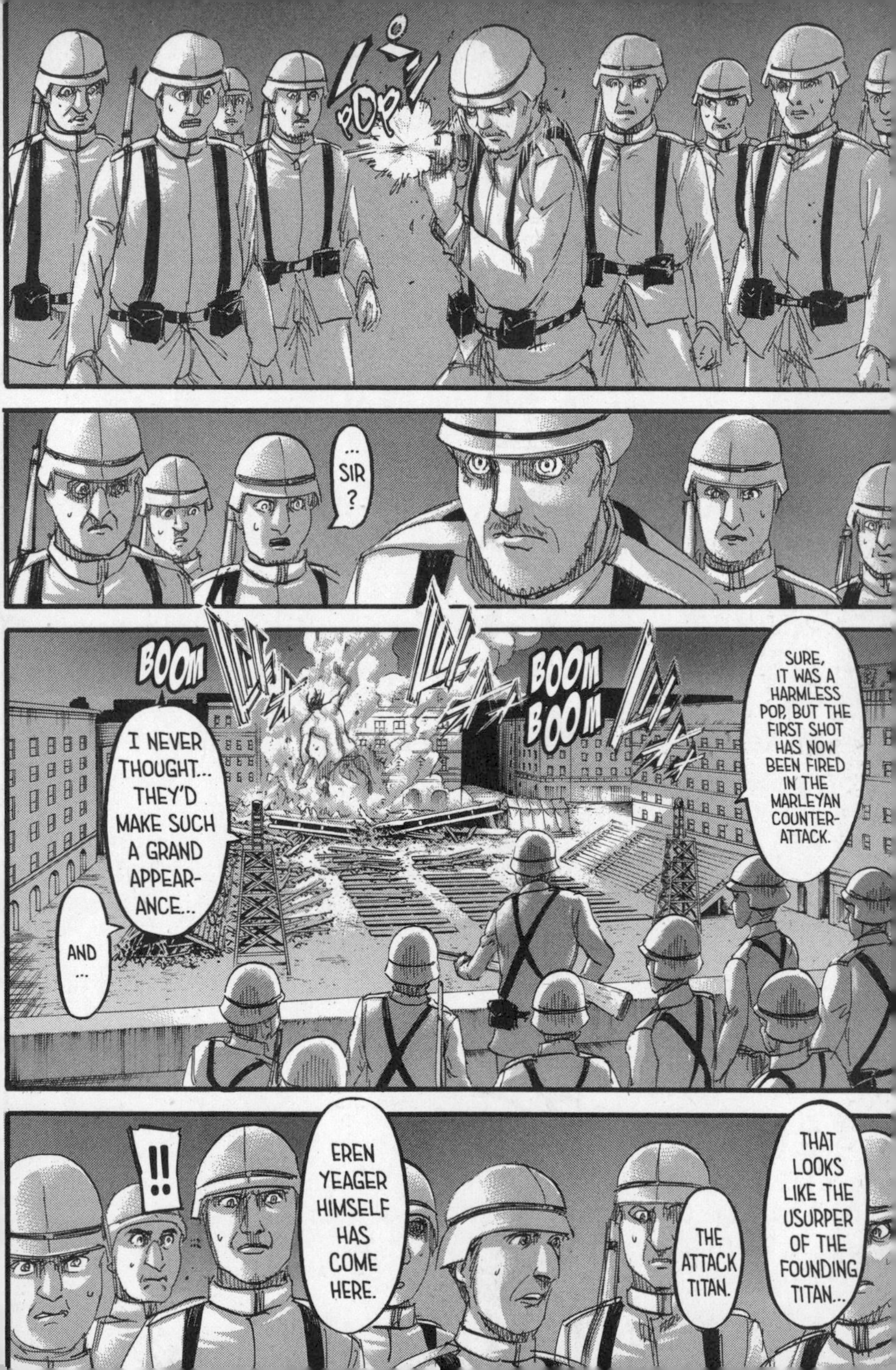
POP
... SIR ?
SURE, IT WAS A HARMLESS POP, BUT THE FIRST SHOT HAS NOW BEEN FIRED IN THE MARLEYAN COUNTER-ATTACK.
BOOM BOOM
BOOM
I NEVER THOUGHT... THEY'D MAKE SUCH A GRAND APPEARANCE...
AND ...
THAT LOOKS LIKE THE USURPER OF THE FOUNDING TITAN...
THE ATTACK TITAN.
EREN YEAGER HIMSELF HAS COME HERE.
!!

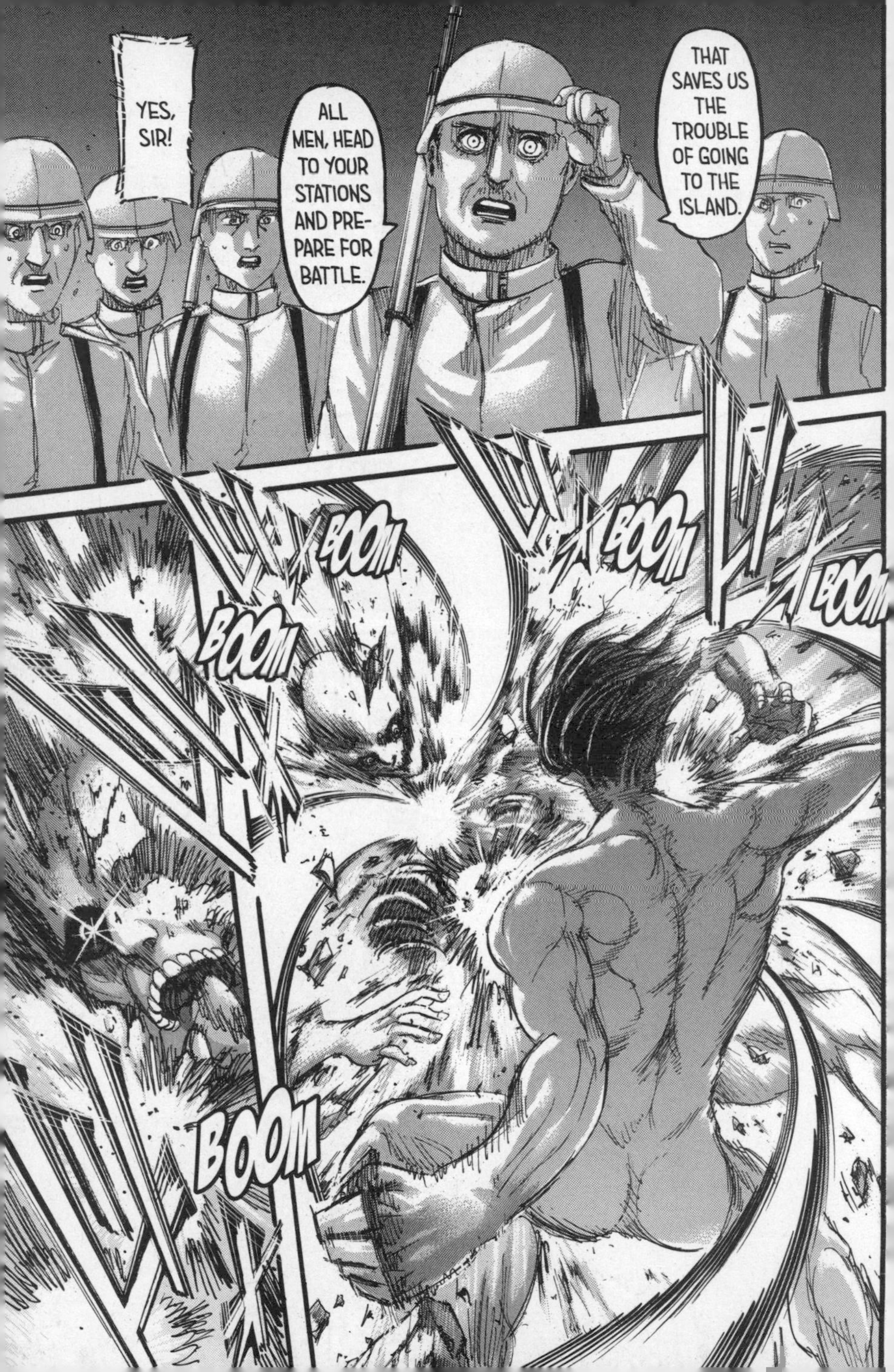
THAT SAVES US THE TROUBLE OF GOING TO THE ISLAND.
ALL MEN, HEAD TO YOUR STATIONS AND PRE-PARE FOR BATTLE.
YES, SIR!
BOOM
BOOM
BOOM
BOOM
BOOM

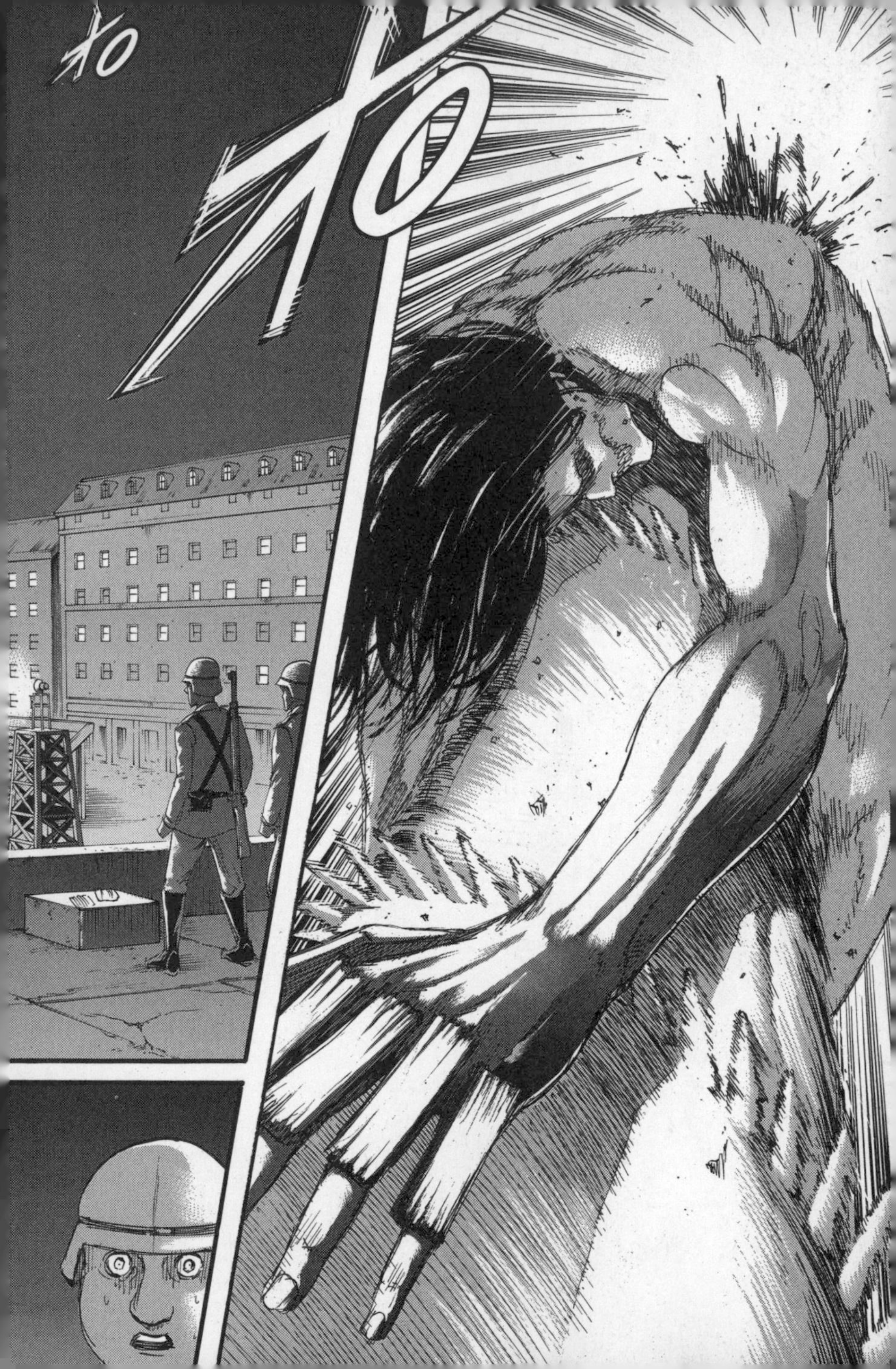

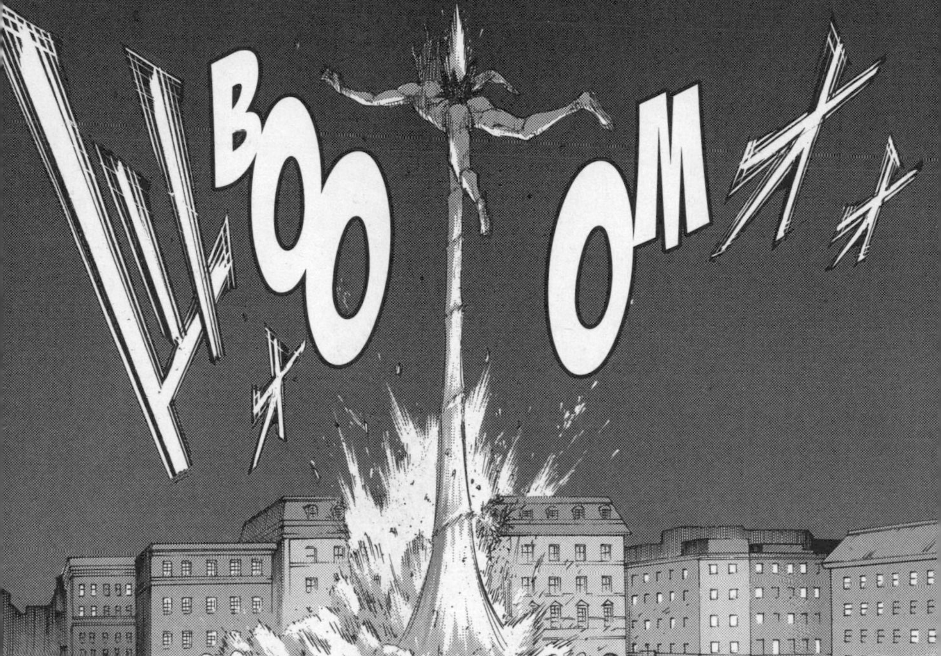
BOOOM

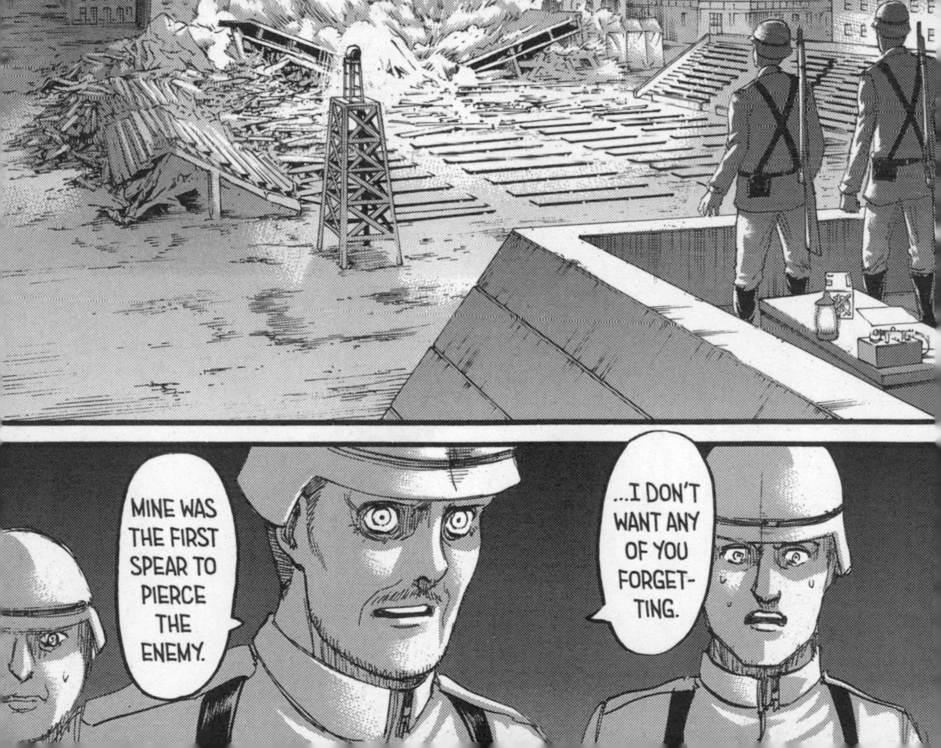
...I DON'T WANT ANY OF YOU FORGET-TING.
MINE WAS THE FIRST SPEAR TO PIERCE THE ENEMY.

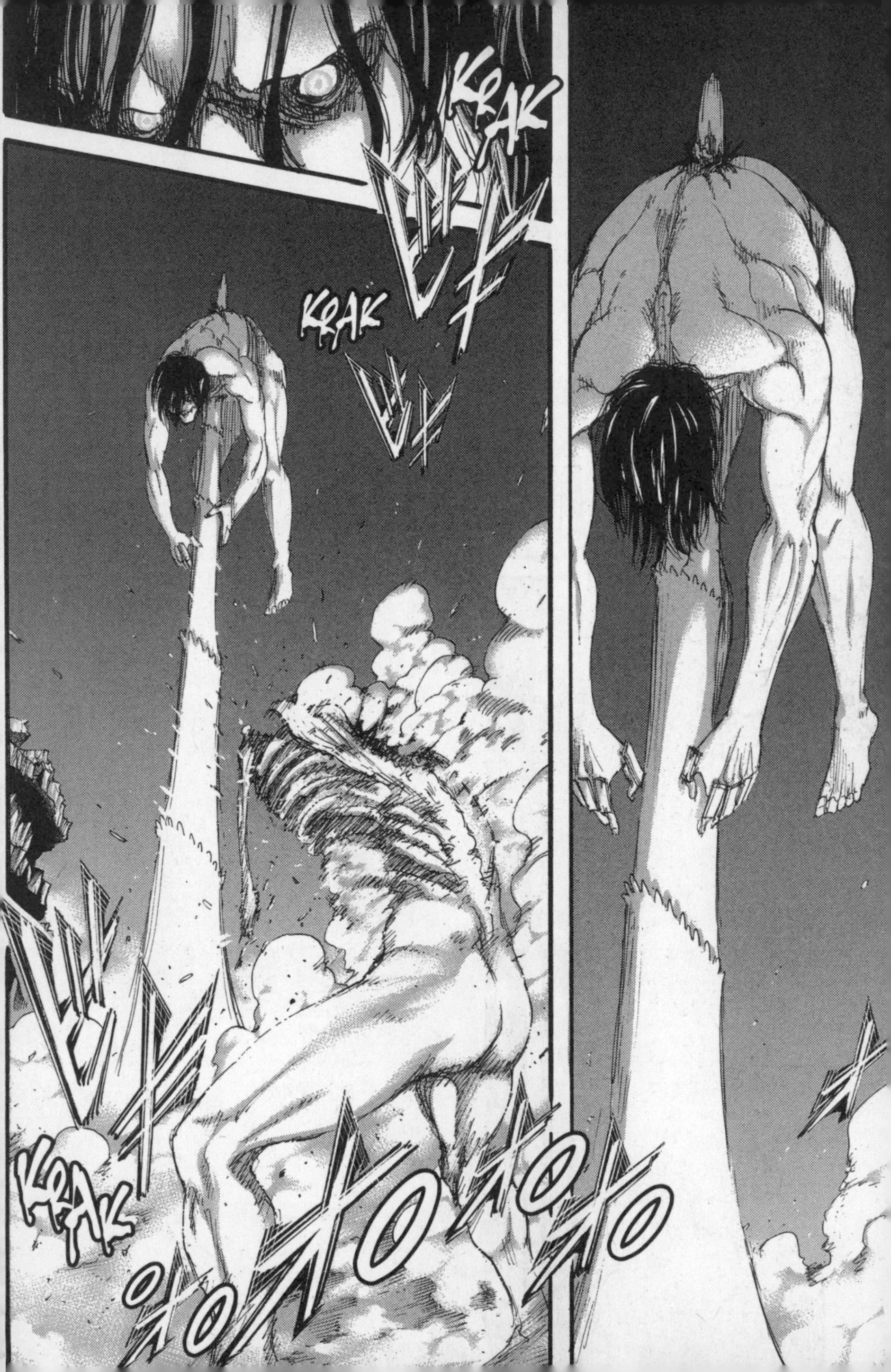
KRAK
KRAK
KRAK

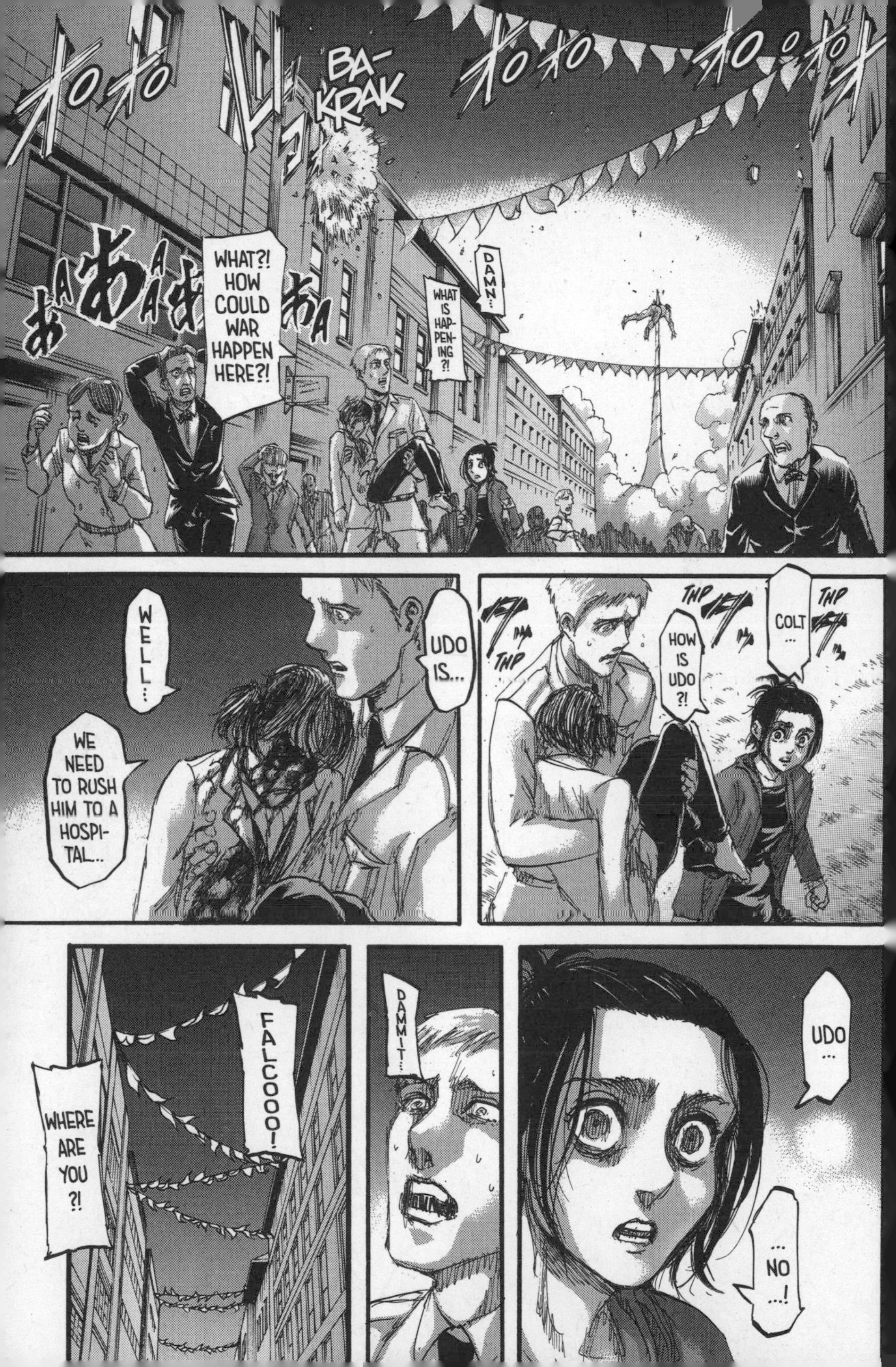
BA-KRAK
DAMN...
WHAT IS HAPPENING?!
WHAT?! HOW COULD WAR HAPPEN HERE?!
THP
COLT...
HOW IS UDO?!
UDO IS...
WELL...
WE NEED TO RUSH HIM TO A HOSPITAL...
UDO...
...NO...!
DAMMIT...
FALCOOO!
WHERE ARE YOU?!

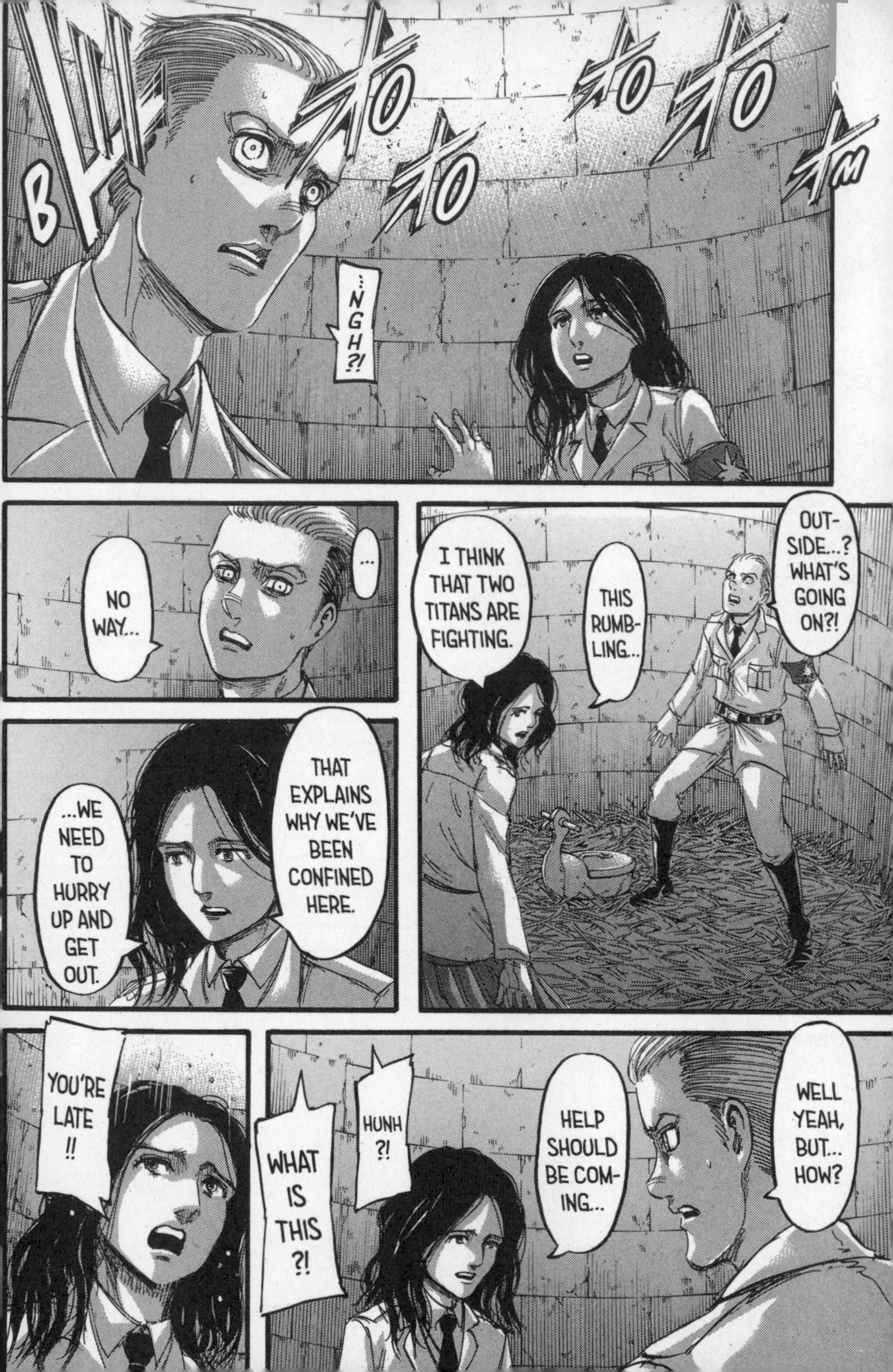
...NGH?!
OUT-SIDE...? WHAT'S GOING ON?!
THIS RUMB-LING...
I THINK THAT TWO TITANS ARE FIGHTING.
...
NO WAY...
THAT EXPLAINS WHY WE'VE BEEN CONFINED HERE.
...WE NEED TO HURRY UP AND GET OUT.
WELL YEAH, BUT... HOW?
HELP SHOULD BE COM-ING...
HUNH?!
WHAT IS THIS?!
YOU'RE LATE!!

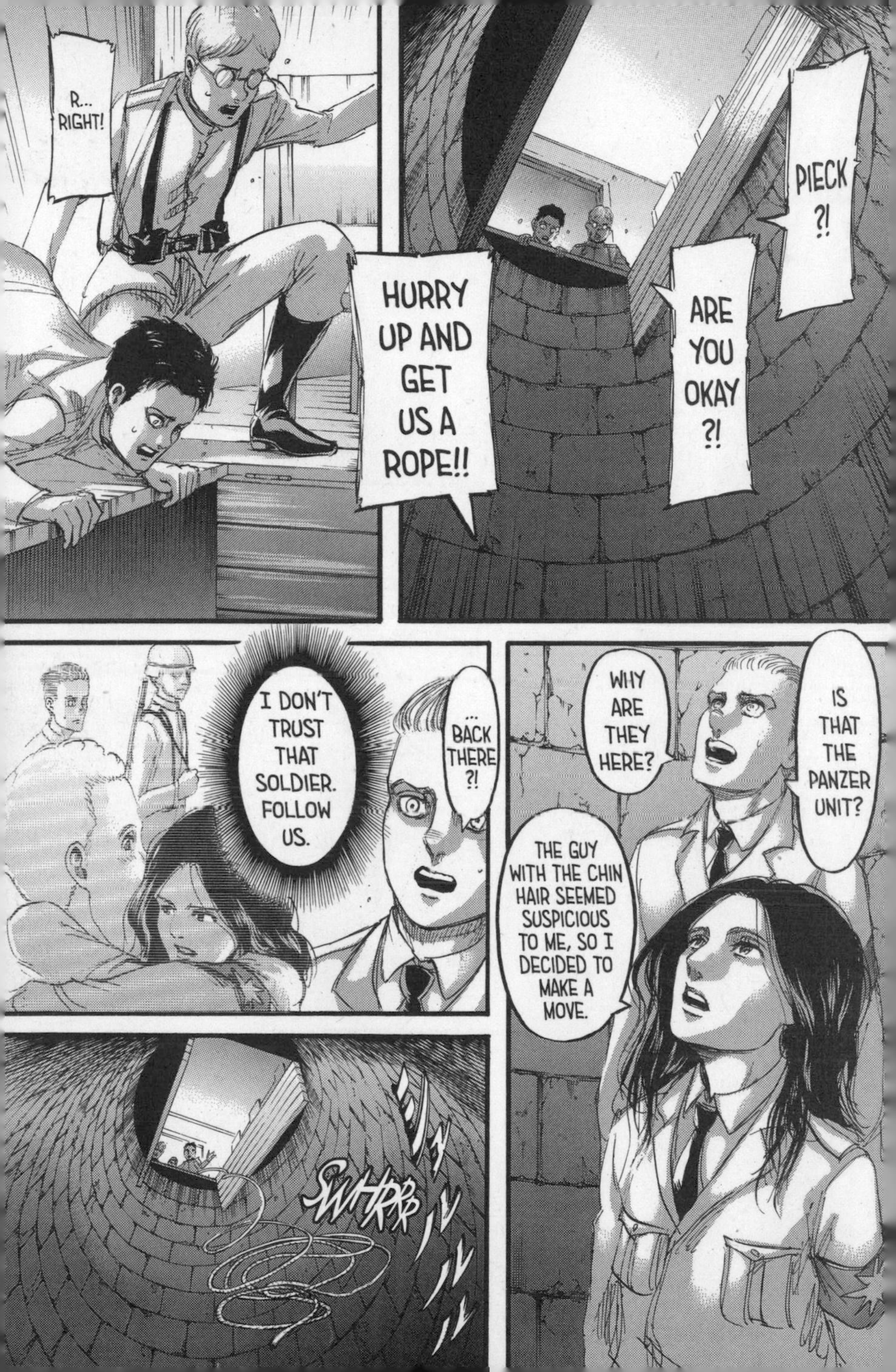
PIECK ?!
ARE YOU OKAY ?!
HURRY UP AND GET US A ROPE!!
R... RIGHT!
IS THAT THE PANZER UNIT?
WHY ARE THEY HERE?
THE GUY WITH THE CHIN HAIR SEEMED SUSPICIOUS TO ME, SO I DECIDED TO MAKE A MOVE.
... BACK THERE ?!
I DON'T TRUST THAT SOLDIER. FOLLOW US.
SWHRRR

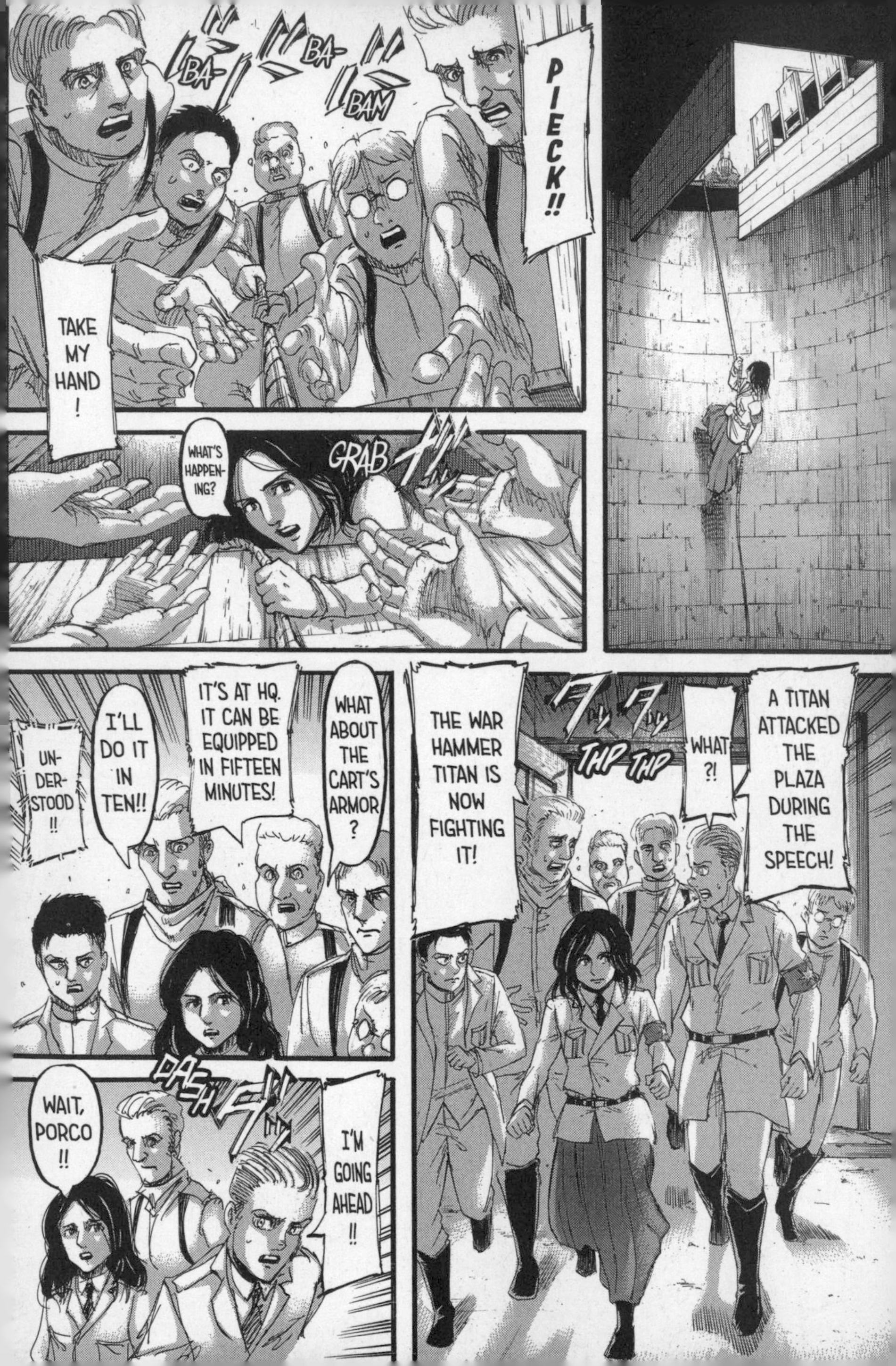
PIECK!!
BA- BA- BAM
TAKE MY HAND!
GRAB
WHAT'S HAPPEN-ING?
A TITAN ATTACKED THE PLAZA DURING THE SPEECH!
WHAT?!
THP THP
THE WAR HAMMER TITAN IS NOW FIGHTING IT!
WHAT ABOUT THE CART'S ARMOR?
IT'S AT HQ. IT CAN BE EQUIPPED IN FIFTEEN MINUTES!
I'LL DO IT IN TEN!!
UN-DER-STOOD!!
I'M GOING AHEAD!!
DASH
WAIT, PORCO!!

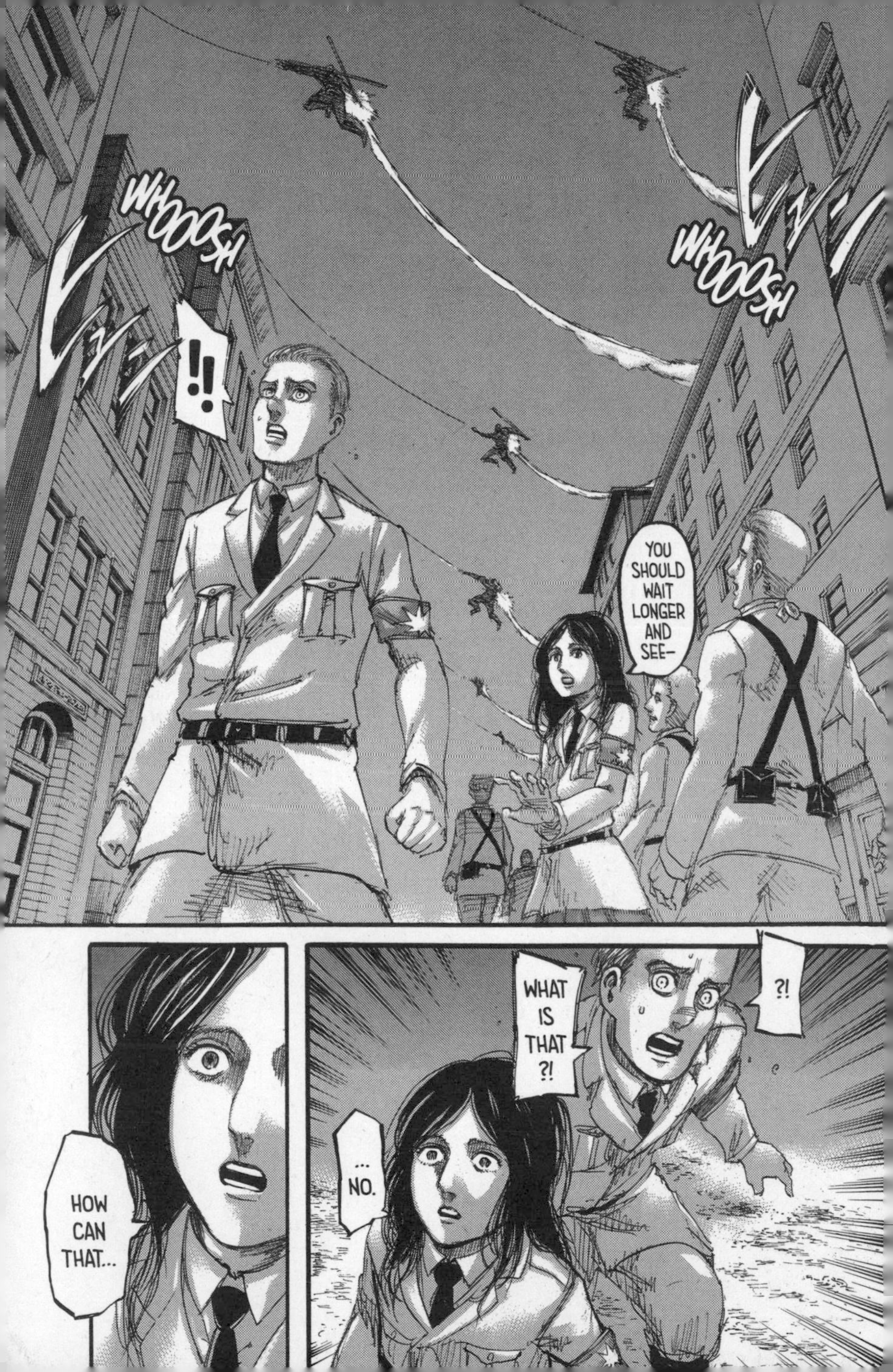
WHOOOSH
WHOOOSH
!!
YOU SHOULD WAIT LONGER AND SEE—
?!
WHAT IS THAT ?!
... NO.
HOW CAN THAT...

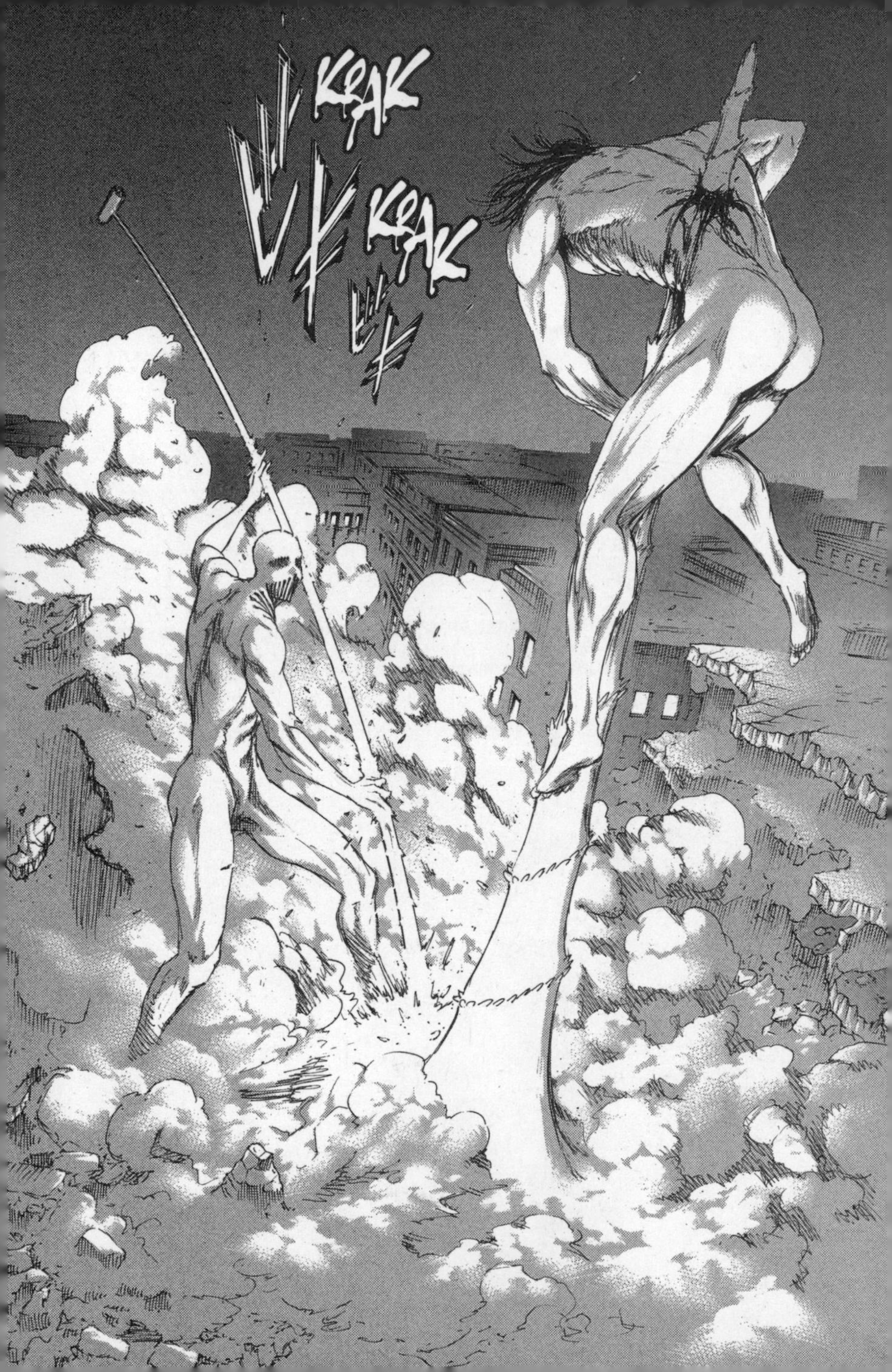
KRAK
KRAK

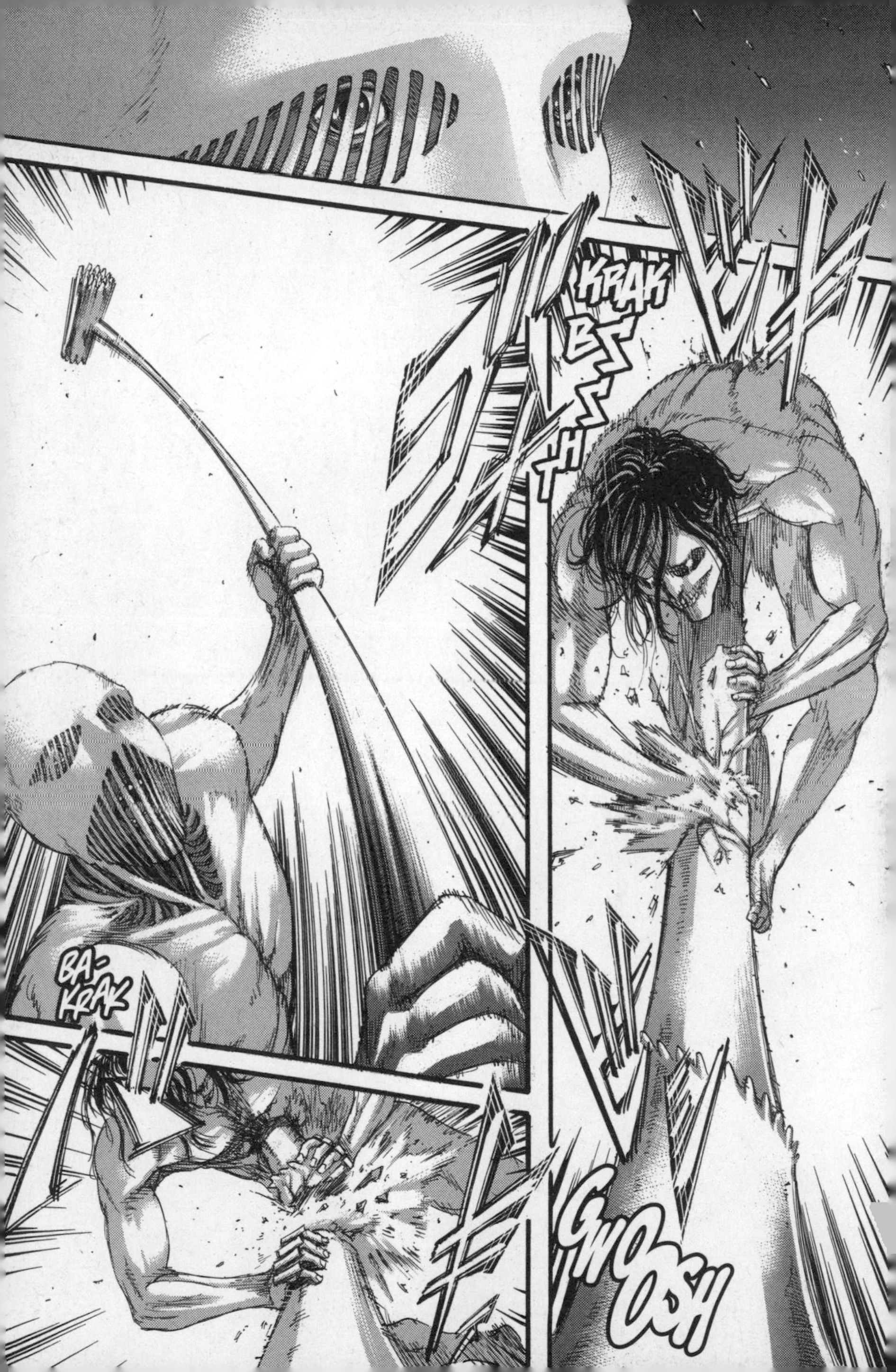
KRAK
BSSTH
GWOOOSH
BA-KRAK

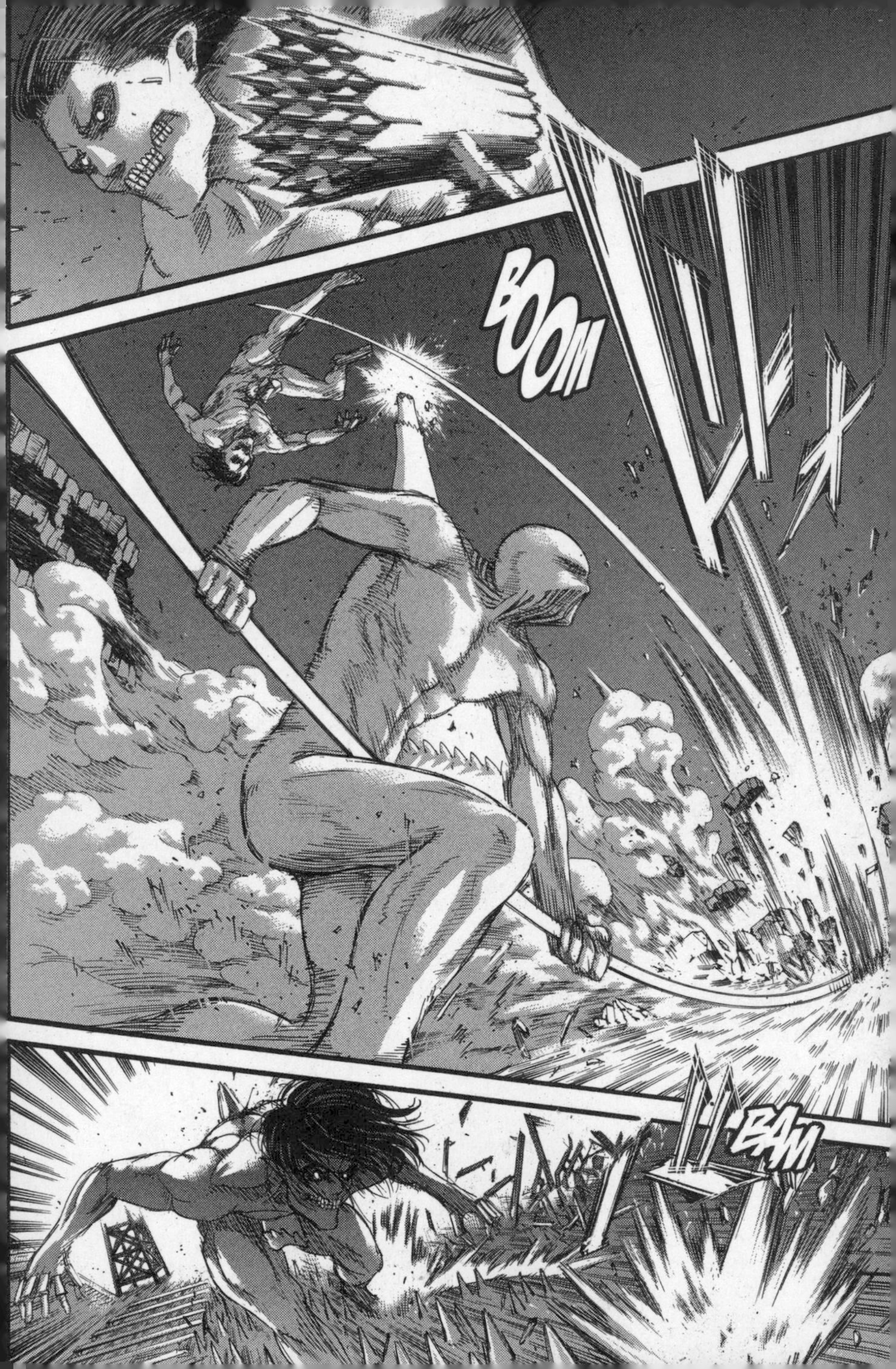
BOOM
BAM

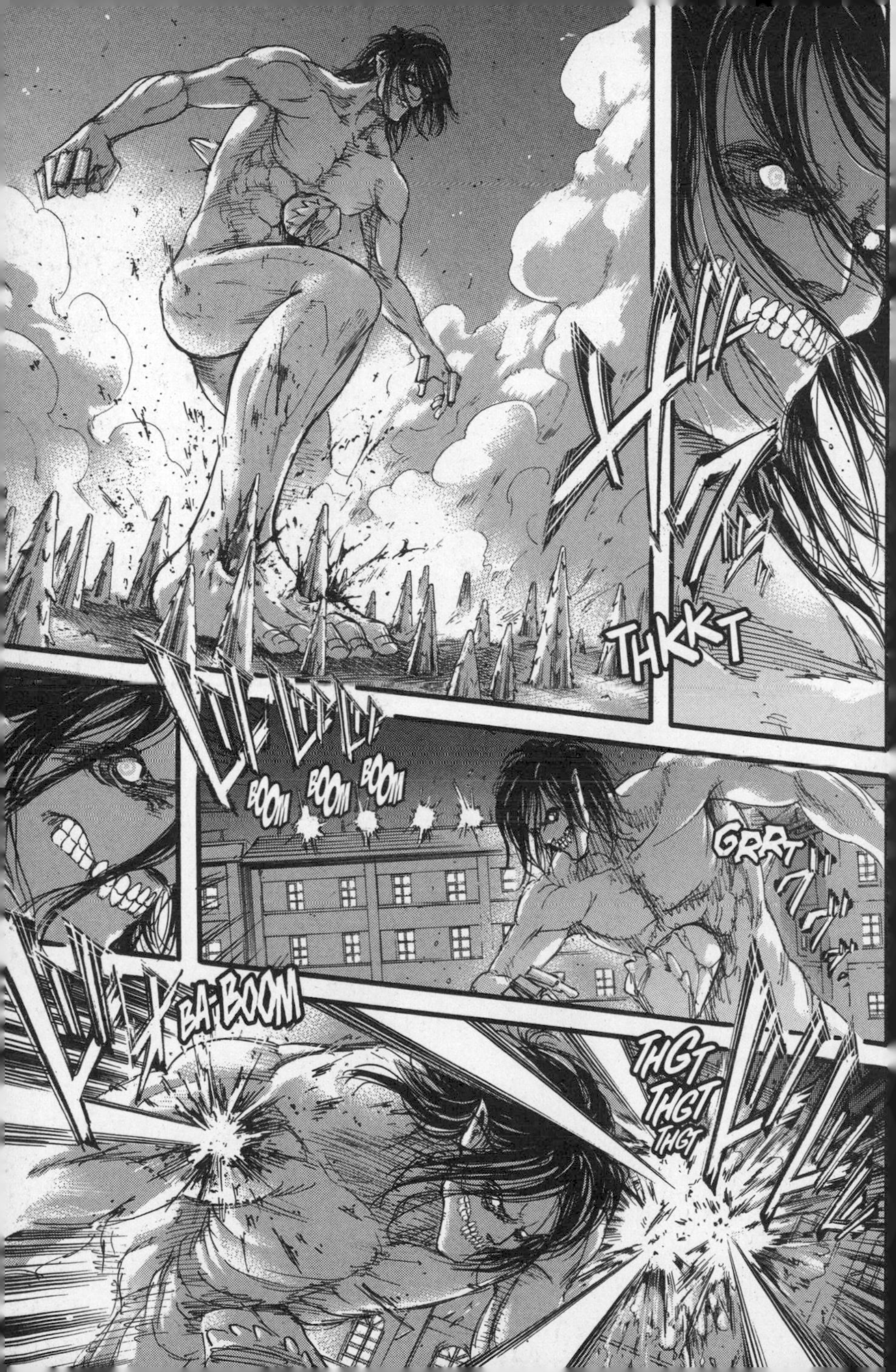
THKKT
GRRT
BOOM
BOOM
BOOM
THGT
THGT
THGT
BA-BOOM

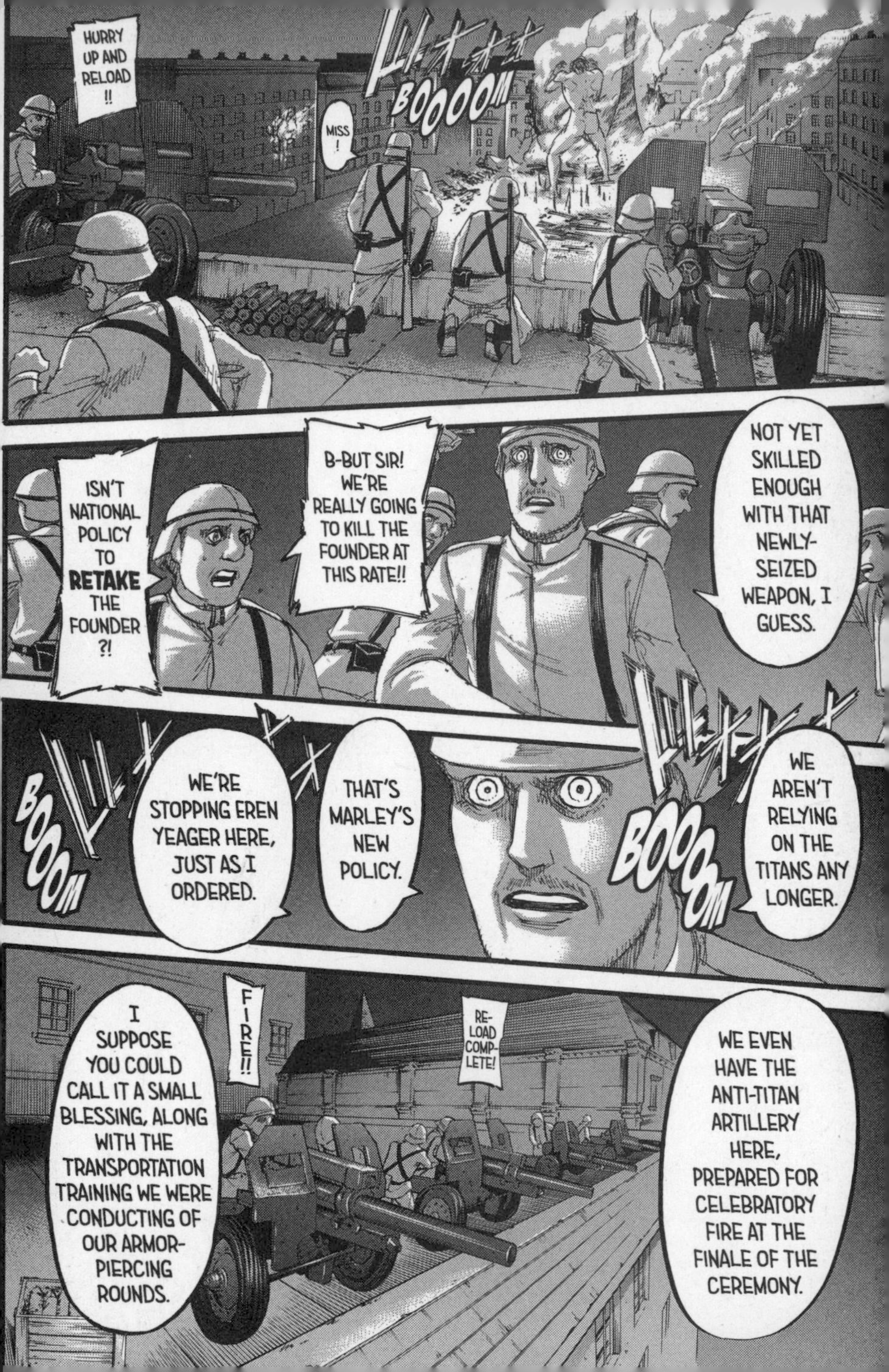
BOOOOM
MISS!
HURRY UP AND RELOAD!!
NOT YET SKILLED ENOUGH WITH THAT NEWLY-SEIZED WEAPON, I GUESS.
B-BUT SIR! WE'RE REALLY GOING TO KILL THE FOUNDER AT THIS RATE!!
ISN'T NATIONAL POLICY TO **RETAKE** THE FOUNDER?!
BOOOOM
WE AREN'T RELYING ON THE TITANS ANY LONGER.
THAT'S MARLEY'S NEW POLICY.
WE'RE STOPPING EREN YEAGER HERE, JUST AS I ORDERED.
BOOOOM
WE EVEN HAVE THE ANTI-TITAN ARTILLERY HERE, PREPARED FOR CELEBRATORY FIRE AT THE FINALE OF THE CEREMONY.
RE-LOAD COMP-LETE!
FIRE!!
I SUPPOSE YOU COULD CALL IT A SMALL BLESSING, ALONG WITH THE TRANSPORTATION TRAINING WE WERE CONDUCTING OF OUR ARMOR-PIERCING ROUNDS.

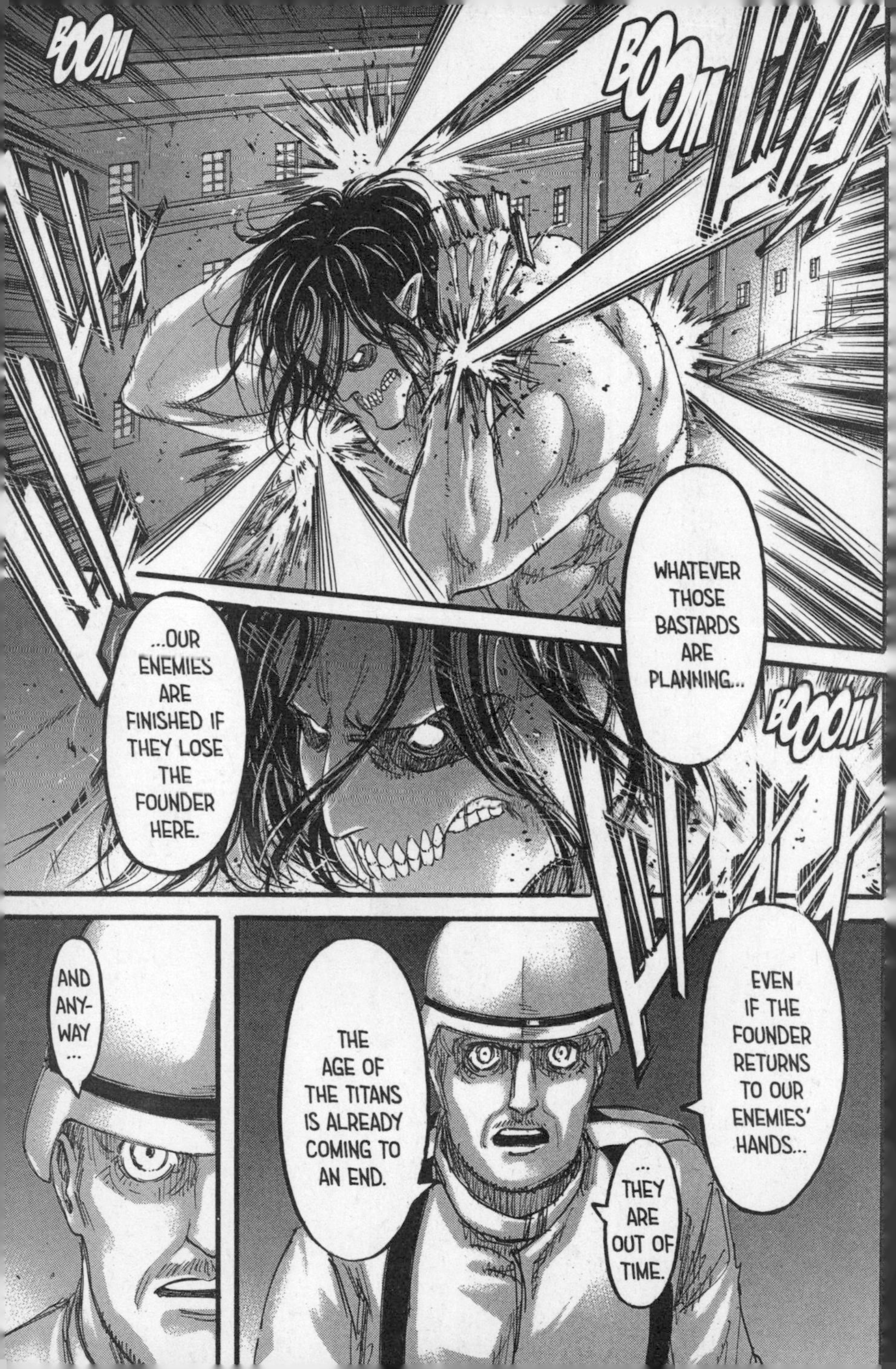
BOOM
BOOM
WHATEVER THOSE BASTARDS ARE PLANNING...
BOOOM
...OUR ENEMIES ARE FINISHED IF THEY LOSE THE FOUNDER HERE.
EVEN IF THE FOUNDER RETURNS TO OUR ENEMIES' HANDS...
...THEY ARE OUT OF TIME.
THE AGE OF THE TITANS IS ALREADY COMING TO AN END.
AND ANY-WAY ...

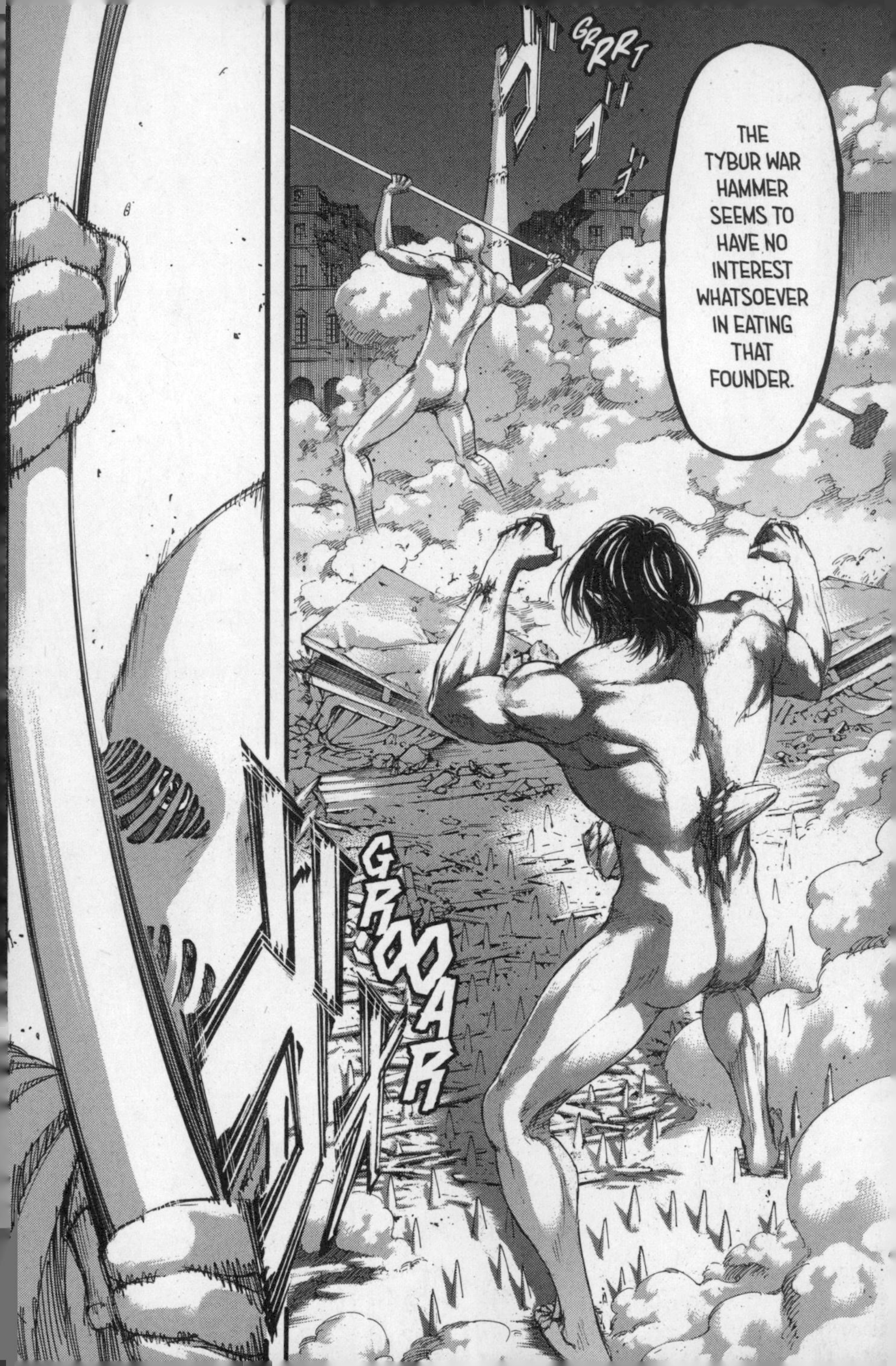
GRRRT
THE TYBUR WAR HAMMER SEEMS TO HAVE NO INTEREST WHATSOEVER IN EATING THAT FOUNDER.
GROOOAR

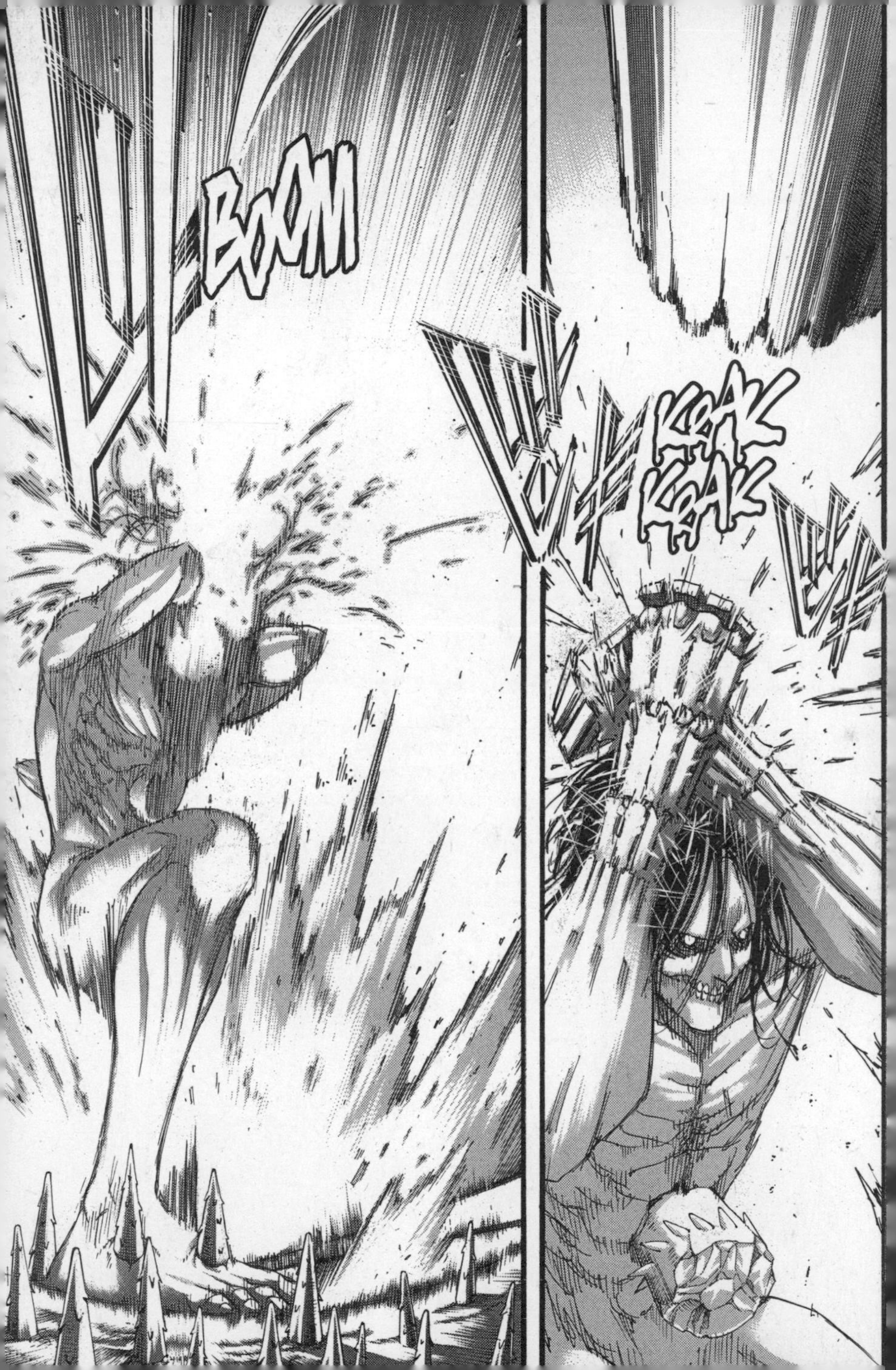
KRAK KRAK
BOOM

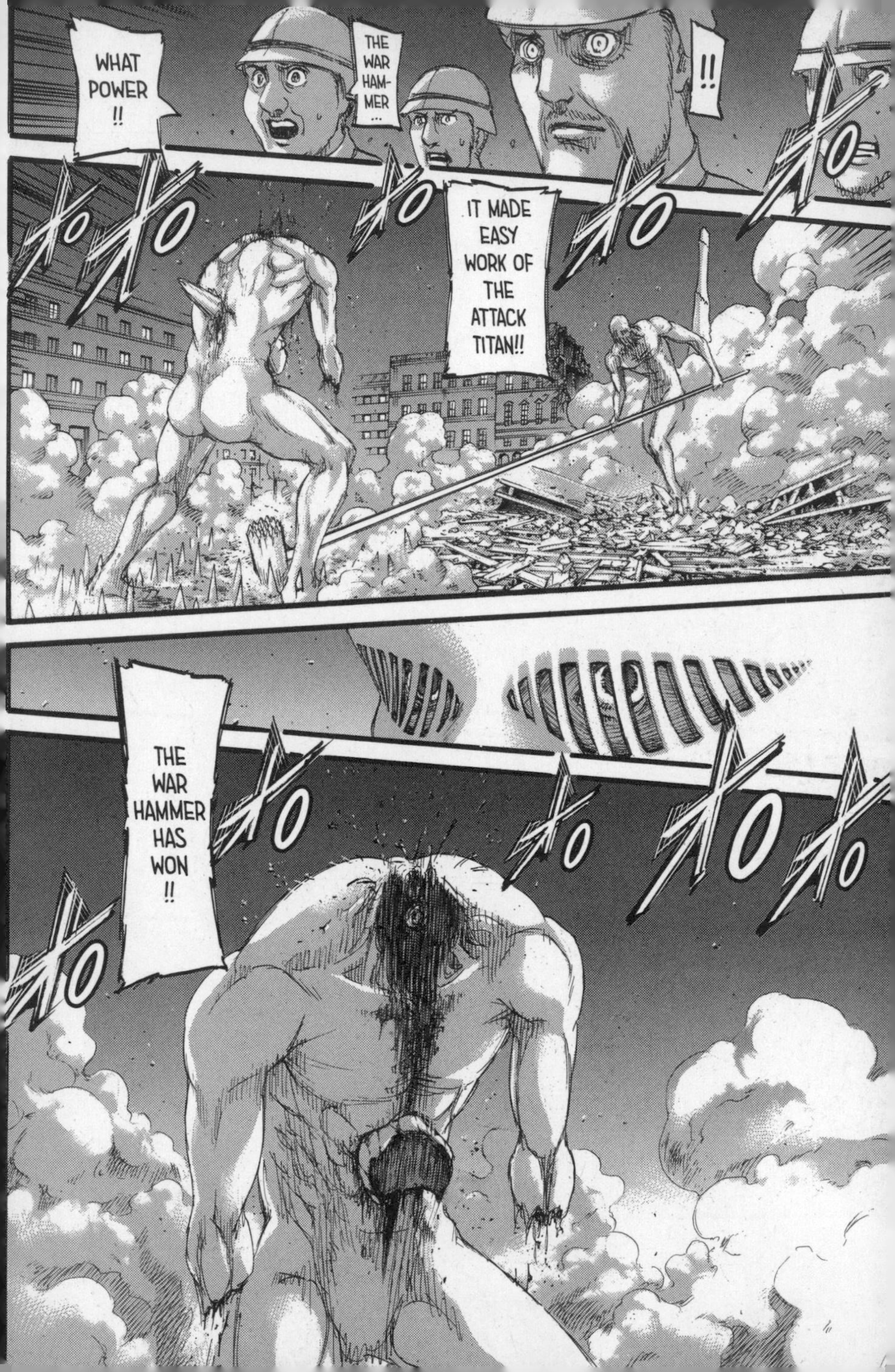
!!
THE WAR HAMMER...
WHAT POWER!!
IT MADE EASY WORK OF THE ATTACK TITAN!!
THE WAR HAMMER HAS WON!!

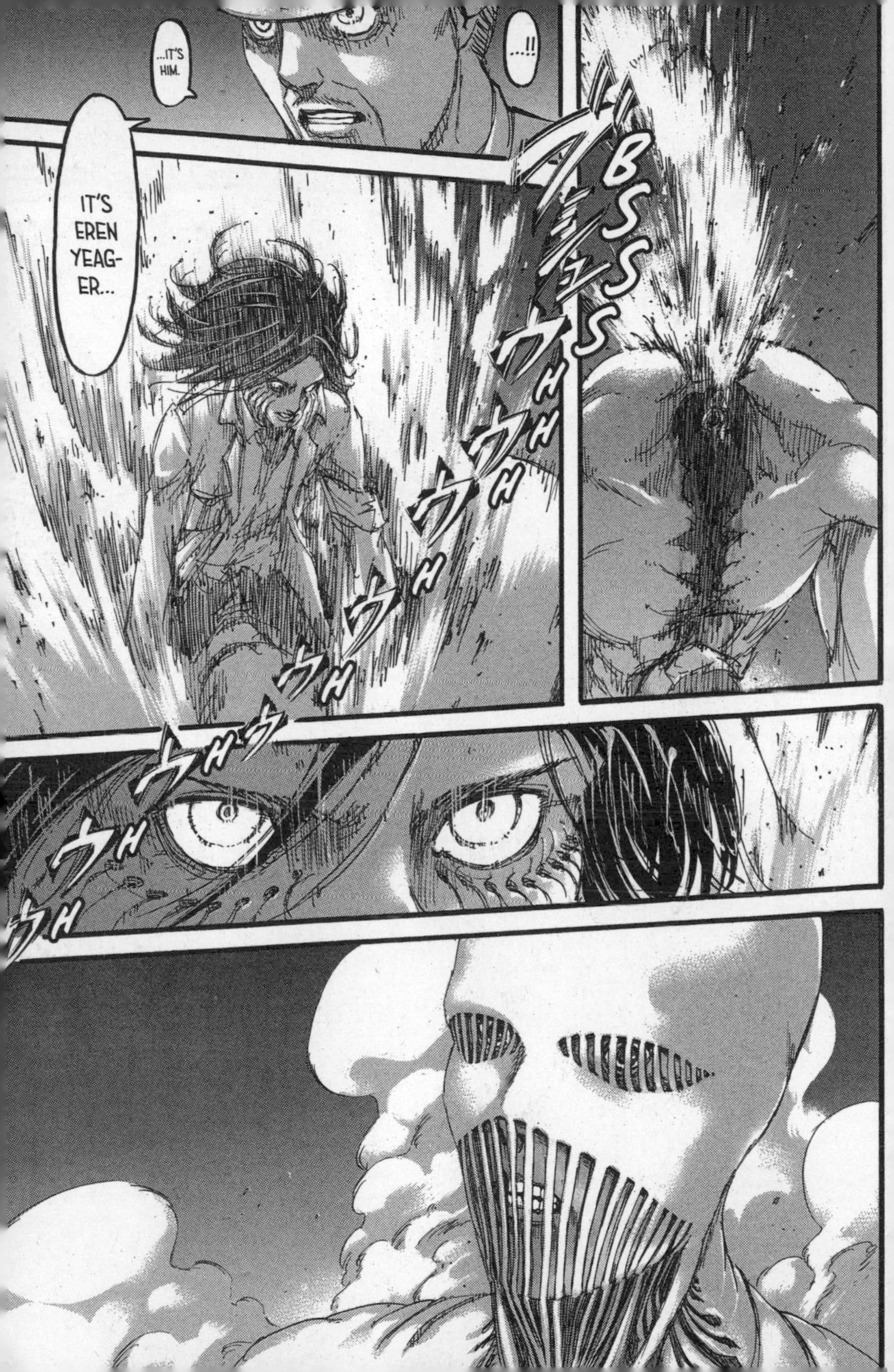

BSSSSS
...!!
...IT'S HIM.
IT'S EREN YEAGER...

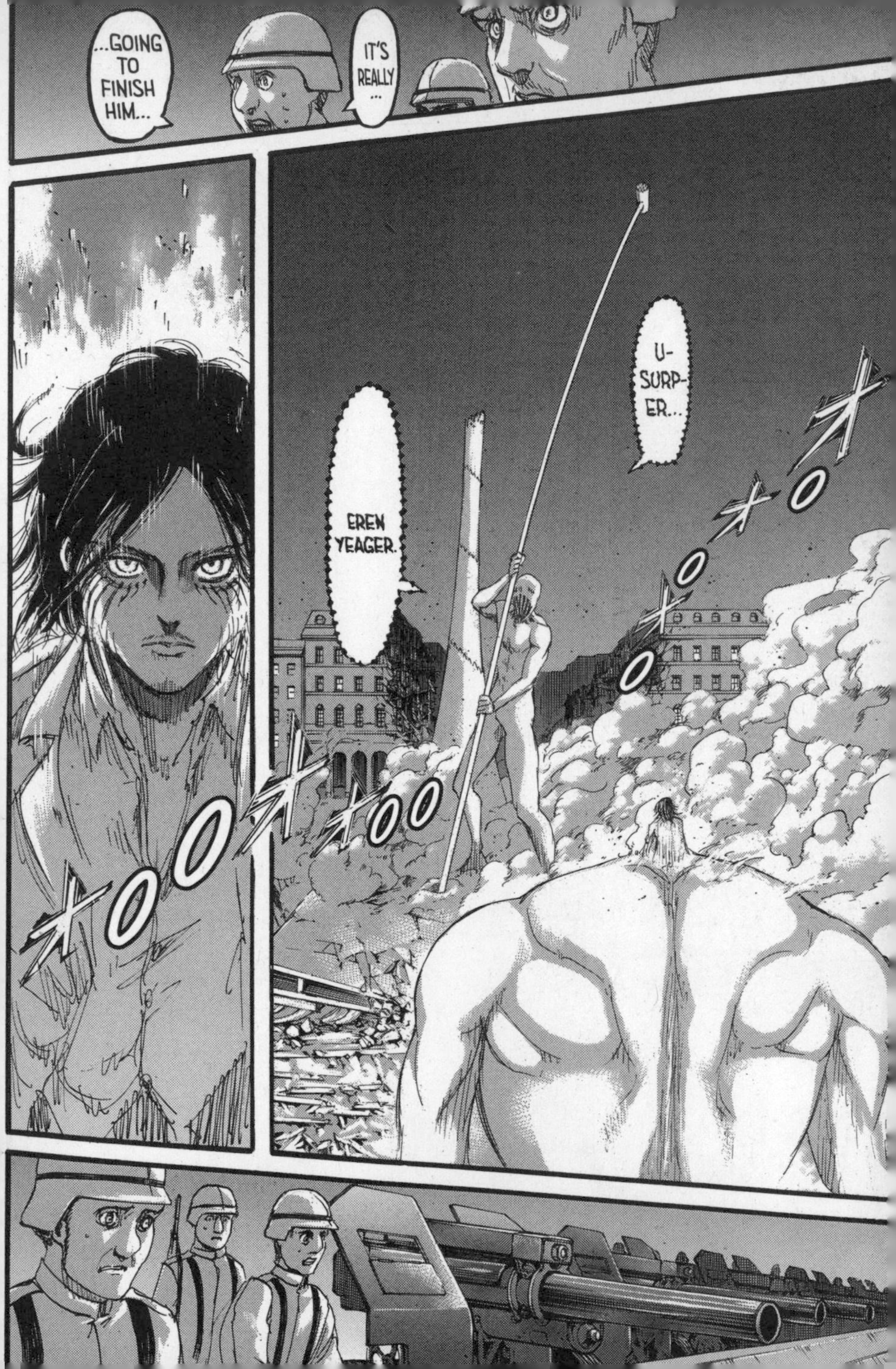
IT'S REALLY...
...GOING TO FINISH HIM...
U-SURPER...
EREN YEAGER.

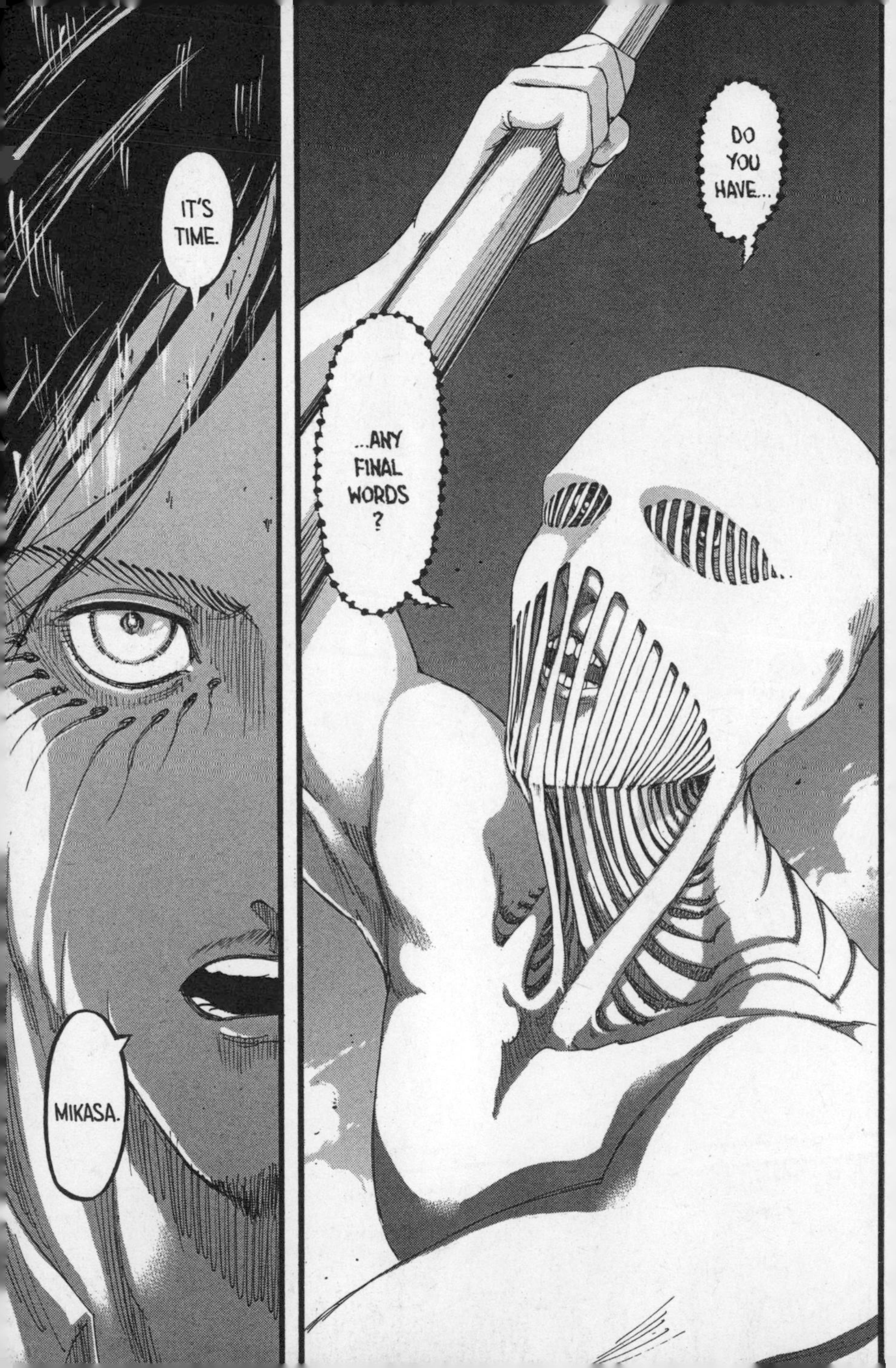
DO YOU HAVE...
...ANY FINAL WORDS ?
IT'S TIME.
MIKASA.

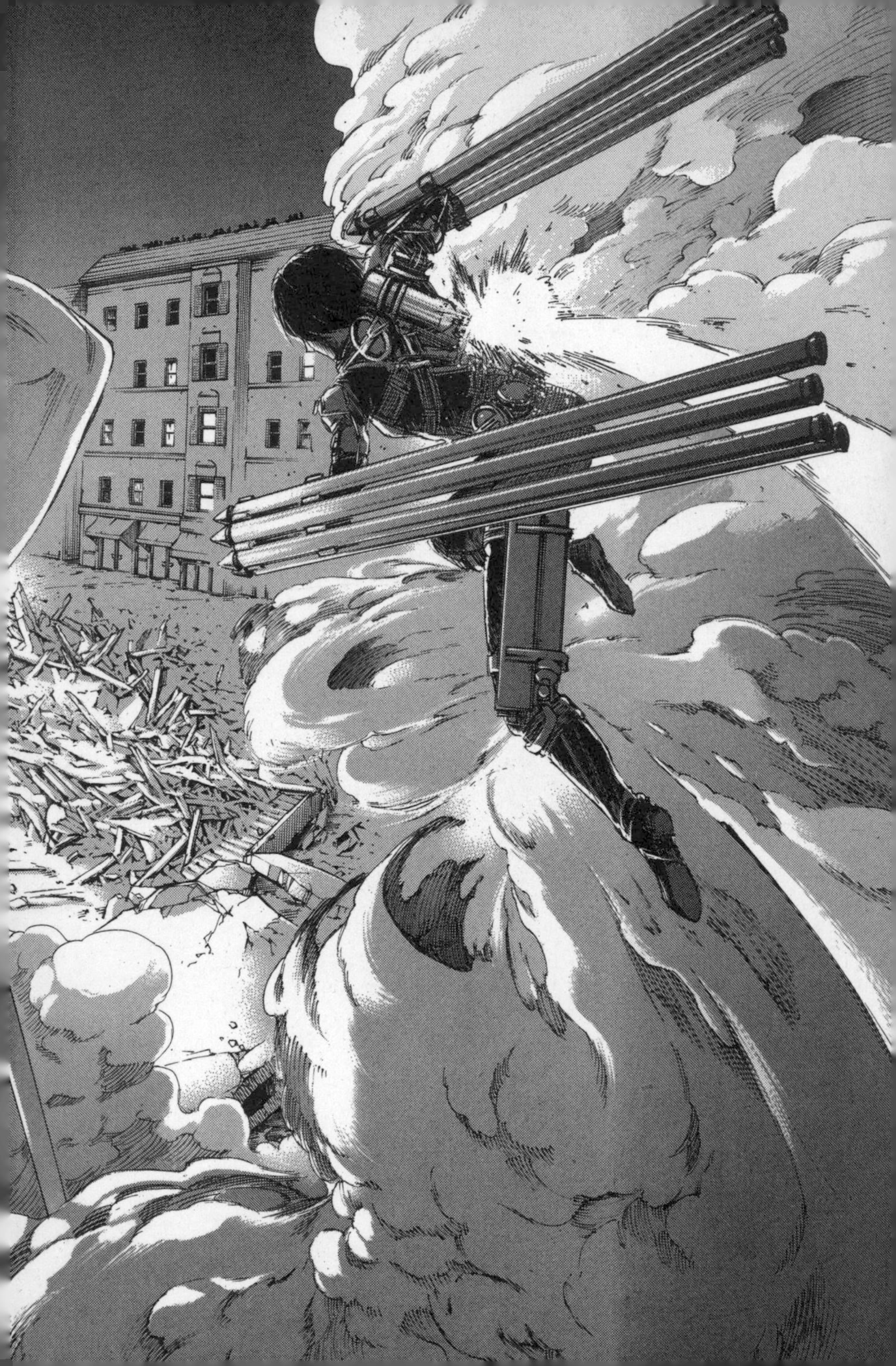

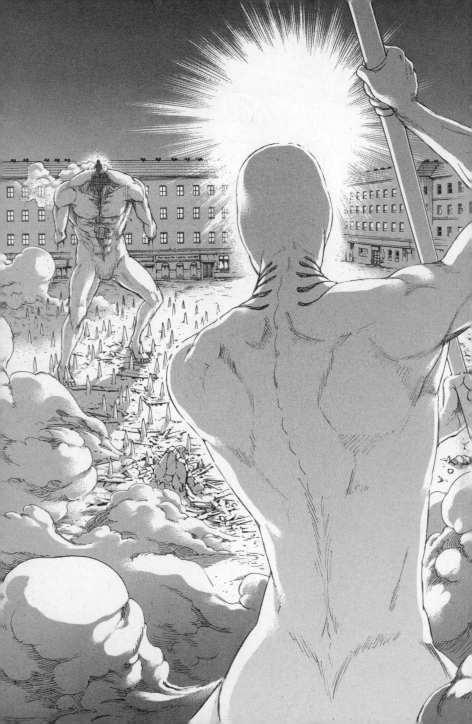

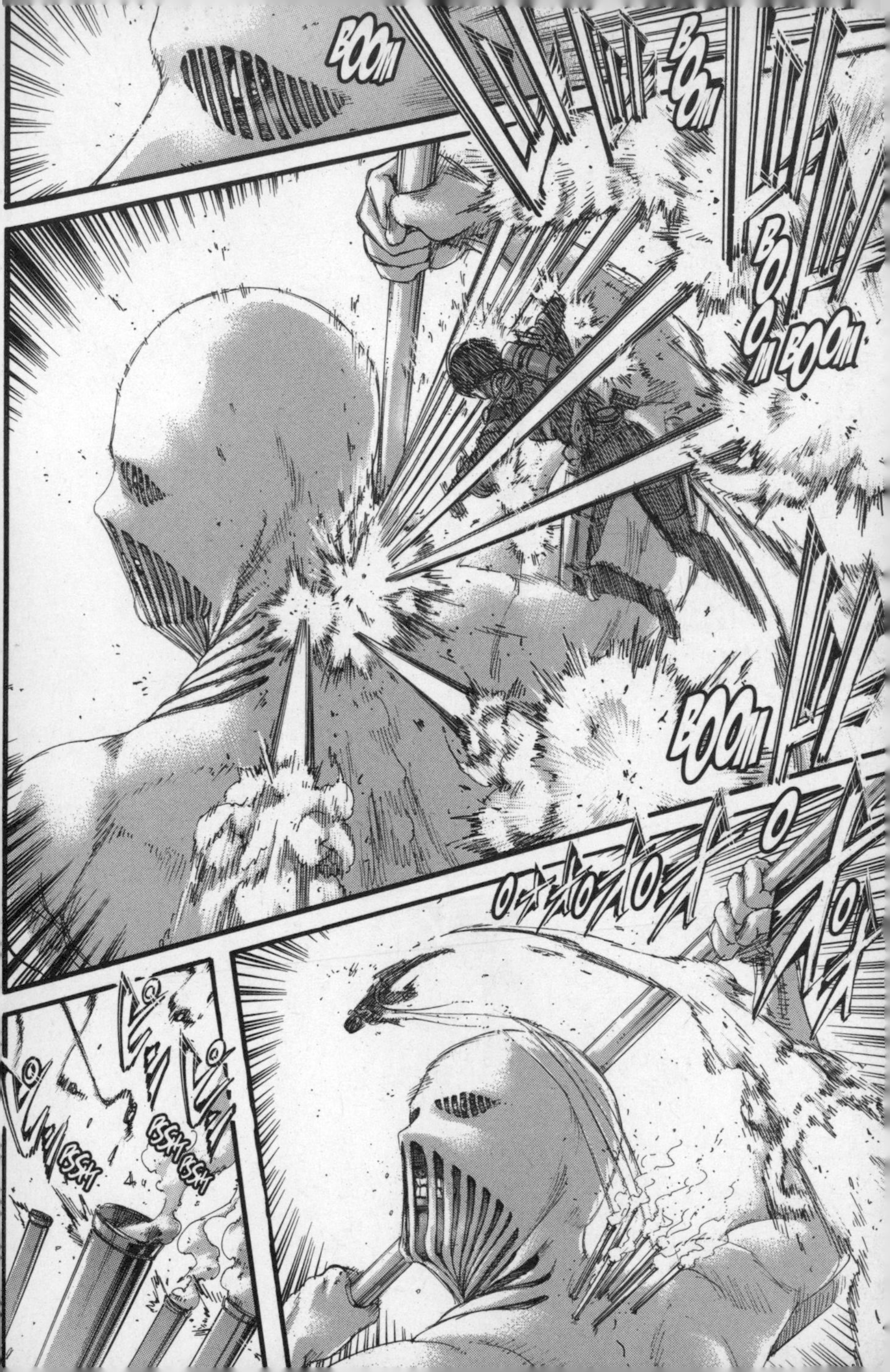
BOOM
BOOM
BOOOM
BOOM
BOOM
BSSH BSSH
BSSH

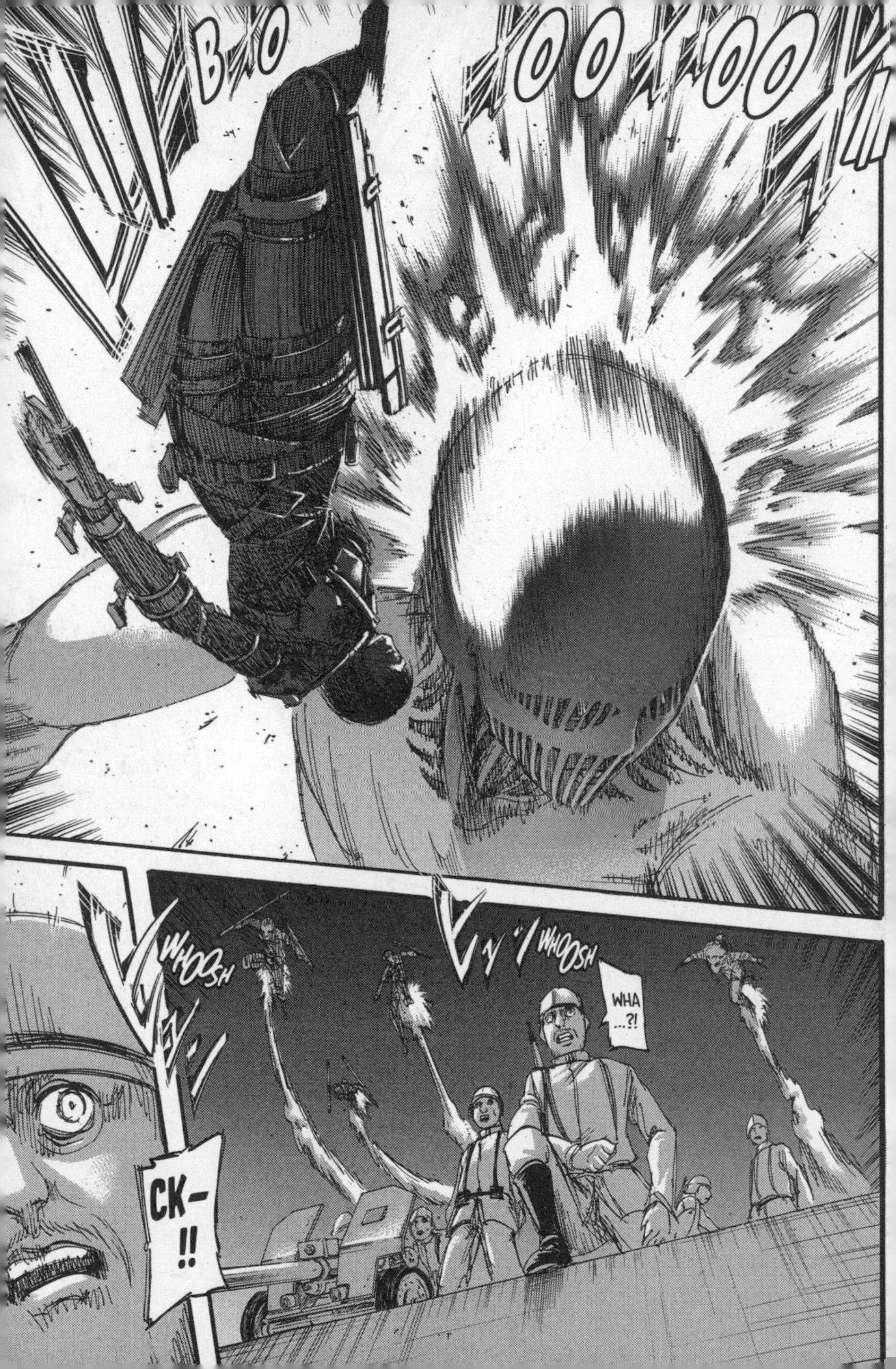
WHOOSH
WHA ...?!
WHOOSH
CK- !!

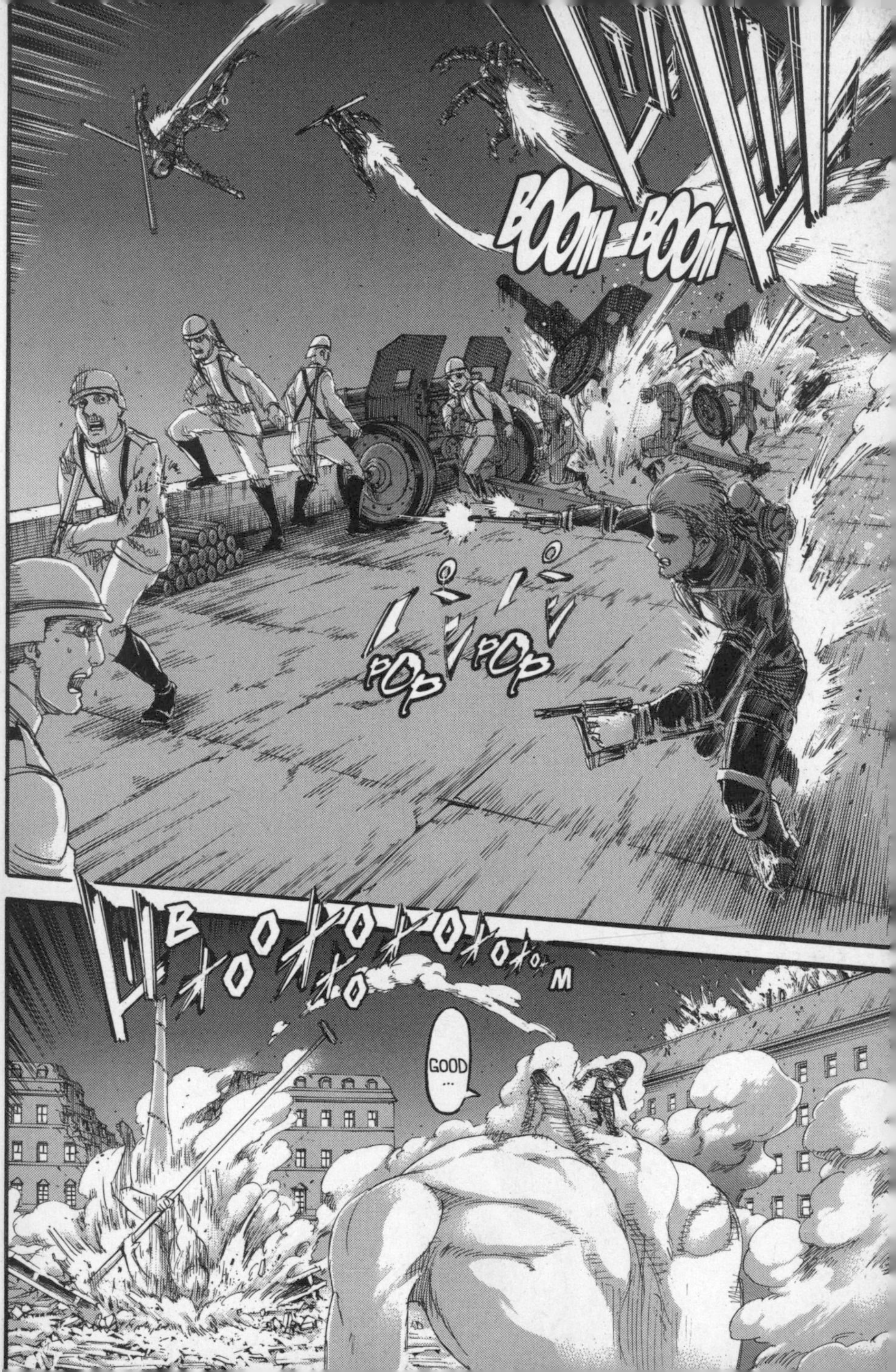
BOOM BOOM
POP POP
BOOOOOOOOOOM
GOOD ...

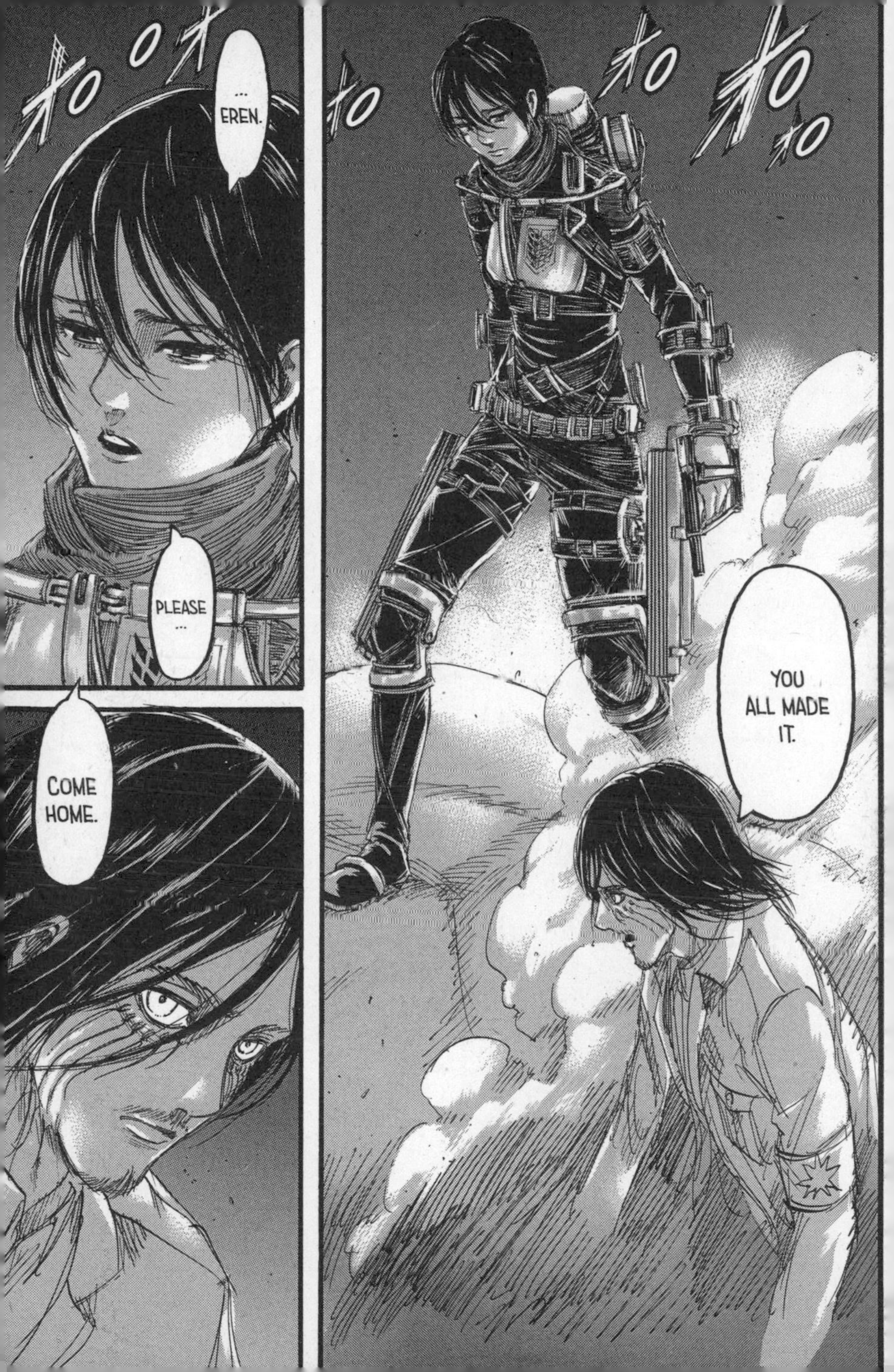
YOU ALL MADE IT.
... EREN.
PLEASE ...
COME HOME.

ATTACK on TITAN

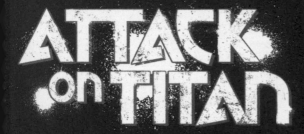

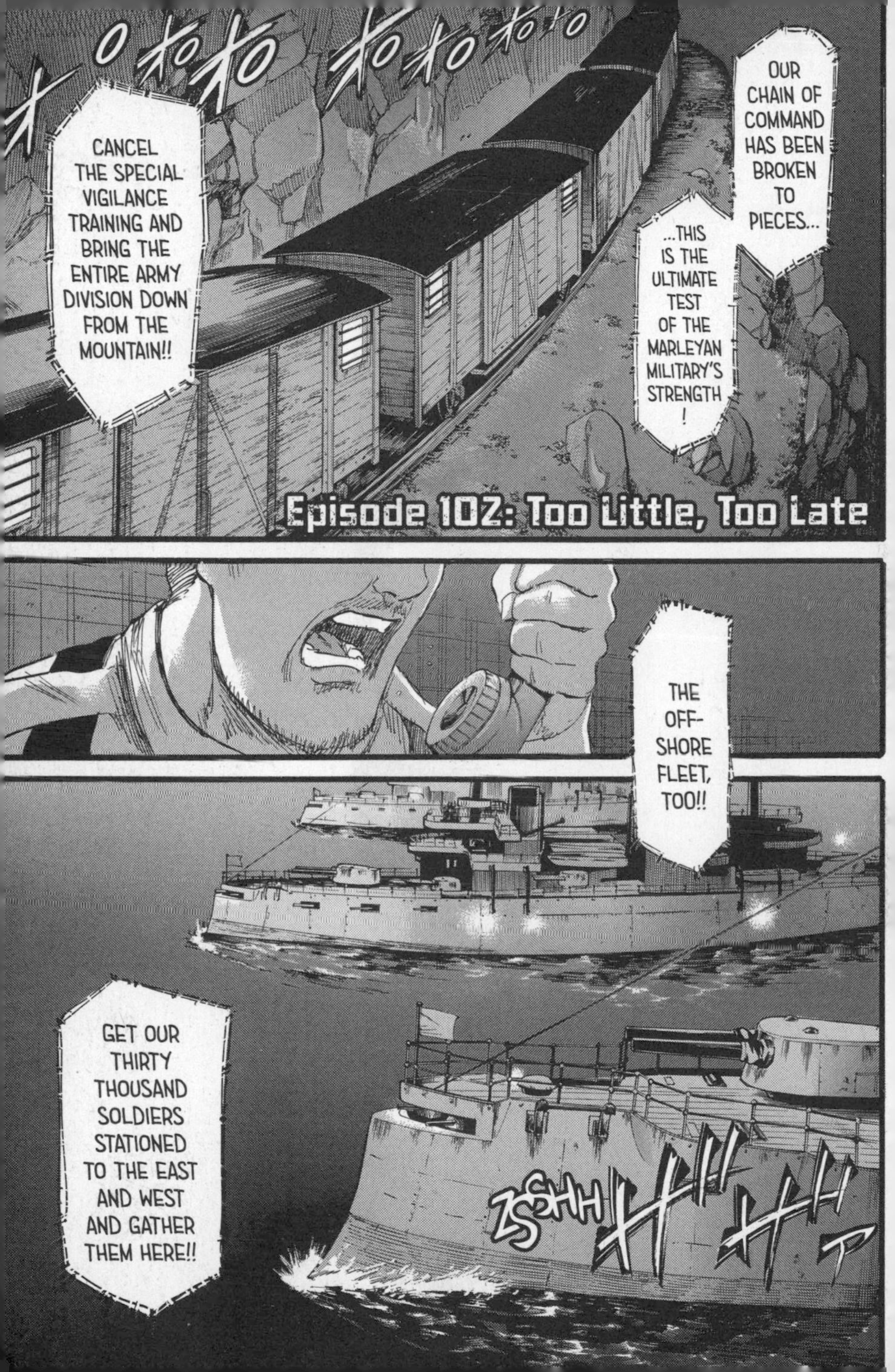
OUR CHAIN OF COMMAND HAS BEEN BROKEN TO PIECES...
...THIS IS THE ULTIMATE TEST OF THE MARLEYAN MILITARY'S STRENGTH!
CANCEL THE SPECIAL VIGILANCE TRAINING AND BRING THE ENTIRE ARMY DIVISION DOWN FROM THE MOUNTAIN!!
Episode 102: Too Little, Too Late
THE OFF-SHORE FLEET, TOO!!
GET OUR THIRTY THOUSAND SOLDIERS STATIONED TO THE EAST AND WEST AND GATHER THEM HERE!!

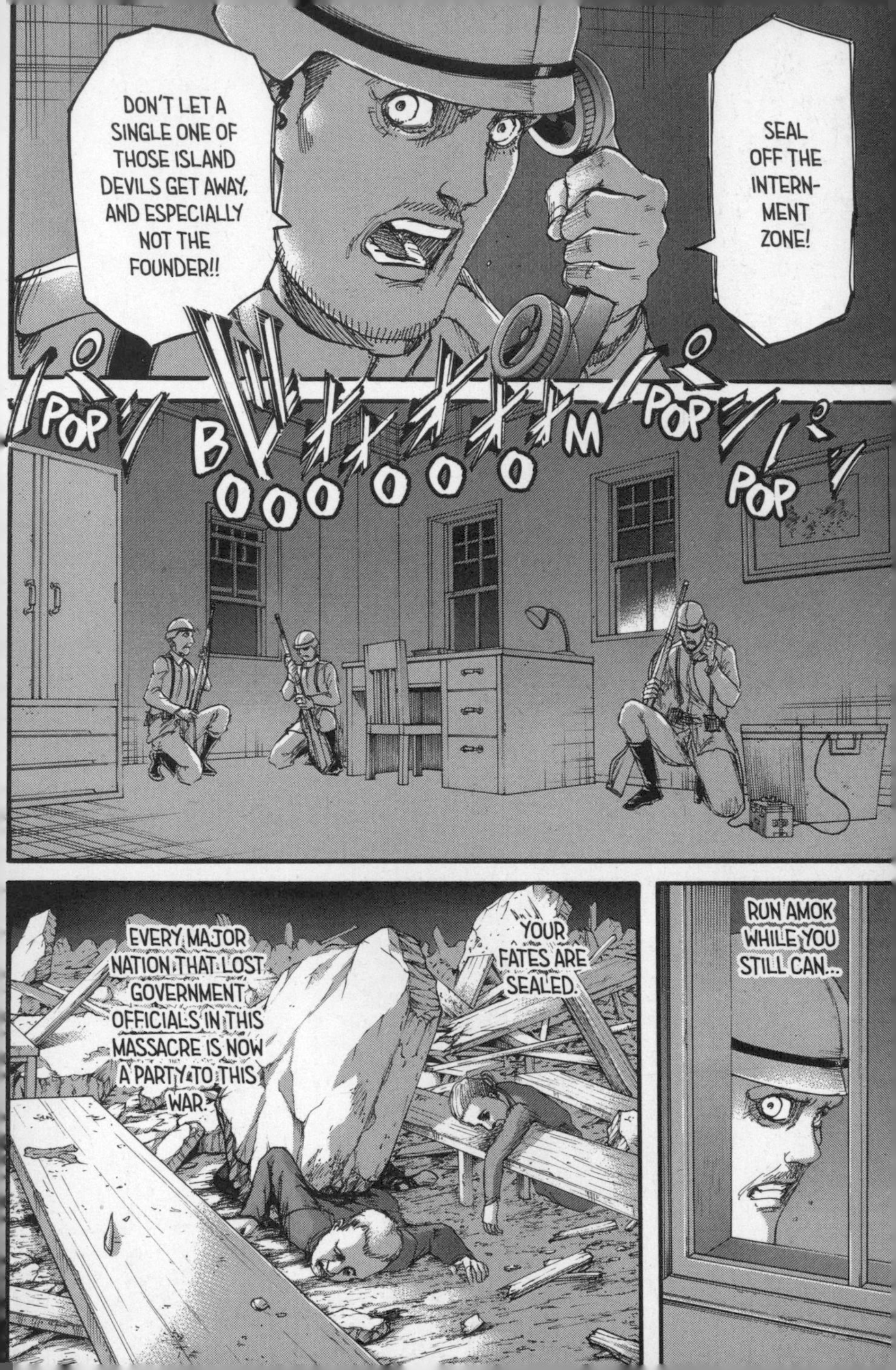

SEAL OFF THE INTERNMENT ZONE!
DON'T LET A SINGLE ONE OF THOSE ISLAND DEVILS GET AWAY, AND ESPECIALLY NOT THE FOUNDER!!
POP
POP
BOOOOOOM
POP
RUN AMOK WHILE YOU STILL CAN...
YOUR FATES ARE SEALED.
EVERY MAJOR NATION THAT LOST GOVERNMENT OFFICIALS IN THIS MASSACRE IS NOW A PARTY TO THIS WAR.

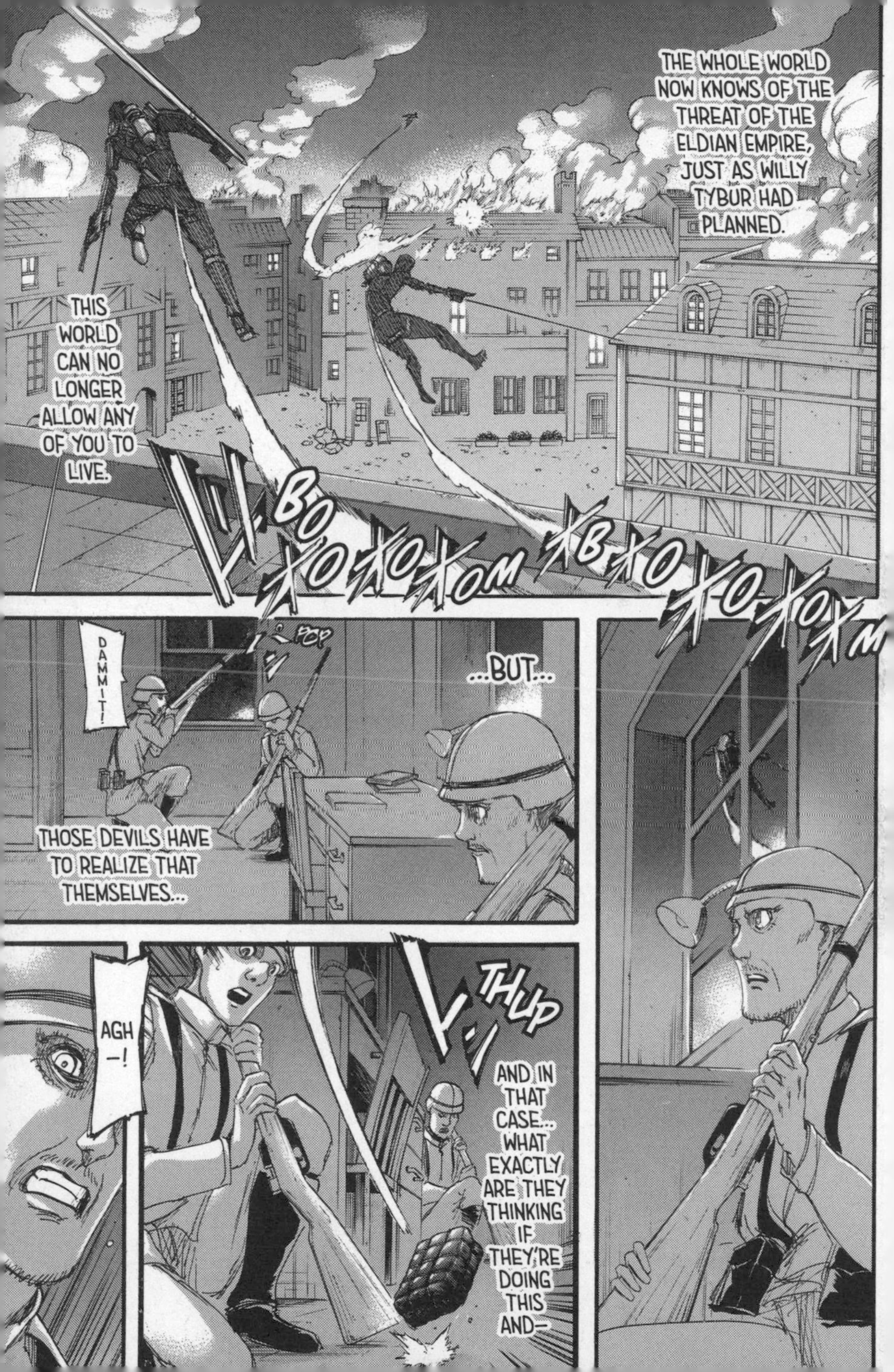
THE WHOLE WORLD NOW KNOWS OF THE THREAT OF THE ELDIAN EMPIRE, JUST AS WILLY TYBUR HAD PLANNED.
THIS WORLD CAN NO LONGER ALLOW ANY OF YOU TO LIVE.
BOOOOOM
BOOOOOM
...BUT...
DAMMIT!
POP
THOSE DEVILS HAVE TO REALIZE THAT THEMSELVES...
AND IN THAT CASE... WHAT EXACTLY ARE THEY THINKING IF THEY'RE DOING THIS AND—
THUP
AGH—!

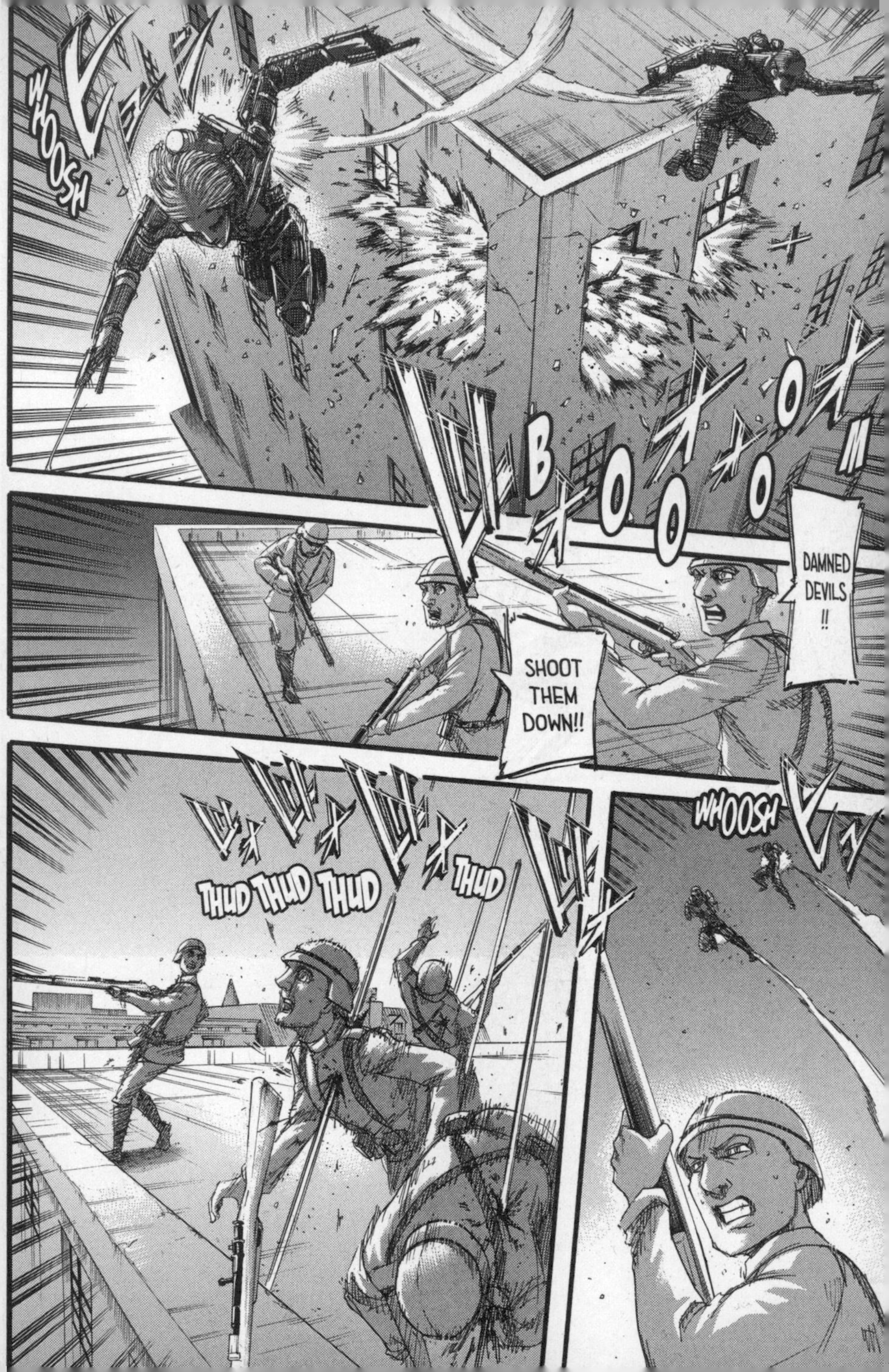

WHOOSH
BOOOOM
DAMNED DEVILS!!
SHOOT THEM DOWN!!
WHOOSH
THUD
THUD THUD THUD

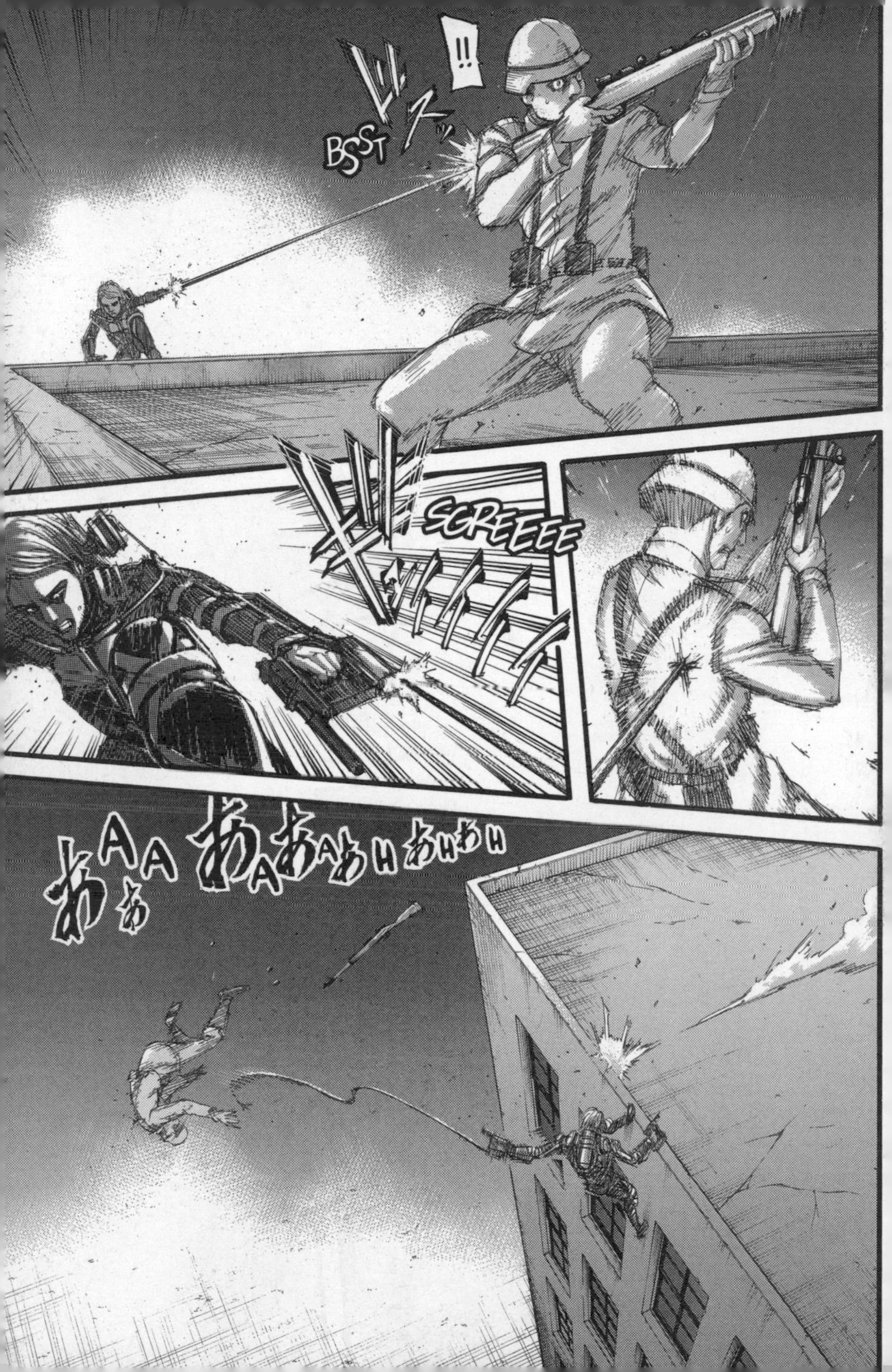
!!
BSST
SCREEEEE
AAAAHHH

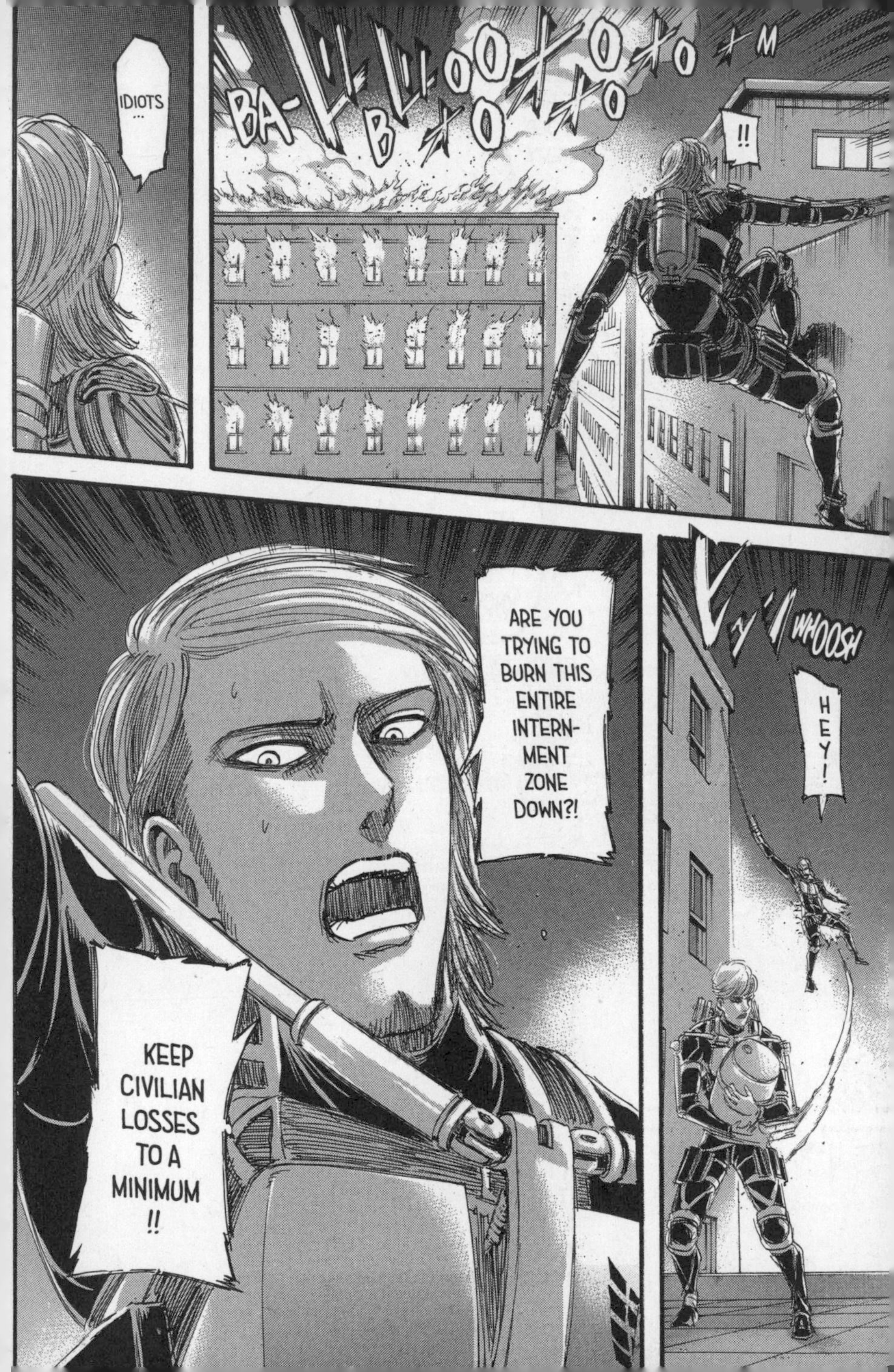
BA-BOOOOOM
!!
IDIOTS...
WHOOSH
HEY!
ARE YOU TRYING TO BURN THIS ENTIRE INTERNMENT ZONE DOWN?!
KEEP CIVILIAN LOSSES TO A MINIMUM!!

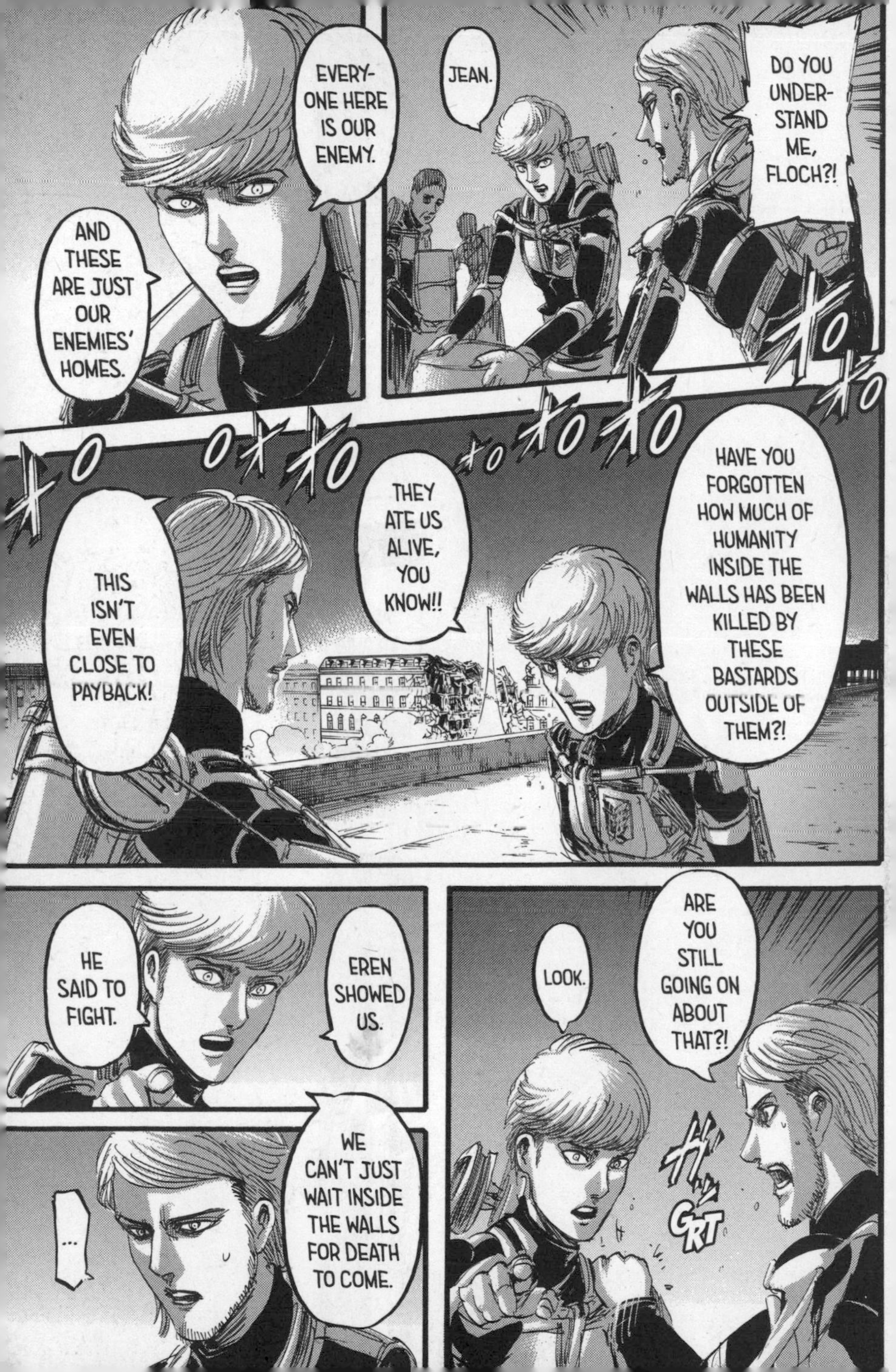
DO YOU UNDER-STAND ME, FLOCH?!
JEAN.
EVERY-ONE HERE IS OUR ENEMY.
AND THESE ARE JUST OUR ENEMIES' HOMES.
HAVE YOU FORGOTTEN HOW MUCH OF HUMANITY INSIDE THE WALLS HAS BEEN KILLED BY THESE BASTARDS OUTSIDE OF THEM?!
THEY ATE US ALIVE, YOU KNOW!!
THIS ISN'T EVEN CLOSE TO PAYBACK!
ARE YOU STILL GOING ON ABOUT THAT?!
LOOK.
GRT
EREN SHOWED US.
HE SAID TO FIGHT.
WE CAN'T JUST WAIT INSIDE THE WALLS FOR DEATH TO COME.
...

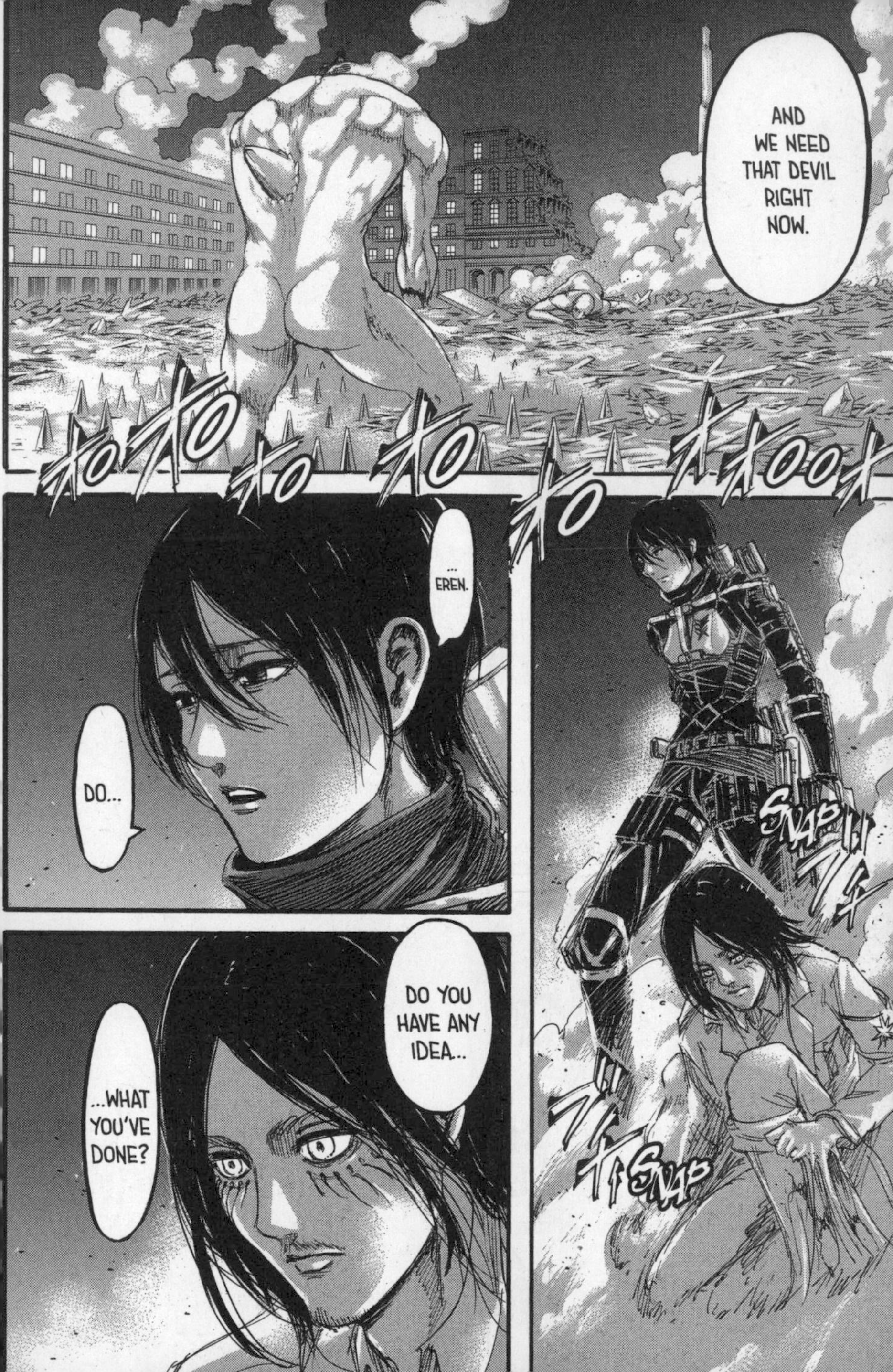
AND WE NEED THAT DEVIL RIGHT NOW.
SNAP
SNAP
...EREN.
DO...
DO YOU HAVE ANY IDEA...
...WHAT YOU'VE DONE?

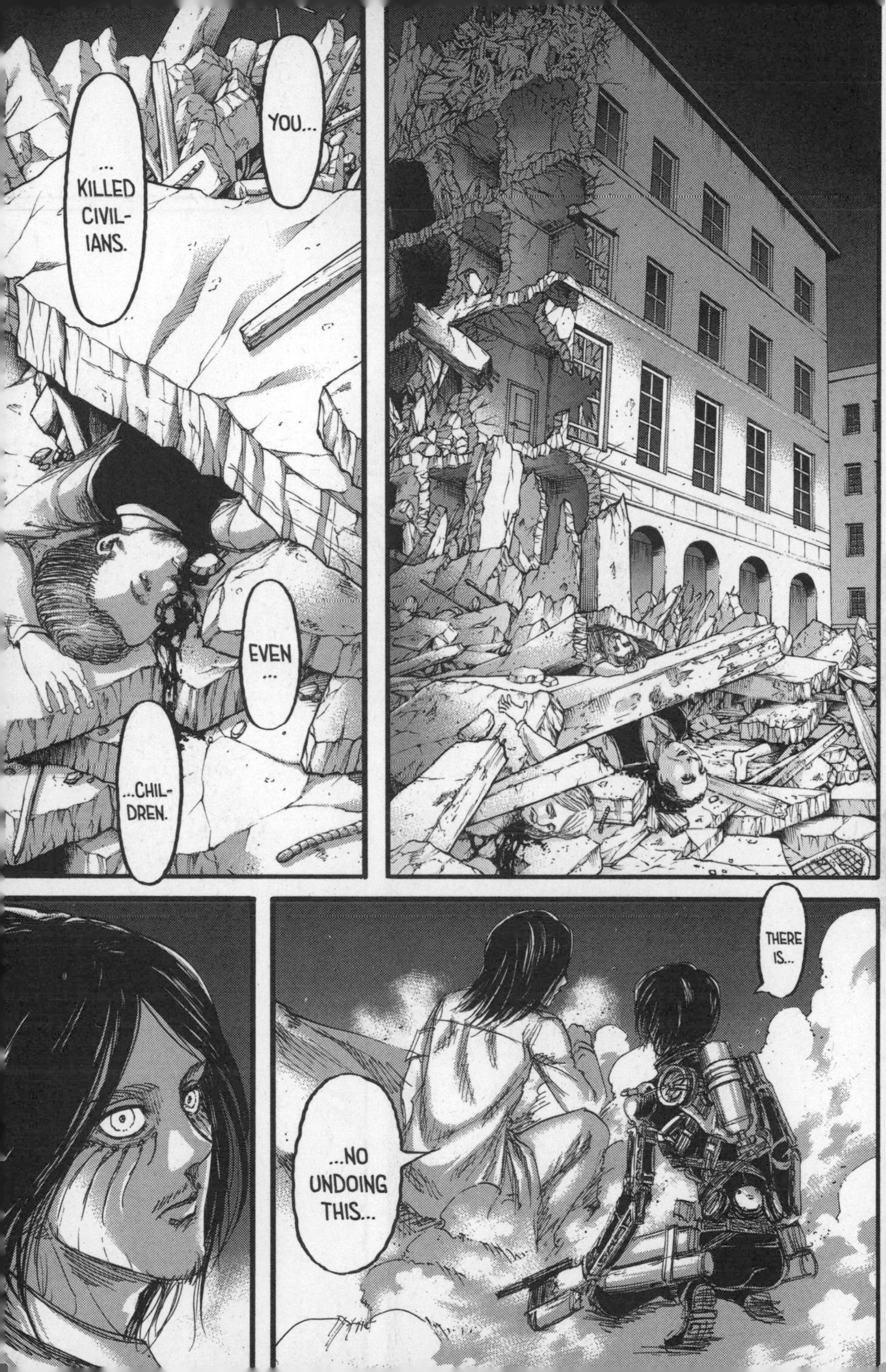
YOU...
...KILLED CIVIL-IANS.
EVEN...
...CHIL-DREN.
THERE IS...
...NO UNDOING THIS...

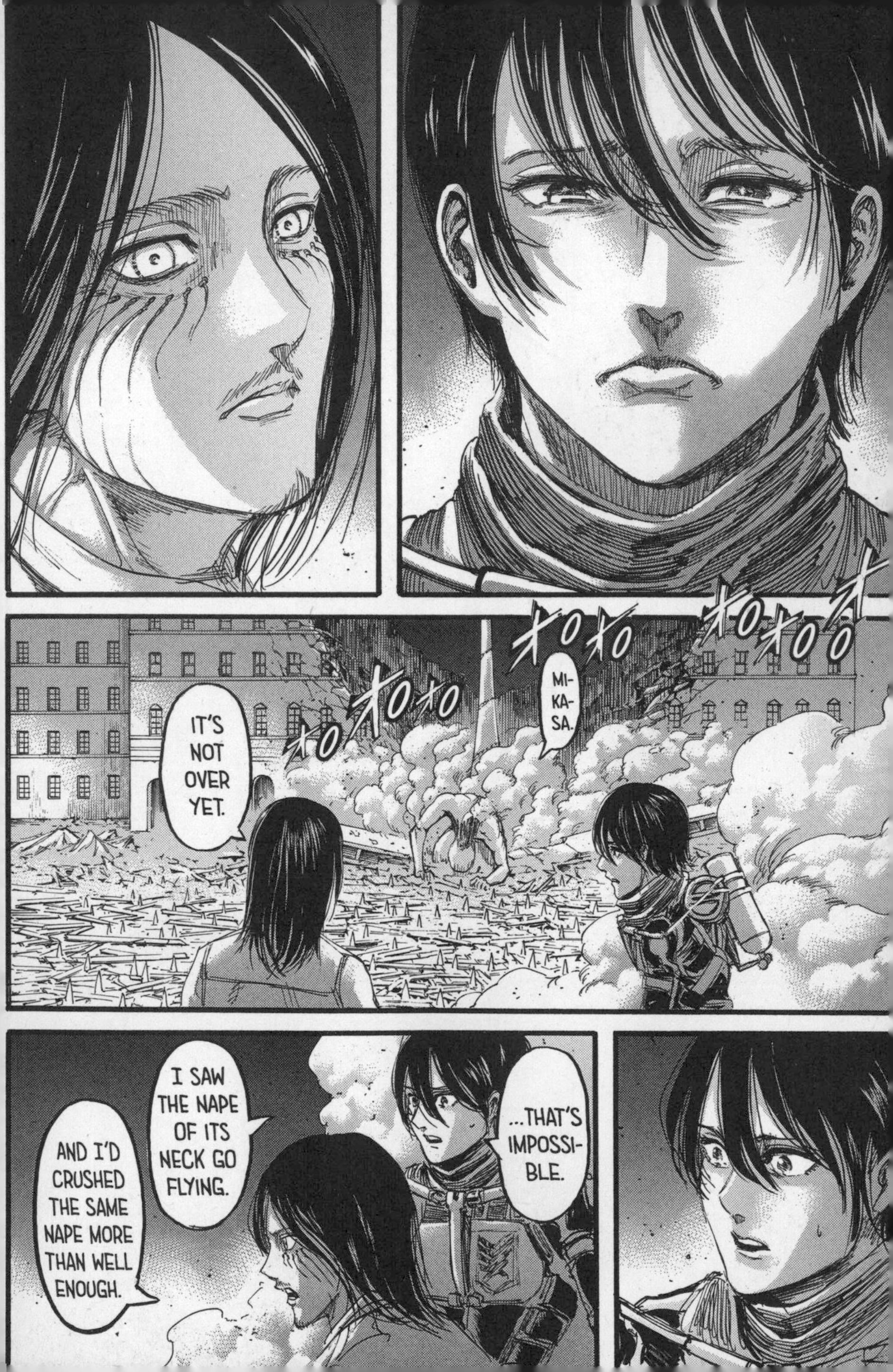
MI-KA-SA.
IT'S NOT OVER YET.
...THAT'S IMPOSSIBLE.
I SAW THE NAPE OF ITS NECK GO FLYING.
AND I'D CRUSHED THE SAME NAPE MORE THAN WELL ENOUGH.

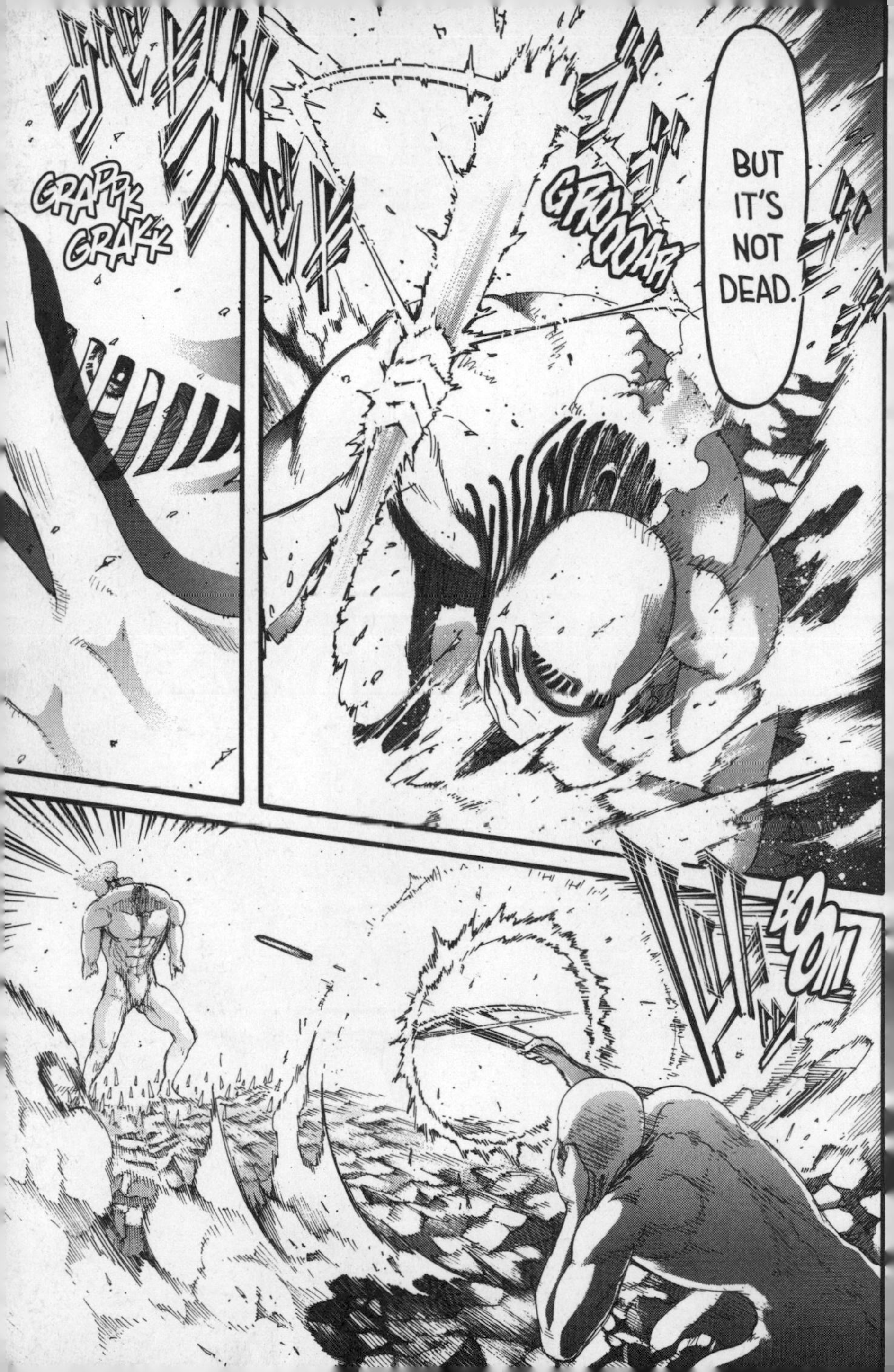
BUT IT'S NOT DEAD.
GROOOAR
GRAPPK
GRAKK
BOOM

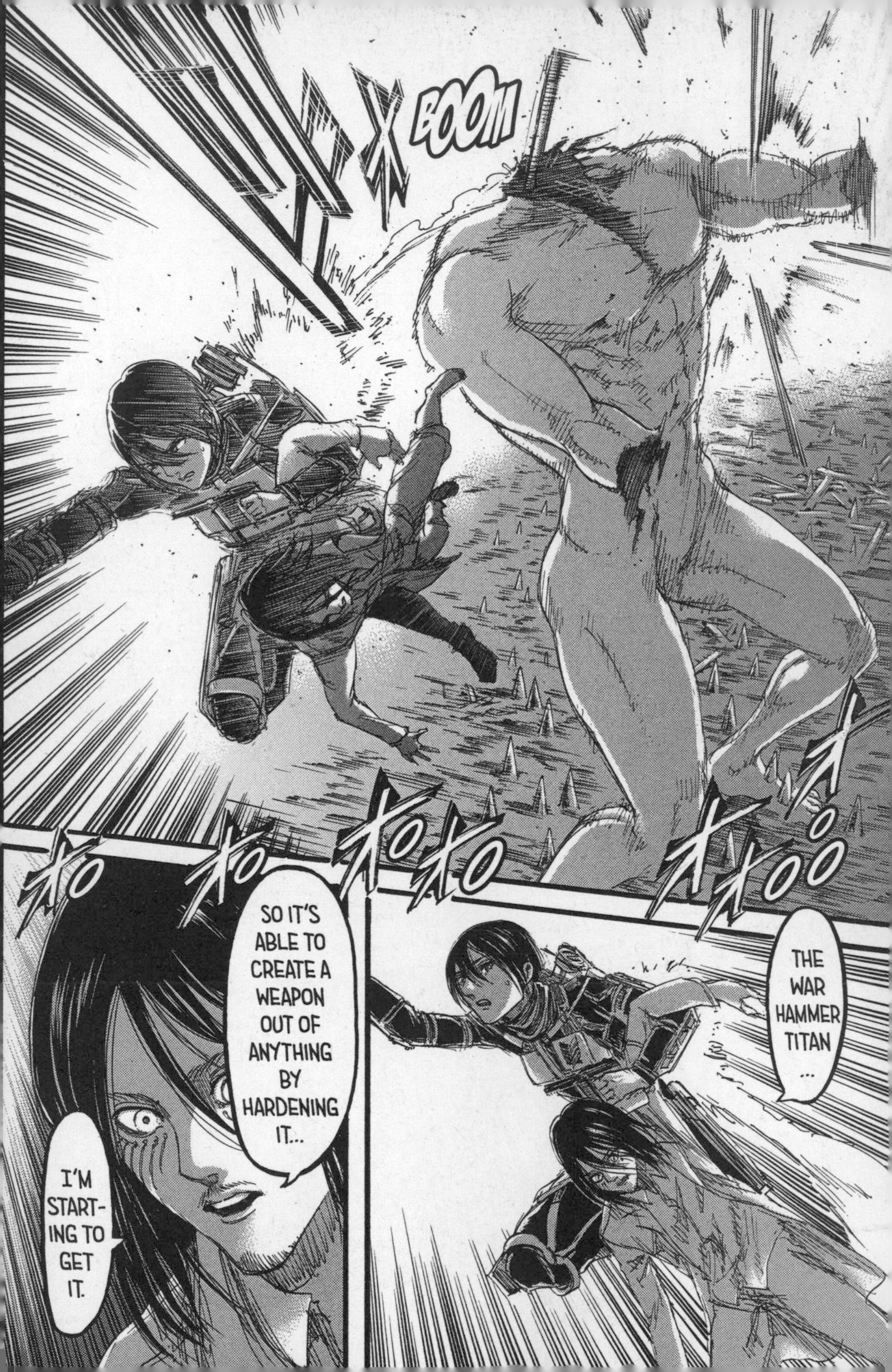
BOOM
THE WAR HAMMER TITAN ...
SO IT'S ABLE TO CREATE A WEAPON OUT OF ANYTHING BY HARDENING IT...
I'M START-ING TO GET IT.

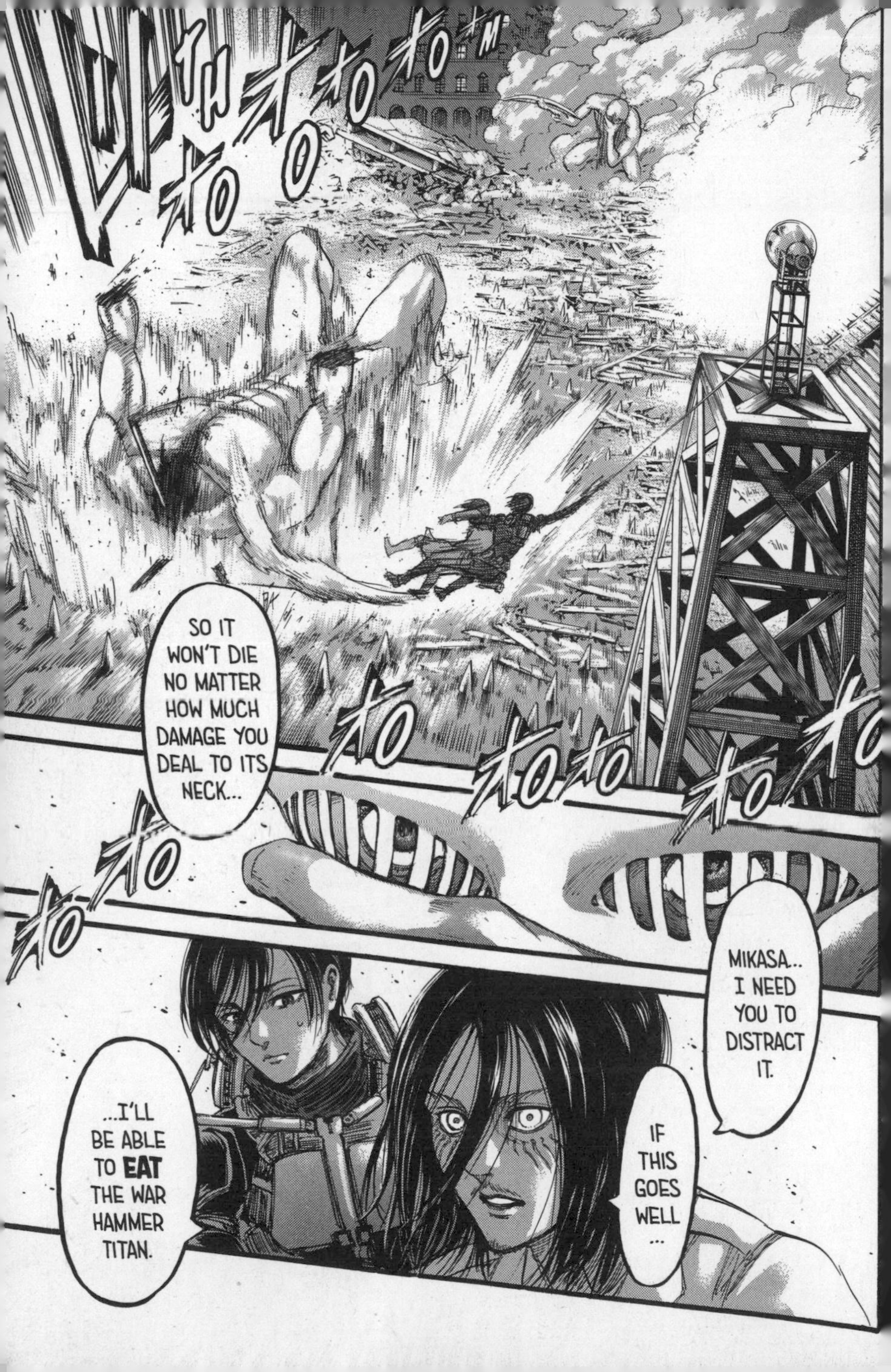
SO IT WON'T DIE NO MATTER HOW MUCH DAMAGE YOU DEAL TO ITS NECK...
MIKASA... I NEED YOU TO DISTRACT IT.
IF THIS GOES WELL...
...I'LL BE ABLE TO **EAT** THE WAR HAMMER TITAN.

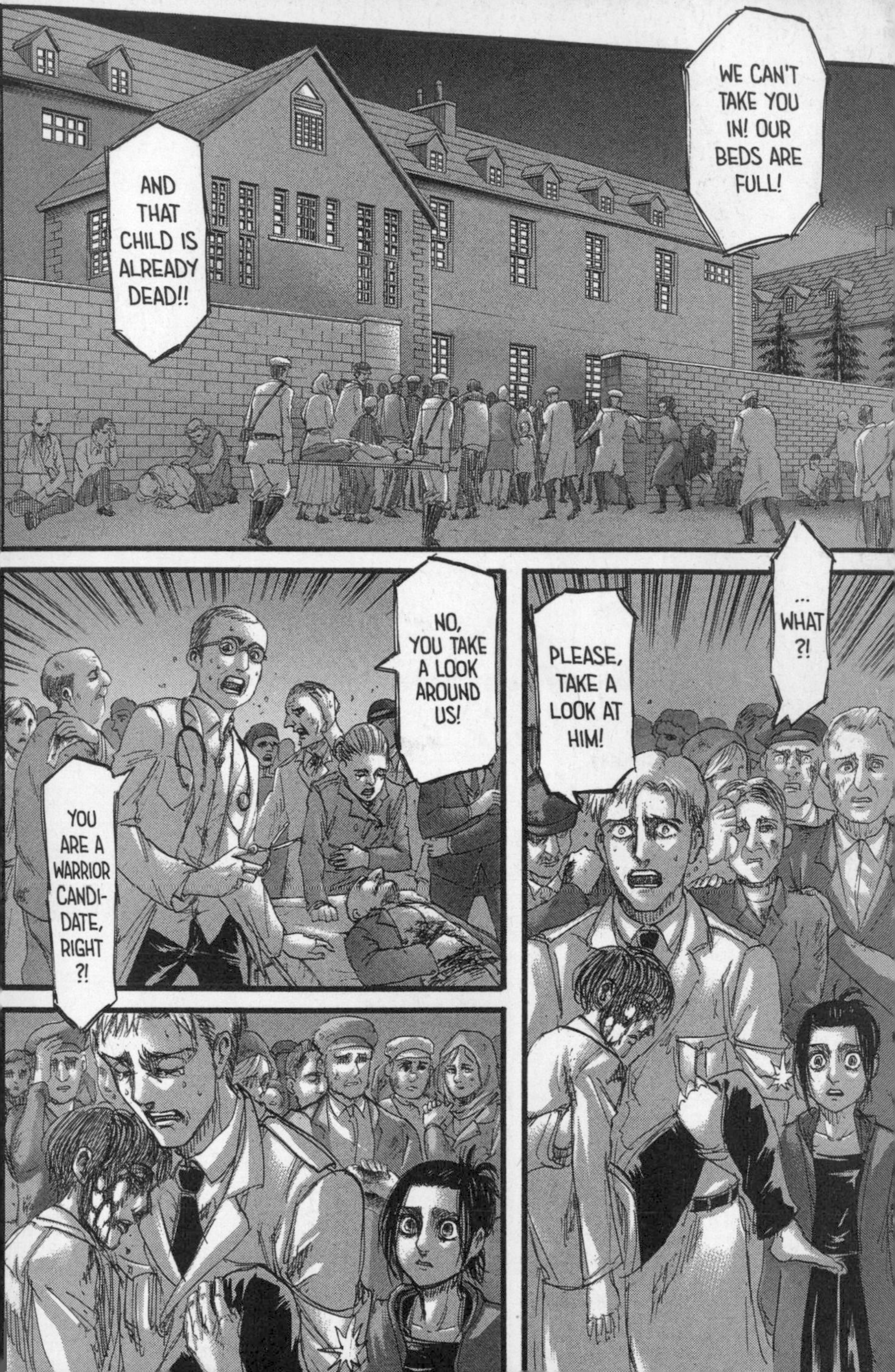
WE CAN'T TAKE YOU IN! OUR BEDS ARE FULL!
AND THAT CHILD IS ALREADY DEAD!!
... WHAT ?!
PLEASE, TAKE A LOOK AT HIM!
NO, YOU TAKE A LOOK AROUND US!
YOU ARE A WARRIOR CANDI-DATE, RIGHT ?!

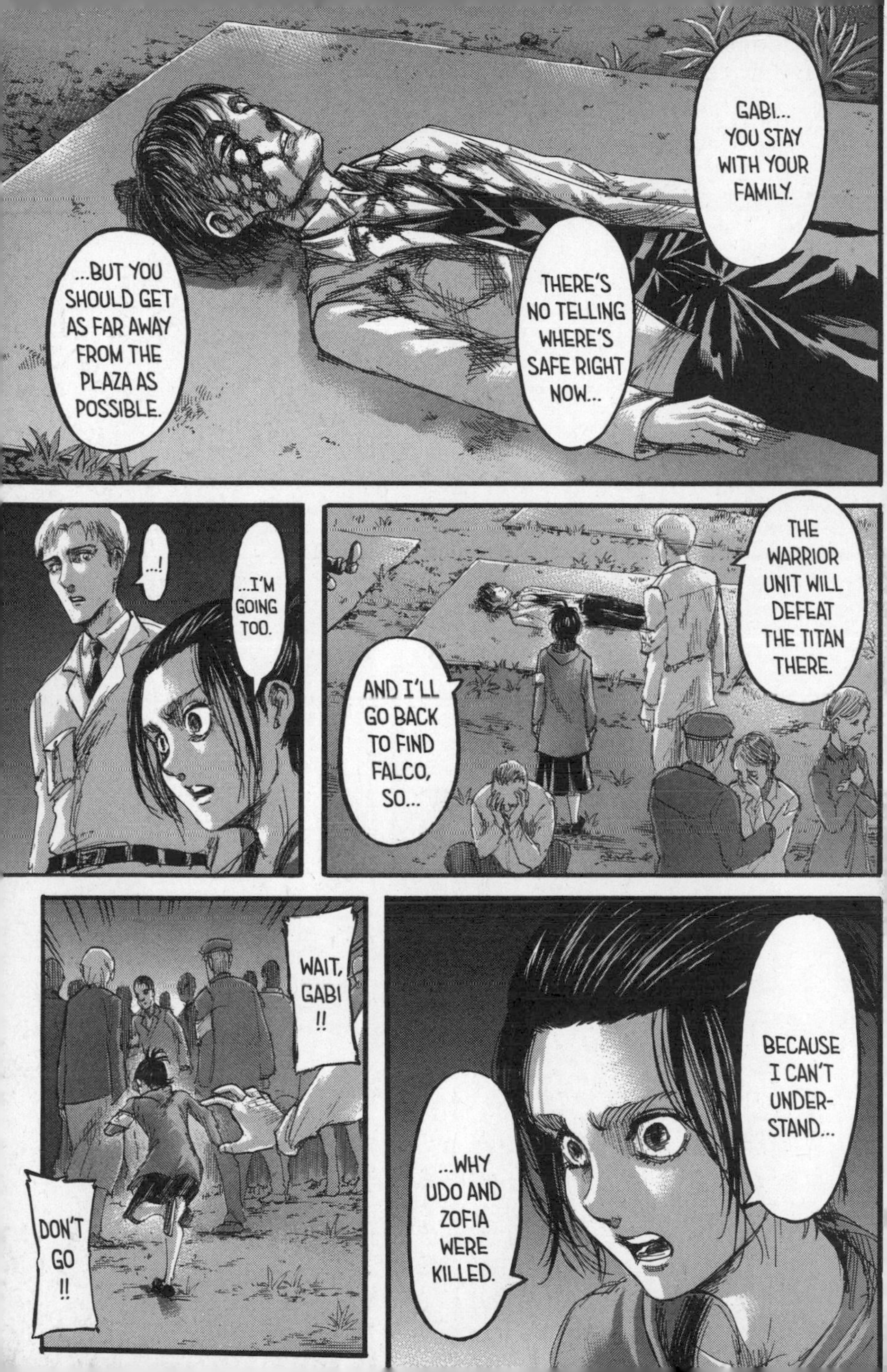
GABI... YOU STAY WITH YOUR FAMILY.
THERE'S NO TELLING WHERE'S SAFE RIGHT NOW...
...BUT YOU SHOULD GET AS FAR AWAY FROM THE PLAZA AS POSSIBLE.
THE WARRIOR UNIT WILL DEFEAT THE TITAN THERE.
AND I'LL GO BACK TO FIND FALCO, SO...
...I'M GOING TOO.
...!
BECAUSE I CAN'T UNDER-STAND...
...WHY UDO AND ZOFIA WERE KILLED.
WAIT, GABI !!
DON'T GO !!

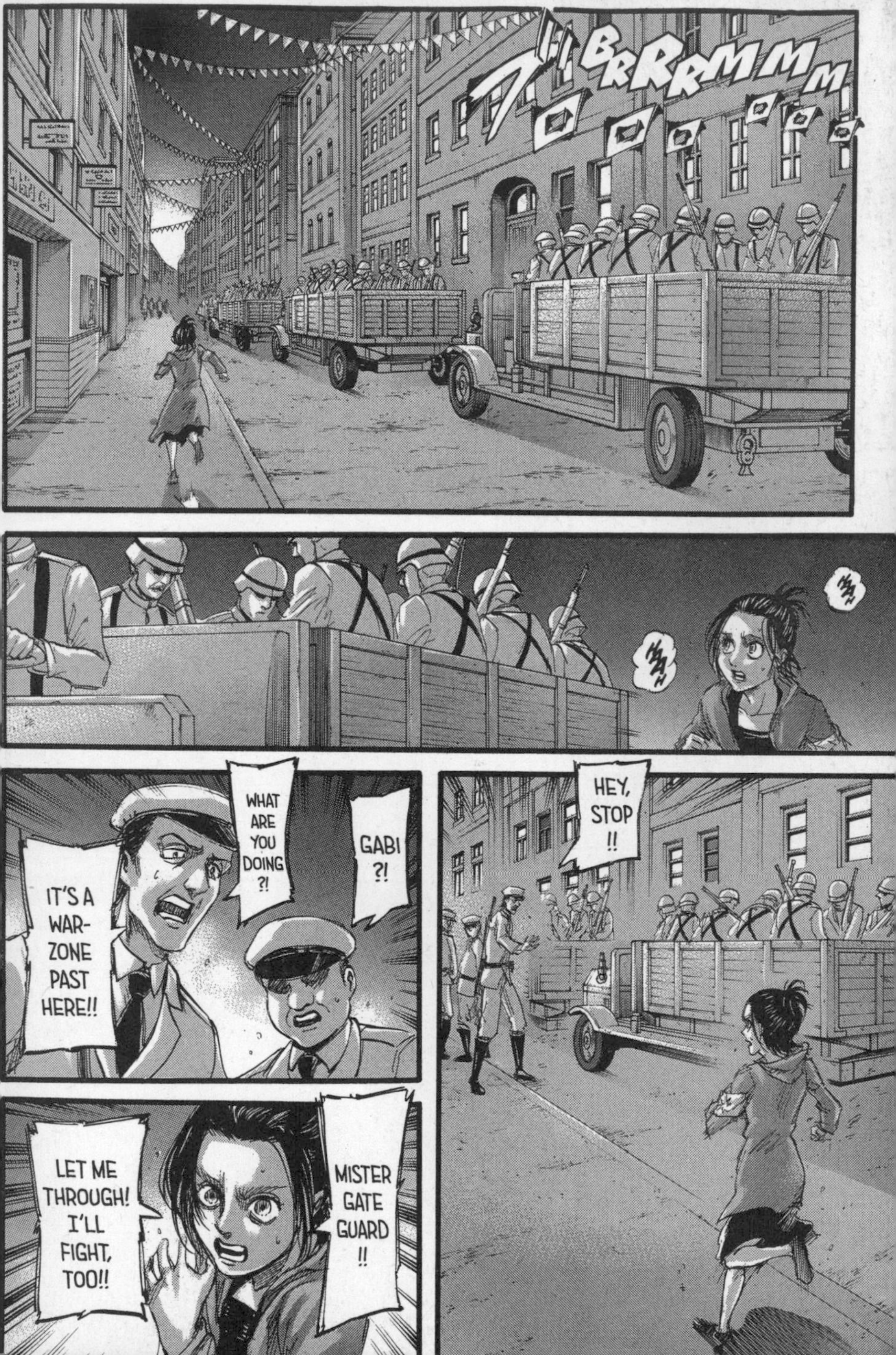
BRRRMMMM
HEY, STOP !!
GABI ?!
WHAT ARE YOU DOING ?!
IT'S A WAR-ZONE PAST HERE!!
MISTER GATE GUARD !!
LET ME THROUGH! I'LL FIGHT, TOO!!

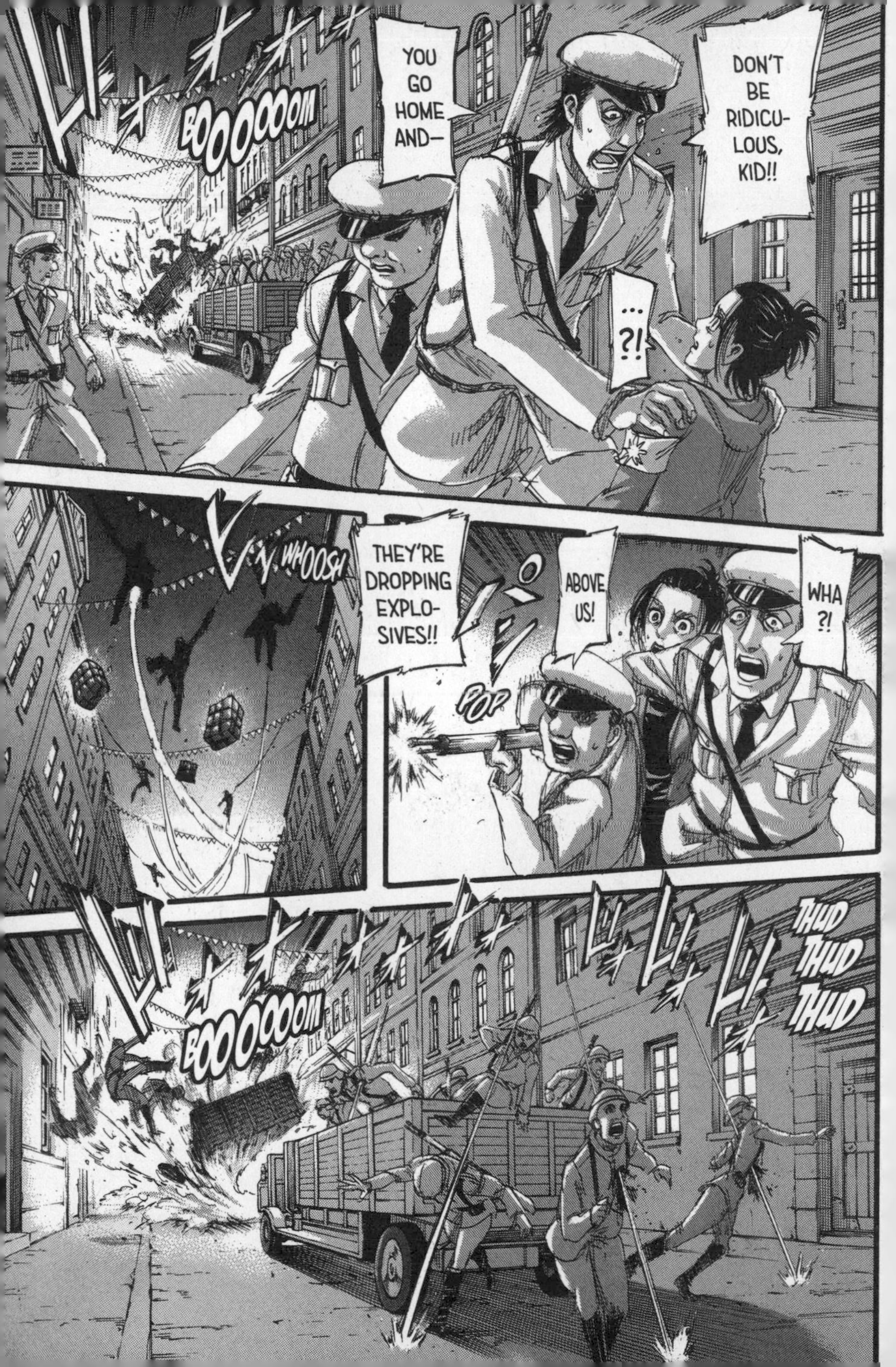

DON'T BE RIDICULOUS, KID!!
YOU GO HOME AND—
...?!
BOOOOOOM
WHA?!
ABOVE US!
THEY'RE DROPPING EXPLOSIVES!!
POP
WHOOSH
THUD THUD THUD
BOOOOOOM

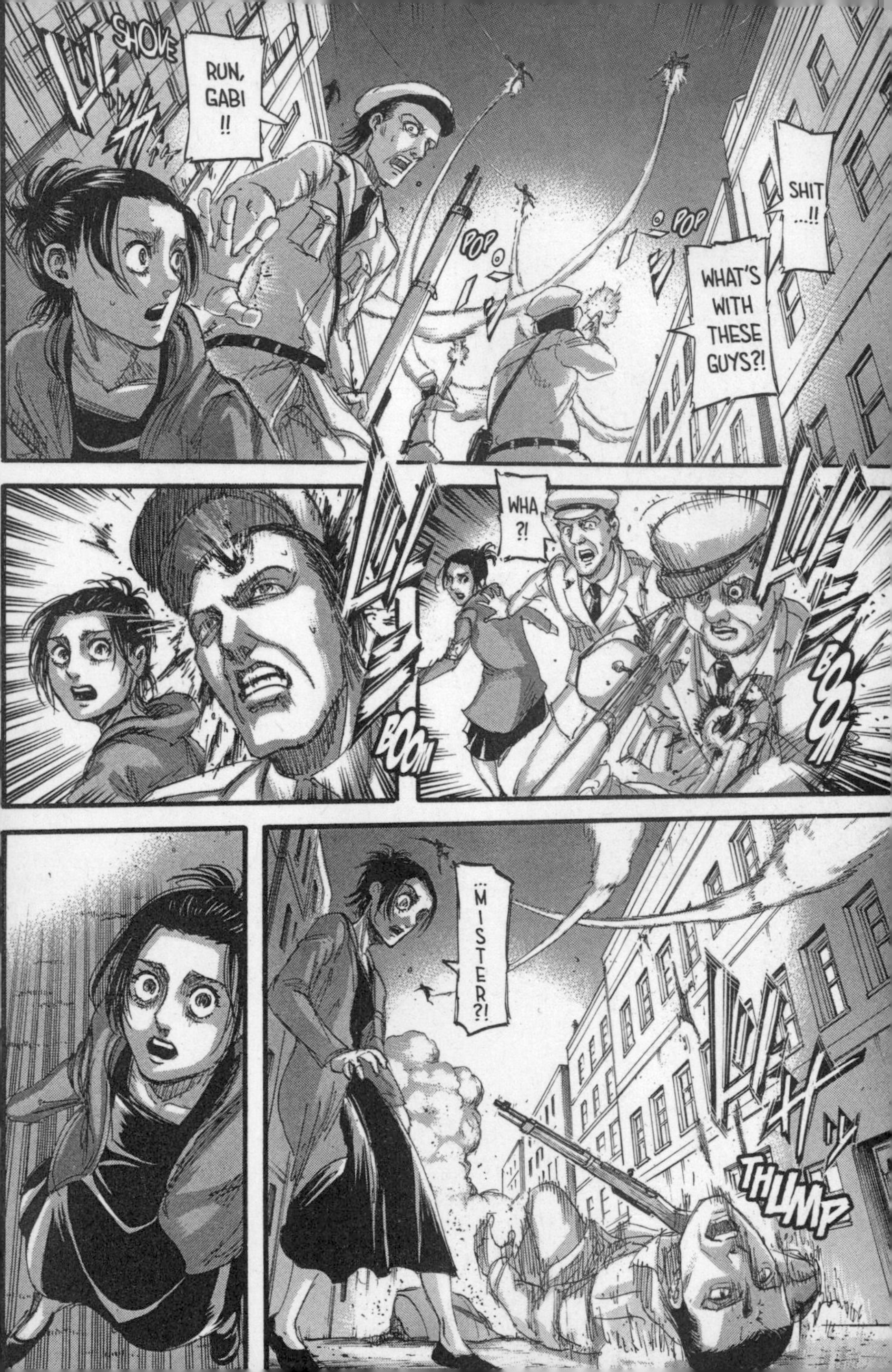
SHIT ...!!
POP
WHAT'S WITH THESE GUYS?!
POP
RUN, GABI !!
SHOVE
WHA ?!
BOOM
BOOM
...MISTER?!
THUMP

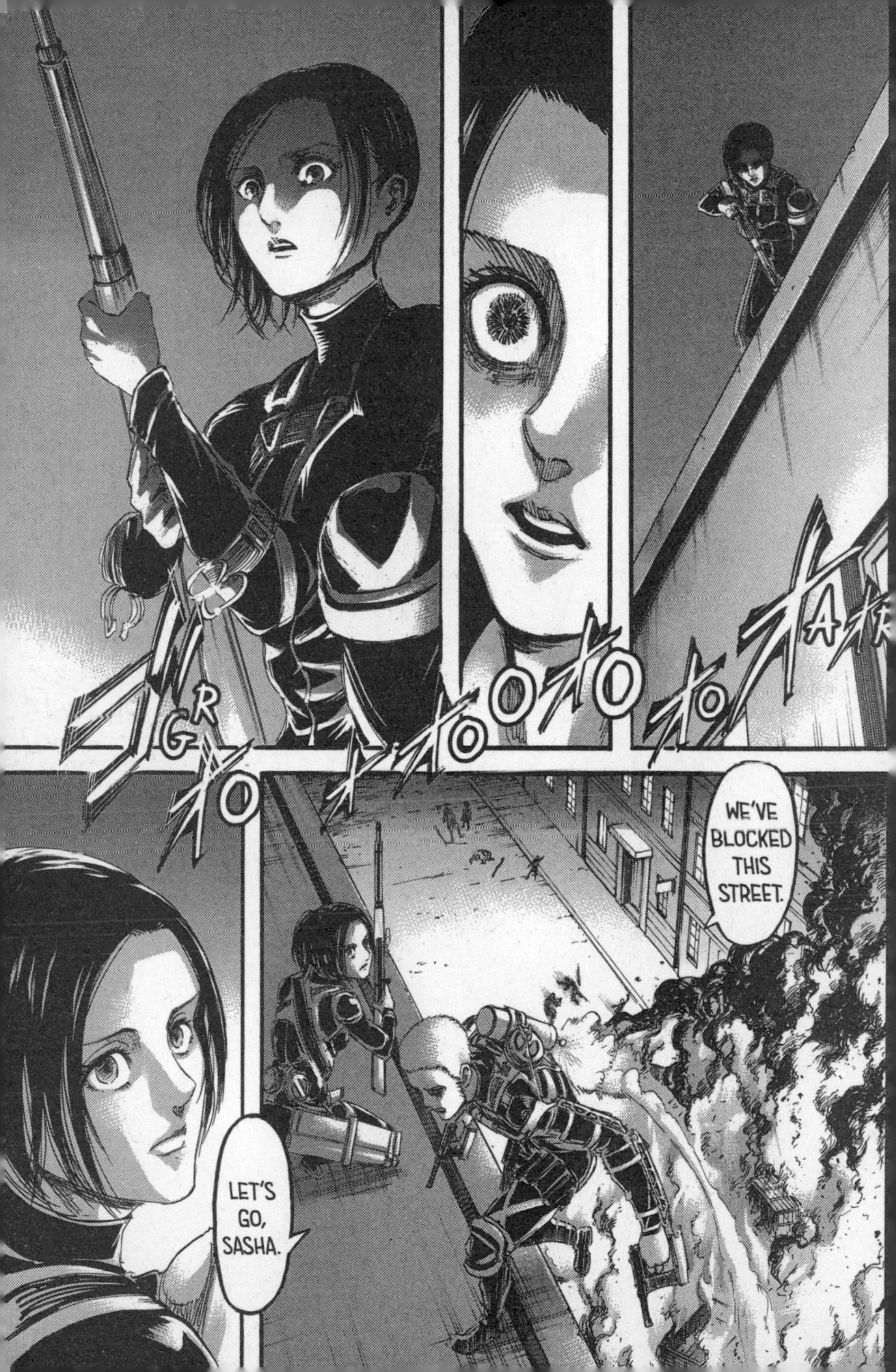
WE'VE BLOCKED THIS STREET.
LET'S GO, SASHA.

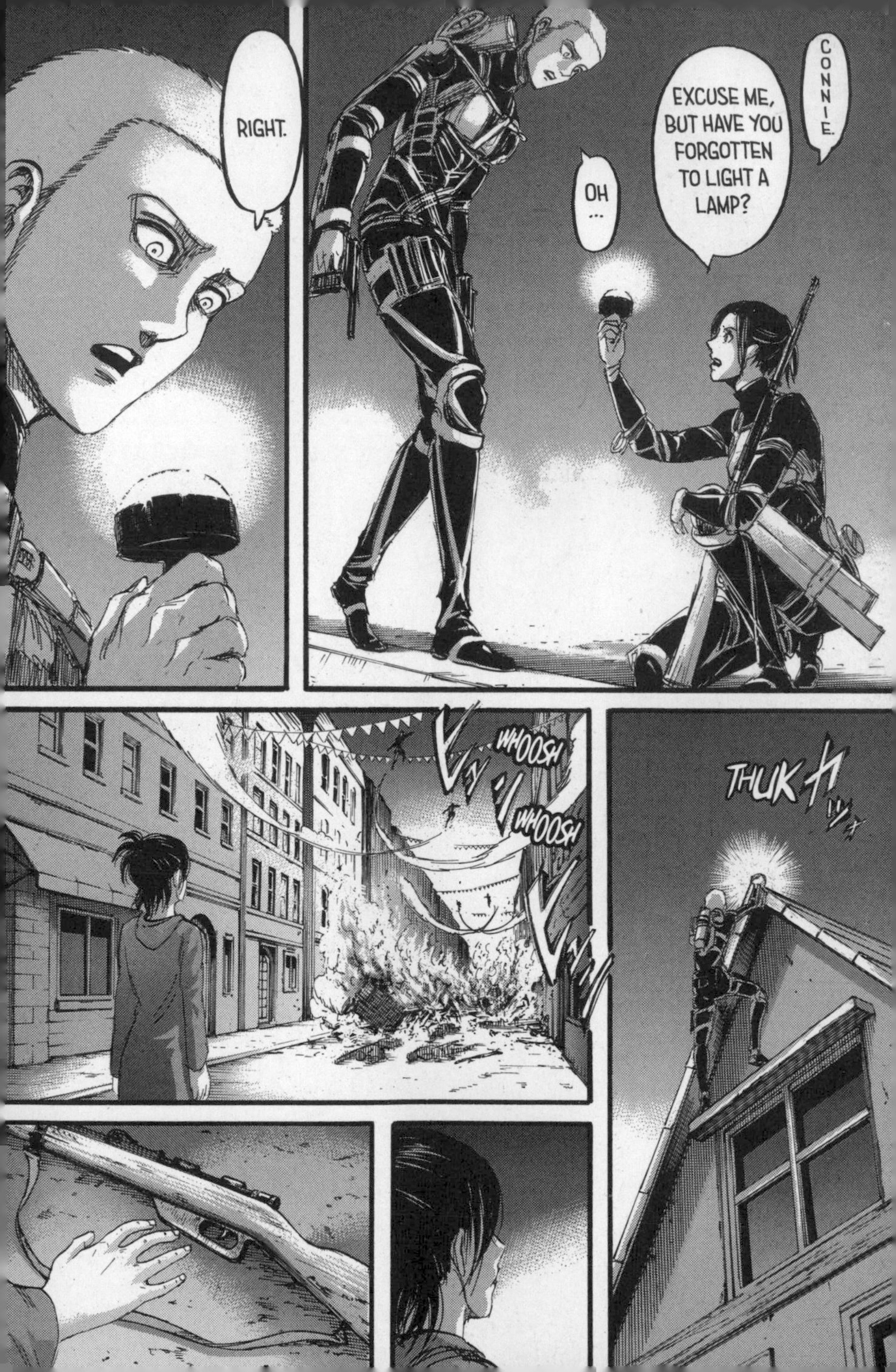
CONNIE.
EXCUSE ME, BUT HAVE YOU FORGOTTEN TO LIGHT A LAMP?
OH ...
RIGHT.
THUK
カッ
WHOOSH
WHOOSH

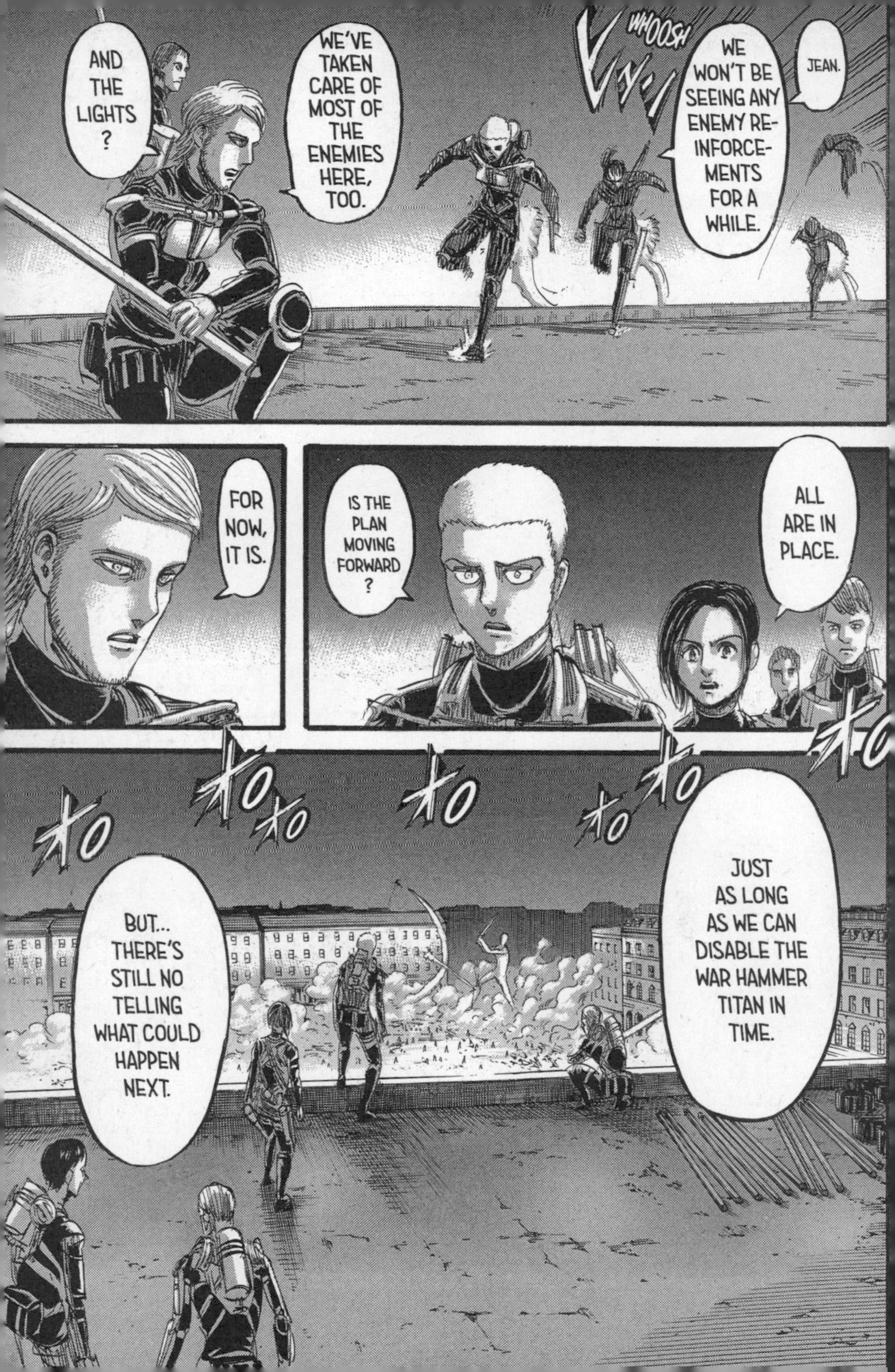
WHOOSH
JEAN.
WE WON'T BE SEEING ANY ENEMY RE-INFORCEMENTS FOR A WHILE.
WE'VE TAKEN CARE OF MOST OF THE ENEMIES HERE, TOO.
AND THE LIGHTS?
ALL ARE IN PLACE.
IS THE PLAN MOVING FORWARD?
FOR NOW, IT IS.
JUST AS LONG AS WE CAN DISABLE THE WAR HAMMER TITAN IN TIME.
BUT... THERE'S STILL NO TELLING WHAT COULD HAPPEN NEXT.

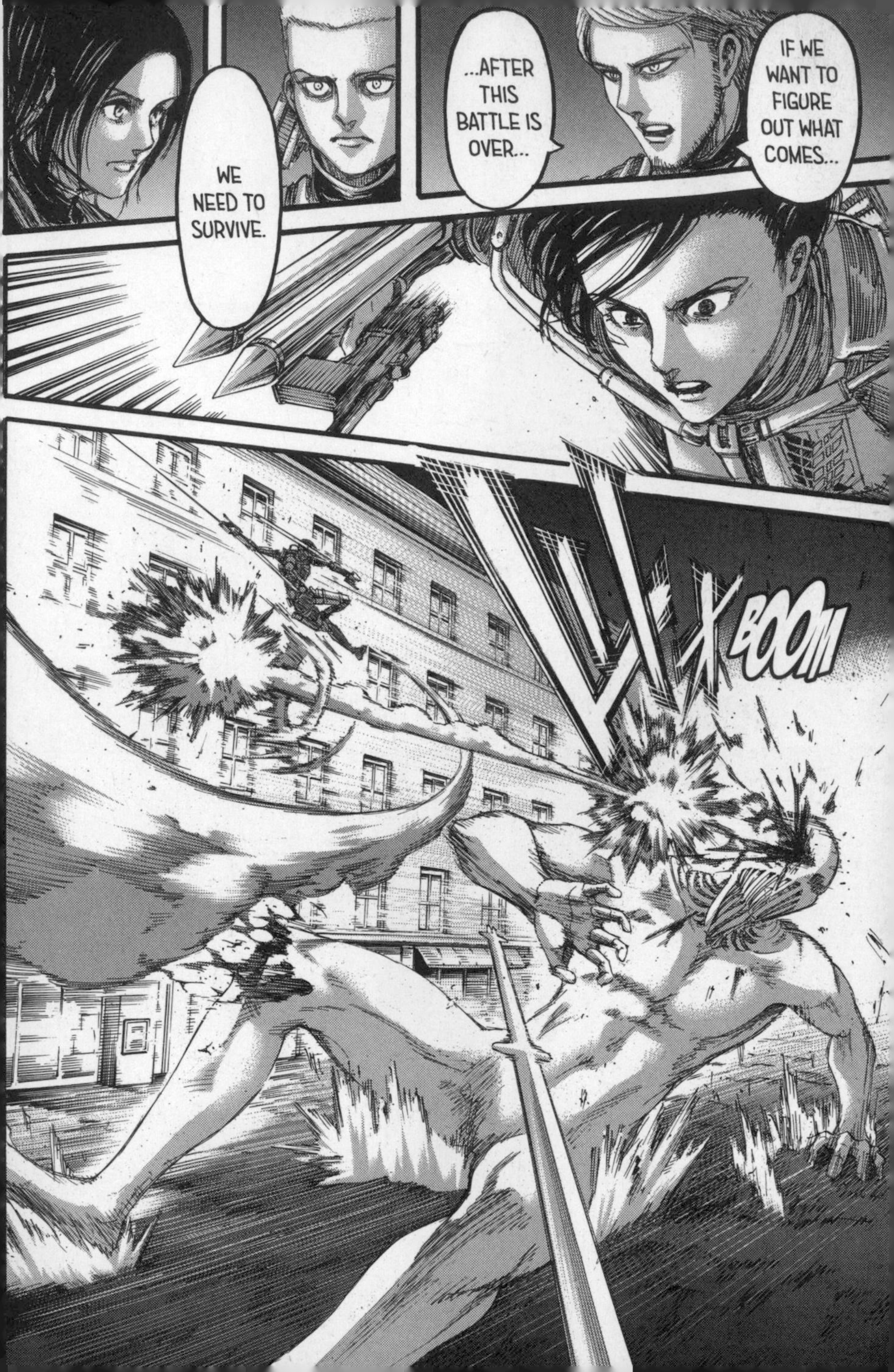
IF WE WANT TO FIGURE OUT WHAT COMES...
...AFTER THIS BATTLE IS OVER...
WE NEED TO SURVIVE.
BOOM

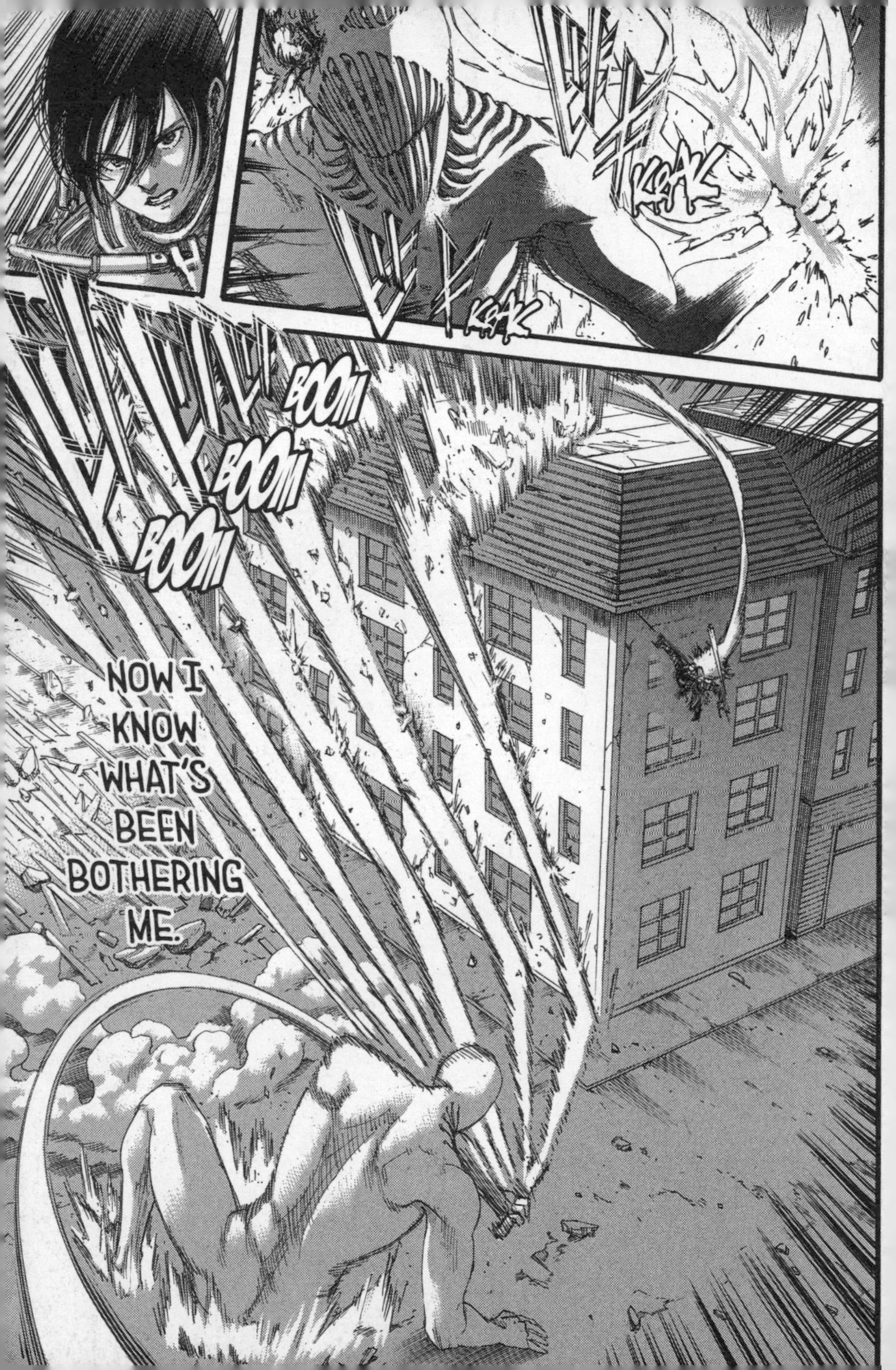
KRAK
KRAK
BOOM
BOOM
BOOM
NOW I KNOW WHAT'S BEEN BOTHERING ME.

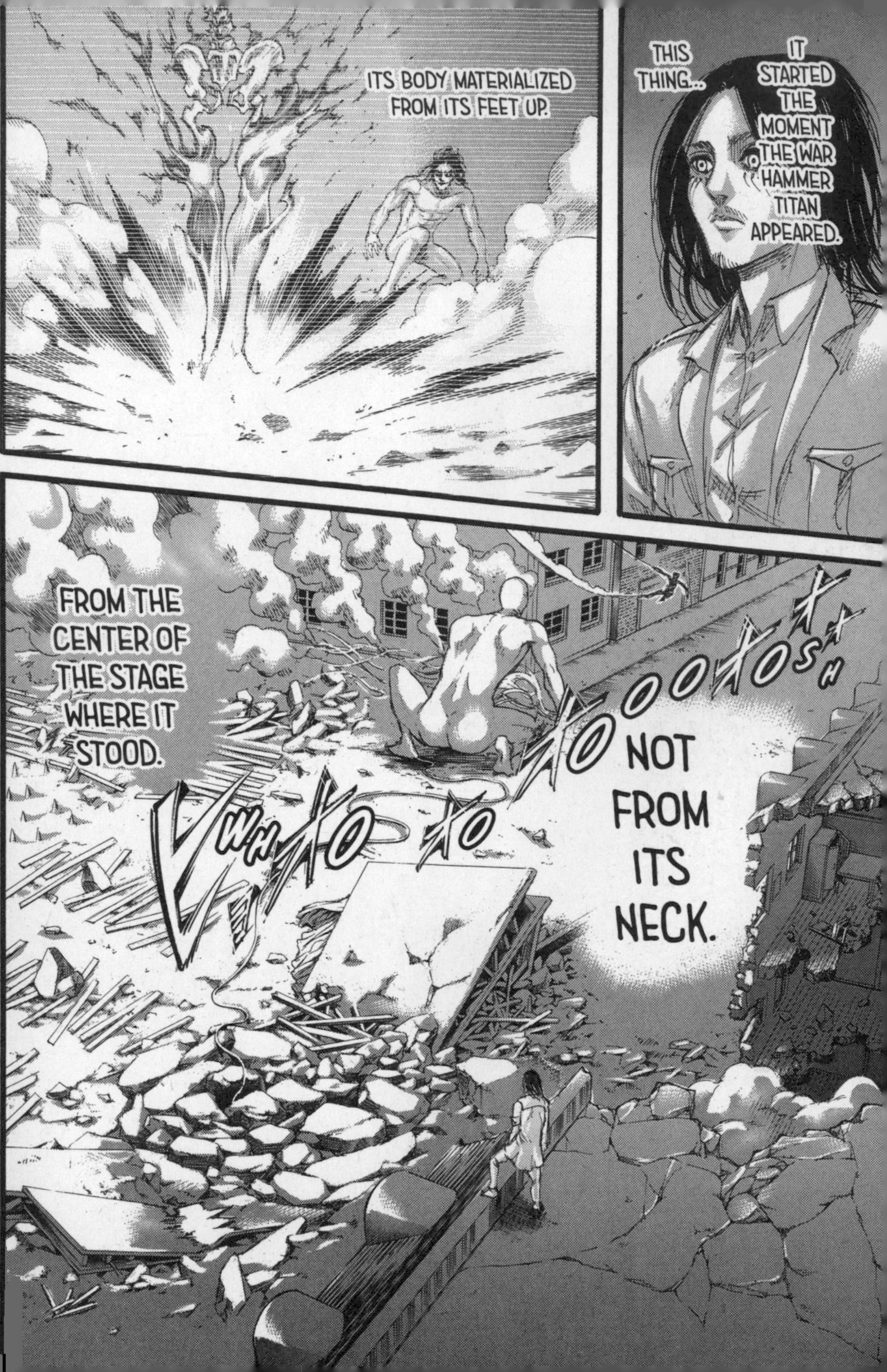
IT STARTED THE MOMENT THE WAR HAMMER TITAN APPEARED.
THIS THING...
ITS BODY MATERIALIZED FROM ITS FEET UP.
NOT FROM ITS NECK.
FROM THE CENTER OF THE STAGE WHERE IT STOOD.

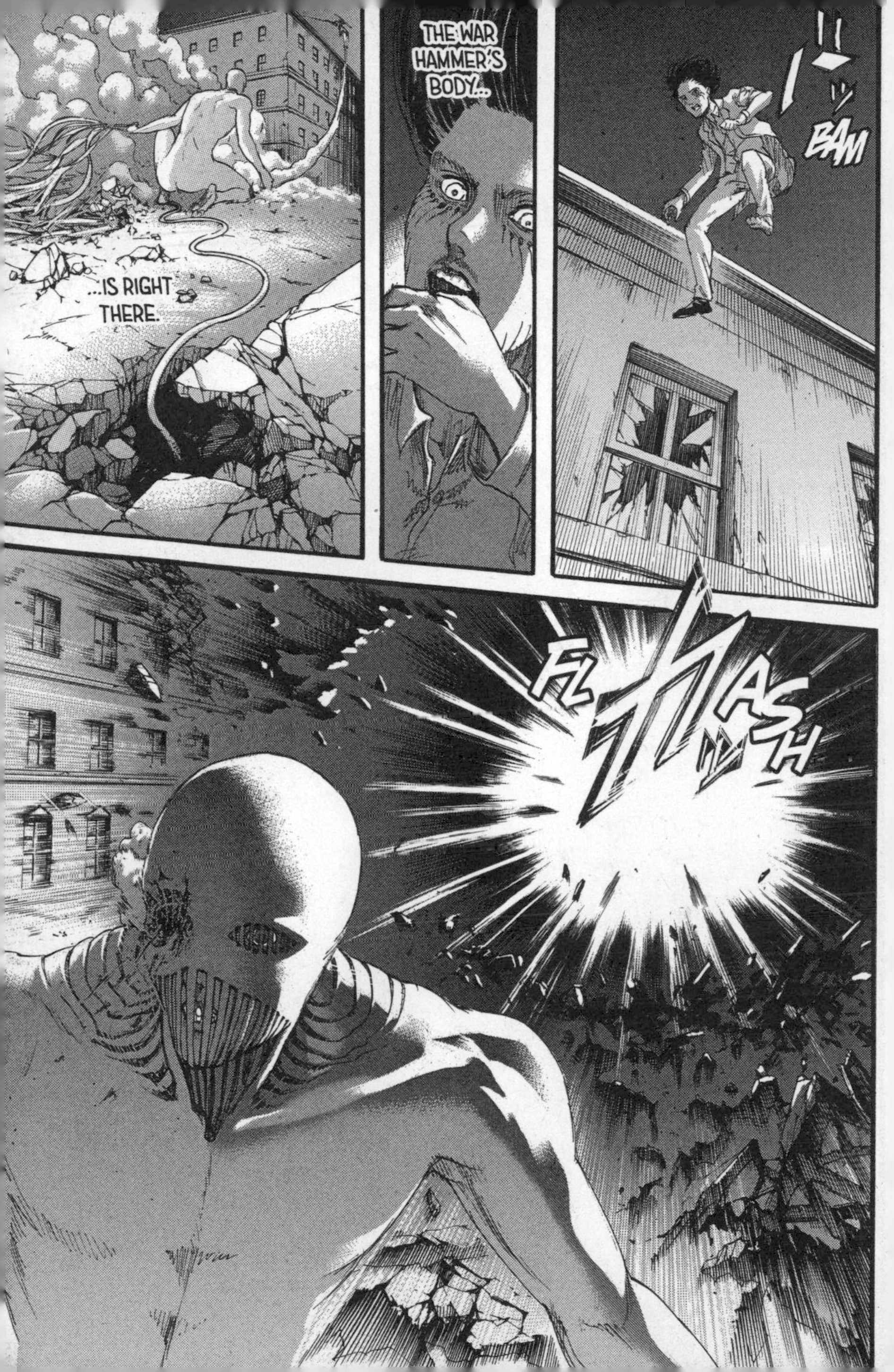
BAM
THE WAR HAMMER'S BODY...
...IS RIGHT THERE.
FLASH

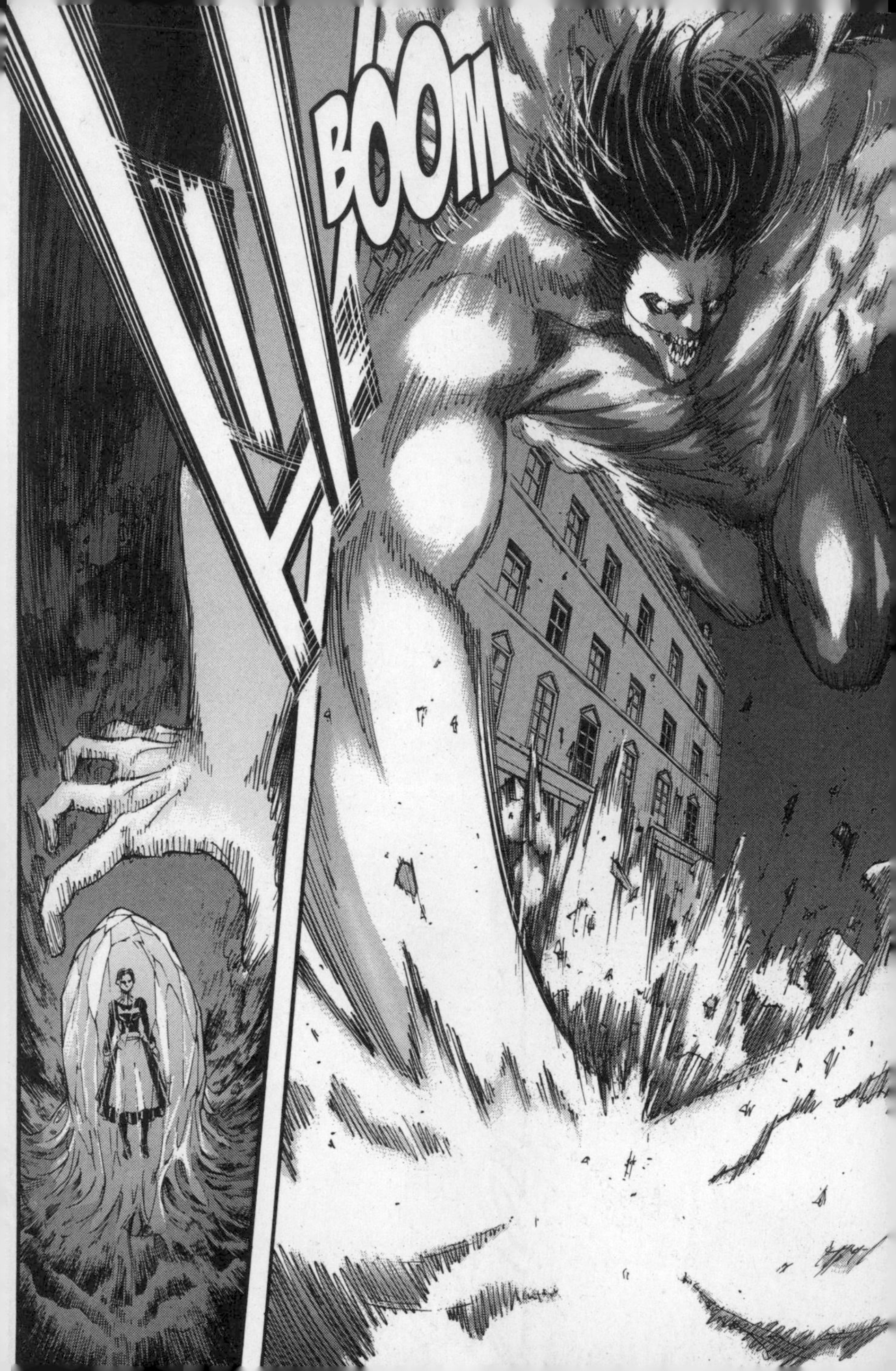
BOOM

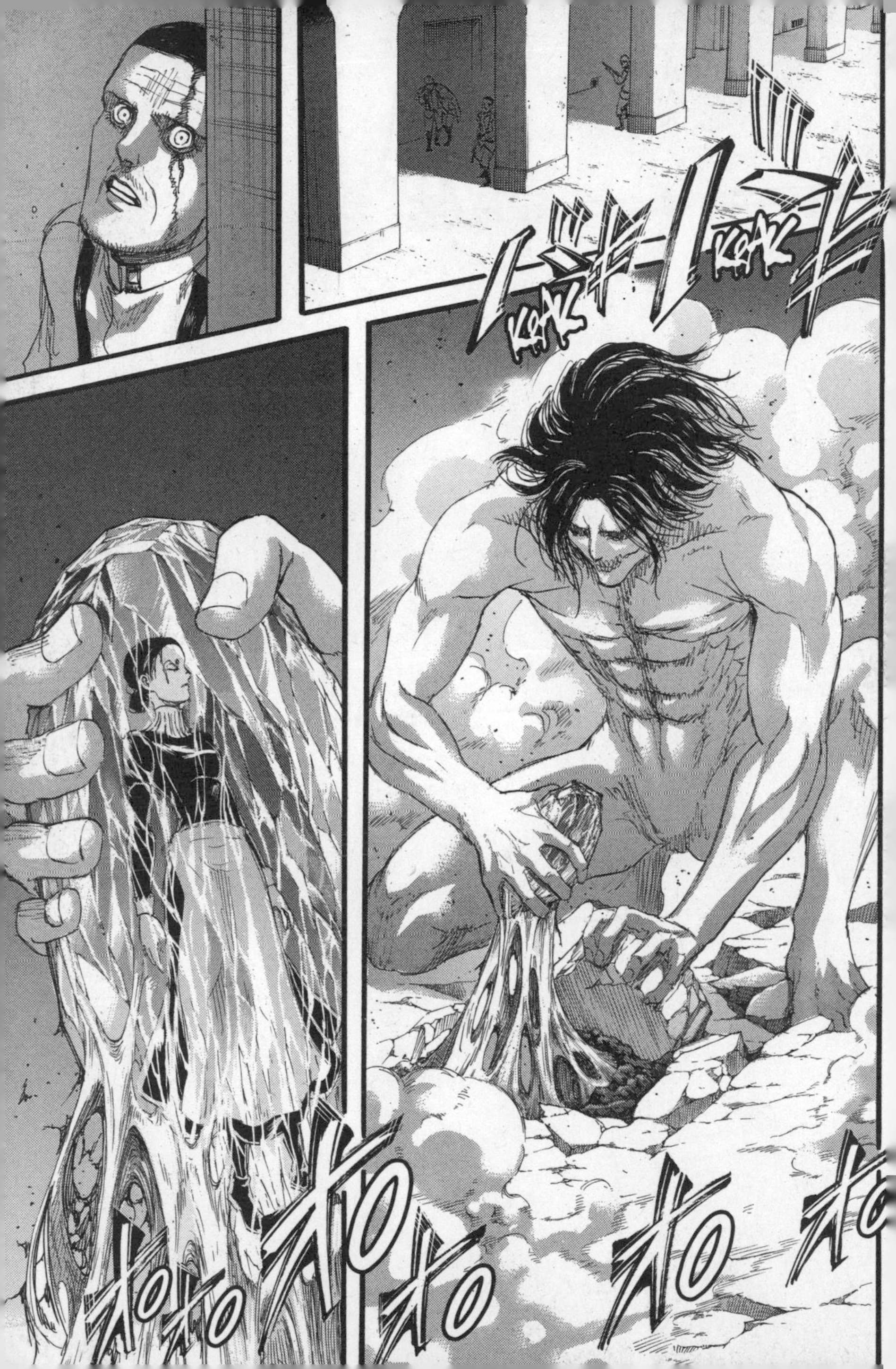
KRAK
KRAK

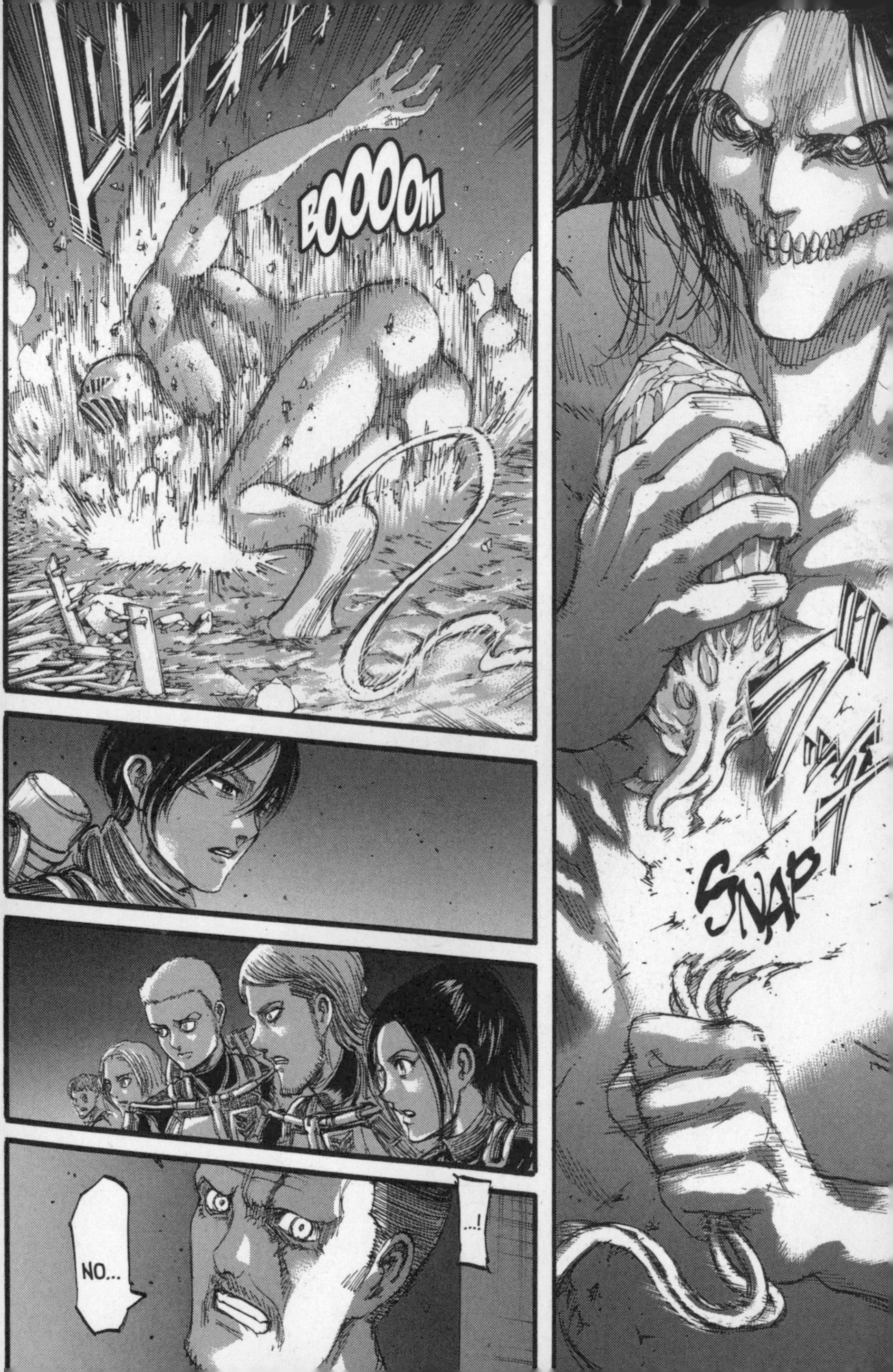
SNAP
BOOOOM
...!
NO...

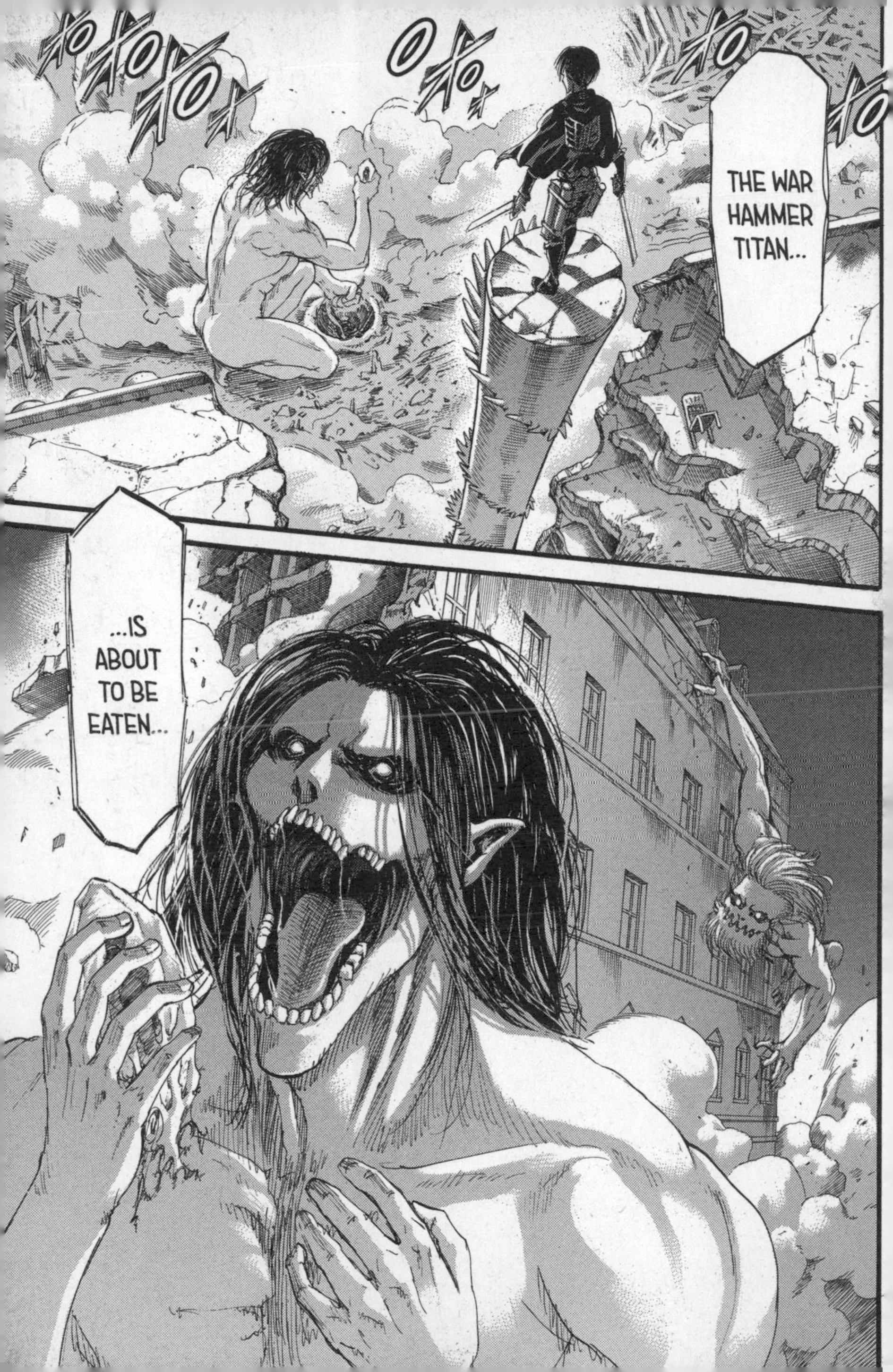
THE WAR HAMMER TITAN...
...IS ABOUT TO BE EATEN...

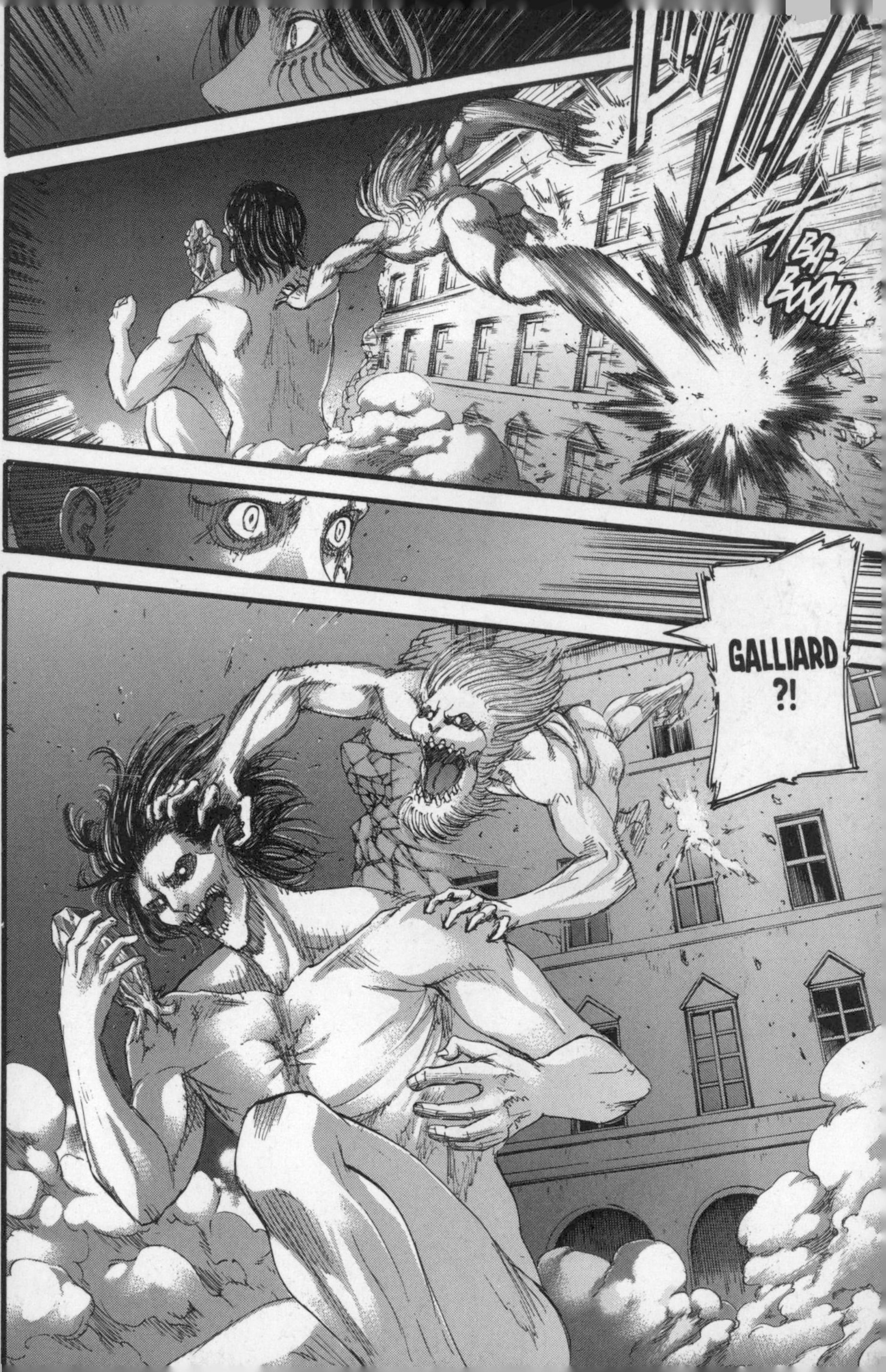
BA-BOOM
GALLIARD ?!

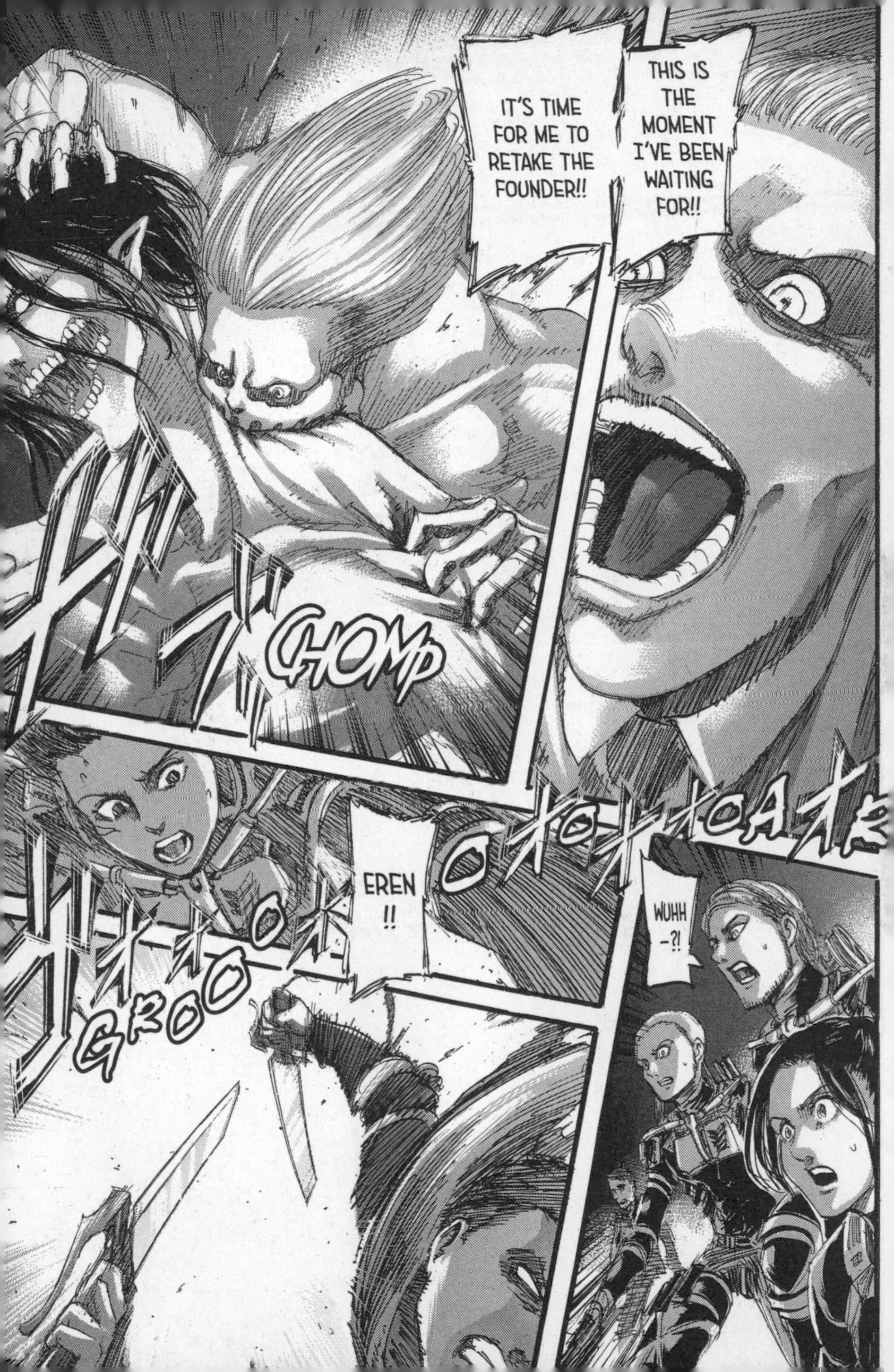
THIS IS THE MOMENT I'VE BEEN WAITING FOR!!
IT'S TIME FOR ME TO RETAKE THE FOUNDER!!
CHOMP
WUHH –?!
EREN !!
GROOOOOOOOAA

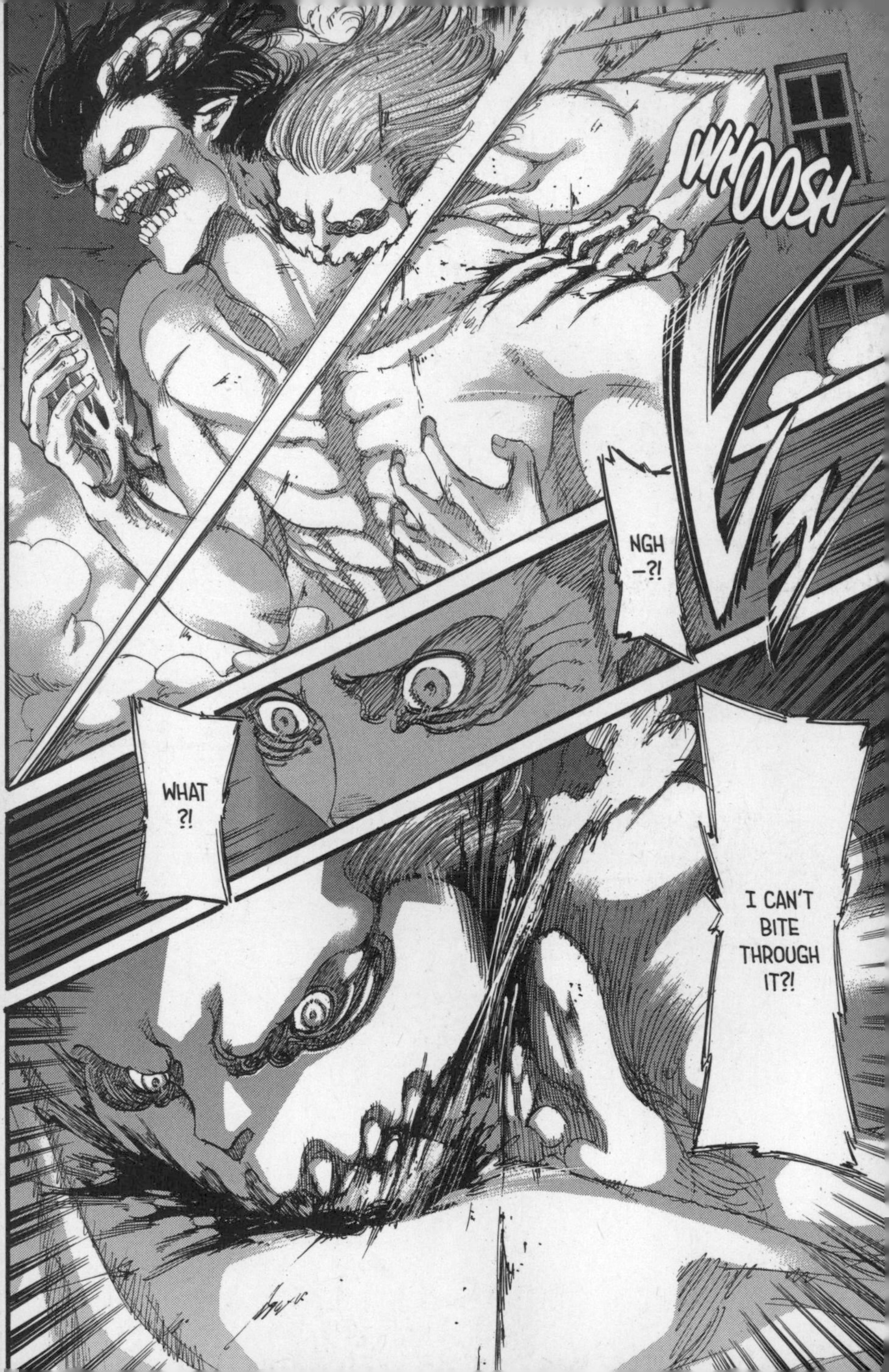
WHOOSH
NGH —?!
WHAT ?!
I CAN'T BITE THROUGH IT?!

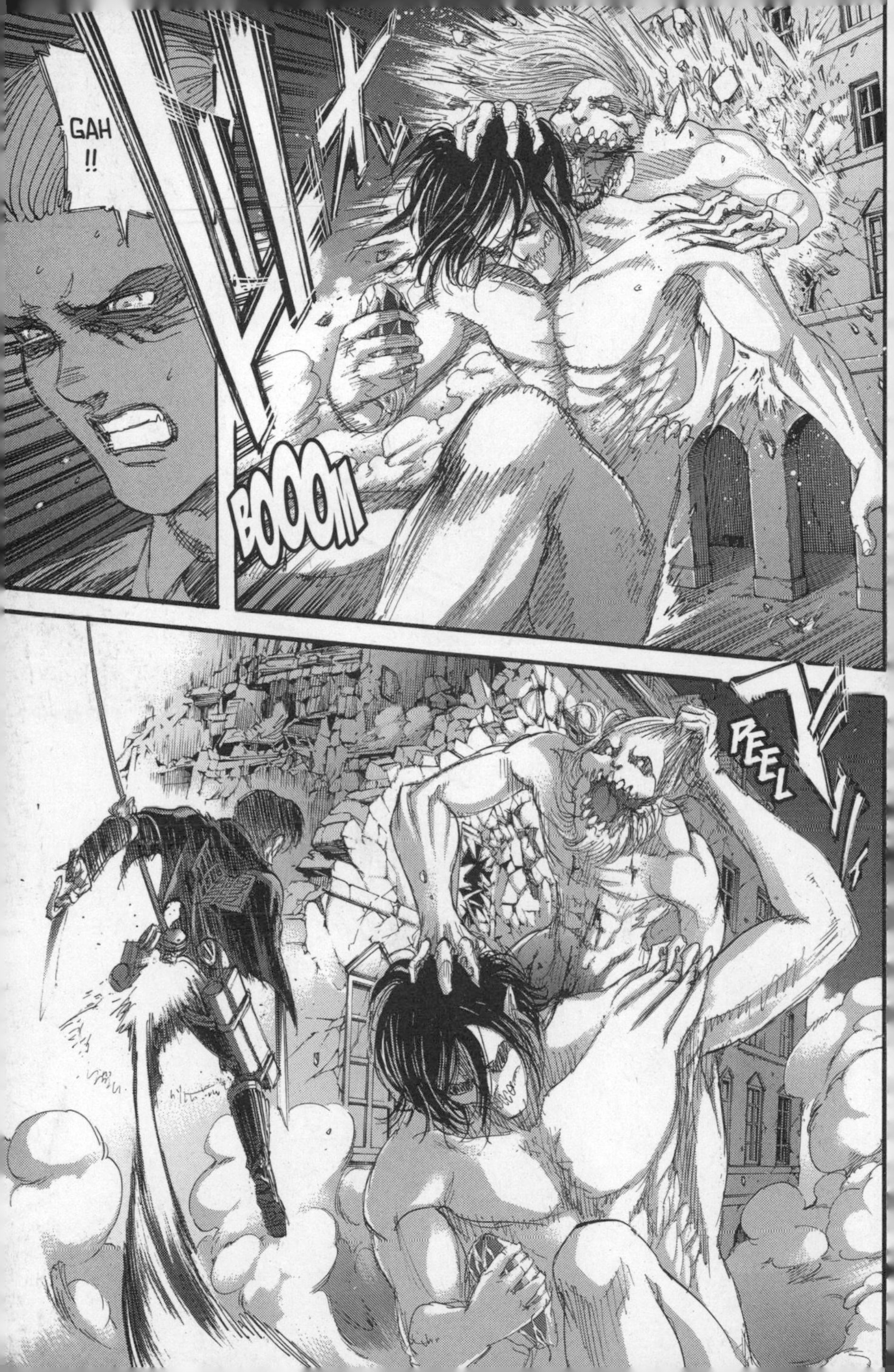
BOOOM
GAH !!
PEEL

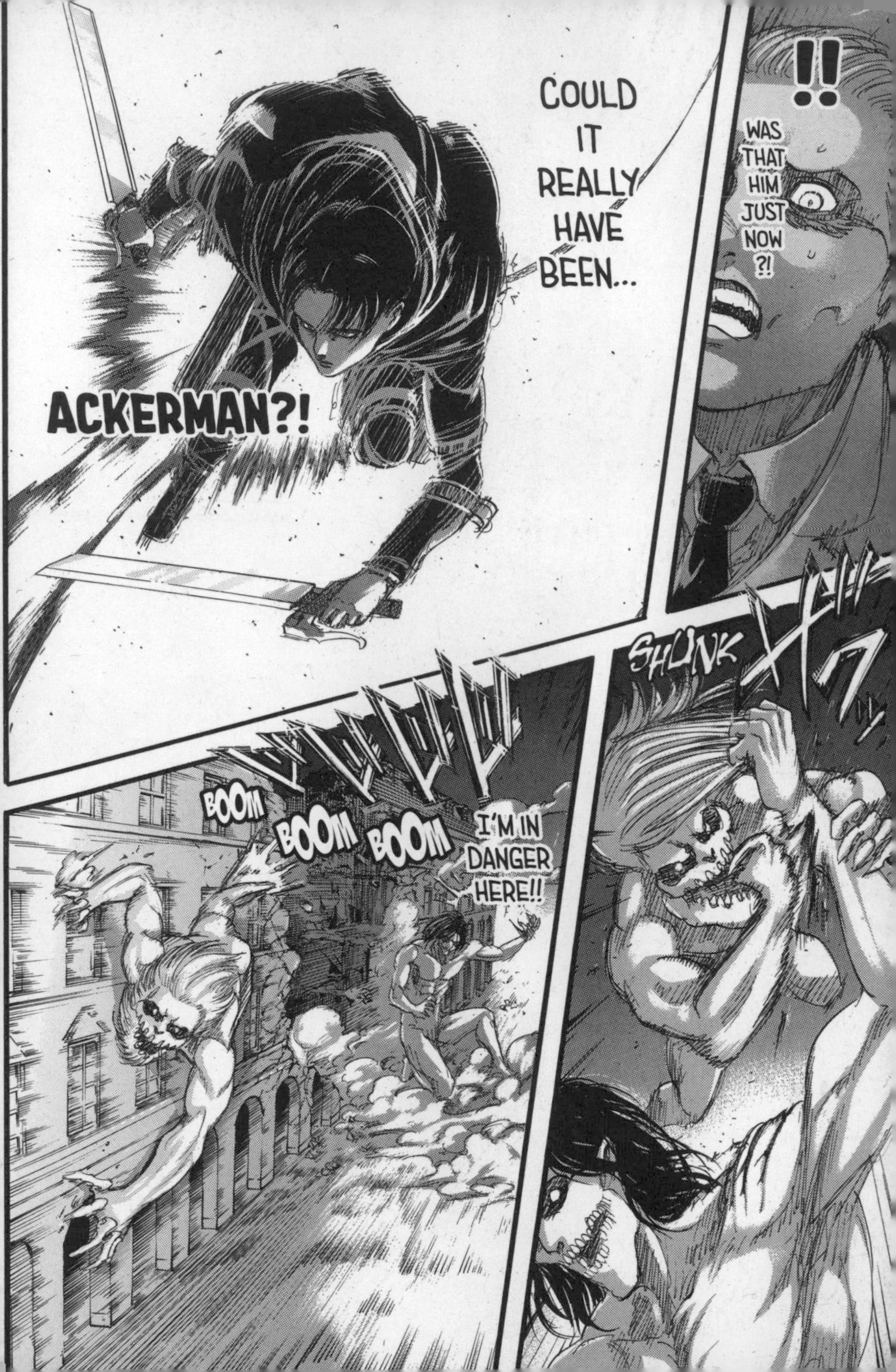

!!
WAS THAT HIM JUST NOW?!
COULD IT REALLY HAVE BEEN...
ACKERMAN?!
SHUNK
BOOM
BOOM
BOOM
I'M IN DANGER HERE!!

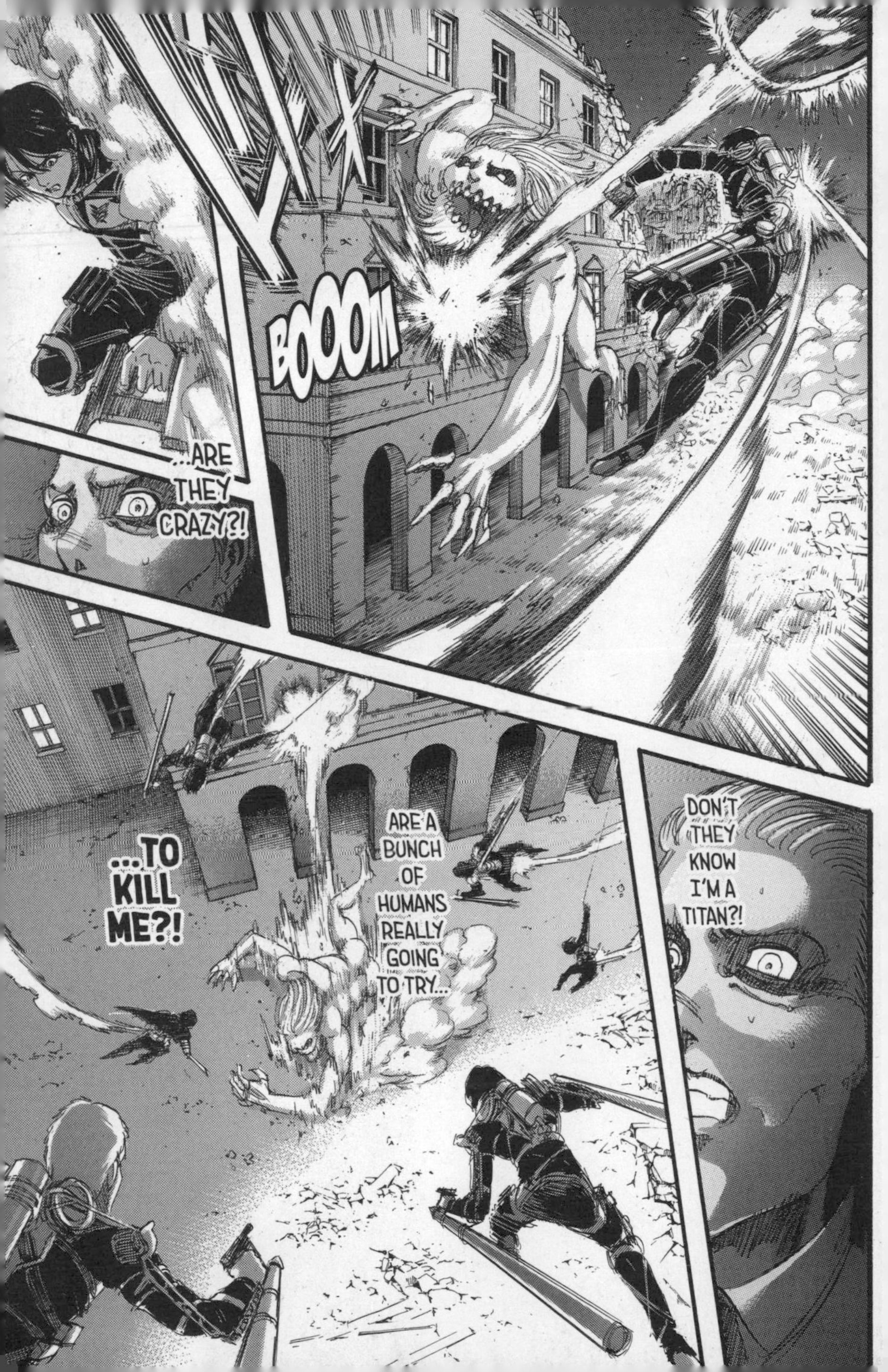
BOOOM
...ARE THEY CRAZY?!
DON'T THEY KNOW I'M A TITAN?!
ARE A BUNCH OF HUMANS REALLY GOING TO TRY...
...TO KILL ME?!

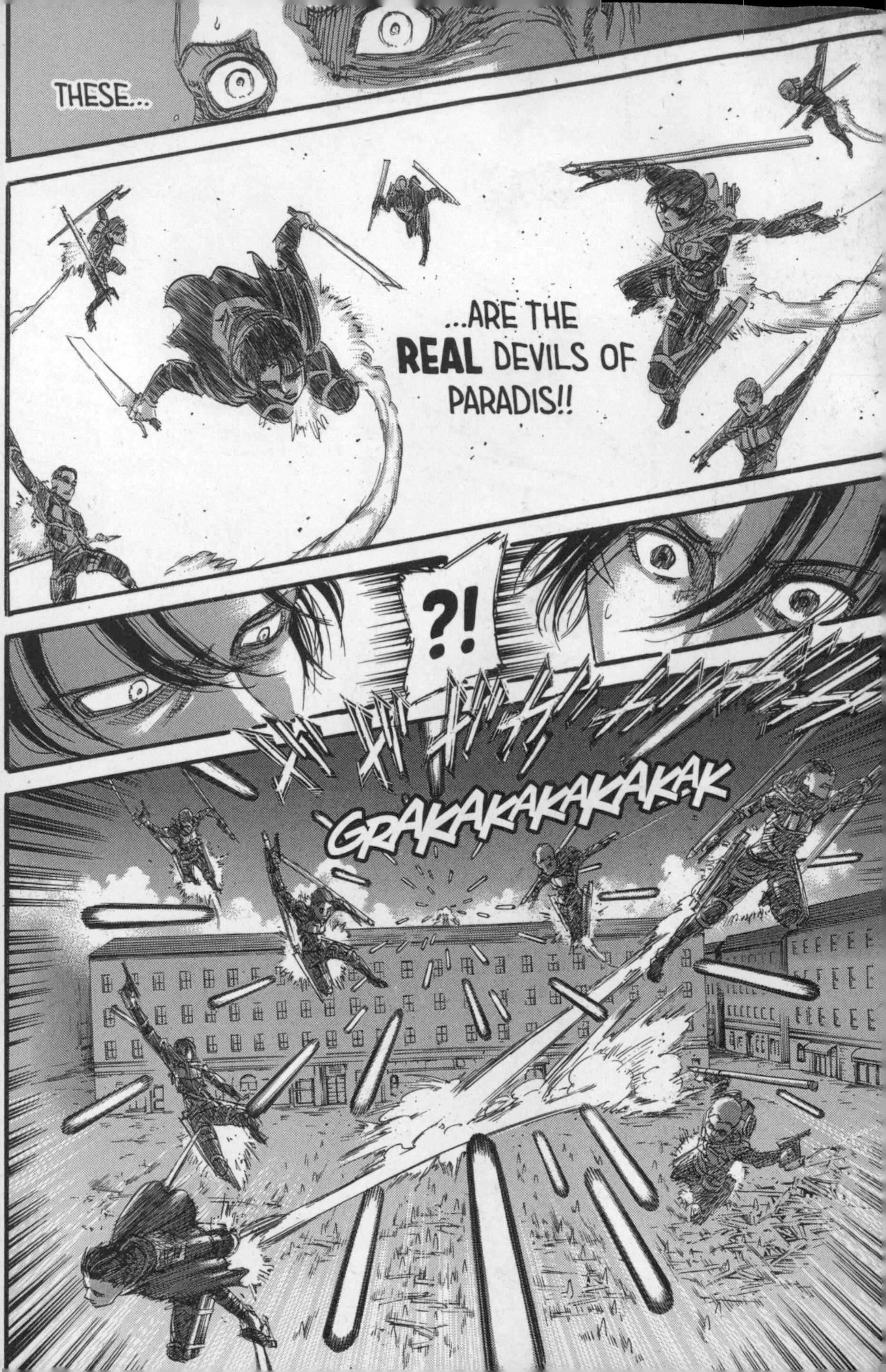
THESE...
...ARE THE **REAL** DEVILS OF PARADIS!!
?!
GRAKAKAKAKAKAK

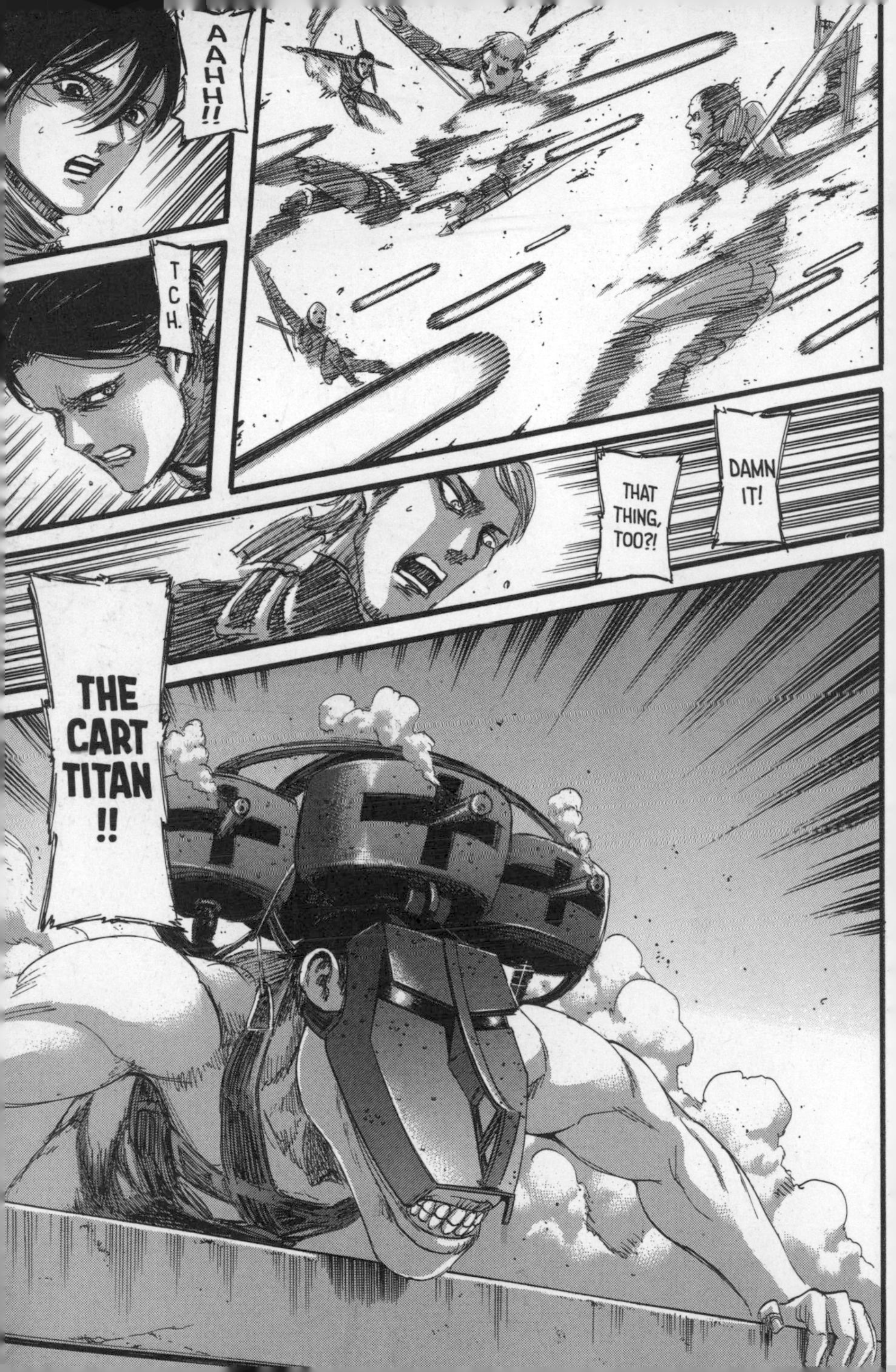
AAHH!!
TCH.
DAMN IT!
THAT THING, TOO?!
THE CART TITAN!!

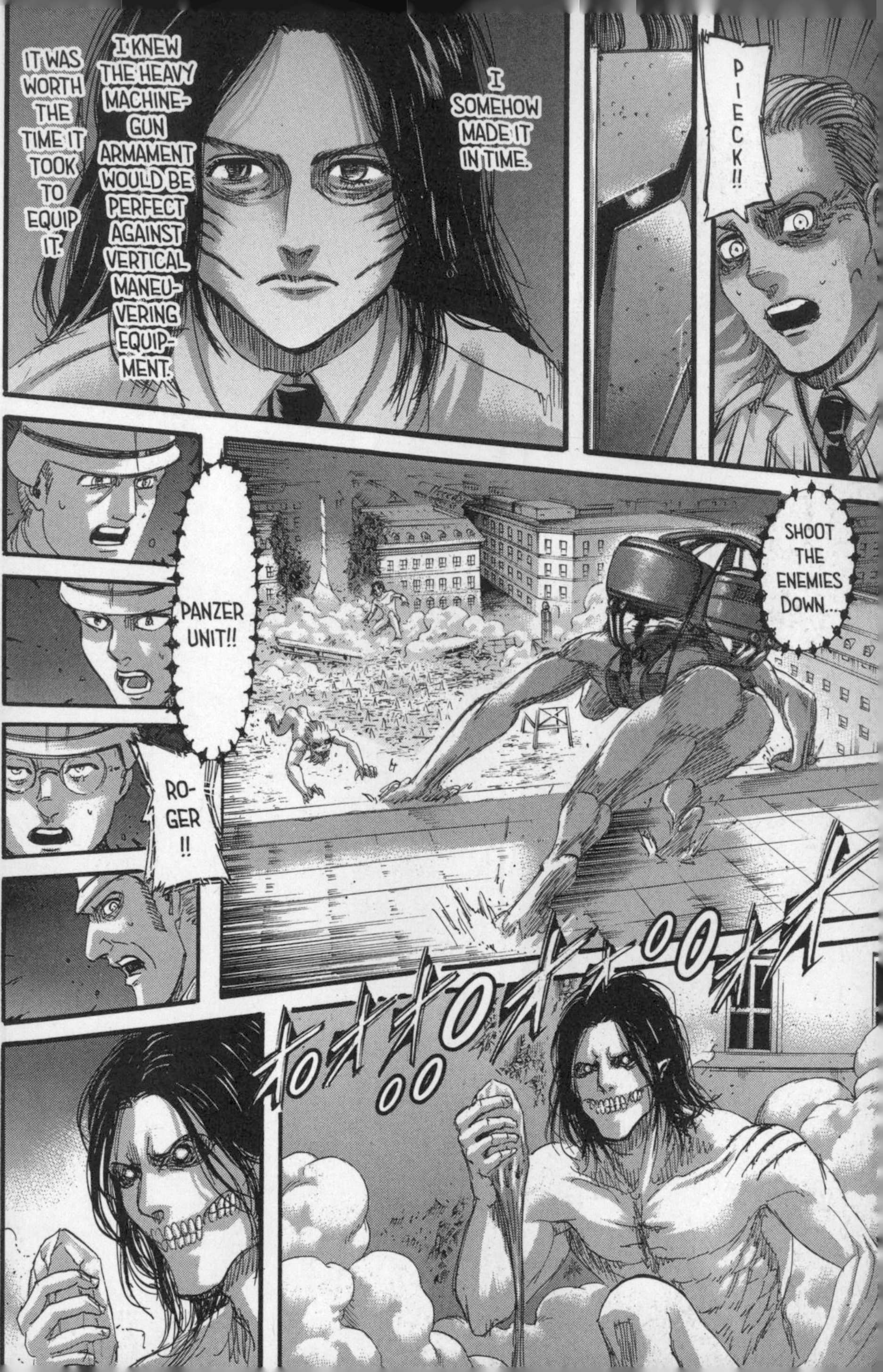
PIECK!!
I SOMEHOW MADE IT IN TIME.
I KNEW THE HEAVY MACHINE-GUN ARMAMENT WOULD BE PERFECT AGAINST VERTICAL MANEUVERING EQUIPMENT.
IT WAS WORTH THE TIME IT TOOK TO EQUIP IT.
SHOOT THE ENEMIES DOWN...
PANZER UNIT!!
ROGER!!

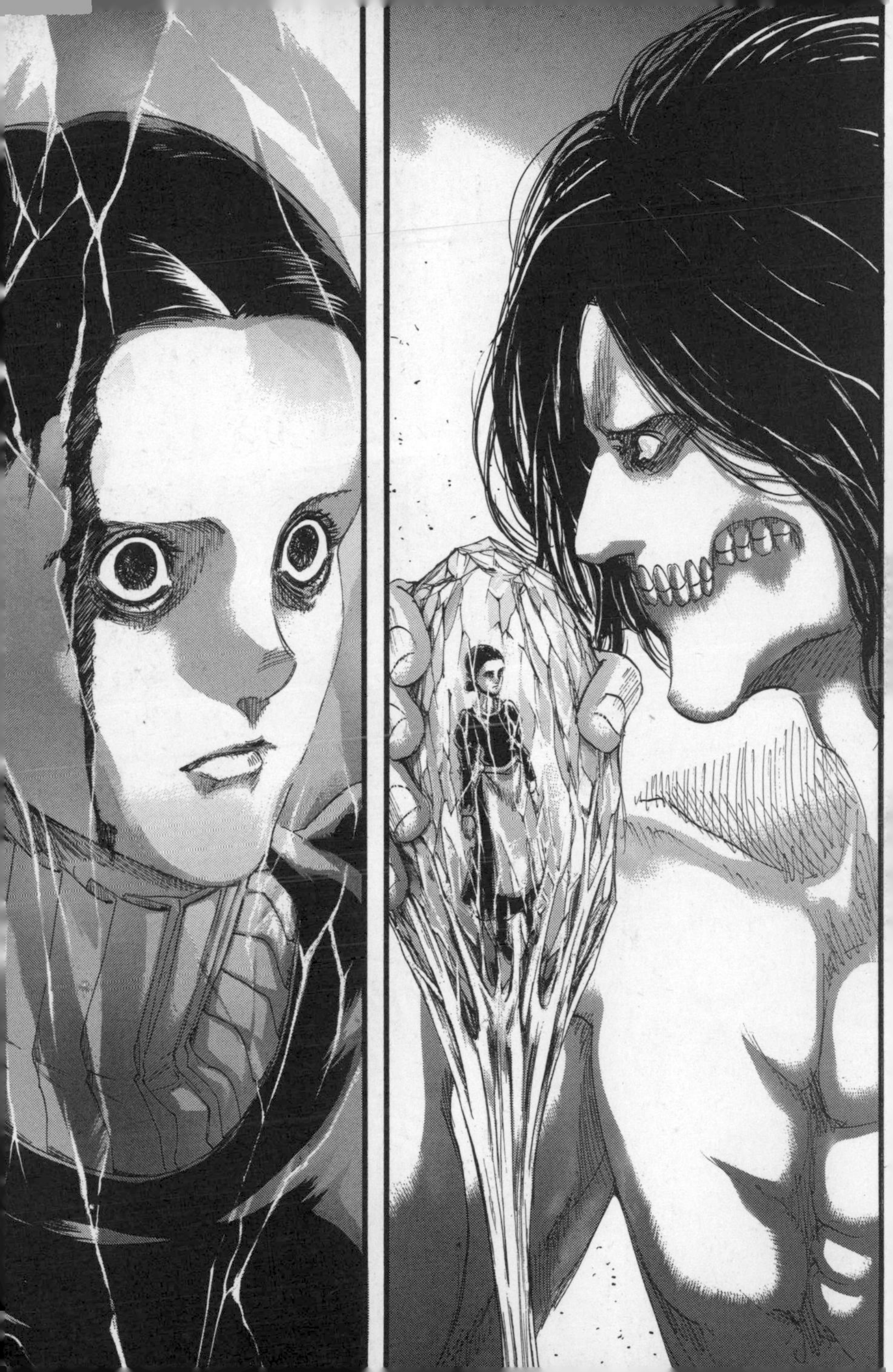

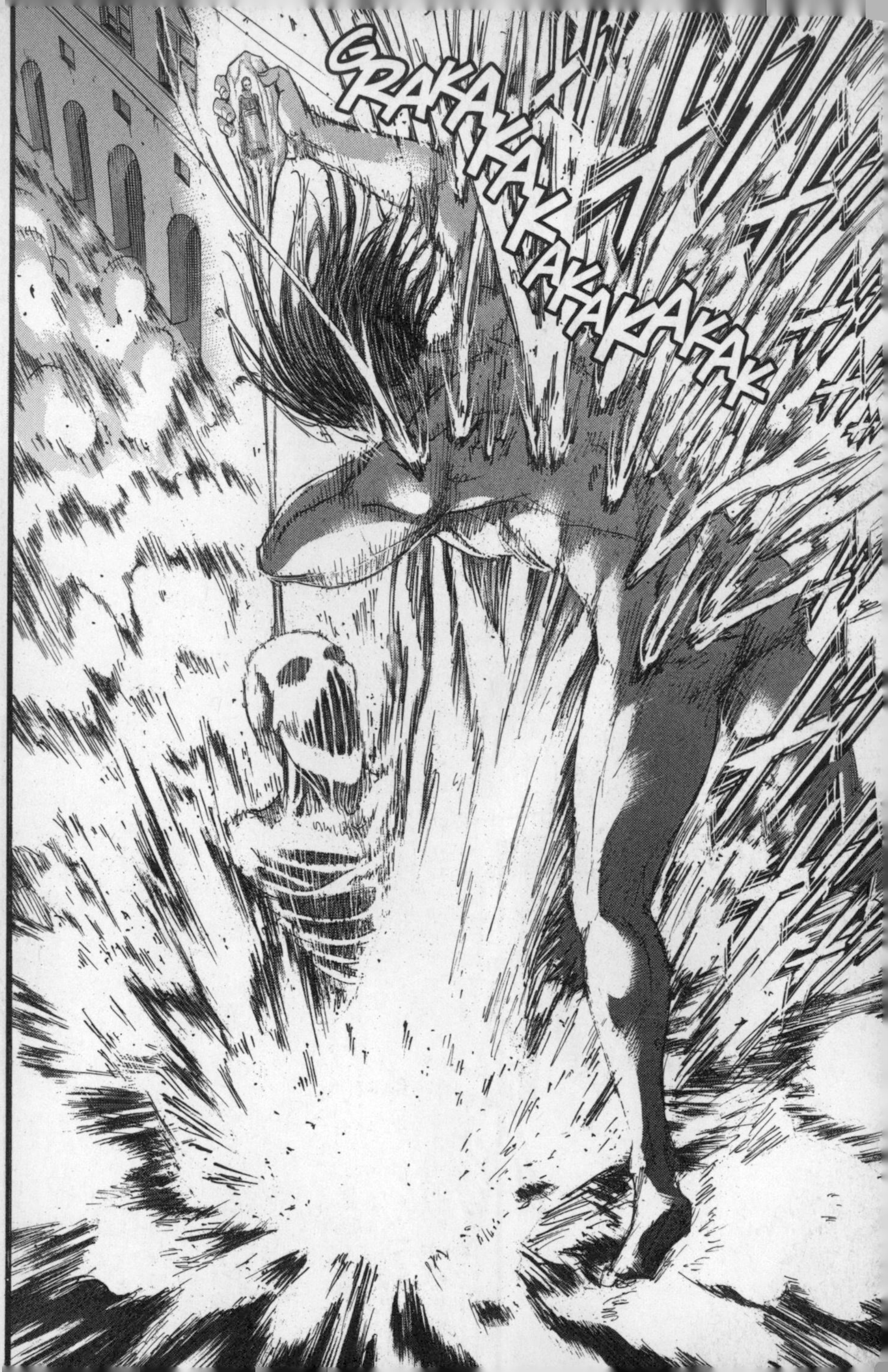
GRAKAKAKAKAKAKAK

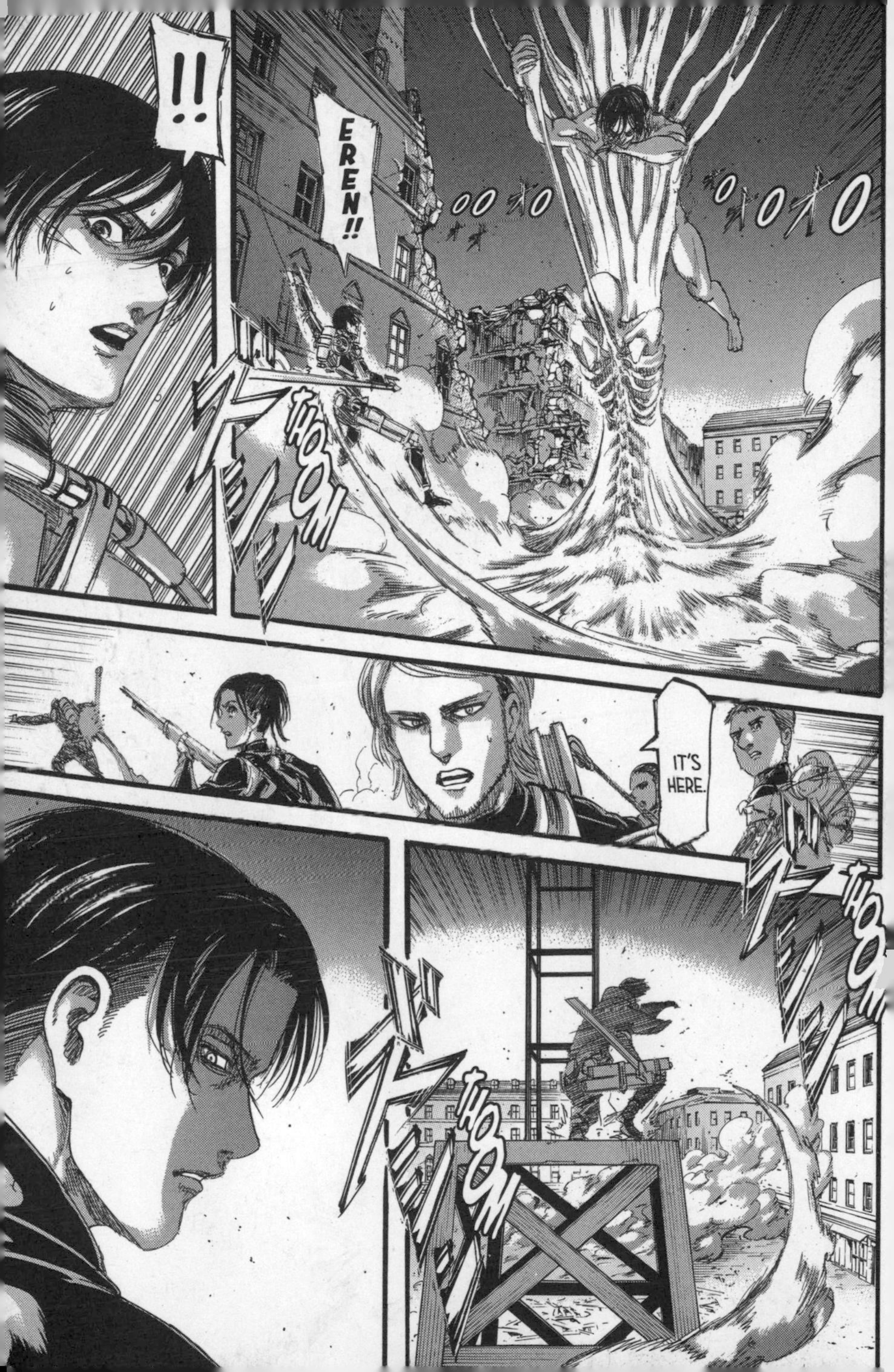

OOO
OOO
EREN!!
THOOM
!!
IT'S HERE.
THOOM
THOOM

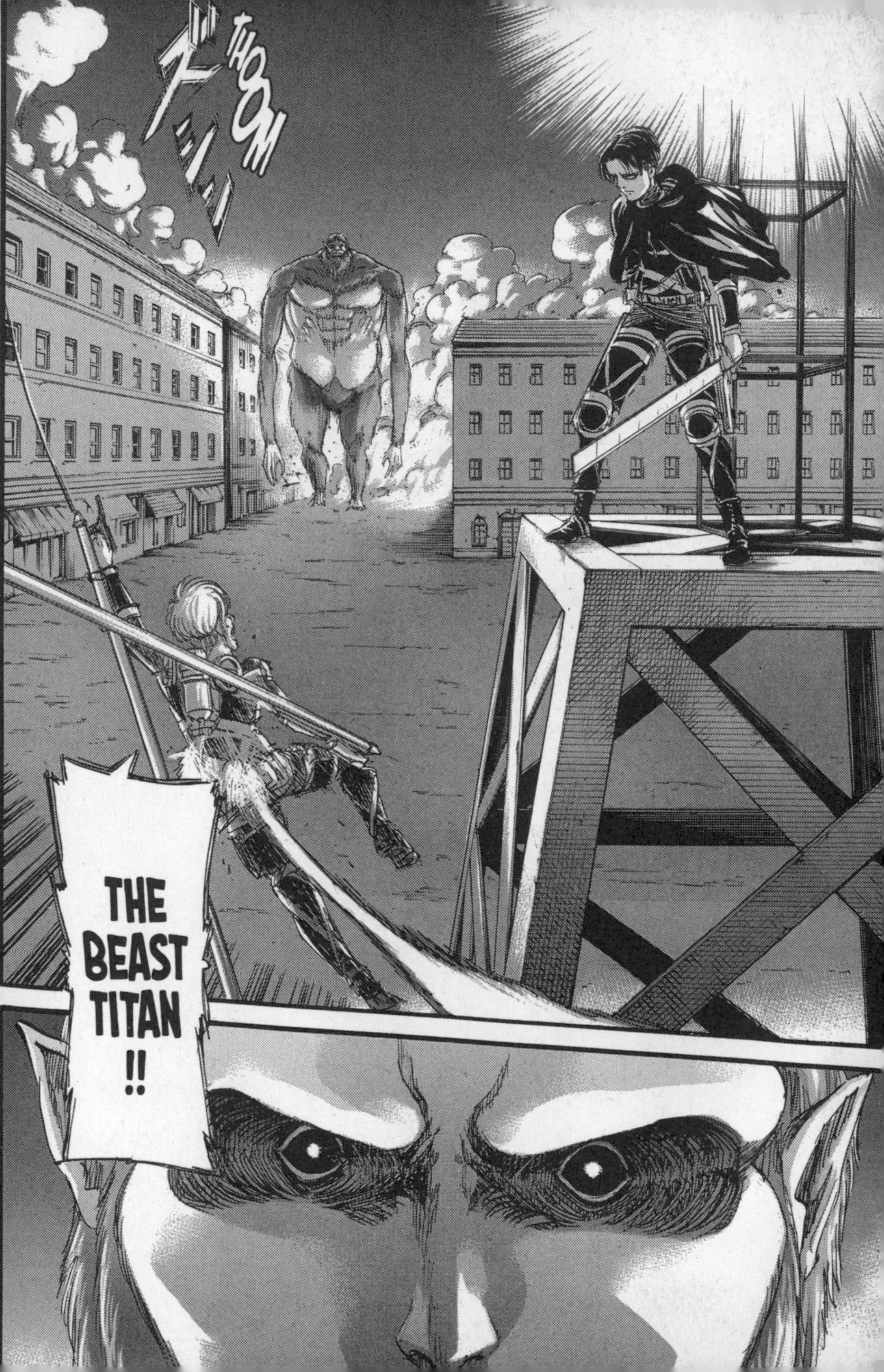
THOOM
THE BEAST TITAN !!

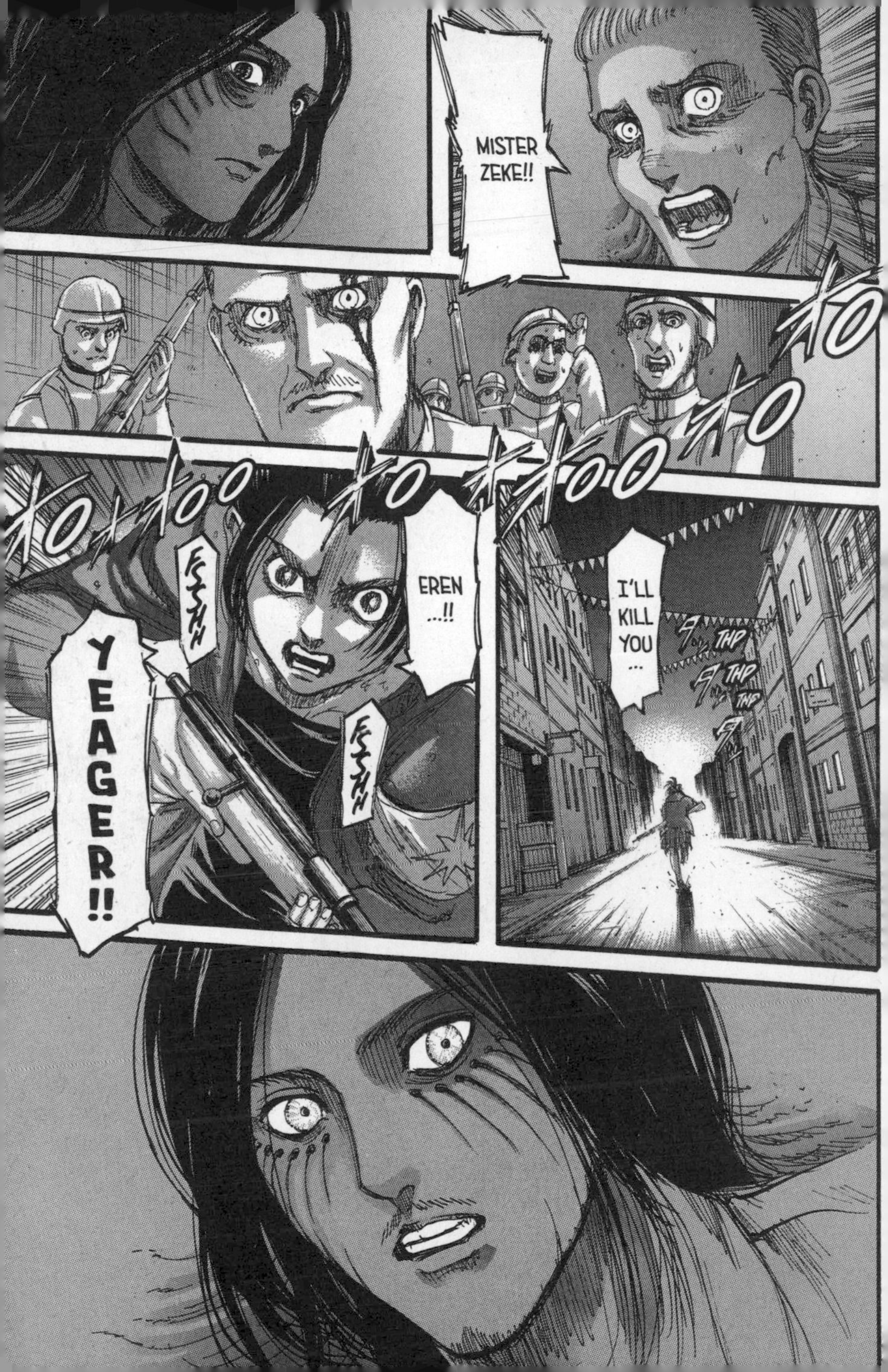
MISTER ZEKE!!
I'LL KILL YOU ...
THP
THP
EREN ...!!
FSSHH
FSSHH
YEAGER!!

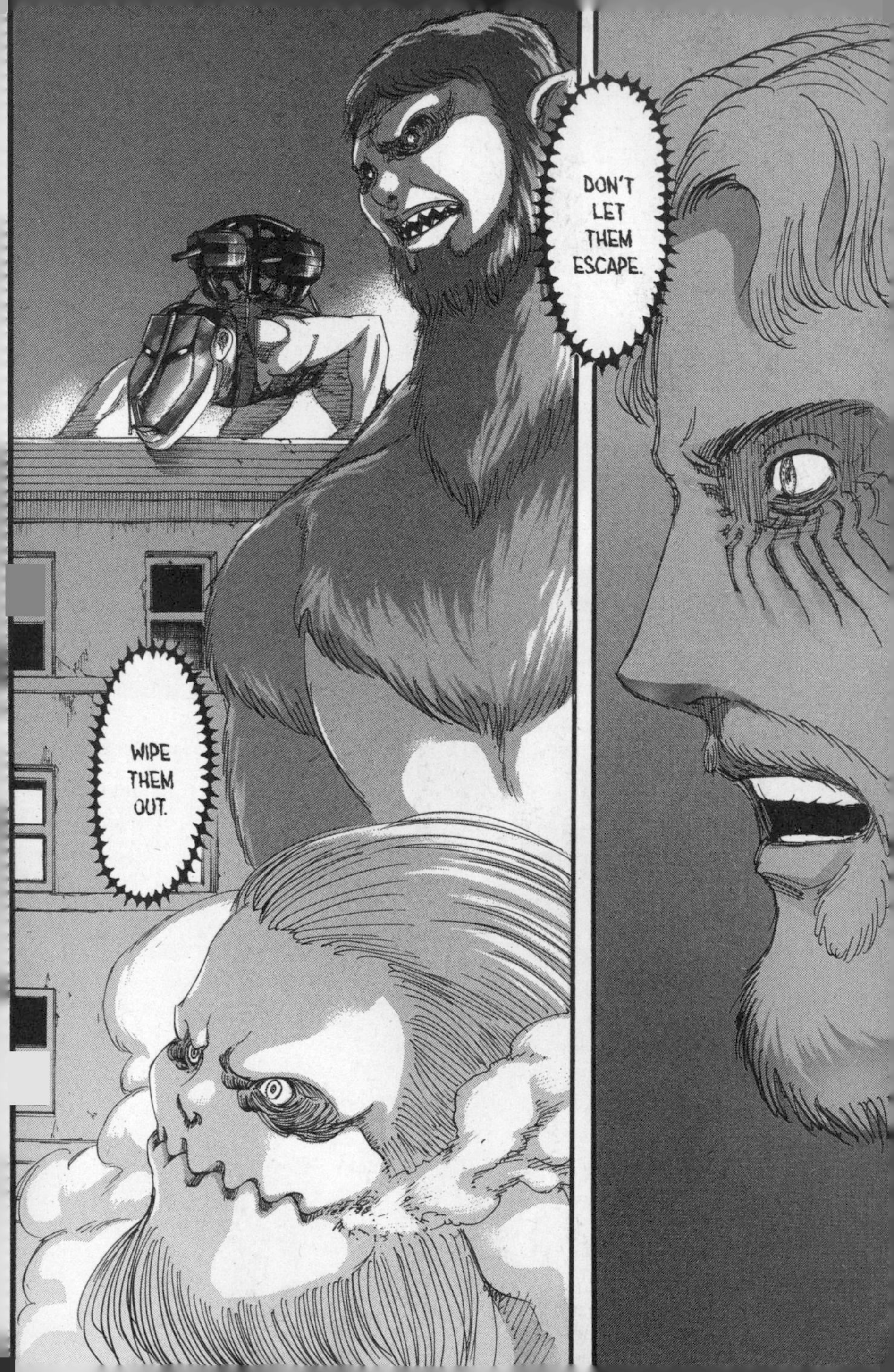
DON'T LET THEM ESCAPE.
WIPE THEM OUT.

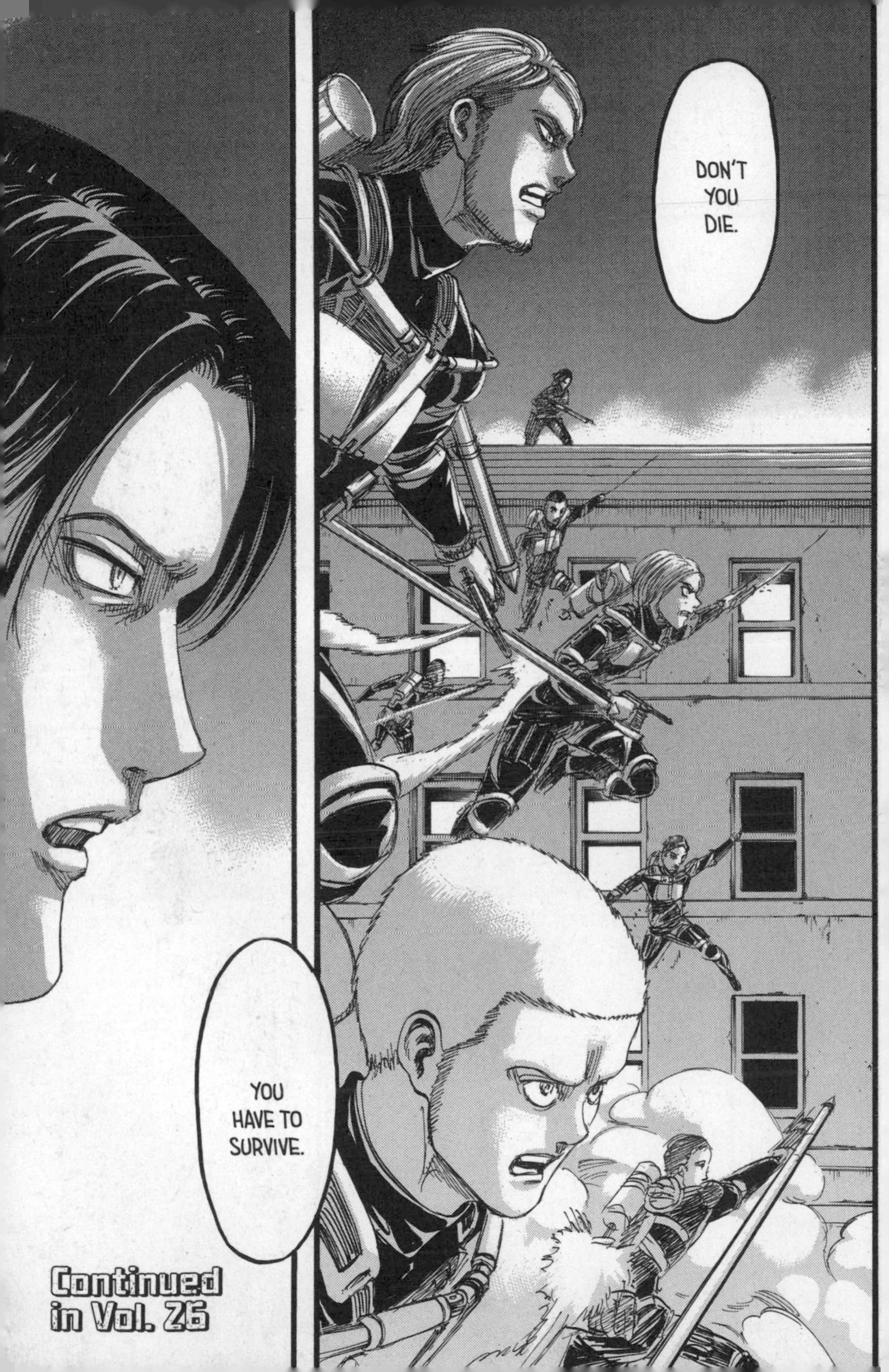
DON'T YOU DIE.
YOU HAVE TO SURVIVE.
Continued in Vol. 26

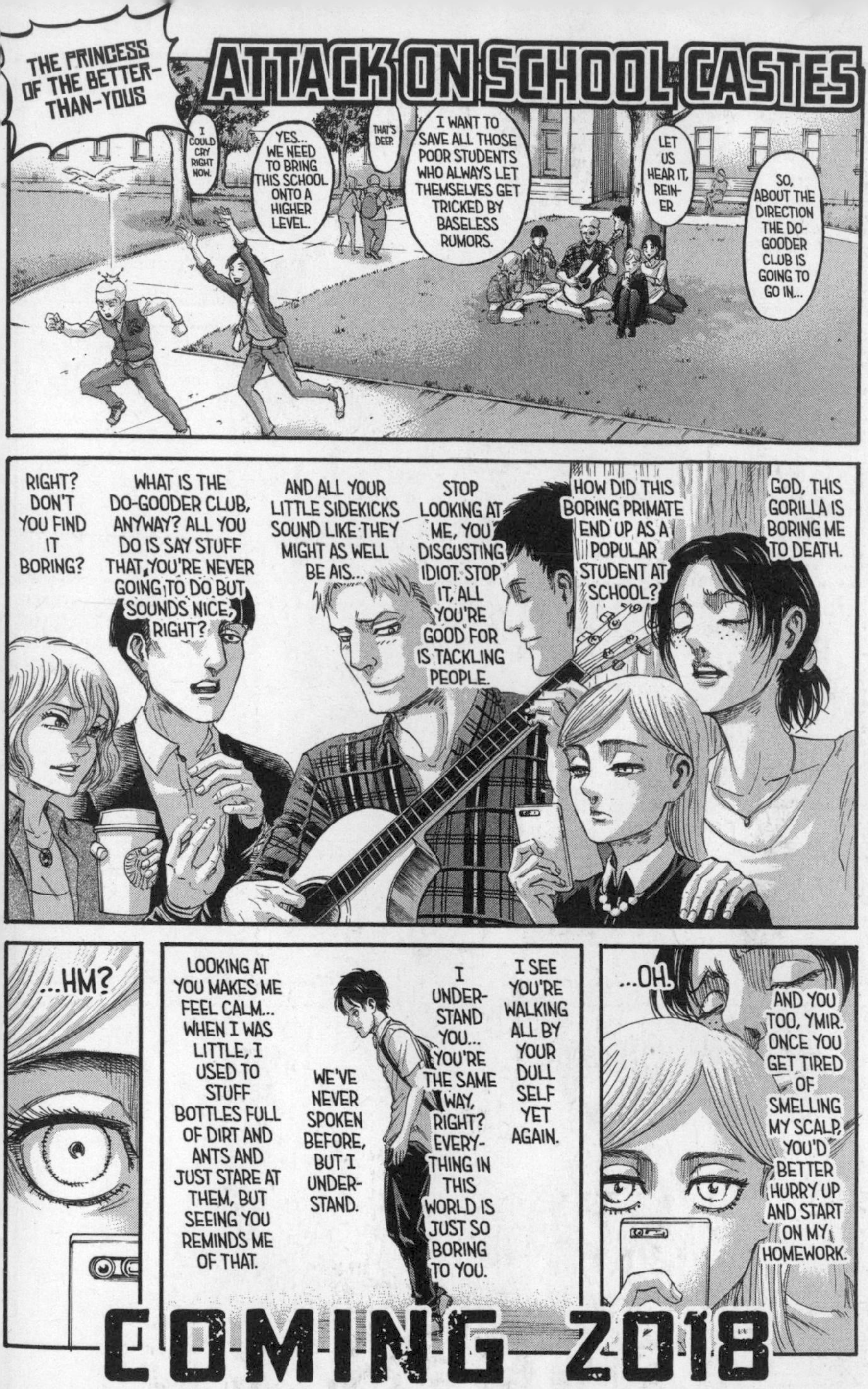
ATTACK ON SCHOOL CASTES
THE PRINCESS OF THE BETTER-THAN-YOUS
SO, ABOUT THE DIRECTION THE DO-GOODER CLUB IS GOING TO GO IN...
LET US HEAR IT, REINER.
I WANT TO SAVE ALL THOSE POOR STUDENTS WHO ALWAYS LET THEMSELVES GET TRICKED BY BASELESS RUMORS.
THAT'S DEEP.
YES... WE NEED TO BRING THIS SCHOOL ONTO A HIGHER LEVEL.
I COULD CRY RIGHT NOW.
GOD, THIS GORILLA IS BORING ME TO DEATH.
HOW DID THIS BORING PRIMATE END UP AS A POPULAR STUDENT AT SCHOOL?
STOP LOOKING AT ME, YOU DISGUSTING IDIOT. STOP IT. ALL YOU'RE GOOD FOR IS TACKLING PEOPLE.
AND ALL YOUR LITTLE SIDEKICKS SOUND LIKE THEY MIGHT AS WELL BE AIS...
WHAT IS THE DO-GOODER CLUB, ANYWAY? ALL YOU DO IS SAY STUFF THAT YOU'RE NEVER GOING TO DO BUT SOUNDS NICE, RIGHT?
RIGHT? DON'T YOU FIND IT BORING?
...OH.
AND YOU TOO, YMIR. ONCE YOU GET TIRED OF SMELLING MY SCALP, YOU'D BETTER HURRY UP AND START ON MY HOMEWORK.
I SEE YOU'RE WALKING ALL BY YOUR DULL SELF YET AGAIN.
I UNDERSTAND YOU... YOU'RE THE SAME WAY, RIGHT? EVERYTHING IN THIS WORLD IS JUST SO BORING TO YOU.
WE'VE NEVER SPOKEN BEFORE, BUT I UNDERSTAND.
LOOKING AT YOU MAKES ME FEEL CALM... WHEN I WAS LITTLE, I USED TO STUFF BOTTLES FULL OF DIRT AND ANTS AND JUST STARE AT THEM, BUT SEEING YOU REMINDS ME OF THAT.
...HM?
COMING 2018

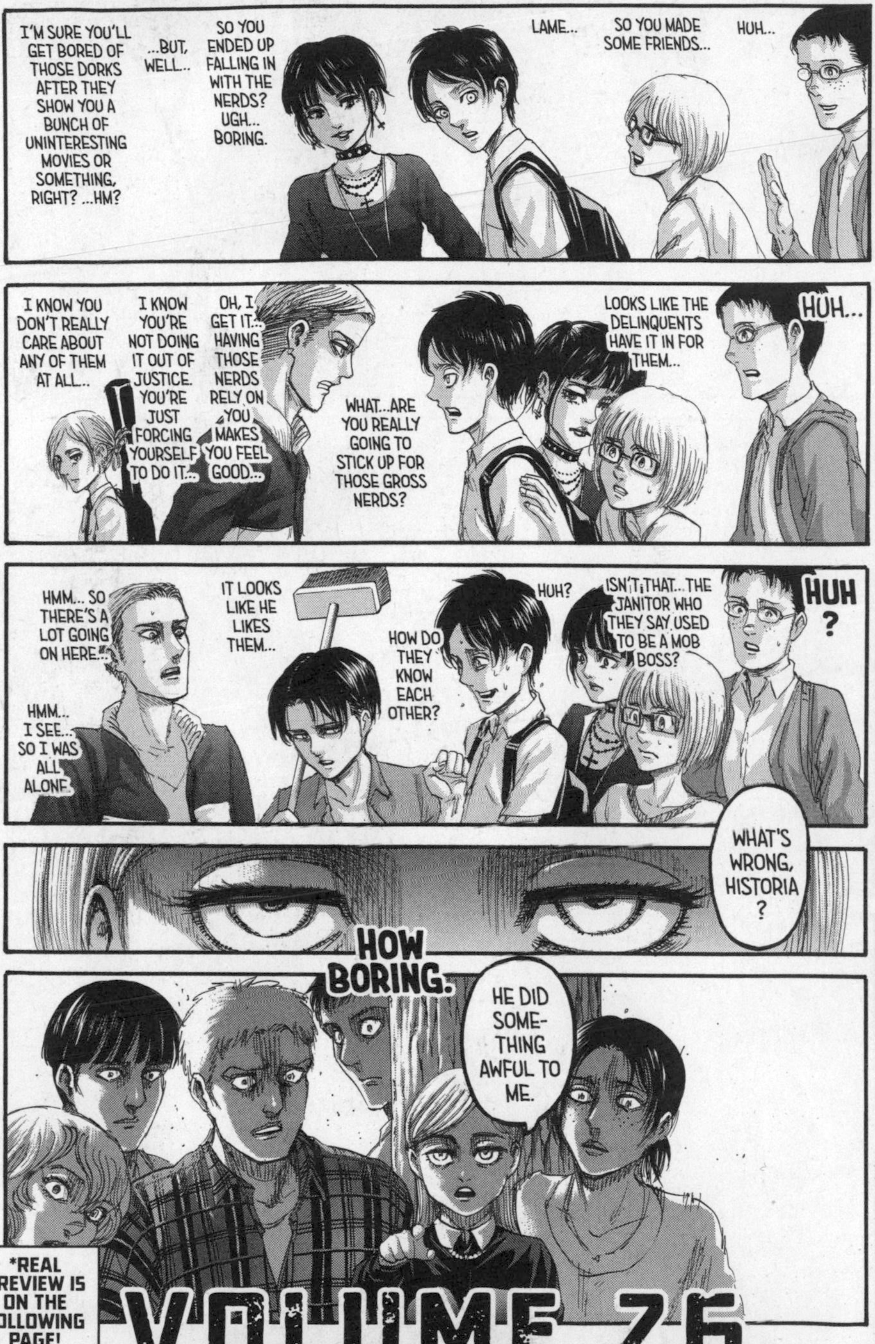
HUH...
SO YOU MADE SOME FRIENDS...
LAME...
SO YOU ENDED UP FALLING IN WITH THE NERDS? UGH... BORING.
...BUT, WELL...
I'M SURE YOU'LL GET BORED OF THOSE DORKS AFTER THEY SHOW YOU A BUNCH OF UNINTERESTING MOVIES OR SOMETHING, RIGHT? ...HM?
HUH...
LOOKS LIKE THE DELINQUENTS HAVE IT IN FOR THEM...
WHAT...ARE YOU REALLY GOING TO STICK UP FOR THOSE GROSS NERDS?
OH, I GET IT... HAVING THOSE NERDS RELY ON YOU MAKES YOU FEEL GOOD...
I KNOW YOU'RE NOT DOING IT OUT OF JUSTICE. YOU'RE JUST FORCING YOURSELF TO DO IT...
I KNOW YOU DON'T REALLY CARE ABOUT ANY OF THEM AT ALL...
HUH ?
ISN'T THAT... THE JANITOR WHO THEY SAY USED TO BE A MOB BOSS?
HUH?
HOW DO THEY KNOW EACH OTHER?
IT LOOKS LIKE HE LIKES THEM...
HMM... SO THERE'S A LOT GOING ON HERE...
HMM... I SEE... SO I WAS ALL ALONE.
WHAT'S WRONG, HISTORIA ?
HOW BORING.
HE DID SOME-THING AWFUL TO ME.
*REAL PREVIEW IS ON THE FOLLOWING PAGE!
VOLUME 26

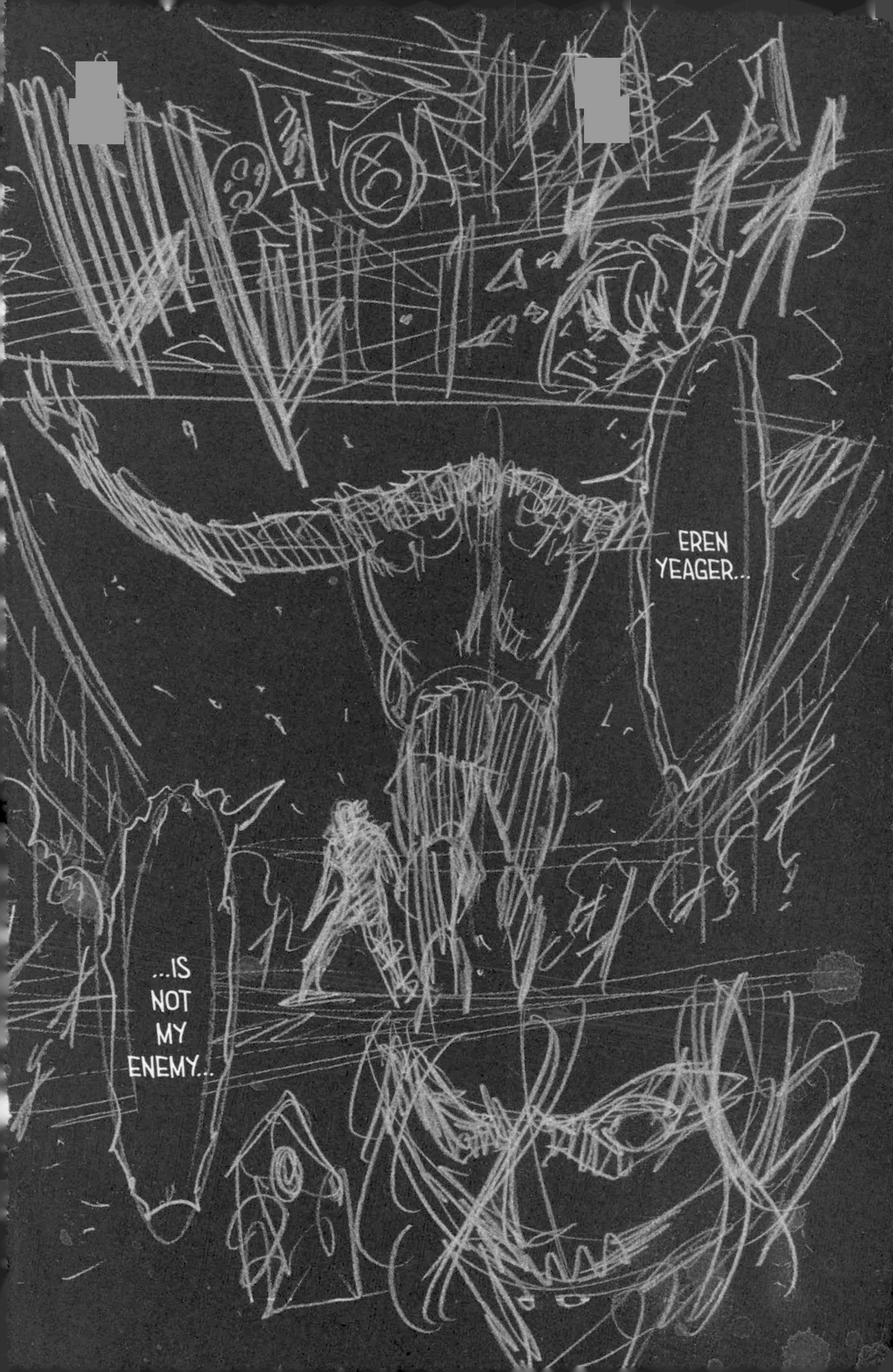
EREN YEAGER...
...IS NOT MY ENEMY...

VOLUME 26 COMING 2018!

HUMANITY'S MOST POWERFUL AND MOST DESTRUCTIVE GATHER.

WHAT WILL BE LEFT AFTER THE BATTLE ONCE EVIL FALLS...?

Attack on Titan 25 is a work of fiction. Names, characters, places, and incidents are the products of the author's imagination or are used fictitiously. Any resemblance to actual events, locales, or persons, living or dead, is entirely coincidental.

A Kodansha Comics Trade Paperback Original

Published in the United States by Kodansha Comics, an imprint of Kodansha USA Publishing, LLC, New York.

Publication rights for this English edition arranged through Kodansha Ltd, Tokyo.

First published in Japan in 2018 by Kodansha Ltd., Tokyo as *Shingeki no kyojin*, volume 25.

ISBN 978-1-63236-613-9

Original cover design by Takashi Shimoyama (Red Rooster)

Printed in the United States of America.

www.kodanshacomics.com

9 8 7 6 5 4 3 2 1
Translation: Ko Ransom
Lettering: Steve Wands
Editing: Ben Applegate
Kodansha Comics edition cover design by Phil Balsman

GIRDING FOR BATTLE

Eren and everyone he has ever known have lived on the island of Paradis. For many years, the Marleyans have been threatening Paradis in an attempt to monopolize the power of the Titans and keep the world trembling before their military might. In an effort to prove their worth and cement their truth, the Marleyans prepare for the ultimate declaration of war on Paradis. But when the time for deliverance comes, neither side is equipped for the shocking drama that unfolds.

PRAISE FOR THE HIT ANIME

"A visceral and fantastically intense action / horror story."
—Anime News Network

"Japan's equivalent of *The Walking Dead*."
—i09

KODANSHA
COMICS

T AGES 16+   USA $10.99   CAN $14.99

www.kodanshacomics.com
ISBN 978-1-63236-613-9

EAN

51099

9 781632 366139